Charles Tilly was one of the great sociologists of the last fifty years, and social change today makes his work all the more important. Castañeda and Schneider clearly present the scope of Tilly's contributions and make his work accessible to a new generation of social scientists.

—Craig Calhoun, London School of Economics and Political Science

No scholar in the past half century has more deeply shaped historical and political sociology, and no volume more effectively brings together a better sampling of his prodigious opus. This collection not only demonstrates how Tilly has shaped the agenda in many of sociology's liveliest themes, but also captures his uncanny ability to seamlessly weave together theory, method, and substance. For the novice or the senior scholar, it is essential reading for anyone seeking to understand collective violence, contentious politics, and social change.

—William Roy, University of California, Los Angeles

Castañeda and Schneider have brought together some of Tilly's most influential and compelling pieces. In this moment of great change, Tilly offers us tools to understand the present and shape the future. This collection will satisfy both new readers and current followers of Tilly's work.

—Lesley J. Wood, York University

Over the course of several decades, Tilly sent a great many ships (ideas/ pieces of scholarship) into a great many seas. Some of us would follow a ship or three. Others would sit in the middle of an ocean or at a port to see what Chuck would send by. This volume serves as an amazing guide/companion/navigation device/travel log as one attempts to fathom all of the journeys taken by our dear friend.

—Christian Davenport, University of Michigan

This collection by Ernesto Castañeda and Cathy Schneider provides the ideal entryway into Tilly's work. As Tilly would have hoped, it will help young scholars generate more questions, new research, and better explanations.

—Ann Mische, U̶n̶i̶v̶e̶r̶s̶i̶t̶y̶ ... me

Collective Violence, Contentious Politics, and Social Change

Charles Tilly is among the most influential American sociologists of the last century. For the first time, his pathbreaking work on a wide array of topics is available in one comprehensive reader. This manageable and readable volume brings together many highlights of Tilly's large and important oeuvre, covering his contribution to the following areas: revolutions and social change; war, state making, and organized crime; democratization; durable inequality; political violence; migration, race, and ethnicity; narratives and explanations.

The book connects Tilly's work on large-scale social processes such as nation-building and war to his work on micro processes such as racial and gender discrimination. It includes selections from some of Tilly's earliest, influential, and out of print writings, including *The Vendée; Coercion, Capital and European States;* the classic "War Making and State Making as Organized Crime;" and his more recent and lesser-known work, including that on durable inequality, democracy, poverty, economic development, and migration. Together, the collection reveals Tilly's complex, compelling, and distinctive vision and helps place the contentious politics approach Tilly pioneered with Sidney Tarrow and Doug McAdam into broader context. The editors abridge key texts and, in their introductory essay, situate them within Tilly's larger opus and contemporary intellectual debates. The chapters serve as guideposts for those who wish to study his work in greater depth or use his methodology to examine the pressing issues of our time. Read together, they provide a road map of Tilly's work and his contribution to the fields of sociology, political science, history, and international studies. This book belongs in the classroom and in the library of social scientists, political analysts, cultural critics, and activists.

Ernesto Castañeda is assistant professor of sociology at American University in Washington, DC. He is the editor of *Immigration and Categorical Inequality: Migration to the City and the Birth of Race and Ethnicity* (Forthcoming Routledge, 2017), and co-author with Charles Tilly and Lesley Wood of *Social Movements 1768–2018* (Forthcoming Routledge, 2018), as well as articles on social movements, immigration, borders, and homelessness. He holds a PhD in sociology from Columbia University.

Cathy Lisa Schneider is associate professor in the School of International Service at American University in Washington, DC. She is the author of *Police Power and Race Riots: Urban Unrest in Paris and New York* (University of Pennsylvania Press, 2014, 2017 pbk.), *Shantytown Protest in Pinochet's Chile* (Temple University Press, 1995), and assorted articles on military and police repression, social movements, and ethnic and racial discrimination. She holds a PhD in government from Cornell University.

Collective Violence, Contentious Politics, and Social Change

A Charles Tilly Reader

EDITED BY
**ERNESTO CASTAÑEDA AND
CATHY LISA SCHNEIDER**

Routledge
Taylor & Francis Group

NEW YORK AND LONDON

First published 2017
by Routledge
711 Third Avenue, New York, NY 10017

and by Routledge
2 Park Square, Milton Park, Abingdon, Oxon, OX14 4RN

Routledge is an imprint of the Taylor & Francis Group, an informa business

Library of Congress Cataloging-in-Publication Data
Names: Tilly, Charles, author. | Castañeda, Ernesto, editor. | Schneider,
Cathy Lisa, 1955– editor.
Title: Collective violence, contentious politics, and social change: a Charles
Tilly reader / edited by Ernesto Castañeda, Cathy Lisa Schneider.
Description: New York, NY: Routledge, 2017.
Identifiers: LCCN 2016047481 | ISBN 9781612056715 (pbk.) |
ISBN 9781612056708 (hbk)
Subjects: LCSH: Social conflict. | Social movements. | Political violence. |
Political sociology. | Social change.
Classification: LCC HM1121 .T539 2017 | DDC 303.6—dc23
LC record available at https://lccn.loc.gov/2016047481

ISBN: 978-1-6120-5670-8 (hbk)
ISBN: 978-1-6120-5671-5 (pbk)
ISBN: 978-1-315-20502-1 (ebk)

Typeset in Avenir and Dante
by codeMantra

Contents

Credits   *ix*

Introduction   1
Ernesto Castañeda and Cathy Lisa Schneider

PART I
Revolutions and Social Change   **23**

1 The Vendée   25
2 Strikes in France 1830–1968   48
3 Does Modernization Breed Revolution?   55
4 From Mobilization to Revolution   71
5 Contentious Performances   92
6 Pernicious Postulates   100

PART II
State Making   **121**

7 War Making and State Making as Organized Crime   123
8 Coercion, Capital, and European States, A.D. 990–1990   140

PART III
Democracy   **155**

9 Democracy Is a Lake   157
10 Where Do Rights Come From?   168
11 Democratization and De-democratization   183
12 Trust and Democratic Rule   208

PART IV
Durable Inequality   **225**

13 Durable Inequality   227
14 Poverty and the Politics of Exclusion   249

PART V
Political Violence   **265**

15 Contentious Conversation   267
16 The Politics of Collective Violence   275
17 Terror, Terrorism, Terrorists   293

PART VI
Migration, Race, and Ethnicity   **305**

18 Transplanted Networks   307
19 Social Boundary Mechanisms   326
20 From Segregation to Integration   342

PART VII
Narratives and Explanations   **369**

21 Why Give Reasons?   371
22 Credit, Blame, and Social Life   383

    Index   *397*

Credits

Chapter 8
Excerpts from *Coercion, Capital, and European States, AD 990–1990* by Charles Tilly. © 1990 Wiley Blackwell. Reprinted with permission.

Chapter 9
Excerpts from *Roads from Past to Future* by Charles Tilly. © 1997 Rowman & Littlefield. Reprinted with permission.

Chapter 10
Excerpts from *Where Do Rights Come From?* by Theda Skocpol. © 1998 Cornell University Press. Reprinted with permission.

Chapter 11
Excerpts from *Democracy* by Charles Tilly. © 2007 Charles Tilly. Published by Cambridge University Press. Reprinted with permission.

Chapter 12
Excerpts from *Trust and Rule* by Charles Tilly. © 2005 Charles Tilly. Published by Cambridge University Press. Reprinted with permission.

Chapter 13
Excerpts from *Durable Inequality* by Charles Tilly © 1998 by the Regents of the University of California. Published by the University of California Press. Reprinted with permission.

Chapter 14
Excerpts from *Moving Out of Poverty: Cross Disciplinary Perspectives on Mobility* by Deepa Narayan and Patty Petesch. © 2007 The International Bank for Reconstruction and Development / The World Bank. Reprinted with permission.

Chapter 15
© 1998 The New School. This article was first published in "Contentious Conversations" *Social Research* 65, 491–510. Reprinted with permission by Johns Hopkins University Press.

Chapter 16
Excerpts from *The Politics of Collective Violence* by Charles Tilly. © 2003 Charles Tilly. Published by Cambridge University Press. Reprinted with permission.

Chapter 17
"Terror, Terrorism, Terrorists"
Vol. 22, No. 1, Theories of Terrorism: A Symposium (2004), pp. 5–13. © *Sociological Theory* journal. Reprinted with permission.

Chapter 18

Excerpts from *Immigration Reconsidered: History, Sociology, and Politics* by Virginia Yans-McLaughlin. © 1990 by The Statue of Liberty Ellis Island Foundation. Published by Oxford University Press. Reprinted with permission.

Chapter 19

Philosophy of the Social Sciences 34,2: 211–236. © 2004 Sage Publications. Reprinted with permission.

Chapter 20

Excerpts from *Why?* by Charles Tilly. © 2006 by Princeton University Press. Reprinted by permission.

Chapter 21

Excerpts from *Why? Credit and Blame* by Charles Tilly. © 2008 by Princeton University Press. Reprinted by permission.

Introduction

Ernesto Castañeda and Cathy Lisa Schneider

Charles Tilly (1929–2008) is one of the most influential contemporary American social scientists. He was instrumental in the establishment of the subfields of historical sociology, social science history, social movements, and contentious politics. Tilly had a prolific career in which he published more than fifty-one books and over seven hundred academic articles. He has deeply influenced sociologists, political scientists, historians, policy makers, and the general public through his methodological and theoretical innovations, and his training of generations of scholars.

Charles H. Tilly was born on May 27, 1929, in Lombard, Illinois—a suburb of Chicago. He grew up in a working-class family; his paternal grandfather was a German immigrant, and his mother was an immigrant from Wales. He pursued his education with the help of scholarships and various jobs that included as noted in his CV "newsboy, grocery clerk, office boy, factory hand, construction laborer, janitor, night watchman, camp counselor, and psychiatric-hospital researcher." Tilly's humble background informed his analytical perspective. He disliked historical accounts centered on kings, great men and elites and argued that social change was the inadvertent consequence of perennial clashes between ordinary people, armed actors, and political regimes.

Tilly graduated *magna cum laude* from Harvard University in 1950. He served in the U.S. Navy during the Korean War. He then did post-graduate work at Oxford and the Catholic University of Angers, France. Tilly obtained his doctoral degree in 1958 from Harvard's Department of Social Relations founded and chaired by Talcott Parsons (1902–1979). The department's curriculum offered a mix of sociology, social anthropology, and social psychology. At the time, the Department of Social Relations and the international field of sociology were largely dominated by Parsons's theoretical framework called "structural functionalism." Yet, Tilly was very critical of functionalism's systemic quasi-tautological explanations.

His dissertation co-directors were George Homans and Barrington Moore. George C. Homans (1910–1989) was a social psychologist and behavioral sociologist, who also taught medieval history, and is known for books such as *The Human Group* (1950). Barrington Moore Jr. (1913–2005) was a political sociologist and an early master of comparative-historical analysis, best known for his *Social Origins of Dictatorship and Democracy: Lord and Peasant in the Making of the Modern World* (1966). Coming from a working-class background, Tilly often stood in awe of Homans's and Moore's privileged backgrounds and quasi-aristocratic lifestyles (Tilly 2006a). Tilly identified more with Pitirim A. Sorokin (1889–1968), a Russian émigré, who witnessed firsthand the revolution of 1917 and was secretary to Russian Prime Minister Alexander Kerensky. Sorokin was exiled by the Soviet regime and immigrated to the United States. Sorokin, who founded the Department of Sociology at Harvard in 1930, was an ardent critic of Parsonian structural functionalism. Tilly was often Sorokin's teaching assistant and he had a great influence on Tilly, encouraging him to pursue his interest in combining sociology and history into the systematic study of revolutions and social change. Tilly referred to Sorokin as "his great teacher" (Tilly 2008a:19).

Tilly taught at Delaware, Harvard, Toronto, Michigan, The New School, and Columbia. While at the University of Delaware, he conducted surveys of local immigrant populations and worked on empirical problems related to urban sociology for governmental agencies in Delaware. He also wrote *The Vendée*, about the bloody and failed counterrevolution in France. Tilly returned to Harvard before moving to the University of Toronto where he received tenure. In 1969 he moved to the University of Michigan, where he pioneered the creation of "event catalogues." This quantitative approach to historical events consists of coding and constructing databases of recorded collective action events across time. Information contained in event catalogues could consist of the number of people participating in protests, claims made, type of protests, and the responses of police and local authorities. In 1984 Tilly founded the Center for the Study of Social Change at the New School for Social Research in New York. Ira Katznelson, Eric Hobsbawm, Perry Anderson, Louise Tilly, Vera and Aristide Zolberg, Richard Bensel, Talal Asad, and Janet Abu-Lughod were among the luminaries that, together with Tilly, made the New School one of the most exciting centers of critical research in the world (Mische 2011).

In 1996, Tilly moved to Columbia University, where he was the Joseph L. Buttenwieser Professor of Social Science, and where he spent his final twelve years and directed over fifty doctoral dissertations. Hundreds of those he taught or mentored throughout five decades remember his kindness and generosity. His contentious politics seminars in New York were open to the scholarly community at large. Tilly was able to pull together a true community of scholars to which he dedicated much time. He developed an online scholar community that continues to allow scholars around the world to share research findings and analyses of ongoing events and social movements.

In the spirit of social history, it bears mentioning that Tilly, with his wife and later colleague Louise Tilly, raised four children: Chris (an economist and professor), Kit (a research microbiologist), Laura (an attorney), and Sarah (a psychologist). Reports from the junior Tillys note that "Charles Tilly spent a great deal of time in the office, but cooked a tasty *quiche lorraine*, had a wicked volleyball spike, and organized frequent family expeditions."

During the span of his academic career he was visiting professor at the most prestigious French universities including the *Sorbonne*, the School for Advanced Studies in the Social Sciences (the *École des Hautes Études en Sciences Sociales*), the Paris Institute of Political Studies (*Sciences-Po*), and the prestigious *Collège de France*; as well as other European institutions. He received eight honorary doctorates from universities across the world. Tilly was a member of the National Academy of Sciences, the American Academy of Arts and Sciences, the American Philosophical Society, the Sociological Research Association and the *Ordre des Palmes Académiques*. His numerous awards include the Hirschman Prize from the Social Science Research Council and the Career of Distinguished Scholarship Award from the American Sociological Association.

Tilly: A Creative Theorist and Methodologist

While the late Tilly was extremely erudite and one of the world's most influential scholars, the early Tilly was partly an autodidact. Without any training in historical archival research (Merriman 2008), he went into the archives of a French province to gather data for his dissertation and he was able to make history and sociology meet in his first and groundbreaking book *The Vendée* (1964). In the same way, he would later develop original methods, models, and theories to answer important questions and empirical puzzles. His fresh approach led him to make original contributions to urban sociology, demography, immigration, politics, inequality, and fiscal, cultural, and military studies.

Tilly's main professional affiliation was sociology but he incorporated history and politics into his work, having a significant impact in currents inside contemporary history, political science, and international relations. Like other social scientists of this period such as E. P. Thompson, Fernand Braudel, and Eric Hobsbawm, Tilly was critical of top-down history. In a paper discussing the work of sociologist Paul Lazarsfeld and the nascent field of public opinion research, Tilly sought to understand how we can know what regular folk and people who did not keep diaries cared about before the twentieth century "in the absence of elections, surveys and social movements"? Tilly's argues that contentious performances of popular collective action "gave ordinary people extensive means of speaking their minds" and that records of public protest "yield rich information about the interests, grievances, and aspirations of our predecessors in this world. Even today we can reasonably look to the language of popular collective action as a complement to the knowledge offered us by elections and surveys" (Tilly 1983:477). His innovative event catalogue data gathering technique lent itself to comparisons, across time and space, between phenomena such as revolutions, social movements, strikes, protests, revolts or civil wars (Tilly 2008a). From these comparisons he observed how old repertoires of collective action transformed into new ones given changing structural arrangements,

> Why the prevailing repertoire of popular collective action underwent the change from relatively parochial and patronized to relatively national and autonomous is simple to state in principle and complex to show in practice. In principle, the shift occurred because the interests and organization of ordinary people shifted away from local affairs and powerful patrons to national affairs and major concentrations of power and capital. As capitalism advanced and national states became more powerful and centralized, local affairs and nearby patrons mattered less to the fates of ordinary people. Increasingly, holders of large capital and national power made the decisions that affected them. As a result, seizures of grain, collective invasions of fields, and the like became ineffective, irrelevant, obsolete. In response to the shifts of power and capital, ordinary people invented and adopted new forms of action, creating the electoral campaign, the public meeting, the social movement, and the other elements of the newer repertoire. Although the shift in repertoires followed the logic of change in power and capital, each form and each actor had a particular history. The

demonstration that we know, for example, took shape in Great Britain as a series of modifications in the sending of delegates, in the holiday parade, and in other older forms. It issued, furthermore, from 40 years of confrontation between radical activists and authorities. The firm-by-firm strike took on its recognizable characteristics in concrete labor-management struggles as capital concentrated in locality after locality. Because the particular histories are quite different, the common processes creating the demonstration and the strike only appear in perspective, at a distance. Nevertheless, in case after case it is clear that the common processes involved concentration—concentration of capital, concentration of political power.

(Tilly 1983:467–8)

Thus national electoral campaigns and social movements appeared as the national arena impacted more and more economic conditions and power relations in towns and localities.

While influential in historical sociology, Tilly is less often cited in the subfields of migration, inequality, and urban sociology not for lack of quality but partly because he is primarily associated with the study of revolutions, social movements, and contentious politics. Charles Tilly's contributions to historical sociology, state-formation, and especially social movements and contentious politics are among the most well-known because, in great part, these fields formed around Tilly's work. In terms of methodology, he followed Barrington Moore and others in pushing for the historical comparative method across a limited number of cases, and the use of event catalogues (Tilly 2008a). His work was problem- and theory-driven. He avoided purely scholastic or technical explanations for what he called "superior stories" (Tilly 2006b) accompanied by contextualized vignettes, charts, diagrams, and two-by-two tables. As Craig Calhoun said when presenting the Hirschman prize to Tilly,

[Charles Tilly and Albert Hirschman] wrote clear books that made complicated and nuanced analyses seem almost obvious—but only after their lucid formulations. Both men combined a passion for social science with a determination not to let this be owned by narrow disciplinary agendas or internal academic debates that lost purchase on the big issues in the larger world.

(Calhoun 2008)

Tilly was always an empiricist, relying heavily on historical records, primary and secondary sources. Yet his theoretical contributions are of such breadth, depth, and scope that he is often considered among the most important contemporary social theorists (Ashforth 2009, Demetriou 2012, Goldstone 2010, Krinsky and Mische 2013). His theories were elegant and parsimonious (Brubaker 2010) and often could be summarized in two-by-two tables and graphs. Building on Harrison White's (2009 [1965]) concept of catnets (categorical networks), Tilly advocated for a relational sociology that emphasizes social relations as the crux of social life; many have fruitfully used this approach (Diani 2007, Emirbayer 1997, Mische 2011, Tilly 2002:72, Zelizer 2012). These empirical and theoretical concerns remained constant across his academic career (Krinsky and Mische 2013).

Tilly pioneered a relational approach to the study of national states, one that focused on contentious interactions between states, subjects, and citizens. He maintained a certain detachment when analyzing collective violence. State violence might be used for regressive and extractive purposes, but rebellions and violent clashes could result in more representative states or equitable societies. Tilly warns us not to attach a priori moral judgements to an analysis of historical or contemporary events. Rather than considering violence by the state as legitimate and justified, while that by non-state actors as illegitimate and dangerous, Tilly empirically examined actual struggles over power and resources at historical conjunctions. Legitimate and illegitimate violence, he notes, are often mirror-images of each other, with official legitimacy gained by the winning side only after the fact.

Contributions and Implications

To equate Tilly to only one of his articles or books is myopic. Instead of waiting until a text reached "perfection," Tilly was willing to publish and be proven wrong or only partially right. Each work was designed to correct errors he believed he had made in his previous work. He had a burning passion to get it right. This is exemplified in his first book *The Vendée* (1964), which was a refutation of his dissertation.

Although the size of Tilly's oeuvre and his work in a wide variety of academic fields makes a comprehensive compilation of his work difficult, his research in one area contributed to and reinforced his thinking in other areas. In this book, we include what we consider Tilly's most seminal work on six areas: Revolutions and Social Change; State Making; Democratization; Durable Inequality; Collective Violence; Migration, Race, and Ethnicity; and

Narratives and Explanations. We have selected key snippets of Tilly's work to highlight some of the major themes, theories, and methods that he contributed to social science, but clearly this tome is not exhaustive. Here is a brief summary of the sections included in this first edition.

Part I: Revolutions and Social Change

Tilly began his career in the 1960s by looking not at the revolutionary heroes of 1789 but at the 1793 armed counter-revolutionaries in the mainly rural Vendée region of France. Tilly wanted to know why this region revolted against the Republic. While Tilly's dissertation partly attributed the counter-revolution to the "backward" nature of peasants, *The Vendée* looks at large-scale social change from the perspective of local actors in provincial France. Here he emphasized the impact of urbanization on changing economic relations, and how that set the stage for armed conflict. Chapter 1 is taken from *The Vendée*, a book that

> portrays a coalition of peasants, rural artisans, priests, and nobles lining up in different ways ... against a bourgeoisie which had been gaining economic strength during the eighteenth century, and which rapidly seized control of the local and regional apparatus during the early years of the Revolution. As they did elsewhere in France, the bourgeois who came to power in the Vendée received strong support from their fellow bourgeois in the national government. Unlike their counterparts in most other regions, they lacked the allies and power base in the countryside to crush their enemies, neutralize the disaffected, and generate active support among the rest of the population. Why and how that happened are the book's central problems.
> (Preface to the 1976 Harvard paperback edition)

Tilly rejected accounts that "stuff[ed] a standard set of motives into the skulls of peasants" and explained peasant revolts as driven by ignorance, fanaticism, or uncritical loyalty to the king. He also challenged the dominant theories that focused on anomie, frustration, and individuals unmoored from social restraints, as Samuel Huntington (1968), Ted Gurr (1970), and James Davies (1974) had argued. Instead, in cataloging their most oft-stated grievances, Tilly found that peasant revolts were driven by anger over taxes and military conscription. Tilly would build on this insight throughout his career. William H. Sewell Jr. sees the Vendée as "The Model" on how to best do social history,

> Here was a work of historical sociology that incorporated serious the-oretical reasoning and made use of quantitative methods but that was also recognizable as a thoroughly historical study. It tackled a major problem of historical interpretation, contained splendidly detailed archival research about ordinary people, and told a cracking good story—and it did all this from a distinctly sociological standpoint … it supplied a brilliant model of the sort of detailed local social-historical inquiry that I had in mind. It appeared in a flurry of other books that also helped inspire my research. E. P. Thompson's *The Making of the English Working Class* was published in 1963. Stephan Thernstrom's *Poverty and Progress* (a phenomenally influential work in its day) and E. J. Hobsbawm *Labouring Men* were published in 1964, the same year as *The Vendée*. These were glory years in the emergence of social his-tory. But it was *The Vendée* that I chose as my model.
>
> (Sewell 2010)

In Chapter 2, "Strikes in France 1830–1968," Tilly and Edward Shorter pro-vide further evidence to counter "breakdown" theories of social mobiliza-tion. Using event catalogues, maps, and statistics, they point out that strikes occurred not where workers experienced dislocation and deprivation but rather where they were well organized, where workers' organizations had been created during prior waves of collective action. Indeed, strikes followed a predictable geographical pattern: they emerged where prior organiza-tions existed, and previous labor struggles had been fought. The dominant theories that focused on individual frustration, relative deprivation, or rising expectations could not explain the mechanisms that resulted in thousands of people marching on the same street, at the same time, to protest the same grievance. Tilly and Shorter concluded that organization and communica-tion networks were essential for even the smallest mobilizations.

In Chapter 3, "Does Modernization Breed Revolution?," Tilly disproves Huntington's argument that the gap between rapid socio-economic change (modernization) and stymied political change causes praetorianism and rev-olution. Tilly points out that the state is the most common perpetrator of violence and that most revolutions occur when groups that are excluded or losing ground politically organize as challengers. Revolutions result from the clash between existing states, defending existing power relations, and challengers organizing alternative states and power arrangements. After regime change, before the new state is able to institutionalize power and construct an effective coercive apparatus, criminal and politically displaced groups may threaten both the new state and the relatively powerless citizenry with increasingly violent actions.

In Chapter 4 taken from his widely cited book, *From Mobilization to Revolution*, Tilly looks at a wider array of social movements and revolutions and again shows that movements do not erupt when there is a breakdown in established order but rather when new networks, organizations, and states are established. Starting from his empirical work in France and Britain, Tilly now puts forth a more fully developed theoretical framework for understanding both protest and revolution in general as rational and political. Tilly's "polity model" is the first to view protest as a form of political claim making, shaped by the interactions between government, organized challengers, other members of the polity, and coalitions forged during struggles. With this work Tilly revolutionized social movement theory, which would become a critical impetus to the creation of social movement studies as a field.

One of the advantages of Tilly's model is that in contrast to the literature of the day, it did not presuppose a society with particular fully formed national geographical borders. Thus it is less prone to methodological nationalism, and more historically accurate since it does not start with current-day political borders. This often-cited theoretical book highlights the incapacity of existing theories to explain mobilization across various geographical and historical contexts. Advancing a Resource Mobilization Model, Tilly argues that successful mobilization depended on available resources (land, labor, capital) and the creation of social movement organizations (SMO). The model marries a neo-Marxist structural approach with elements of game theory, rational choice theory, and the concept of imperfect information. Graphs in the original text, but not presented here, include theoretical return curves, theoretical path analysis graphs, and zero-sum assumptions. In the first chapters of this book, social movement groups and activists are treated as rational, strategically calculating agents who take into account resources, opportunities, and threats. In the last chapters of *From Mobilization...* Tilly qualifies such approaches as useful but reductionist. He emphasizes, instead, the importance of context specific meanings in which participants imbue their actions, and the cultural development and diffusion of repertoires of contention. Here we see the beginning of Tilly's shift from a focus on macro structures such as states, international systems, and modes of production to "relational realism," micro processes and relational mechanisms like brokerage, boundary activation, and identity shifts. It also presages his later interest in political ethnography and personal narratives (Castañeda 2009). While some claim that Tilly moved dramatically from a material structuralist to a culturalist understanding later in life, a fuller reading of *From Mobilization* ... shows that he always saw both elements as important and complementary.

Chapter 5 is drawn from one of his later books, *Contentious Performances*. In this more fully dynamic model, Tilly shows how the contentious performances and arguments of one movement campaign affect the next one. He uses the term campaign not in the electoral sense but as a predecessor to our concept of social movements, which he discusses in the next chapter of *Contentious Performances* and in his book *Social Movements*. In another methodological innovation, seen in the unabridged version of this chapter and in his book on Great Britain, Tilly analyses verbs used in historical records to describe contentious gatherings and claim-making in England to show how contention moves from the direct intimidation of local political enemies to protests that pressure parliament to implement desired legislation. An example of this process is the expansion of rights for Catholics in Anglican Britain.

Chapter 6, "Pernicious Postulates," drawn from *Big Structures, Large Processes, Huge Comparisons*, presents Tilly's discussion of eight pernicious postulates (deceiving assumptions) in social theory. In one of his clearest meta-theoretical statements, Tilly questions the validity of macro-comparative quantitative research which compares nation-states as "coherent, independent units" (for more on this, see Babones 2014). Such work starts from the present and works backward, assuming that prior state leaders deliberately created the institutional features of the modern state, and that one could draw a straight line from past to future. In contrast, Tilly insists that modern states were created by dynamic processes, structural constraints, and contingencies beyond the awareness of those actors commonly credited with making history. To paraphrase Marx, ordinary people, not statesmen, made history, and they did so not as they pleased but under circumstances created by war, changing modes of production, urbanization, and resistance.

Part II: State Making

Part II addresses the topic of state making from a historical, comparative, and theoretical perspective. The readings included in Chapters 7 and 8 are drawn from Tilly's provocatively titled article "State Making as Organized Crime" and his more fully developed book on this theme *Coercion, Capital, and European States, A.D. 990–1990*. In both, Tilly challenges Mode of Production, Statist, World System and Geopolitical accounts of the relationship between state-making, war-making, exploitation, and organized crime. States, he argues, were not created by extraordinarily smart individuals with long-term designs for their nations. Rather, they emerged as an unintended by-product of banditry and war. A thousand years ago, armed bandits and pirates fought each other for control of land, resources, and waterways. Their need to conquer or rule conquered territories led to the development of bureaucratic systems, or states. Repeated clashes over territory and control of global trade routes led states to seek greater resources for war-making. The search for resources led European armies to conquer territories in Africa, Asia, and the Americas. As rulers sought to cement control over given territories they created censuses, passports, customs, and accounting systems. A thousand years of warfare forged modern European national states. Conquering European armies and colonialism created states in Africa, Asia, and the Americas.

In Chapter 7, an abridged version of Tilly's famous essay "State Making as Organized Crime," Tilly compares state-formation with the criminal activity of the mafia, which likewise demand payment (taxes) for protection from violence that they themselves create. Indeed, the first states were constructed by bandits, pirates, and other criminal organizations that preyed on peasant communities. Rather than perpetually raid such communities to steal resources, criminal gangs and predators conquered such villages either enslaving the peasants or forcing them to pay tribute. To extract payments, prevent rebellion, and fight-off contending armed groups, the conquering bandits were forced to create coercive administrative structures. European areas rich in agricultural land and waterways—that facilitated trade—attracted other bandits. Increased resources were needed to fend off such attacks and make war. When conquered people rebelled, newly born states, lacking the resources to simultaneously make war against rival armies and suppress domestic unrest, bargained with local populations.

Depending on the terrain, the bargains led to very different institutional arrangements. Rich agricultural land located on waterways led to trade and the accumulation of capital. In city-states, pirates struck bargains with wealthy merchants, receiving money for protective services. Pirates became navies and the city-states were governed by a committee of merchants, for what Tilly calls the capital-intensive path. Where large expanses of land were available but with only a few waterways, tribute-taking empires gave armed bandits large tracts of land and serfs to work the land, for what Tilly calls a coercion-intensive path. Bandits became feudal lords, kings ruled through them via indirect rule. Both states were fatally flawed. City-states lacked the landmass to field standing armies and depended on mercenaries. Tribute-taking empires were vulnerable to betrayal, succession, and revolution. Both eventually disappeared, as they lost wars against states with both rich waterways and large landmasses.

"War made the state, and the state made war," Tilly argues (1975:42). The needs of war eventually drove European states to seek a continually expanding supply of resources. High taxes, grain requisition, and forced conscription sparked massive rebellions. In 1789, punishingly high taxes to pay off war debts sparked a revolution in France and led to the creation of the first national state. Other European states created similar institutions, including a national language and standardized education. States created citizen armies, contracted outside protection services, or were defeated in war. The new national state was a formidable war machine partly due to the war-making capacity of citizen armies, whose loyalty to the state was based on popular sovereignty and national identity, and partly due to the resources, and subsequent technological advances, generated through bargains struck between states and citizens.

Tilly argues that European states emerged as an unintended by-product of violent conflict and war. European monarchies fought each other for control of land, resources, and waterways, and, as war-making grew more expensive, for control over colonies and global trade routes. The urgency to finance these wars led to the development of bureaucratic systems to control militias, govern territories, generate wealth, collect taxes, and administrate estates in a rational manner. In order to do so, censuses, passports, customs, and accounting systems were developed. These processes, Tilly argues, led unintentionally to the construction of national states.

European states soon conquered the globe. In Chapter 8, drawn from the final chapters of *Coercion, Capital, and European States*, Tilly looks at the devastating impact of this process on states outside Europe. In areas without Europe's long experience in warfare, no organization could withstand its conquering armies. By 1914, most of the globe was controlled by Europe. If European states bargained with their local population for the wherewithal for war, colonial states used the resources of European armies to conquer and repress domestic populations and extract resources in the Americas, Asia, and Africa. Absent the need for continuous military mobilization and without the crucial mechanism of bargaining between the rulers and ruled, transplanted European institutions would not yield democratic outcomes outside of the West, but predatory relationships instead.

Part III: Democracy

The work in this part shows Tilly's conception of democracy as a process not as a "tradition," an "institution," nor the result of a constitutional convention. To him, democracy depends on the creation of trust networks and governments that broker and stand above particular *trust networks*. In Chapter 9, "Democracy Is a Lake," he reminds us that democracy is a process that depends on broad, equal, protected, and mutually binding consultation. To maintain democratic legitimacy, the state must establish direct relations with the broadest segments of its population, standing above particular trust networks and representing all groups impartially even in categorically unequal societies. In Chapter 10, "Where Do Rights Come From?," Tilly grounds rights in popular demands, social mobilization, and bargaining between nascent nation-states and inhabitants over taxes and conscription. Again, he emphasizes the crucial role played by war in constructing the modern national state, its externally-oriented standing professional national armies and its internally-oriented national police.

In Chapter 11, "Democratization and De-democratization," drawn from *Democracy*, Tilly uses the examples of France, India, and Switzerland to advance an ambitious mechanism-oriented argument about the non-linearity of the democratization processes. The knitting of trust networks between states and citizens and between categories of citizens, as well as the reduction of categorical inequalities, is critical to the creation of democratic regimes. Regimes may also experience democratic decay. Here Tilly introduces a relatively novel concept—de-democratization. A regime is democratic to the degree that "political relations between the state and its citizens feature broad, equal, protected, mutually binding consultation." Changes in the breadth, equality, protection, and scale of mutually binding consultation between states and citizens are evidence of increasing or decreasing levels of democracy. In Chapter 12, "Trust and Democratic Rule," drawn from *Trust and Rule*, Tilly continues to expand on the relationship between trust networks and democratization. For democracy to exist, states must stand above particular trust networks. Where those belonging to particular trust networks withdraw from binding agreements, even mature liberal democracies can experience reversals. The retreat of the wealthy to gated communities and private schools, the capture of regulatory agencies by those they are designed to regulate, the denial of civil rights and civil liberties, and the increased policing and surveillance of minorities and immigrants can even lead to democratic collapse.

Tilly's preference for relational approaches over methodological individualism results in a rich sociological account of democracy. Democracy is a process that involves categories and networks of ordinary people through bargaining, contention, and compromise with state authorities and other power-holders. Tilly's work is a corrective to the ethnocentrism of theories that see emulation of Western institutions as necessary and sufficient for democratic development. Despite having published works contributing to French and British historiography, Tilly recognized that understandings of democracy and state-making were unduly influenced by the particular trajectories of France and Britain, an emphasis that led some theorists to blame sloth and backwardness for the fragility of democracy in southern Europe, Latin America, Africa, and Asia. Instead, Tilly drew attention to the negative impact of colonialism on the relationship between states and citizens, and on the relative power and autonomy of the repressive apparatus.

Part IV: Durable Inequality

Part IV discusses another important Tillyian contribution, the concept of categorical inequality. Chapter 13 includes selections from the book *Durable Inequality*, where Tilly introduces his highly original and influential relational theory of inequality. Written during a fellowship at the University of Uppsala, Sweden, the book pondered the persistence of categorical inequality in democratic states like Sweden, where elected leaders had worked assiduously to eradicate it. Why was work and compensation not arrayed along a gradient based on ability, but instead clustered in highly unequal categories that tied particular kinds of work to large differences in remuneration, trust, and prestige? Tilly asked. And why were such clusters paired with particular categories of people characterized by race, ethnicity, gender, religion, citizenship status, nationality, and the like?

Tilly's answer was that the installation of categories and categorical boundaries facilitates and stabilizes exploitation, which he defines in classic Marxist terms as occurring when "some well-connected group of actors controls a valuable, labor demanding resource from which they can extract returns by harnessing the effort of others, whom they exclude from the full value of that effort." Exploitation, however, is a fundamentally unstable process: the large exploited majority could band together to expropriate the means of production. The installation of categorical boundaries, pitting different exploited groups against each other, helps diminish the likelihood of rebellion. Opportunity hoarding, where members of a certain category have greater opportunities for advancement and income, in return for greater loyalty and trust, helped make such categories durable, stabilizing exploitation, forestalling the development of a united opposition. Networks form along each side of a given boundary and those on one side of the boundary claimed "solidarity with others on the same side … and invoke a certain sort of relationship to those on the opposite side." Members tell stories about the boundary with those pertaining to dominant categories justifying their more privileged position. Over time both sides "attribute hard and durable and even genetic reality to the categories they inscribe."

Durable Inequality (1998) has garnered interest from the subfield of social stratification and inequality with the growing interest in social boundaries. Erik Olin Wright was among the first to praise Tilly's book (2000) and called it a crucial contribution to Marxist theory. Douglas Massey's 2007 *Categorically Unequal: The American Stratification System* "is heavily indebted to Charles Tilly's" *Durable Inequality* (Bobo 2010). Michael B. Katz's *Why Don't American Cities Burn?* (2012) and Cathy L. Schneider's *Police Power and Race Riots: Urban Unrest in Paris and New York* (2014) explain why race riots erupt in some locations and time periods and not others, drawing explicitly on Tilly's work on boundary activation and deactivation. Kim Voss (2010) used this work to understand stratification dynamics and gender inequality. Cecilia Ridgeway also used the framework presented in *Durable Inequality* to explain gender inequality in her 2013 Presidential Address to the American Sociological Association (Ridgeway 2014).

In Chapter 14, "Poverty and the Politics of Exclusion," Tilly elaborates on his relational view on inequality citing work interested in understanding poverty from the point of view of the poor and not that of technocrats, favoring ethnographic work over technical accounts. This chapter discusses processes fostering or reducing exclusion and categorical inequality. He proposes a set of policy implications derived from seeing poverty as relational; and brings up factors to keep in mind in order to prevent negative unintended consequences, and misusing resources in unsuccessful anti-poverty interventions.

Part V: Political Violence

In his later work on political violence, Tilly built on the theoretical work he pioneered in *Durable Inequality*. Specifically, he made boundary activation, as well as mechanisms like brokerage (uniting the members of several categories, violent entrepreneurs, and violent specialists against a rival coalition), central to understanding a wide array of violent conflicts. In Chapter 15, "Contentious Conversation," Tilly emphasizes the dialectical and relational nature of conflict. Warfare and conflict among categorical groups can be studied as a conversation in the language of violence. In Chapter 16, drawn from *The Politics of Collective Violence* (2003), Tilly places all forms of collective violence along a two-by-two axis of coordination and salience. The most damaging form of violence is coordinated destruction. Here, violent entrepreneurs connect armies and citizens along an activated us/them boundary with the intention of destroying all those on the other side of a given boundary. Where both sides are equally matched you have war. Where the more powerful side engages in total destruction of the other, you have genocide or politicide. Where the weaker side launches the attack, you have coordinated terror. Tilly also includes smaller forms of collective violence in his discussion, ranging from brawls, broken negotiations, and scattered attacks to opportunism.

In Chapter 17, "Terror, Terrorism, and Terrorists," Tilly attempts to unpack the war on terror. He asks, what exactly is "terror"? Is a war on terror a war against a strategy or against a specific group of people? Originally terror, Tilly points out, was used to describe the aftermath of the French revolution as in "the reign of terror." The term referred specifically to the action of states, the institution most capable of inflicting large-scale violence. Yet now, the term terrorist is applied only to small groups of conspirators that compensate for their weakness through attacks on soft targets, particularly civilians. The concept of a "war on terror" is slippery, and dangerously so. It is not clear whether we are to fight a tactic, a small transnational group, or a group of states. The result is an endless war, one with ever-multiplying enemies.

Just four days after September 11, 2001, Tilly intuited how the events of those days had been derived from a decentralized network, with members who did not know each other personally but who shared a political ideology, and were trying to make a political statement through non-conventional, violent means. Tilly predicted the terrible consequences to come of the international politics of George W. Bush. He feared that a discursive barrier would now be constructed between the two large groups, the self-nominated "us" versus "them." A resulting armed attack against a certain region blamed for the attacks would change the power relations within these given groups, amplifying radicalization amongst the group labeled as "them." This would then intensify their attacks, aggravating the situation, leading to escalation, and thus further justifying the confrontation between these groups. This division would call for the creation of new international alliances, which would obligate the excluded parties to unite within themselves, and paradoxically make room for the creation of new routes and opportunities for drug trafficking and international organized crime—as ultimately happened in Afghanistan. The result of a war declared against an enemy who is invisible, and at the same time categorical, would end up giving more power and outside support to dissident groups inside countries. Meanwhile, US policy makers deciding to invade Iraq chose to condone the violence and terror perpetrated by allied states such as Saudi Arabia, Bahrain, Yemen, or Pakistan, and by US military forces and armed contractors. As a result, the level of democracy would decrease, as much in these countries as in the West; a product of major militarization of the forces of security and the reduction of civil liberties and human rights for both citizens and foreigners. Regrettably, such predictions were on target, although as he explains in his model, these democratic setbacks can be rectified when citizens voice opposition to expensive foreign incursions.

Part VI: Migration, Race, and Ethnicity

Part VI deals with Tilly's less-known contributions to immigration and race and ethnic relations. While traditionally not considered a migration scholar, Tilly was actually one of the first social scientists to note the role played by social networks in chain migration. As a result of chain migration, immigrants concentrate in certain localities and economic niches (Tilly and Brown 1967). Their concentration increases their visibility, helping promote stereotypes about them. Cities, in particular, are the factories of ethnicity.

In Chapter 18, "Transplanted Networks" (1990), Tilly provides a masterful explanation of the causes behind migration, a typology of migration, and how migration into cities creates ethnicity in the US. He then discusses what is at stake when talking about assimilation in terms of race relations and categorical inequality. Tilly's understanding of migration has stood the test of years of ethnographic and quantitative research on migration, and anticipated the use of networks to understand migration flows and spatial concentration that Douglas Massey and colleagues would later popularize.

Chapter 19, "Social Boundary Mechanisms," further develops Tilly's theoretical work on race relations and us/them boundaries by focusing on the case of Bolivian immigrants in Argentina, showing how social boundary mechanisms work to exclude newcomers and perpetuate inequality. Chapter 20, "From Segregation to Integration," uses examples from different geographies and historical periods to compare bottom-up and top-down religious and ethnic trust networks and show how they have, or have not, been integrated into larger polities.

Deeply influenced by the work of Harrison White and the New York relational school (Mische 2011), Tilly wanted to explain the role that intergroup dynamics played in cementing power differentials and categorical inequality based on gender, race, ethnicity, and geography (Wellman 2008). Different categories attain particular characteristics at specific times and places as a consequence of a networked sorting and legitimation processes, rather than the innate properties of certain individuals. Tilly's work on urbanization, the birth of ethnicity in cities, and migration dynamics builds on this insight as well as on the work of Viviana Zelizer (Zelizer 2005, Zelizer 2012). For Tilly and Zelizer, remittances are a way to fulfill family obligations, tangible proof of the importance of social relations despite distance (Tilly 2007, Zelizer and Tilly 2006).

Part VII: Narratives and Explanations

This part showcases the type of work that Tilly also carried out toward the end of his career. Reflecting on decades of work, he argues that social processes are the result of accidents and unintended consequences. He contrasts this with our need to tell simplified stories that attribute credit and blame at the individual or categorical level. In his last books, Charles Tilly analyzes daily behaviors and discursive processes. For example, he examines why we see the need to give reasons and tell stories in our social life (Tilly 2006c), why we assign blame and give credit to people around us (Tilly 2008c), and how researchers can reconcile the study of culture and the critiques brought up by post-modernism with a research agenda that generates high-quality and useful scientific social knowledge (*The Oxford Handbook of Contextual Analysis* Goodin and Tilly 2006). His goal was to draw "a tunnel under the post-structuralist challenge" (Mische 2011). He wanted to take discursive, epistemological, constructivist, cultural, and socio-psychological challenges to positivism seriously, without throwing the baby out with the bathwater. He wanted social scientists to explain the "how" of social construction and how narratives impact everyday social thinking and practice. Tilly then realizes that he has been using vignettes, negative cases, and superior storytelling to make his empirical and theoretical arguments for decades. Stories are easier to remember, and they are the way we naturally convey information and moral values. A superior story has many actors, is nonlinear, and in its complexity it conveys social science in a way that mathematical formulas, diagrams, timelines, or elite histories cannot.

Chapter 21, "Why Give Reasons?," the introduction to his book *Why?*, starts with powerful reactions to the 9/11 attacks on the World Trade Center and how people scrambled to understand the events as they unfolded, and provides an explanation of why they happened. Tilly then argues that people give reasons in order to form and keep social relations. For example, reasons as to why we are late or absent from a party, whether factual or not, underline our intention to continue investing in a social relationship. In Chapter 22, the abridged first chapter of *Credit and Blame* (2008), Tilly continues his analysis of the importance of rhetorical and narrative devices in our understanding of social reality, in the attribution of credit or blame, and their implications for politics.

We have drawn broadly from Tilly's work, abridging selected texts to include a larger sampling of his oeuvre. Those interested in more details should refer to the original texts. We hope that these selections encourage readers to explore Tilly's work in greater depth and to apply, critique, and build on his theoretical and methodological contributions.[1]

Acknowledgments

The Tilly family and Chris Tilly in particular have been very helpful, supportive of this project, and trusting of our choices. We thank all the book and journal publishers who did not object to the reproduction here of portions of Tilly's work. We would like to thank the unwavering support and continuous encouragement of Dean Birkenkamp at Routledge. Amanda Yee's editorial assistance was also key to the publication of this book.

The authors wish to thank the many scholars who filled out the online survey on their use and knowledge of Tilly's work. Special thanks to Sid Tarrow, Marie Kennedy, Viviana Zelizer, Craig Calhoun, Gil Eyal, Bill Roy, Ron Aminzade, Michael Hanagan, Mauricio Font, Javier Auyero, Jeff Goodwin, John Krinsky, Roy Licklider, Marco Giugni, Mario Diani, Jeff Broadbent, Randa Serhan, Andreas Koller, Nicholas Toloudis, Angela Alonso, Anne Mische, Laleh Khalili, Lesley Wood, among many others for conversation at the early stages of this and related book projects for their support, inspiration, and encouragement to take on this daunting task.

In particular, the authors are grateful to Charles Tilly. Cathy Schneider first met Tilly in 1985, shortly before conducting dissertation field research in Chile. For the next thirty-three years, until his death, she maintained a regular email correspondence and friendship. His optimism and unstinting generosity, the joy he took in the craft of research, his ability to cut through extraneous material to the most impenetrable root of a problem, have long inspired her work. As a junior scholar, Ernesto worked on this reader because he took three graduate courses with Tilly at Columbia, attended the Contentious Politics seminar on and off for seven years, and co-taught with Tilly his last course, titled "Revolutions, Social Movements, and Contentious Politics," at Columbia College during the Spring of 2007. Furthermore, he was lucky to have the late Tilly co-direct his MA thesis and dissertation proposal. It took him many years to understand the range, importance, and complexity of Charles Tilly's work, and he is still learning from it. Adrienne LeBas and Maura Fennelly provided feedback on this introduction. Matt Marquez and Jonathan Klassen provided administrative help early on. Elana Lipkin, Natali Collazos, and Johandra Delgado helped us compiling the references for each chapter. All errors and omissions remain our own.

We hope that this reader helps others learn about Tilly's work, theories, and methods to facilitate their own research and understanding of large-scale social change.

Note

1   A number of books directly expand on Tilly's work, for example: Hanagan, Michael and Chris Tilly. 2011. *Contention and Trust in Cities and States*: Springer Netherlands, a co-edited volume by Michael Hanagan and Chris Tilly, includes chapters by renowned social scientists assessing Tilly's work on cities. Kousis, Maria, Tom Selwyn and David Clark. 2011. *Contested Mediterranean Spaces: Ethnographic Essays in Honour of Charles Tilly*: Berghahn Books, applies Tilly's theories to understand contested politics in the Mediterranean region through ethnographic methods, following up on a 2008 special issue on the Mediterranean of the *American Behavioral Scientist*. Tilly, Charles. 2008b. "A General Introduction to the Special Issue: Mediterranean Political Processes in Comparative Historical Perspective." *American Behavioral Scientist* 51(10):1467–71. Tarrow, Sidney. 2015. *War, States, and Contention: A Comparative Historical Study*: Cornell University Press. explicitly aims to connect Tilly's work on contention and war to that on state-building. Castañeda, Ernesto. 2017. *Immigration and Categorical Inequality: Migration to the City and the Birth of Race and Ethnicity*: New York, Routledge, is an edited volume that builds upon Tilly's theoretical conceptualizations around migration, urbanization, social boundaries, and race and ethnicity.

References

Ashforth, Adam. 2009. "Charles Tilly." *Proceedings of the American Philosophical Society* 153(3):372–80.

Babones, Salvatore J. 2014. *Methods for Quantitative Macro-Comparative Research*. Thousand Oaks, CA: SAGE Publications.

Bobo, Lawrence D. 2010. "Inequality and U.S. Society: Review of Douglas S. Massey's Categorically Unequal: The American Stratification System." *Du Bois Review: Social Science Research on Race* 7(1):30–34.

Brubaker, Rogers. 2010. "Charles Tilly as a Theorist of Nationalism." *The American Sociologist* 41(4):375–81.

Calhoun, Craig. 2008, "A Voice We Will Miss" *Tributes to Charles Tilly*: Social Science Research Center. (http://www.ssrc.org/essays/tilly/calhoun).

Castañeda, Ernesto. 2009. "Charles Tilly: Connecting Large Scale Social Change and Personal Narrative." *Sociological Research Online* 14(5):24.

Castañeda, Ernesto. 2017. *Immigration and Categorical Inequality: Migration to the City and the Birth of Race and Ethnicity*. New York, NY: Routledge.

Davies, James Chowning. 1974. "The J-Curve and Power Struggle Theories of Collective Violence." *American Sociological Review* 39(4):607–10.

Demetriou, Chares. 2012. "Processual Comparative Sociology: Building on the Approach of Charles Tilly." *Sociological Theory* 30(1):51–65.

Diani, Mario. 2007. "The Relational Element in Charles Tilly's Recent (and Not So Recent) Work." *Social Networks* 29(2):316–23.

Emirbayer, Mustafa. 1997. "Manifesto for a Relational Sociology." *American Journal of Sociology* 103:281–317.

Goldstone, Jack A. 2010. "From Structure to Agency to Process: The Evolution of Charles Tilly's Theories of Social Action as Reflected in His Analyses of Contentious Politics." *The American Sociologist* 41(4):358–67.

Goodin, Robert E. and Charles Tilly. 2006. *The Oxford Handbook of Contextual Political Analysis*. Oxford: Oxford University Press.

Gurr, Tedd Robert. 1970. *Why Men Rebel*. Princeton, NJ: Princeton University Press.

Hanagan, Michael and Chris Tilly. 2011. *Contention and Trust in Cities and States*: Springer Netherlands.

Homans, George C. 1950. *The Human Group*. New York, NY: Harcourt.

Huntingon, Samuel. 1968. *Political Order in Changing Societies*. New Haven, CT: Yale University Press.

Katz, Michael B. 2012. *Why Don't American Cities Burn?* Philadelphia, PA: University of Pennsylvania Press.

Kousis, Maria, Tom Selwyn and David Clark. 2011. *Contested Mediterranean Spaces: Ethnographic Essays in Honour of Charles Tilly*: Berghahn Books.

Krinsky, John and Ann Mische. 2013. "Formations and Formalisms: Charles Tilly and the Paradox of the Actor." *Annual Review of Sociology* 39(1):1–26.

Merriman, John. 2008, "I Went up to Amiens Today" *Tributes to Charles Tilly*. (<http://www.ssrc.org/essays/tilly/merriman>).

Mische, Ann. 2011. "Relational Sociology, Culture, and Agency." pp. 80–97 in *The Sage Handbook of Social Network Analysis*, edited by J. Scott and P. Carrington. London: Sage Publications.

Moore, Barrington. 1966. *Social Origins of Dictatorship and Democracy: Lord and Peasant in the Making of the Modern World*. Boston, MA: Beacon Press.

Ridgeway, Cecilia L. 2014. "Why Status Matters for Inequality." *American Sociological Review* 79(1):1–16.

Schneider, Cathy Lisa. 2014. *Police Power and Race Riots: Urban Unrest in Paris and New York*. Philadelphia, PA: University of Pennsylvania Press.

Sewell, William H. 2010. "Charles Tilly's Vendée as a Model for Social History." *French Historical Studies* 33(2):307–15.

Tarrow, Sidney. 2015. *War, States, and Contention: A Comparative Historical Study:* Cornell University Press.

Tilly, Charles. 1964. *The Vendée.* Cambridge, MA: Harvard University Press.

Tilly, Charles and Harold C. Brown. 1967. "On Uprooting, Kinship, and the Auspices of Migration." *International Journal of Comparative Sociology* (8).

Tilly, Charles. 1975. *The Formation of National States in Western Europe.* Princeton, NJ: Princeton University Press.

Tilly, Charles. 1983. "Speaking Your Mind without Elections, Surveys, or Social Movements." *The Public Opinion Quarterly* 47(4):461–78.

Tilly, Charles. 2002. *Stories, Identities, and Political Change.* Lanham, MD: Rowman & Littlefield.

Tilly, Charles. 2006a. "In Memoriam: Barrington Moore Jr." *Canadian Journal of Sociology Online.*

Tilly, Charles. 2006b. *Why?* Princeton, NJ: Princeton University Press.

Tilly, Charles. 2007. "Trust Networks in Transnational Migration." *Sociological Forum* 22(1).

Tilly, Charles. 2008a. *Contentious Performances.* Cambridge: Cambridge University Press.

Tilly, Charles. 2008b. "A General Introduction to the Special Issue: Mediterranean Political Processes in Comparative Historical Perspective." *American Behavioral Scientist* 51(10):1467–71.

Voss, Kim. 2010. "Enduring Legacy? Charles Tilly and Durable Inequality." *The American Sociologist* 41(4):368–74.

Wellman, Barry. 2008. "Review of Charles Tilly, Identities, Boundaries & Social Ties. Boulder, CO and London: Paradigm Publishers, 2005. 269 pp." *American Journal of Sociology* 113(5).

White, Harrison C. 2009 [1965]. "Notes on the Constituents of Social Structure." *Sociologica* 1.

Zelizer, Viviana A. 2005. *The Purchase of Intimacy.* Princeton, NJ: Princeton University Press.

Zelizer, Viviana A. 2012. "How I Became a Relational Economic Sociologist and What Does That Mean?" *Politics & Society* 40(2):145–74.

Zelizer, Viviana A. and Charles Tilly. 2006. "Relations and Categories." pp. 1–31 in *The Psychology of Learning and Motivation*, Vol. 47. Categories in Use, edited by A. Markman and B. Ross. San Diego, CA: Elsevier.

Revolutions and Social Change

1

The Vendée   1

Charles Tilly

Preface to the Second Printing

In preparing the book which was to refute my earlier theses, I turned away
from the common notion of a general and irreversible evolution from
"backward" to "progressive" politics toward a more careful consideration
of the political consequences of urbanization. Urbanization seemed relevant
because cities clearly played different roles and had gone through different
recent histories in the revolutionary and counterrevolutionary sections of
western France, and because so many of the collective conflicts in the region during the early Revolution pitted groups based in the country against
groups based in the city.

Textile production plummeted in 1789 and 1790. Riots over supplies and
prices constantly gnawed at local officials in the region, frequently toppled
them, and probably drove them toward more stringent controls over both
supplies and prices. Popular participation by riot had a political force of its
own. Furthermore, the industrial artisans of town and country alike were
acutely vulnerable to both unemployment and food shortages, and regularly
struck out against suspected hoarders and profiteers. In fact, a great many
incidents of the so-called Peasant Revolt of 1789 in the West turn out, on
close inspection, to involve nuclei of rural or semiurban workers rather than
peasants.

In addition to helping account for one of the critical events of the Revolution, I hoped to contribute to the sociologist's understanding of large-scale
changes in societies. There seemed to be two openings for such a contribution. The first was to show the advantages of first-hand work with historical

materials in the verification or refinement of ideas sociologists have been applying to contemporary evidence or second-hand historical accounts. The second was to examine the relations between the way cities grew and the nature of other changes in the organization of communities in the case of western France, with the hope that some of the connections which showed up there might apply more generally. This meant addressing two audiences at once: people concerned with the French Revolution but unmoved by sociological problems, people concerned with contemporary social change but unmoved by eighteenth-century France.

CHAPTER 1

Introduction

In 1793 a great uprising in the West of France threatened the very life of the Revolution. Country people in adjacent sections of Poitou, Anjou, and Brittany seized staves, scythes, pitchforks, and muskets, then joined to attack the forces of the Republic. They remained masters of their territory for more than six months, and a threat to the authority of successive political regimes in the West for more than six years. We call the uprising of 1793 and its aftermath the War of the Vendée, the Vendée counterrevolution, or more simply, the Vendée.

The memory of the Vendée has never stopped inspiring histories in great volume and variety. In the minds of its many devotees it looms as large as the Civil War does in the United States. No doubt there is room in their enthusiasm, as well as in the technical literature of the Revolution as a whole, for new and more accurate general accounts of the Vendée. But this book says very little about what happened once the counterrevolution began. Instead, it fixes on the nature of eighteenth-century society in the West and on local developments between the coming of the Revolution in 1789 and the outbreak of the counterrevolution in 1793.

I have reversed the usual recipe, one part background to ten parts military history, out of a triple interest: in the effects of modernization on rural areas, in the sources of resistance to the Revolution, and in the origins of the Vendée. These interests have much more to do with each other than is apparent at first glance. They keep overlapping, intertwining, melting into each other; when we come to that trenchant question, "Why the Vendée, and not somewhere else?" we shall find that they are indistinguishable. Because these concerns have brought the book into being, most of its pages deal with events and social arrangements before the great rebellion. Even here, however, it may be useful to begin with a review of the events that made Vendée memorable.

The Counterrevolution in Capsule

The counterrevolution known as the Vendée began in mid-March, 1793, breaking out almost simultaneously in several parts of the area between Nantes, La Rochelle, Poitiers, and Angers. Although observers were astonished at the rapidity, force, and apparent spontaneity of the uprising, it was the climax of four years of growing tension. As elsewhere, in the West the convocation of the Estates General, proclaimed late in 1788, caused great commotion. The establishment of Provincial Assemblies in 1787 had already helped form the nuclei of revolutionary parties; the local and regional meetings of 1789 crystallized the "bourgeois" and "noble" factions. Although the people of some of the West—especially the cities—received the Revolution quite eagerly, resistance to political change soon developed in the rural areas south of the Loire. The sale of church property caught the enthusiasm of only a few, and the Revolutionary reorganization of the church aroused widespread opposition. The parish clergy were soon uniformly opposed to the Revolution, and the great majority of their parishioners stood with them.

In 1791 and 1792, numerous local incidents—meetings, processions, even armed attacks—showed the growing restiveness of local feeling. Most of these fracases involved the priests named to replace those who had not accepted the church reforms, and almost all of them showed that the officials charged with local administration lacked the confidence and support of the rural population.

For many of their troubles, the administrators blamed the rebellious clergy. As a result, law was piled upon law to control the clergy, until the climax of August, 1792: the decree of immediate deportation of all priests who had refused the oath of submission. But with the deportation of a large portion of the nonconformist clergy and the disappearance of the rest into hiding, agitation only grew. The Revolutionary chiefs in the Vendée were talking fearfully of counterrevolution long before March, 1793. In fact, six months before then their fears were justified by a full-scale attack on Bressuire and Chitillon (in the department of Deux-Sevres), an attack foreshadowing the counterrevolution in both motives and personnel.

The great rebellion came in short order. The government's call for 300,000 men to meet the menace on France's frontiers caused bitter agitation in the

Vendée. The publication of the call to arms in the first days of March, 1793, was the signal for armed demonstrations, rioting, disarmament of patriots, and the flight into the country of the young men eligible for service.

For the first few days of March, everything rumbled, but nothing exploded. Riots at Cholet on the 4th cost a few lives, without becoming open warfare. On the 11th, 12th, and 13th everything seemed to blow up at once. At St. Florent, Chanzeaux, Machecoul, and Challans, armed troops appeared to the ringing of the tocsin, shouting of war and vengeance. The rebellion soon found leaders, and rapidly swept the region.

It would be an exaggeration to say the rebels stormed and took towns in the first days of the rebellion: they swarmed over them unresisted. ... By that time the rebel mass had not only a name (the Catholic, or Catholic and Royal, Army) but also a body of recognized leaders (Bonchamp, d'Elbée, Stofflet, many others).

There were three stages in the great war of 1793: 1) rebel expansion (until the end of June), 2) check and attrition (until mid-October), 3) flight (until year's end). The dividing points are the defeats of the Vendeans at Nantes (29 June) and at Cholet (17 October).

Rebel expansion was in fact fairly well contained after the first few weeks of the revolt. After that, it was basically a tale of capture, relinquishment, and recapture of cities along the borders of the Vendée, culminating in the taking of Saumur (9 June) and of Angers (12 June). The Vendeans did not occupy these cities; they took them, sacked them, organized shadowy provisional governments, then decamped. During all this period the Republican government was changing plans, placing and replacing generals, shouting treason, sending investigatory missions, generally failing to meet the rebellion firmly and directly.

The high command of the Catholic and Royal Army increased in organization and decreased in daring. The gradual encirclement and exhaustion of the Vendeans ended in their defeat at Cholet, which drove the despairing rebels into exile north of the Loire.

Then came flight: the hopes of the counterrevolution were broken, the armies shattered. In a blind drive up to Granville, "to meet the English," the rebels—now an inchoate mass of men, women, children, carts, animals, household goods—entered and then left Laval, Mayenne, and Avranches. Turned away at Granville, the remaining fragments moved back toward the Loire. They were repulsed at Angers, but still were able to take La Flèche and then Le Mans. After trying to recross the Loire into their homeland, the remaining Vendeans were smashed at Savenay just before Christmas. That was the end of the great war.

It was not, however, the end of the Vendée. The remaining leaders patched together an army that troubled the Republicans for another year. This "second war" ended with an amnesty and the treaty of La Jaunais (February, 1795), but soon after, the leaders—spurred by promises of aid from *émigrés* and English—began again. Moving only from disaster to disaster, they were quieted definitively by March, 1796. Neither of these insurrections, nor any of those to follow, approached the first war in magnitude.

North of the Loire, the Vendée left more than a memory. About the time the rebel remnants were wandering in that neighborhood, late in 1793, *Chouannerie* began. The Chouans were guerrilla bands, aiming to harass the Republicans whenever and however possible. In its mood and its personnel, Chouannerie had a great deal in common with the more general warfare south of the Loire. But it was more varied in form, on a smaller scale; it flourished (unlike the great counterrevolution) in Brittany, Maine, Normandy, and northern Anjou.

The Traditional History of the Vendée

With such a splendid series of adventures, it is not surprising that there is a rich folklore and an abundant literature concerning the Vendée; Balzac, Hugo, Dumas, Scott, Trollope, Michelet, Carlyle, and Taine all devoted melodramatic pages to its pageantry. It is not even surprising that scholars and laymen alike continue to argue their favorite heroes, battles, and causes. Yet the importance of the counterrevolution is not simply that it was colorful. It is an essential part of the history of the Revolution itself. In 1793, Bertrand Barère called it "the political fire consuming the heart of the nation" (Walter 1953:225).

Peasants opposed the Revolution. Why? The easiest answer is to stuff a standard mentality and a standard set of motives into the skulls of all the peasants of the region, preparing the mentality and motives mainly from general ideas of peasant character and the motives that could have opposed people to the Revolution (see Tilly 1963). The analyst's attitude toward the Revolution as a whole is likely to govern his choice of appropriate motives.

The assumption of this procedure is that the counterrevolution was the result of the mental state of the peasantry at the point of rebellion, and that the causes one must look for are those influences or events which brought about that mental state. As evidence of the mental state, the historian may take the observations of witnesses and the statements of the rebels themselves.

Tradition has called for the recognition of only a few possible "motives" for the counterrevolution: 1) royalism, 2) resistance to conscription, 3) support of religion (variously called "fidelity," "fanaticism," and "subservience"), 4) self-interest among the leaders, plus uncritical loyalty among the bulk of the rebels (see Bois 1960: 579–594). Each writer has made his choice among these "motives" or offered some combination of them.

There was no great delay in assigning causes to the counterrevolution. By the year III, Lequinio, a member of the Convention, was declaring:

> The first causes of that disastrous war are known; 1. the ignorance, fanaticism and subservience of the country people; 2. the pride, wealth and perfidy of the former nobles; 3. the criminality and hypocrisy of the priests; 4. the weakness of the government administration, the special interests of the administrators and their illegal favors to their relatives, farmers and friends (Year III: 10–11).

The assertion that the causes of the counterrevolution are well known is among the most common introductions to its histories. Nevertheless, it is precisely on this question of motivation that the great debates on the Vendée have arisen.

The thesis of *royalism* has taken this form: the peasants were oppressed by the new regime and shocked by the abolition of the monarchy and the death of the king, so they revolted. As can well be imagined, only writers strongly identified with both the nobility and the counterrevolution have presented this theory in pure form.

What unites these various explanations of the Vendée is that they all claim to identify the motives, by and large, the conscious motives at that, of the participants in the rebellion of March, 1793. No doubt every reconstruction of historical events implies some propositions about human motives; no doubt part of the historian's burden is to describe the motives of participants in crucial actions of the past. Yet it is possible to shift the emphasis. One may begin with questions about the organization and composition of the groups that supported the Revolution and the counterrevolution, about the relations among the principal segments of the population before and during the Revolution, about the connection between the rapid, drastic changes of Revolution and counterrevolution and the more general, more gradual social changes going on in eighteenth-century France. These questions occur naturally to a sociologist faced with an ebullient social movement. These questions have guided my inquiry into the origins of the Vendée.

A Sociological View

A concern with social organization calls for a comparative approach. We need a systematic comparison of the counterrevolutionary West with those sections of France that supported the Revolution. Such a comparison ought to include at least three elements: 1) most generally, the ways in which those major social changes which prepared France for revolution had affected the Vendée and the revolutionary segments of the country; 2) the major divisions of the population and the relations among them; 3) the organization, composition, and relations of the parts of the population that supported the Revolution, and those that resisted it. There is one more essential part of the analysis of the Vendée which does not require so direct a comparison: 4) the relationship between events before 1793 and the counterrevolutionary outbreak itself. These are the four problems one ought to solve in dealing with the Vendée.

This way of posing the problem of revolution and counterrevolution has a special virtue. It makes it easier to see the relevance for the Vendée of a great deal of sociological thinking on the nature of rural society and of social change.

Two lines of thinking about modern society form the frame of this analysis of the Vendée. The first concerns the set of broad social changes which has commonly accompanied the growth in size and influence of cities—the process of urbanization. The second deals with the organization of rural communities.

The growth of the size, number, and influence of cities is only one cluster in a set of changes that have occurred together in the growth of modern societies. I shall call the whole set of the changes "urbanization," but not out of any conviction that the growth of cities *causes* all the rest.

A general view of urbanization serves very well in the analysis of the relationship between general features of the social organization of western France and the nature of its response to the Revolution. But it leaves out the means by which general social changes touch the individual. It is convenient to deal with this part of the analysis through a conception of community organization. The immense majority of the citizens of the West lived in rural, predominantly peasant, communities. I shall stress the divisions and relationships within the rural community, and the ways they varied from one type of community to another, from region to region, in western France.

This is precisely the point at which the two lines of analysis come together. Urbanization implies changes in community organization. The changes that will command our attention are ones that follow from the increased involvement of the members of rural communities in sets of activities, norms, and social relationships that reach beyond the limits of their own localities. For example, production for a national market, participation in politics, and exposure to mass communication seem to have crudely regular effects on the organization of rural communities.

One further question to which this path leads us is the nature of the changes in western France during the Revolution itself. Some of the most important changes—the centralization of governmental power, the increase in importance of the bourgeoisie, the redistribution of property, and so on—were in many respects accelerated continuations of the general process of urbanization. But they were in large measure introduced or imposed from outside the West, and the groups which brought them in tried to make them operate more or less uniformly throughout the region. Where the prerequisites for such a further, rapid transformation already existed—that is, where urbanization had gone furthest—the process went relatively smoothly, but where the prerequisites were missing, it produced ardent conflict. Now, this statement is also no more than an approximation, and one with an air of circularity to it. Yet it, too, helps bring some order into the study of the Vendée and social change in the West.

Prospectus

In trying to answer the kinds of questions I have posed here, one might seek to assemble detailed information on all sections of the West from published sources, and thus learn the answers for all the region at once. I found the published sources too unreliable and too incomplete to make this course feasible. One might also try to glean an essential minimum of information about each section from both archival and published sources. But that procedure assumes that the investigator begins with a detailed master plan, knows in advance what information will be both crucial and available, and can easily reach a wide range of sources. The present study met none of these conditions. I chose a third course: to go far into the records available for one small, but important part of the West, and even farther into the records of a few communities there, and then to determine how well the most significant conclusions reached this way applied to other sections of the West. This study is based largely on the analysis of documents, and the documents deal mainly with the part of Anjou south of the Loire river. Southern Anjou offers the advantage of including one section whose inhabitants generally cooperated with the Revolution and avoided the counterrevolution, and another which was the very homeland of the rebellion. In addition to studying this one area intensively, I have devoted a good deal of effort to ascertain whether the conditions which appeared in southern Anjou also appeared elsewhere in the West.

Revolution

A favorite tautology among students of political upheaval is that for a revolution to occur there must be a "revolutionary situation." Often this has been taken to mean that throughout the revolution-prone society (except, perhaps, in the incumbent elite) there are demands for radical change. However, a society is not like a cheese which, however thinly sliced, tastes like cheese throughout.

The Revolution of 1789

Certainly it is hard to imagine that there would have been a great revolution in 1789 if France had consisted of the West, or of territories like the West, alone. It is hard, for that matter, to imagine a Revolution without Paris. De Tocqueville (1955: 76–77), fresh from the experience of Louis Napoleon's *coup d'état,* opined that "chief among the reasons for the collapse of all the various governments that have arisen in France during the past forty years are this administrative centralization and the absolute predominance of Paris."

And what was the nature of the revolutionary changes that impinged on provincial France? Again Tocqueville is helpful. At least when discussing governmental institutions, he emphasized the continuity between the developments of the old regime and the changes of the Revolution. In a sense, the Revolution did not overturn, it accelerated. It accelerated the formation of a "modern" kind of property, free of multiple private rights and obligations, and speeded the transfer of property to the Third Estate. It fostered the preeminence of Paris. It hastened the construction of a centralized nation-state, uniform in its administration, demanding widespread participation. It added impetus to the growth of political associations, newspapers, means of communicating and opinionating. It extended a kind of economic rationalization and market expansion, combining the eradication of personal and local controls with the fortification of national controls. It intensified many of the general changes associated with urbanization. In these respects, the great French Revolution anticipated the powerful "modernizing" and "nationalizing" revolutions of such countries as Egypt, Japan, or Argentina.

Of course, the Revolution also *reversed* some trends in French society: the attempts of the high nobility to reaffirm its influence in French government and to shut off the access of new men to lofty positions of honor and power, the reassertion of fiscal rights by noble landlords, the decadence of monasticism. Still, on the whole, the Revolution continued the work of the old regime. It seems to be generally true that as a consequence the Revolution found its most willing reception in the most urban sectors of French society. Again, "urban" is an elastic term, for it applies to great cities more than small ones, city more than country, but also trading areas more than commercially stagnant ones, people involved in trade and industry more than those involved in the land, holders of "capitalistic" property more than holders of "feudal" property, communicators and coordinators more than those they served or controlled, the mobile more than the immobile.

No doubt the proper retort to such a sweeping summary is "Which Revolution do you mean?" After all, Georges Lefebvre (1947) distinguished four overlapping revolutions—aristocratic, bourgeois, popular, and peasant—without moving past 1789. Yet there is a rough kind of unity in the major changes of the early Revolution. That complex unity, in the last analysis, is probably best conveyed by the fabulous watchword: Liberté, Égalité, Fraternité.

One of the bases of this unity was surely the prominence of France's bourgeoisie in the events and reforms of the Revolution. There was continuity with the old regime in this respect as well. The bourgeoisie (the observation is at least as old as Guizot) was gaining strength and self-awareness throughout the eighteenth century; the Revolution swiftly augmented that class's political power. As Marx would have it, the "feudal" class system was crumbling, and the "capitalistic" class system arising from its dust. As Marx would also have it, the bourgeois were the principal agents and beneficiaries of the Revolution.

My reasons for stating these unsubtle and largely commonplace generalities are to put the experience of western France back into its historical setting, to characterize the external changes to which the West had to respond during the early Revolution, and to suggest that the Vendée was not the kind of region in which one could have expected to find enthusiastic support for the Revolution. One of the most self-consciously Marxist of recent historians (Guérin 1946: 10) summed up the distinction in this way: "The archaic conditions of land ownership and of agriculture in certain regions like the

Vendée and Brittany had helped keep these provinces in the darkness of servitude." Hippolyte Taine (1876: 32), with an enormously different bias, spoke of the Vendée as one of the few "remnants of the good feudal spirit" left in the France of 1789.

Both statements are quite wrong in detail. Both statements are quite right in signaling the distinctiveness of the Vendée's social situation. Less urban as a whole than the rest of France yet supplied with newly growing cities, its bourgeoisie weaker than elsewhere yet aware of growing strength, the Vendée was not ready for revolution, but it was ripe for turmoil.

The West's Experience

We may begin the detailed discussion of the Revolution with the relatively unconventional date of 1787. In that year, Loménie de Brienne's reform established a series of assemblies, uniformly organized throughout France, at the level of the individual community, the election, the province, and the generality. In addition, there were "interim commissions," executive bodies designed to carry on the work of the provincial assemblies between their meetings. As precedent and as practical training, these new arrangements were exceedingly important. As precedent, because (even though the projected elections were never actually held) the reform established the principle of representative assemblies throughout the nation, as well as combined the double representation of the Third Estate with the vote by head instead of by estate. As practical training because (even though the assemblies generally accomplished very little, and were probably intended to do no more than ratify new taxes) the new arrangement gave a whole generation of the ambitious Third Estate its first taste of public office.

Those agents, who up until then had been no more than the delegates of the residents, received only a mandate limited to keeping accounts, sending out notices for the corvée, taxes, conscription, under the authority of the royal officers, the subdelegate, even the lord, and at the risk of arbitrary fines. The new election made of them all at once true representatives of the community, intermediaries between it and the central power, endowed with their own authority, which left servile relationships to subordinates. Everywhere that it was possible, these modest functions, until then forced on simple peasants, were for the first time accepted proudly, even sought with eagerness by the small number of petty nobles, or officials, seneschals, rentiers, notaries, landowners "who mattered in terms of wealth or upbringing" in their parish.

The new-found eminence of "those who mattered" carried over into the first phase of the Revolution. The administrative reform of 1787 may have been much more important to the local history of the early Revolution—and not only in southern Anjou—than it has been customary to recognize.

No one, on the other hand, has missed the importance of the Estates General of May, 1789, the local and regional assemblies which preceded that national congress, or the drawing up of the *cahiers de doléances*—Statements of Grievances—that accompanied these meetings.

That brings us to a major effect of the calling of the Estates General: that it helped "politicize" local issues and personal alignments, in the sense of making them appear relevant to national issues and alignments. It is a momentous day in the growth of a modern state when people in its rural villages begin to recognize the connection between what goes on at home and what goes on in the nation at large. A whole series of events of the early Revolution—the reorganization of local government, the Civil Constitution of the Clergy, the changes in taxes, universal military conscription, and frequent elections as well as the calling of the Estates General—made French villagers unavoidably aware of the fact of citizenship. In Anjou, as elsewhere, the sudden proliferation of pamphlets and newspapers reinforced the new awareness.

Response to the Revolution

When it comes to tracing the response of southern Anjou to such exciting events of the early Revolution as the storming of the Bastille or the "abolition of feudalism" on the Fourth of August, some problems appear at once. All the great days of Paris received their ritual recognition, and often more, in Angers, Saumur, and the other important cities. But no one has assembled whatever information may be available on who celebrated what, and how, outside the major cities. For that reason, the many claims that "the Revolution was greeted with joy" in Anjou leave tantalizingly unanswered the question "By whom?" It is clear that there was no substantial and vociferous opposition to the major reforms of the Revolution in southern Anjou before the end of 1790.

There was no concerted response in southern Anjou to other major events of the first half year of Revolution. ... Nor does the nationalization of church properties seem to have incited a general hue and cry, despite the shouting that began a year later as the sales of those properties approached.

Taxes were another story. Many Angevins, like many other French-men, felt that if there had been a revolution, then it followed obviously that taxes had been abolished. Especially the onerous salt tax. At the end of August, 1789, the authorities at Beaupréau reported that "everyone is seeking to avoid any payment of taxes. There have been armed bands near the Loire which have engaged in every sort of violence toward the officers of the Gabelle, whom they have disarmed. People are going to Brittany to fetch salt, which they are selling publicly in a number of bourgs" (A.D. M-et-L C 186). When official word came that this extralegal abolition of the salt tax was not only premature but financially intolerable, commu-nities throughout Anjou sent delegates to a meeting of protest on the 6th of October, and the protest was carried effectively to the top of the national government (Port 1878: I, 83–85). Likewise, the hopes for revolutionary revision or abolition of taxes incited not only increased resistance to tax collection but also numerous disputes over the proper distribution of the taxes. In the Saumurois, significantly, there were a number of demands that "former privileged persons," i.e., basically the nobles, should be taxed more heavily.

Another set of revolutionary changes that received a decisive response in southern Anjou was the reorganization of the territorial arrangements of government. Like the changes in taxation, this reorganization provided a splendid opportunity for the "politicizing" of local affairs; local rivalries and ambitions took on national meanings (see Tilly 1961, 1962).

The assignment of whole Statements of Grievances to major political ten-dencies in this way is useful, but it tells us little about the specific issues that mattered in 1789. For that reason, I have gone back to the Grievances to iden-tify the most common complaints and proposals, and to see how *they* varied from one part of southern Anjou to another.

Let us take all the items mentioned by at least 10 percent of the Griev-ances, and add to them both the sale of church properties and the reform of "feudal" rights, which were not proposed very often, but are interesting anyway. That gives us a list of 24 items, which fall under four general head-ings: 1) taxes, 2) government, 3) lords, 4) clergy. A separate table for each heading will keep the number of items under discussion small enough to be manageable. (In evaluating the Grievances, I gave a full score on a given item to explicit proposals or complaints, and a half score to indirect ones; that is why some of the percentages in the tables to follow are based on 9.5 or 10.5 cases.)

The first, and most commonly discussed, category is taxes. Table 1.1 pres-ents the distribution of complaints by district.

Table 1.1 Taxes: percent of statements mentioning the Grievance, by district

Grievance	Angers	Vihiers	Cholet	St. Florent	Total
General reform of taxes is needed	67	94	76	47	57
All three Estates should pay the same taxes	88	62	85	67	75
The salt tax	100	94	92	93	94
Abolish duties on movement of goods within the country	83	59	89	88	83
Complaints against the tax on legal transactions	75	81	61	47	62
Complaints against franc-fief	67	53	88	70	73
Number of cases	12	16	33	30	91

The first message of the table is: everyone complained about taxes. There was far more agreement on these items than on any others that appeared in the Grievances. The salt tax, that infamous gabelle, was apparently the most unpopular of all. Complaints about duties on internal trade, the *Traites*, were also widespread, and three quarters of the communities inveighed against the inequitable distribution of taxes among the Estates. When it comes to the franc-fief, which burdened the commoner who held "noble" land, there is a plausible correlation between the intensity of the complaints and 1) the extent of noble property, 2) the presence of wealthy bourgeois managers of property. Almost 90 percent of the Grievances of the District of Cholet, where noble property was almost certainly the most extensive, protested against the franc-fief. Otherwise, aside from a slight tendency for the communities of St. Florent to complain less than the rest, there were no systematic differences among the four areas on the subject of taxation.

There were four common items among the Grievances that can be grouped under government: the objections to *jurés-priseurs*, military conscription, and the malfunctioning of the royal courts, as well as the need for general reform in government. The jurés-priseurs were the petty officials who seized property in cases of court judgments and indebtedness; they were the scourge of the poor. The question of military conscription deserves special mention because a number of authors (no doubt influenced by the knowledge that the first violence of the counterrevolution in March, 1793, was in the form of resistance to the draft) have postulated an extraordinary hatred of military service among the people of the Vendée. The other two items, the malfunctioning of the courts and the need for general reform, are perhaps self-explanatory. The distribution of grievances appears in Table 1.2.

The fourth, and final, phase of the Grievances consists of recommendations concerning the clergy. The range of such recommendations was wide, but there was less agreement on any particular proposal or plaint than there was in regard to taxes, government, or the nobility. Parish priests and higher clergy drew approximately equal attention, but some of the recommendations concerning the parish priests were meant to improve their position, while no such thought entered the comments on the higher clergy. For both the tithe and the sale of church properties, it is not hard to separate the Grievances directed at the parish priests from those intended for the higher clergy, so a rough comparison of attitudes toward the two groups is possible. Table 1.3 gives the relevant figures.

Table 1.2 Government: percent of statements mentioning the Grievance, by district

Grievance	Angers	Vihiers	Cholet	St. Florent	Total
Objections to jurés-priseurs	75	62	52	50	56
Military conscription	17	62	48	37	43
Malfunctioning of royal courts	67	69	39	65	57
The need for general reform in government	33	19	15	7	15
Number of cases	12	16	33	30	91

Table 1.3   Clergy: percent of statements mentioning the Grievance,
by district

Grievances	Angers	Vihiers	Cholet	St. Florent	Total
The revenues of religious communities should be reduced	21	50	39	20	32
Religious communities should be reformed or abolished	8	25	21	8	16
Against absentee holders of benefices	25	12	12	4	11
Against the tithe collected by curés	4	19	15	5	11
Against the tithe collected by outsiders	17	34	12	10	16
Properties of the higher clergy should be sold	12	12	2	7	7
Properties of the curés should be sold	0	0	0	0	0
Curés should have higher incomes	8	41	15	13	18
The lot of vicars should be improved	25	66	30	17	31
Number of cases	12	16	33	30	91

What is the general significance of these *cahiers de doléances*? First, the comparison of Val-Saumurois and Mauges confirms the conclusions drawn from our earlier inspection of Le Moy's categories of Grievances. Opposition to the traditional privileges of the noble landlord was much more common in Val-Saumurois, as was outright support of the "bourgeois" party in the dispute between Walsh and his enemies. Furthermore, the Grievances of Val-Saumurois more commonly include comprehensive programs for reform. These programs probably reflect greater, politically focused, dissatisfaction with the old regime and greater participation in the political debates that preceded the Estates General, as well as the direct influences of the model Grievances that were circulating.

The issues closest to formal politics—taxes and governmental administration—attracted far more comment and far greater agreement than the problems of the nobility and the clergy. I think the explanation is that the authors of the Grievances were not so sure that the traditional positions of these classes were proper matters for legislation and public policy or safe matters on which to take a public stand. They were not, I suspect, simply less concerned about the priests and nobles. The place of these groups in French society was not yet clearly a political issue. Yet the spokesmen of Val-Saumurois were much more willing to treat it as such, and in that limited sense were much closer to making revolutionary demands.

That leads to the more general point: proposals for fundamental reforms were significantly more common in Val-Saumurois than in the Mauges. Judging from their Statements of Grievances, the Mauges were less ready for revolution.

The Grievances were in no simple sense the voice of the peasantry. They did not unanimously propose fundamental reform. The peasants as a group never became strongly committed to the success of the Revolution, any more than they ever really became committed to its defeat as a political revolution.

Military Service

To return to the question of "attitude" toward the Revolution itself, we may investigate the willingness of citizens to enter the military service of the nation. Frenchmen had a whole series of opportunities to do so: in the militia units that formed in a number of cities as the first revolutionary news from Paris spread; in the various forms of the National Guard that were organized, more widely, later; then, in the enlistments for the revolutionary armies of 1791; still later, in the response to the draft of 1793 (which was the beginning of open civil warfare in the Vendée), and then to the *levées en masse,* the attempts at mass conscription for the prosecution of the European war. As an ensemble, the civilian response to these calls to service is still awaiting its historian, both for the French nation and for Anjou. When the accounts are written, they will surely be of interest to more than the military historian. The enthusiasm of enlistments must have something to do with the extent of working patriotism, and the response to conscription ought to be a gauge of the strength of the principle of citizenship.

The evidence I have been able to assemble for southern Anjou is distressingly weak for 1789 and 1790, the years before the struggle between prorevolutionary and antirevolutionary parties became so open and general as to transform the entire meaning of volunteering to serve the fatherland. It is much fuller for 1791 and later. As far as it goes, the evidence does not reveal unanimity or widespread enthusiasm. Instead, it anticipates the final chapters of this book in emphasizing the deep divisions of classes, subregions, and parties in southern Anjou before the counterrevolution broke into the open.

Before 1791, the organization of a Militia or National Guard was almost entirely the affair of the cities. ... The higher ranks in these groups were prizes the citizens were willing to squabble over. And at times the squabbles had strong overtones of class, party, or factional conflict. For example, at Saumur in February, 1790, the citizens of the "districts des ponts et château" complained that the "aristocrats" had perverted the purposes of the Militia by forming a special, privileged group with distinctive uniforms, "looking on other citizens as scum" (A.N. D IV 10). About the same time, there were similarly angry reports from Montreuil-Bellay (A.N. D XXIX 58). There are signs that the substantial citizens of Cholet sought to exclude mere peasants from their Guard (A.N. D IV 40). Even if lamentable, these teapot tempests are not very surprising. Their only importance to us is that they tell us that in many of the cities of southern Anjou the distinctions the early Revolution had Gardes, and 3 from Le May are accounted for, there are only 13 more enlistments to apportion among all the other communities of the district. That is, the cities and the principal bourgs of the textile industry, which were also the centers of revolutionary zeal, supplied almost all the recruits. The correlation between revolutionary fervor and enlistments holds up.

The next logical question is the identity of the recruits. It is possible to answer that question in great detail for the Second Battalion, which was recruiting from January to October, 1792 (A.D. M-et-L 1 L 598 bis). The well-kept registers described the recruits carefully, right down to the color of their eyebrows, sometimes even to the tint of their patriotism. The great majority were young men, and single ones. Of the 268 admitted to the battalion from southern Anjou, there is occupational information for 221.

Table 1.4 gives the occupational distribution of recruits by district.

Considering the actual distribution of these occupational categories in the general population, it is obvious that the artisans and, especially, the bourgeois contributed much more than their share of recruits, while the peasants were greatly underrepresented. This is not a bad description of all kinds of support for the Revolution.

Table 1.4   Occupational distribution of recruits, 1792

District	Total number of enlistments	Percent of recruits*			
		Bourgeois	Artisan	Peasant	Other
St. Florent	30	5.9	94.1	0.0	0.0
Cholet	52	35.7	54.8	7.1	2.4
Vihiers	11	25.0	50.0	0.0	25.0
Angers	0	—	—	—	—
Saumur	175	29.9	55.8	4.6	9.7
Total, southern Anjou	268	29.0	58.4	4.5	8.1

*Calculated on the basis of the 221 recruits identified by occupation.

The data, and the conclusions they suggest, call for a pair of demurrers. First, there is no need to exaggerate the mechanical accuracy with which divisions of class or region separated the True Believers of the Revolution from the rest of the population. ... There were patriots on both sides in the open country as well as in the cities. Some bourgeois were avid counterrevolutionaries, and others were unable to make up their minds. There were peasants who supported the Revolution. Many features of the analysis of community organization in earlier chapters—for example, the investigation of marriage patterns—suggest other variables which unquestionably affected personal alliances and party alignments. The most microscopic information we have on communal politics in southern Anjou resists forcing into categories of class and locality alone, and calls for hunches about kinship, family friendships, the residues of old feuds, and the like. ... The lesson: categories of class, locality, and party explain a great deal, but they do not explain everything.

The second demurrer has to do with the character of the supporters of the Revolution. It is tempting to think of them as fiery-eyed, fearless "radicals." (After all, they were helping make a major revolution.) The fact is that, like all other political groupings, they displayed a tremendous range of zeal, conviction, and assurance. In regard to military service, one of the gripes of the first counterrevolutionaries of March, 1793, was that revolutionary public officials had neatly shielded themselves from genuine military service by assuming office.

Emigration

One other kind of evidence has a place in this discussion. Except for the deportation of many priests and the occasional return of the nobles of Anjou from the company of the émigrés, emigration has not been discussed in connection with the Vendée very often. It is hard to interpret crude rates of emigration. Do they measure antipathy to the Revolution? Or do they reflect the amount of internal conflict in the area?

I lean toward the second interpretation. Donald Greer (1951) has shown without question the general relationship in France between political turbulence during the Revolution and departmental rates of emigration. Revolutionary storm centers like Bordeaux, Lyon, and Toulon had many émigrés, just as counterrevolutionary departments like Mayenne did. The correlation deserves attention. People seem to have fled conflict as much as they fled the Revolution.

The departments of the West were a bloc with exceptionally high emigration; however their lists of emigrants were swollen both by the exceptional number of exiled priests and by the inclusion of many counterrevolutionaries who had not left the country but had fled their homes, gone into hiding, or died in combat. It is interesting to ask, therefore, whether it was the counterrevolutionary sections of these departments that supplied most of the names on their lists of emigrants. For southern Anjou, the answer is: No.

To find that answer, I have simply applied Greer's procedure in miniature to the cantons and districts of southern Anjou. That is, I have taken the general list of émigrés through October, 1793, for the Department of Maine-et-Loire (A.D. M-et-L 15 Q 271–280, 1 L 398 bis), and assigned the persons named to cantons and districts. I struck out the persons identified as being placed on the list for serving on counterrevolutionary committees in 1793. There may well have been more such nonemigrants left on the list; their inclusion would probably inflate the totals for the cantons of the Mauges, where the rebels were able to organize committees everywhere. But the great majority were surely genuine emigrants, for the great majority were priests and nobles.

At the beginning, groups like the peasants of the Mauges were not so much in opposition as unaware of politics altogether. Gradually, local life became more and more openly political. The pace quickened around the end of 1790, with the local application of major religious reforms. Opposition parties formed and filled out. Party positions hardened. The uncommitted found it impossible to remain uncommitted. Conflict between the supporters of the Revolution and their opponents became open and general. This is, in the last analysis, what it means to say that the "attitude of the people of southern Anjou toward the Revolution" changed deeply from the time of the Estates General to the time of the War of the Vendée.

The First Year of Revolution

While pursuing the problem of "attitude" I have had to wander beyond the bounds of the Revolution's first year. It may now be helpful to pause for a backward look. What was the state of Anjou a year or so after the Bastille fell? To commemorate the event, Federation Day of July, 1790, brought delegates from all over France to Paris for one of the first of the great modern political rallies. Southern Anjou's representatives were there—in what strength, it would be worth knowing. There were some things for Angevins to celebrate. The salt tax had disappeared. The tithe was gone (but the financial advantage of that change went mainly to the owners of property). The pettier vestiges of traditional noble privileges had been swept away. Some of the more irritating excise taxes were being abolished, even if the general tax load was far from being lightened.

The 1787 reorganization of the municipalities, the Estates General, the revolutionary re-reorganization of the municipalities, the local elections of 1790, the formation of cantons, districts, and departments comprised the most drastic, thorough, and rapid administrative reformation Frenchmen had ever known. By the middle of 1790 the official correspondents of southern Anjou were already writing of The Revolution, although sometimes in the past tense. A new corps of public officials, from petty to great, was at work. Of course, the corps included many who had helped run the old regime, but *it* also included many whom the older traditions would never have called to public service. Villagers could now see their local notary, or the rich merchant of the bourg, serving as a member of the district's increasingly powerful administration. Lord and curé had been toppled from automatic eminence in the commune, and prosperous clothiers or wealthy farmers had often stepped into their places. Outsiders and newcomers were arriving in office. Furthermore, the administration with which the local political officials had to deal had been transformed, in personnel, outlook, and formal structure. It was an administration with which the traditional ways of mediation of lord and curé were decreasingly likely to be effective, with which the local bourgeoisie was well prepared, by taste, skill, and personal acquaintance, to deal. In other words, the commune—the political aspect of the community—was in the process of moving toward greater formal differentiation from other aspects of the community, greater specialization in its formal positions, greater involvement in political movements pervading all of French society, a new elite.

The events of the first year of Revolution probably disturbed the position of the lord more than that of any other figure in most communities of southern Anjou. They came close to destroying the social arrangements that gave him distinction and privilege outside the community. They also sapped his usefulness as liaison between community and outside, for influence with grandees, King and Court rapidly became insignificant in getting things done, and handsome traditional titles were fast becoming a liability. The response of most of the nobles was withdrawal. ... Emigration had already gained plenty of momentum by mid-1790. For the rest, it was withdrawal to inconspicuous privacy in their town houses or manors. When they were once again able to function as leaders in activities that went beyond the mean and confining range of local politics, the nobles were ready to return. In the meantime, the political elite of the community was being transformed.

Both the national church and the individual parish were likewise being transformed. By the anniversary of the Bastille, the church properties were "at the disposition of the nation," already inventoried and under the surveillance of the local revolutionary administration. The preparations for their sale were underway. Monks, their vows dissolved by the National Assembly, were leaving their monasteries. Those who remained found local officials empowered to inquire with unheard-of freedom into the operation of the religious establishments.

After a year of Revolution, the tithe had been abolished in principle, if not yet in fact, and the curé had an ill-defined promise of payment by the revolutionary authorities to replace it. He was now obliged to read governmental decrees at Sunday Mass (which was not really much of a change from his news-dispensing functions of before the Revolution, when he often announced auctions and decrees as well as blessed events). He no longer belonged to the communal council ex officio, but he still officiated in many communities as mayor or as president of the electoral assembly. His small properties had been enumerated and placed, at least technically, under the control of the government. And it was especially the local bourgeois, the ambitious ones, the upstarts, the outsiders, who were presuming to regulate the curé's actions. This was enough to make him abundantly aware of the scope of the nation's political changes. But the most serious attempts of the Revolution to intervene in the actual exercise of his functions, and the most serious threats to his position in the community, were not to begin until later in 1790.

References

Bois, Paul. 1960. *Cahier de doléances du tiers état de la sénéchaussée de Château-du-Loir pour les États Généraux de 1789.* Gap: Imprimerie Louis-Jean.

Greer, Donald. 1951. *The Incidence of the Emigration during the French Revolution.* Cambridge, MA: Harvard University Press.

Guérin, Daniel. 1946. *La Lutte des classes sous la premiére république: bourgeois et "bras nus" (1793–1797),* 3rd ed., vol. I. Paris: Gallimard.

Lefebvre, Georges. 1947. *The Coming of the French Revolution* (R. R. Palmer, tr. and ed.). Princeton: Princeton University.

Port, Célestin. 1878. *Dictionnaire historique, géographique et biographique de Maine-et-Loire,* 3 vols. Paris and Angers.

Taine, Hippolyte Adolphe. 1876. *The Ancient Regime* (John Durand, tr.). New York: Henry Holt and Company.

Tilly, Charles. 1961. "Local Conflicts in the Vendée before the Rebellion of 1793." *French Historical Studies* 2(2):209–31.

Tilly, Charles. 1962. "Rivalités De Bourgs Et Conflits De Partis Dans Les Mauges De 1789 À 1793." *Revue du Bas-Poitou et des Provinces de l'Ouest* LXXIII:268–80.

Tilly, Charles. 1963. "The Analysis of a Counter-Revolution," *History and Theory,* III. No. 1,1, 30–58.

Tocqueville, Alexis de. 1955. *The Old Regime and the French Revolution* (Stuart Gilbert, tr.). New York: Anchor Books.

Walter, Gérard. 1953. *La Guerre de Vendée.* Paris: Plon.

Strikes in France 1830–1968

2

The Interplay of Organization, Location, and Industrial Conflict

Edward Shorter and Charles Tilly

A Review of the Argument

Several broad assertions have recurred through the discussion so far, and have borne up well against repeated assaults by evidence. The first is that the scale and intensity of strike activity in a setting depend closely on the prior organization of the workers in the setting, on the availability of a structure which identifies, accumulates and communicates grievances on the one hand, and facilitates collective action on the other. Although that sort of conclusion is self-evident from several points of view, it contradicts two widely held interpretations of industrial conflict: (1) the reading of the level of strike activity as an index of worker 'discontent'; (2) the attribution of a large weight to momentary impulse or accidents of local leadership. To be sure, we have presented precious little evidence concerning the day-to-day dynamics of individual strikes and the week-to-week waxing of conflict within particular workplaces. Our evidence has taken the form of general correspondences between unionization and strike activity, demonstrations that strike waves tend to draw disproportionately from those industries which already have high propensities to strike in ordinary years....

A second recurrent assertion has combatted the idea of strikes as direct responses to dislocation and deprivation. We have not denied that workers had real grievances, that wage cuts often incited walkouts, that craftsmen resisted dequalification by various forms of concerted action or that the appearance of new industries made a difference to the qualities of industrial conflict. Our time-series analysis, in fact, led us to modify our original argument by conceding that economic downturns tend to stimulate strike activity in the short run. But we have argued that in general dislocation and severe deprivation tend to *reduce* the propensity of workers to strike—except in the important case where they touch groups which already have a high degree of solidarity and internal organization. Our reasoning is threefold: (1) dislocation and deprivation fix the attention of workers on survival from day to day, leaving them little disposed to risky collective action; (2) dislocation and deprivation reduce the resources available for any sort of collective action; (3) for a number of different reasons (well known to the nineteenth-century employers who preferred docile recent migrants over the tough old hands, just so long as the work didn't require a very high level of skill or experience) dislocation and deprivation generally go along with an unfavorable bargaining position for workers.

To support this line of argument, we have pointed to the tendency of French strike activity to rise in times of prosperity, to the generally lower levels of strike activity in fast-growing cities, to the fact that the average strike brings out lower proportions of the whole workforce in large plants than in small ones (despite the fact that large plants have strikes more frequently) and to other evidence of that kind.

Third, we have asserted that struggles for power among groups of workers, employers, local authorities and segments of the national government strongly influenced the rhythm, distribution and character of French industrial conflict throughout its history, despite the fact that the bulk of the explicit grievances in strikes had to do with wages and hours. We have argued, furthermore, that over the century after 1850 strikes became increasingly oriented to the *national* political position of labor; we claim to have detected a particularly strong shift in that direction some time between the Popular Front and the end of the Second World War. Here the evidence has been flimsier than in the case of the first two assertions, for we have had to reason mainly from information about strikes themselves rather than about the wielding of power in general. Still, our analyses of year-to-year covariation of political conflicts and strikes, of the character of governmental intervention and mediation in strikes and of the political timing of strike waves all appear to move in the same direction.

Our fourth persistent argument has rested on the distinction among three types of industrial organization: (a) the type depending on the interaction of well defined crafts, (b) the type characterized by semi-skilled workers, machine-tending and bureaucratic control, (c) the type applying complicated technologies and requiring high levels of formal training of its personnel. The schema goes something like this:

		Professional solidarity	
		Low	High
Scale and bureaucratization of workplace, labor organization	Low	NONE	Craftsmen
	High	Factory proletarians	Skilled professionals in science sector

(The big NONE for the low-low category means we expect no significant labor organization or strike activity where producing units are small, informal and staffed by heterogeneous and/or unskilled workers.) With due recognition of the incompleteness and overlap of these categories, we have called attention to the implications for industrial conflict of the general historical shift from artisanal to proletarian to professional as dominant sectors of the labor force. We have claimed that each produces a characteristically different form of worker organization, and consequently a different pattern of industrial conflict. In the chief period under observation—from the 1890s to the 1960s—we see the shifts from artisanal to proletarian exemplified in the increasing size and frequency of the strike, its increasing orientation to national politics and a number of other features. Only in the 1960s do we begin to see traits which one might reasonably attribute to the increasing prominence of the science sector.

Let us rest our case here. The French experience points directly away from explanations of territorial differences in strike activity that invoke marginality, peripheralness and isolation. Our study of the geographical dimension of conflict indicates rather the strategic role of the central place and of exposure to diversity in eliciting militant organization. The French cities with the highest intensities of conflict and the most efficient mobilization of participants were places where a riot of experiences and of possibilities for association crowded in upon the working man. They were places where people could meet easily, communicate swiftly and above all be confident of attracting the attention of the powerful in their public demonstrations and protests. They were the loci of extensive working-class organization.

French strikers were not, by and large, marginal workers on the periphery of social life. They were bearers of the core traditions of working-class protest, skilled craft workers in the hearts of classic urban centers. Genuine proletarians were only able to overcome the sizable obstacles to organization set by homogeneity of rank, lack of skill and large size of enterprise by drawing upon the resources of the metropolis. It is a nice irony of the French experience that precisely the structures which Kerr and Siegel saw as producing "integration" were those making for conflict.

Pinning Down the Differences among Departments

If we are right, we should be able to show that the variables we stressed in earlier discussions actually provide a plausible statistical account of area-to-area differences in strike activity....

In this last analysis, we take the total strike activity in a department over a substantial block of years as the object to be explained, and attempt to specify the simultaneous effects of a number of departmental characteristics on that strike activity. The analysis breaks into two parts. The first concentrates on the explanation of the sheer number of strikes in the department without regard to the size, shape or other characteristics of those strikes. The second deals mainly with the relationship among different characteristics of the strikes occurring within a department. In both cases the analysis begins with simple correlation coefficients covering several sets of years, and then moves rapidly to path diagrams representing the most important relationships (and non-relationships) revealed by the correlations.

We have computed (in tables too bulky to present here) correlations among a number of characteristics of departments, including the extent of their strike activity, in three substantially different five-year periods: 1910 to 1914 (a time of high militancy and mass strike activity in modern industry, including the famous railroad strike crushed by Briand in 1910), 1920 to 1924 (covering the last part of the strike wave of 1919–20 and a few relatively quiet years), 1925 to 1929 (except for the flurry of 1926, a time of moderate industrial conflict).

The first feature of these data is their remarkable similarity. Some of the similarity, to be sure, comes from the repetition of precisely the same variables from one period to the next. But the set of strikes under consideration in each case is quite different, yet the data representing measures of strike activity display approximately the same relationships for all three periods.

The principal exception is the relationship of strike activity to urban growth, which is moderate to strong in 1910–14 and 1925–9 but practically nonexistent in 1920–4 and over the long period 1915–35. That pattern we will have to examine carefully (also, because it reverses the negative correlations between urbanization and strikes we found at the level of the municipality). Otherwise, similar numbers show up in all the data: strong associations of strike activity with the size of the industrial labor force, the number of union members, the total number of years that individual Bourses du travail had existed, the number of steam engines installed in the department (our crude measure of the presence of highly mechanized industry) and the number of workers in establishments employing more than 100 persons. Some of these are obviously no more than matters of scale: more workers, more strikes. The path analysis will sort them out. Still, the stability of these associations over a variety of periods provides assurance that they are more than coincidence.

The correlation matrices also identify a cluster of variables one might call "industrialism." The size of the industrial labor force, the number of union members, the total commune-years of Bourse du travail presence, the number of steam engines and the number of workers in large establishments tend to vary together. It is their persistent association with each other and with the level of strike activity, in fact, which accounts for the stability of the general pattern of correlations.

The correlations, finally, give us some faint indications of associations among large-scale industry, unionization, "offensive" strikes (strikes, that is, in which workers demanded new advantages, especially shorter hours and higher wages, rather than resisting speedups, wage cuts and the like) and success in strike activity.

The diagram relating characteristics of strikes in the same period (Figure 2.1), on the other hand, does offer some evidence of an impact of the scale of industry and the extent of unionization on the kinds of strikes that occurred in a department. Let us disregard the strong coefficients representing effects of scale alone, like the 0.87 linking the number of strikes with unions involved to the total number of strikes. The path analysis shows us a small, unreliable effect of the number of union members on the frequency of strikes, a small but reliable effect on the number of strikes involving unions and no direct relationship at all to the frequency of success or failure in strikes. There appears, however, to be an important indirect effect: offensive strikes were strongly associated with strikes involving unions; where

A. Determinants of total number of strikes

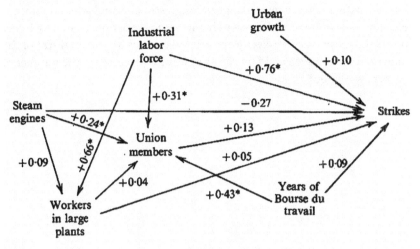

B. Characteristics of strikes

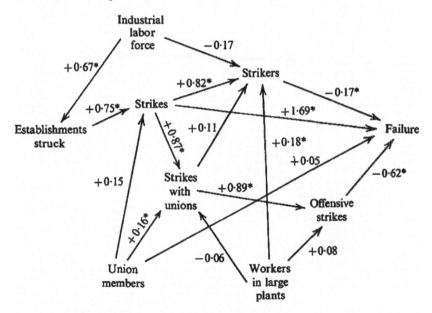

* Coefficient at least two times its standard error

Figure 2.1 Path Analysis at Departmental Level, 1910–14

offensive strikes were frequent, failures were relatively infrequent. Another indirect path is equally interesting: although size of plant had no significant effect on the offensive or defensive character of a department's strikes, larger plants did mean more strikers (even after allowance for the total size of the industrial labor force), and failures were less frequent where the number of strikers was larger.

Does Modernization Breed Revolution?   **3**

Charles Tilly

A Sicilian Revolution

Eighteen forty-eight was one of Europe's vintage years for revolution. The first truly revolutionary situation of the year did not develop in the industrializing centers of France, Germany, or England. It formed in poor old Sicily. During the three decades since the settlement that had closed the Napoleonic Wars, Sicily had occupied a position subordinate to Naples in the newly created Kingdom of the Two Sicilies. Its bourgeoisie had long been pushing for Sicilian autonomy. Some of them, in tune (and, to some extent, in concert) with liberals elsewhere in Italy, had lately been entertaining ideas of political reform. And other groups of Sicilians opposed any strong government whatsoever.

Early in January 1848, the closing of the university, after student riots centering on calls for a new constitution, freed the young and educated for political action. The government decreed the arrest of some of the city's prominent liberals. Then the call for a revolt on the occasion of King Ferdinand's birthday celebration—January 12—began to spread through Palermo. A manifesto, passed from hand to hand on 9 January, read as follows:

> Sicilians! The time of useless supplications is past. Protests, requests, and peaceful demonstrations are useless. Ferdinand has scorned them all. Are we, a freeborn people reduced to shackles and misery, to delay any longer in reconquering our legitimate rights? To arms, sons of Sicily. The force of the people is omnipotent: the unity of the people

will bring the fall of the king. The day of 12 January 1848, at dawn, will bring the glorious epoch of universal regeneration. Palermo will receive with delight those armed Sicilians who offer themselves in support of the common cause: to establish reforms and institutions proper to the progress of this century, reforms and institutions desired by Europe, by Italy, and by Pope Pius. Union, order, subordination to our leaders. Respect for property: theft is a declaration of betrayal of the cause of the nation and will be punished as such. He who lacks means will be given them. With these principles Heaven will support the just cause. Sicilians, to arms!

(Candeloro 1966: 122)

The declaration was a little grander than the events that followed, but the Palermitani did, indeed, begin a revolution on 12 January.

As Frederico Curato sums up for the Sicilian revolution:

This insurrectional movement was based on economic causes not dissimilar to those prevailing elsewhere in Europe, but it had some special features which made it an unusual movement in the history of that year's insurrections. In fact it embodied not only a reaction against Naples ... but also a reaction of the incipient Sicilian bourgeoisie to the introduction by the Neapolitan government of a unitary economic system for the two parts of the Kingdom which, combined with the free coastal trade established in 1824, damaged the development of local industries which were incapable of meeting the competition of mainland industries. In Sicily, in the last analysis, the bourgeoisie sought power not because it had become the most important class and sought juridical and political recognition of its strength, but on the contrary in order simply to survive.

(Curato 1969: 682)

The special features matter. Yet behind the particular interpretation of the Sicilian revolution we see a standard form of historical analysis that consists of identifying the principal actors, attributing to them appropriate incentives, outlooks, or calculations, and then settling them into motion. The conception is dramatic: the stage, the players, the impulses, the action. Revolution becomes a work of art.

Large structural transformations like the incipient industrialization of Europe figure only indirectly in this kind of analysis. They are neither actors nor actions. They simply condition the stage, the players, the impulses, the action. They may also result from the action, in the way that the installation of liberal regimes in 1848 facilitated the expansion of trade, the treatment of labor as a commodity, and so on. As a consequence, they tend to enter the account via theories (implicit or explicit) in which structural changes affect mentalities, mentalities guide actions, and actions produce further structural changes.

Those psychological theories are likely to fall into one of two classes. The first class of theory stresses the psychic impact of large-scale change: disorientation, rising expectations, relative deprivation, the diffusion of new ideologies. Thus, one standard interpretation of the revolutions of 1848 emphasizes the junction of two different responses to early industrialism: the bourgeois formation of a liberal-democratic-individualistic ideology and the working-class response of anger and fear. The second class of theory deals with the "fit" between political institutions and social situation, on the general grounds that where the fit is poor, people become dissatisfied, resentful, and rebellious. Another standard interpretation of the events of 1848 brings out the nineteenth-century inappropriateness or decay of political arrangements fashioned in the epic state-building of the preceding two or three centuries. Obviously, one can employ either or both of these lines of explanation in attempting to account for the Sicilian revolution of 1848: the small Sicilian bourgeoisie did share to some extent in the quasi-religious devotion of their mainland brothers to the market and to self-advancement. ...

Some Larger Questions

Despite the fascination of this sort of dramaturgic analysis of particular events, I want this essay to deal with the questions raised by the Sicilian case within a plane that is rather less historical, less colorful, more pretentious. With one eye fixed on the modern European experience, I want to ask myself whether modernization breeds revolution... That first formulation of the question is compact, but ambiguous. We shall, unfortunately, have to put a large part of our effort into the preliminary task of reducing the ambiguities. *Modernization* is a vague, tendentious concept. *Revolution* is a controversial one as well.

Instead of trying to pace off modernization precisely, I shall ordinarily substitute for it somewhat better-defined processes, such as industrialization or demographic expansion. Instead of trying to grasp the essential genius of revolution, I shall offer a rather arbitrary set of definitions that appears to me to have considerable theoretical utility. I shall compensate for my arbitrariness by discussing violence, instability, and political conflict more extensively than a strict concentration on revolution would justify.

There are, furthermore, quite a few different senses in which one can imagine large-scale structural change as breeding, shaping, causing, sparking, or resulting from major political conflicts. Instead of striving to catalog and assess them all, I shall take a critical look at one synthesis of the relationships that are most often proposed and try to communicate my reasons for thinking that (a) available theories that treat protest, conflict, violence, and revolution as direct responses to the stresses of structural change are wrong; (b) the strong effects of large-scale change on conflict run through the structure of power, especially by shaping the organizational means and resources available to different possible contenders for power; and (c) there are nevertheless certain kinds of short-run crises that tend to promote conflict, or even revolution, by affecting the likelihood that major participants in the political system will make or reject claims of great importance for the structure of power.

Pursuit of the first two problems (the conceptual difficulties and the direct relationships between structural change and revolution) will lead to a third set of questions: if the political process is so important after all, what *are* the political conditions for conflict, violence, and revolution? The discussion of that question will fall even shorter of a comprehensive reply than in the first two cases. But at least there will be some suggestions of relationships among war, domestic violence, revolution, and routine contention for power.

Huntington's Synthesis

One of the most sophisticated recent syntheses of the standard views concerning all these matters comes from Samuel Huntington. In his *Political Order in Changing Societies*, Huntington argues that the widespread domestic violence and instability of the 1950s and 1960s in many parts of the world "was in large part the product of rapid social change and the rapid mobilization of new groups into politics, coupled with the slow development of political institutions" (Huntington 1968: 4). He goes on to portray an interaction among these elements:

> If a society is to maintain a high level of community, the expansion of political participation must be accompanied by the development of

stronger, more complex, and more autonomous political institutions. The effect of the expansion of political participation, however, is usually to undermine the traditional political institutions and to obstruct the development of modern political ones. Modernization and social mobilization, in particular, thus tend to produce political decay unless steps are taken to moderate or to restrict its impact on political consciousness and political involvement. Most societies, even those with fairly complex and adaptable traditional political institutions, suffer a loss of political community and decay of political institutions during the most intense phases of modernization.

(Huntington 1968: 85–86)

Huntington deliberately applies this lead-lag model to Western revolutions, treating them as extreme cases of the conflicts that emerge when political institutionalization proceeds too slowly for the paces of large-scale social change (which Huntington treats as more or less identical with modernization) and of mobilization. Moreover, John Gillis has recently argued that the model applies specifically to the European modernizing revolutions of the eighteenth and nineteenth centuries (Gillis 1970: 344–370). It is therefore legitimate to ask how strong a grip on the Western experience with revolutions and violent conflict Huntington's analysis gives us. My answer is that the grip is needlessly weak: weak, because the scheme founders in tautologies, contradictions, omissions, and failures to examine the evidence seriously; needlessly, because several of the main arguments concerning mobilization, political participation, and conflict improve vastly on the usual socio-psychological tracing of "violence" or "protest" back to "strain" or "discontent."

Although it would be worth trying, this chapter will not attempt to wrench Huntington's theory into shape. I shall dwell on it in other ways, for other reasons, because in one manner or another it sums up most of the conventional wisdom connecting revolution to large-scale structural change; because Huntington places an exceptional range of contemporary and historical material within its framework; because the variables within it appear to be of the right kind; and because it is sturdy enough to exempt me from the accusation of having erected, and then burned, a straw man as I build up an alternative line of argument.

Not that I find the theory convincing, even where it escapes tautology. Its plausibility begins to wither as we examine the portion of the argument that deals directly with the political consequences of large-scale structural change: "Not only does social and economic modernization produce political instability, but the degree of instability is related to the rate of modernization. The historical evidence with respect to the West is overwhelming on this point" (Huntington 1968: 45). I beg leave not to be overwhelmed by the available evidence. Almost all the sources habitually cited by Huntington and others in this regard refer to static cross-sectional comparisons of contemporary states during short spasms of recent years or the distribution of support for ostensibly radical political movements like Communists. In order to be even mildly persuaded, one would want to have reliable information on the effects of changes in the rate of "social and economic modernization" within the same countries.

Very few over-time studies of the problem have ever been done. The vast long-run analyses of Sorokin offer no particular support for the thesis that the pace of change governs the degree of instability (Sorokin 1962). Such longitudinal evidence as my collaborators and I have been able to assemble for European countries in the modern period displays plenty of violent conflict in the modern period. But it suggests either no direct relationship with the pace of structural change, or a negative one: rapid change, diminution of political conflict. In France since 1830, for example, we have discovered a broad tendency for times of rapid urbanization to produce *less* collective violence than the rest.

On a smaller scale, the exact connections that are usually alleged to tie instability to rapid structural change also turn out to be dubious. Rapid rural-to-urban migration has no particular tendency to excite protest; marginal urban populations are not the tinder of revolutions; the initial exposure of peasants to factories does not generate high levels of industrial conflict; and so on. Huntington himself happens onto some of the evidence with apparent surprise when he observes that the big-city lumpenproletariat in modernizing countries, contrary to theory, tends to be a passive, or even conservative, political force and when he goes on to speculate that urbanization may be negatively correlated with revolution (Huntington 1968: 278–28, 299). Yet somehow this important qualification does not penetrate to the general statement of the theory.

The danger of circular argument is just as apparent here as before... Huntington does not really escape the fateful circularity of judging the extent of the discrepancy from the character of the revolution that presumably resulted from the discrepancy. He tells us:

> The great revolutions of history have taken place either in highly centralized traditional monarchies (France, China, Russia), or in narrowly based military dictatorships (Mexico, Bolivia, Guatemala,

Cuba), or in colonial regimes (Vietnam, Algeria). All these political systems demonstrated little if any capacity to expand their power and to provide channels for the participation of new groups in politics.

(Huntington 1968: 275)

Suppose we suppress the urge to blurt out questions about England in the 1640s or the United States in the 1860s and stifle suspicions that the implicit standard for great revolutions at work in this passage simply restricts them logically to centralized, authoritarian regimes. We still must wonder how we could have known before the fact of revolution that the expansive capacity of these governments was inferior to that of the many other monarchies, military dictatorships, and colonial regimes that did not experience revolutions.

Huntington does not answer. In its present form, his scheme does not, it appears, give us any social guidance in the anticipation or production of revolution—not even in the weak sense of projecting ourselves back into the France of 1788 or the Sicily of 1847, and saying how we would have gone about estimating the probabilities of revolution within the next few years.

How else could we proceed? We should hold onto several of Huntington's perceptions: (a) that revolutions and collective violence tend to flow directly out of a population's central political processes, instead of expressing diffuse strains and discontents within the population; (b) that the specific claims and counterclaims being made on the existing government by various mobilized groups are more important than the general satisfaction or discontent of those groups and that claims for established places within the structure of power are crucial; (c) that large-scale structural change transforms the identities and structures of the potential aspirants for power within the population, affects their opportunities for mobilization, governs the resources available to the government, and through it to the principal holders of power. Accepting those insights would incline us to set our faces against such aggregate psychological hypotheses as those of James Davies (Davies 1962: 5–19) or Ted Gurr (1970), as well as against gross system-function hypotheses like those of Chalmers Johnson (Johnson 1966) or Neil Smelser (Smelser 1963). It will encourage us to concentrate our analysis on processes of mobilization, on structures of power, and on the changing demands linking one to the other, in the manner of Barrington Moore (1966), Eric Wolf (1969), or William Gamson (1968).

A Model of Political Conflict

First, a simple model of political action. Let us distinguish three kinds of social unit within any specified population. A *government* is an organization that controls the principal concentrated means of coercion within the population; a *contender for power* is a group within the population that at least once during some standard period applies resources to influence that government; and a *polity* is the set of contenders that routinely and successfully lays claims on that government. (We may call these individual contenders *members* of the polity, while *challenger* is a good name for a contender laying claims in an irregular or unsuccessful fashion.) ... A group gains the capacity to contend by mobilizing: by acquiring collective control over resources—land, labor, information, arms, money, and so on—that can be applied to influence the government; it loses that capacity by demobilizing, losing collective control over resources.

Every polity, then, collectively develops tests of membership. The tests always include the capacity to bring considerable numbers of people into action; they may also include the possession of wealth, certified birth, religious stigmata, and many other characteristics. Challengers acquire membership in the polity by meeting the tests, despite the fact that existing members characteristically resist new admissions and employ the government's resources to make admissions more difficult. The members also test one another more or less continuously; a member failing the tests tends to lose membership in the polity. Each change in membership moves the tests in a direction harmonious with the characteristics and capacities of the set of members emerging from the change. The members of the polity come to treat the prevailing criteria of membership as having a special moral virtue. Challengers denied admission tend to define themselves as being deprived of rights due them on general grounds. Members losing position tend, in contrast, to accent tradition, usage, and particular agreements in support of their claims to threatened privileges and resources. Thus contenders both entering and leaving the polity have a special propensity to articulate strongly moral definitions of their situations.

The model is simple and broad. ... There are compensating advantages: the avoidance of that ill-defined entity called a "society" as the basic analytic unit; the well-defined connections among mobilization, contention, and conflict; the easy accommodation to the existence of multiple governments within the same population.

The scheme also permits us to specify the close relationship between collective violence and the central political process: (a) political life consists largely of making collective claims for resources and privileges controlled by governments; (b) collective violence is largely a by-product of situations in which one contender openly lays such claims and other contenders (or, especially, the government) resist these claims; (c) such situations occur with particular frequency when groups are acquiring or losing membership—that is, partly because testing tends to take that form, partly because the moral orientations of the groups whose memberships are disputed encourage the individuals within them to take exceptional risks of damage or injury, partly because the activation of the coercive forces of the government increases the likelihood of damage or injury to other participants; (d) hence collective violence tends to cluster around major or multiple entries and exits; (e) governments themselves act to maintain priority over substantial concentrations of coercive resources, so that a contender accumulating such resources outside the control of the government is quite likely to find itself in acute conflict with the agents of the government.

As a consequence, the common theories of violence that treat it as a product of the willingness of certain kinds of individuals or groups to "resort to violence" to express themselves or accomplish their ends fall wide of the mark. Those equally common theories that distinguish sharply between violent and orderly political actions fail just as badly. The one misses the extent to which collective violence is a contingent outcome of interactions among contenders and governments, in which the agents of government commonly have the greater discretion and do most of the injury and damage. The other misses the great continuity between nonviolent and violent political actions. In Europe of the last few hundred years, at least, the great bulk of collective violence has (a) involved agents of the government, (b) grown from collective actions (such as assemblies, demonstrations, or strikes) that were not intrinsically violent, indeed that usually went on without violence. Lovers of order and defenders of the state have obscured these facts by expanding the word *violence* to include not only physical damage, but also a wide range of illegal, unseemly, and symbolically repugnant behavior. In our own day as well, it is customary to puff up the idea of violence until it has little value as an analytic tool but carries great moral weight.

Revolutions

We now have the means of moving on to television. The multiplication of polities is the key. A revolution begins when a government previously under the control of a single, sovereign polity becomes the object of effective, competing, mutually exclusive claims from two or more separate polities.

A revolution ends when a single polity—by no means necessarily the same one—regains control over the government. This multiple sovereignty can result from the attempt of one polity to subordinate another heretofore independent polity; from the assertion of sovereignty by a previously subordinate polity; from the formation of a bloc of challengers that seizes control of some portion of the government apparatus; from the fragmentation of an existing polity into blocs, each of which controls some part of the government. Many observers would prefer to restrict the label "revolution" to the action by challengers; many others would prefer to call each of these a different major type of revolution: civil war, national revolution, and so on. I begin with an exceptionally broad definition to call attention to the common properties of the various paths through multiple sovereignty.

This labeling is a delicate matter. As with violence, many groups want to define their own political objectives by reference to *revolution*, whether they fear or welcome an overturn of things as they are.

Condition for Revolutions

At one time or another, the building of European states led down all four paths to multiple sovereignty: (1) attempts of one polity to subordinate another independent polity—a standard situation in the dynastic and colonial war making of the sixteenth century and later; (2) the assertion of sovereignty by a previously subordinate polity—the diverse Habsburg Empire was peculiarly subject to this outcome, and the revolutions of the Netherlands and Catalonia are prime examples; (3) the formation of a bloc of challengers that seizes control of some portion of the government apparatus—the purest cases are peasant revolts, but every major revolution included some such action; (4) the fragmentation of an existing polity into blocs, each controlling some part of the government—with the important qualification that coalitions between members and challengers (in this case, especially working-class groups) were frequent and influential. This was the pattern in the Sicilian revolution with which we began, the standard pattern in 1848 as a whole, and, no doubt, the most common pattern among all modern Western revolutions.

What observable political conditions, then, ought to prevail before a revolution begins? Three conditions appear to be necessary, and a fourth strongly facilitating. The three apparently necessary conditions are:

1   The appearance of contenders or coalitions of contenders, advancing exclusively alternative claims to the control over the government currently exerted by the members of the polity;

2   commitment to those claims by a significant segment of the subject population;
3   unwillingness or incapacity of the agents of the government to suppress the alternative coalition or the commitment to its claims.

The strongly facilitating condition:

4   formation of coalitions between members of the polity and the contenders making the alternative claims.

The expansion of commitment to the claims of the alternative bloc occurs both through their acceptance by groups and individuals not belonging to the bloc and through the further mobilization of the bloc itself. The two undoubtedly reinforce each other. Acceptance of the alternative claims is likely to generalize when: the government fails to meet its established obligations; it greatly increases its demands on the subject population; the alternative claims are cast within the moral framework already employed by many members of the population; there is a strong alliance between the existing government and a well-defined enemy of an important segment of the population; and the coercive resources of the alternative bloc increase.

The Marxist account of the conditions for radicalization of the proletariat and the peasantry remains the most powerful general analysis of the process, expanding commitment to a revolutionary bloc (Marx 1958: 243–344). Where it falls down is in not providing for contenders (communities, ethnic minorities, religious groups, and so on) that are not class-based and in obscuring the revolutionary importance of defensive reactions by segments of the population whose established positions are threatened. (Eric Wolf's [1969] superb study of twentieth-century peasant wars makes apparent the revolutionary potential of such defensive responses to land enclosure, expansion of the market, and the encroachment of capitalism; John Womack's [1969] biography of Zapata provides a heroic portrayal of one important leader of that reaction.)

The agents of the government are likely to become unwilling or unable to suppress the alternative bloc and the commitment to its claims when their coercive resources contract, their inefficiency increases, and inhibitions to their use arise. Defeat in a war is a quintessential case, for casualties, defections, and military demobilization all tend to decrease the government's coercive capacity; the destruction of property, disruption of routines, and displacement of population in defeat are likely to decrease the efficiency of the established coercive means; and the presence of a conqueror places constraints on the government's use of coercion. (The routine of modern military occupation, however, tends to substitute the coercive capacity of the victors for that of the vanquished.) The end of any war, won or lost, tends to restore men with newly acquired military skill to most of the contenders in the political system. Where military demobilization proceeds rapidly, it is likely to shift the balance of coercive resources away from the government, and may shift it toward an alternative bloc. Even without war, the increase in the coercive resources of the alternative bloc (which can occur through theft, purchase, training, the imposition of military discipline, and the lending of support by outsiders) is equivalent to the contraction of the government's own coercive resources. The efficiency of governmental coercion is likely to decline, at least in the short run, when the character, organization, and daily routines of the population to be controlled change rapidly; this appears to be one of the most direct effects of large-scale structural change on the likelihood of revolution. Inhibitions to the use of coercion are likely to increase when the coercive forces themselves are drawn from (or otherwise attached to) the populations to be controlled, when new members of the polity act against the coercive means that were employed to block their acquisition of membership, and when effective coalitions between members of the polity and revolutionary challengers exist.

The final condition for revolution—this one strongly facilitating rather than necessary—is the formation of just such coalitions between polity members and revolutionary challengers. Modern European history, for example, provides many examples of temporary coalitions between professionals, intellectuals, or other fragments of the bourgeoisie well established within the polity and segments of the working class excluded from power. The revolutions of 1830 and 1848 display this pattern with particular clarity. The payoff to the challengers consists of a hedge against repression, some protection against the devaluation of their resources, and perhaps the transfer of information and expertise from the member. The payoff to the member consists of an expansion of the resources available for application to the government and to other members of the polity—not least, the ability to mount a credible threat of mass action. This sort of coalition formation is likely to occur, on the one hand, when a challenger rapidly increases the store of resources under its control and, on the other, when a member loses its coalition partners within the polity, or the polity is more or less evenly divided among two or more coalitions, or an established member is risking loss of membership in the polity through failure to meet the tests of other members.

Revolution and Some Other Forms of Conflict

Even the less romantic forms of piracy and banditry that flourished around the Mediterranean for centuries bore some striking resemblances to civil war, for they frequently amounted to de facto claims to sovereignty within particular geographic areas. In regions like southern Italy, the bandits sometimes exercised their claims in collusion with the duly constituted authorities of adjacent territories.

In the case of Italy, it also becomes clear that war and revolution have a good deal in common. We conventionally distinguish the two on the basis of (a) the status of each participant at the beginning and the end of the conflict, and (b) the means employed. But in nineteenth-century Italy, the "national revolution" that brought about unification consisted mainly of military conquests by Piedmont, coupled with risings led by such heroic invaders as Mazzini and Garibaldi, insurrections subsidized or even engineered by Piedmont, and further popular rebellions that broke out very widely after invasion had weakened the grips of the old state and the old elite. War or revolution? Both. The same conjunction appears in the multiple rebellions of conquered territories against Napoleon, the movements of resistance against the Nazis, the anti-Japanese phase of the Chinese Revolution, and a great many other important conflicts.

Not only similarities, but interconnections. I have already pointed out that the extent of damage and injury that results from collective violence depends largely on the organization and tactics of the government's own coercive forces. Within strong states, that relationship goes further. Repression often works. In the European experience of the last two centuries, the substantial periods of respite from collective violence within any particular country have generally been in the tenures of repressive regimes: the Spanish dictatorships of Primo de Rivera and Franco, the Bolsheviks in power, the heyday of Nazism, Italian fascism after 1925, France under Louis Napoleon and—the Resistance notwithstanding—under German occupation. Obviously, I am speaking strictly of collective violence that pits groups of individuals against one another, and not of terror, torture, individual repression, psychic punishment, or external war. The Nazis (among others) engaged in all of these terrible acts while internal collective violence was at its low point. Just as obviously, all these regimes began with widespread collective violence, and most of them ended with it. So the point is not that repressive regimes are kinder to life. It is, rather, that by deliberately demobilizing their most likely opponents and closely controlling the opportunities for collective action by any other contender, repressive regimes greatly reduce the chances that collective violence will grow out of contention for power.

Another connection comes to mind. In the West of the past five centuries, perhaps the largest single factor in the promotion of revolutions and collective violence has been the great concentration of power in national states. (I concede that the rise of the national state depended to such a large degree on the growth of production, the expansion of large-scale marketing, the strengthening of the bourgeoisie, and the proliferation of bureaucracy that such a statement commits a dramatic oversimplification.) This factor shows up most clearly in frequency of tax rebellions in Western countries over those centuries and in the prominence of grievances concerning taxation in revolutions, such as those of the 1640s or the 1840s. The frequency of violent resistance to military conscription points in the same direction. Violent resistance by separatist movements has commonly begun with attempts of national governments to increase their control over the periphery.

The connections are subtler and more debatable when it comes to food riots, land seizures, machine breaking, violent strikes, or religious conflicts, but in those cases as well, I think the influence of the concentration of power in national states is far from negligible. In any case, over that span of European history, one can see a long slope of resistance to central control followed by a fairly rapid transition (mainly in the nineteenth century) to struggles for control *over* the central state. In the records of collective violence, this shows up as a decisive shift away from localized tax rebellions and the like to conflicts involving contenders articulating national objectives, organized on a national scale, and confronting representatives of the national state.

But I have neglected one major connection. States are war makers, and wars are state makers. At least in modern Europe, the major increases in the scope and strength of national states (as indicated by national budgets, national debts, powers of intervention, and sizes of staffs) have, on the whole, occurred as a direct result of war making or preparation for war. What is more, the armed forces have historically played a large part in subordinating other authorities and the general population to the national state. They backed up the collection of taxes, put down tax rebellions, seized and disposed of the enemies of the crown, literally enforced national policy. The relationship was neatly reciprocal: war provided the incentive, the occasion, and the rationalization for strengthening the state, while war makers assured the docility of the general population and the yielding of the resources necessary to carry out the task. The fairly recent division of labor between specialized police forces for domestic control and military forces for the remaining tasks has not fundamentally changed the relationship.

The connection matters here because a series of important relationships between war and revolution also exists. It is not just that they overlap to some extent. In some circumstances, war promotes revolution. That assertion is true in several different ways: the extraction of resources for the prosecution of a war has repeatedly aroused revolutionary resistance; the defeat of states in war has often made them vulnerable to attacks from their domestic enemies; the complicity of some portion of the armed forces with the revolutionary bloc has been absolutely essential to the success of the modern revolution, and the most frequent variety of revolution—the coup—has depended mainly on the alignments of armed forces; the waning phases of major movements of conquest (the weakening of the Napoleonic regimes outside of France, the Nazi regimes outside of Germany, and the Japanese regimes outside of Japan being prime examples) are strikingly propitious for revolution; and the periods of readjustment immediately following large international conflicts also seem favorable to revolution, often with the collusion of major parties to the conflict. All of this suggests a strong connection between realignments in the international system and conflicts within individual countries, a connection mediated by the repressive policies and capacities of the governments involved.

Those who find at least some of the preceding analysis useful and plausible will do well to reflect on the sorts of variables that have been in play. Despite the many recent attempts to psychologize the study of revolution by introducing ideas of anxiety, alienation, rising expectations, and the like, and to sociologize it by employing notions of disequilibrium, role conflict, structural strain, and so on, the factors that hold up under close scrutiny are, on the whole, political ones. The structure of power, alternative conceptions of justice, the organization of coercion, the conduct of war, the formation of coalitions, the legitimacy of the state—these traditional concerns of political thought provide the main guides to the explanation of revolution. Population growth, industrialization, urbanization, and other large-scale structural changes do, to be sure, affect the probabilities of revolution. But they do so indirectly, by shaping the potential contenders for power, transforming the techniques of governmental control, and shifting the resources available to contenders and governments. There is no reliable and regular sense in which modernization breeds revolution.

References

Candeloro, Giorgio. *Storia dell' Italia moderna,* 2nd ed. (Milan: Teltrinelli, 1966), III.

Curato, Federico. "Il 1848 italiano ed europeo," in *Nuove questione di storia del Risorgimento e dell' Unità* (Milan, 1969), I.

Davies, James C. "Toward a Theory of Revolution," *American Sociological Review* 27 (1962): 5–19.

Gamson, William A. *Power and Discontent.* Homewood, IL: Dorsay, 1968.

Gillis, John R. "Political Decay and the European Revolutions, 1789–1848," *World Politics* 22 (April 1970): 344–370.

Gurr, Ted Robert. *Why Men Rebel*. Princeton, NJ: Princeton University Press, 1970.

Huntington, Samuel P. *Political Order in Changing Societies*. New Haven, CT: Yale University Press, 1968.

Johnson, Chalmers. *Revolutionary Change*. Boston: Little, Brown, 1966.

Marx, Karl, "The Eighteenth Brumaire of Louis Bonaparte," in Karl Marx and Frederick Engles, *Selected Works*. Moscow, 1958, I, pp. 243–344.

Moore, Barrington. *Social Origins of Dictatorship and Democracy: Lord and Peasant in the Making of the Modern World*. Boston, MA: Beacon Press, 1966.

Smelser, Neil J. *Theory of Collective Behavior*. New York: Free Press, 1963.

Sorokin, Pitirim A. *Social and Cultural Dynamics III: Fluctuation of Social Relationships, War, and Revolution*. New York: Bedminster, 1962.

Wolf, Eric. *Peasant Wars of the Twentieth Century*. New York: Harper & Row, 1969.

Womack Jr., John. *Zapata and the Mexican Revolution*. Cambridge, MA: Harvard University Press, 1969.

From Mobilization to Revolution

4

Charles Tilly

Interests, Organization, and Mobilization

The Elementary Models

To get anywhere at all, we will have to hew out rough models of interaction among groups, and of a single group's collective action. At first chop, the model of interaction is quite static. Let us call it our *polity model*. Its elements are a population, a government, one or more contenders, a polity, and one or more coalitions. We define a population of interest to us by any means we please. Within that population we search for one or more of the following:

Government: an organization which controls the principal concentrated means of coercion within the population.

Contender: any group which, during some specified period, applies pooled resources to influence the government. Contenders include *challengers* and *members of the polity*. A *member* is any contender which has routine, low-cost access to resources controlled by the government; a *challenger* is any other contender.

Polity: consists of the collective action of the members and the government.

Coalition: a tendency of a set of contenders and/or governments to coordinate their collective action.

Mobilization

The word "mobilization" conveniently identifies the process by which a group goes from being a passive collection of individuals to an active participant in public life. Demobilization is the reverse process.

Thus any group's mobilization program breaks down into these components:

1 Accumulating resources.
2 Increasing collective claims on the resources
   a   by reducing competing claims,
   b   by altering the program of collective action,
   c   by changing the satisfaction due to participation in the group as such.

A successful mobilization program does all of them at once.

Groups do their mobilizing in a number of different ways. We can make crude distinctions among *defensive, offensive,* and *preparatory* mobilization. In defensive mobilization, a threat form outside induces the members of a group to pool their resources to fight off the enemy. Eric Wolf (1969) has pointed out how regularly this sort of response to the representatives of capitalism and state power has preceded peasant rebellions. Standard European forms of rural conflict—food riots, tax rebellions, invasions of fields, draft resistance, and so on—typically follow the same sort of defensive mobilization. This large class of actions challenges the common assumption (made by Etzioni, among others) that mobilization is always a top-down phenomenon, organized by leaders and agitators.

Offensive mobilization *is,* however, often top-down. In the offensive case, a group pools resources in response to opportunities to realize its interests. A common form of offensive mobilization consists of the diffusion of a new organizational strategy. In the late 1820s, for example, the success of O'Connell's Catholic Association in forcing the expansion of the political rights of British and Irish Catholics inspired the creation of political associations aimed at expanding the franchise and guaranteeing rights to assemble, organize, and act collectively. A coalition of bourgeois and substantial artisans arose from that strategy, and helped produce the great Reform Bill of 1832. In this instance, the top-down organizational efforts of such leaders as Francis Place and William Cobbett were crucial. Nevertheless, in parish after parish the local dissidents decided on their own that it was time to organize their own association, or (more likely) to convert their existing forms of organization into a political association.

Preparatory mobilization is no doubt the most top-down of all. In this variety, the group pools resources in anticipation of future opportunities and threats. The nineteenth-century trade union is a classic case. The trade union built up a store of money to cushion hardship—hardship in the form of unemployment, the death of a breadwinner, or loss of wages during a strike. It also pooled knowledge and organizational skills. When it escaped the union-busting of employers and governments, the trade union greatly increased the capacity of workers to act together: to strike, to boycott, to make collective demands. This preparatory mobilization often began defensively, in the course of a losing battle with employers or in the face of a threat of firings, wage reductions, or cutbacks in privileges. It normally required risky organizing efforts by local leaders who were willing to get hurt.

The preparatory part of the strategy was always difficult, since it required the members to forgo present satisfactions in favor of uncertain future benefits. As we move from defensive to offensive to preparatory mobilization, in fact, we see the increasing force of Mancur Olson's statement of the free-rider problem: a rational actor will ride for nothing if someone else will pay the fuel and let him aboard. But if everyone tries to ride free the vehicle goes nowhere. Preparatory mobilization, especially in the face of high risks, requires strong incentives to overcome the reasonable desire to have someone else absorb the costs.

A population's initial wealth and power significantly affect the probability that its mobilization will be defensive or offensive. Common sense says that the rich mobilize conservatively, in defense of their threatened interests, while the poor mobilize radically, in search of what they lack. Common sense is wrong. It is true that the rich never lash out to smash the status quo, while the poor sometimes do. But the rich are constantly mobilizing to take advantage of new opportunities to maximize their interests. The poor can rarely afford to.

The poor and powerless tend to begin defensively, the rich and powerful offensively. The group whose members are rich can mobilize a surplus without threatening a member's other amusements and obligations. A group with a poor constituency has little choice but to compete with daily necessities. The group whose members are powerful can use the other organizations they control—including governments—to do some of their work, whereas the powerless must do it on their own. The rich and powerful can forestall claims from other groups before they become articulated claims, and can afford to seize opportunities to make new claims on their own. The poor and the powerless often find that the rich, the powerful, and the government oppose and punish their efforts at mobilization. (The main exception, an important one, is the powerless group which forms a coalition with a rich, powerful patron; European Fascists of the 1920s mobilized rapidly in that fashion.) As a result, any mobilization at all is more costly to the poor and powerless; only a threat to the little they have is likely to move them to mobilize. The rich and powerful are well defended against such threats; they rarely have the occasion for defensive mobilization.

If, on the other hand, we hold mobilization constant and consider collective action itself, common sense is vindicated. Relatively poor and powerless groups which have already mobilized are more likely to act collectively by claiming new rights, privileges, and advantages. At the same level of mobilization the rich and powerful are more likely to act collectively in defense of what they already have. Thus the well-documented tendency of strikes to become more frequent and more demanding in times of prosperity, when workers have more slack resources to devote to acting together, and employers have more to lose from the withholding of labor.

Military conscription withdraws a man from his obligations to a circle of friends and relatives.

General Conditions for Mobilization

According to our mobilization model, the broad factors within a population affecting its degree of mobilization are the extent of its shared interest in interactions with other populations, and the extent to which it forms a distinct category and a dense network: its interest and its organization. Outside the group, its power, its subjection to repression, and the current constellation of opportunities and threats most strongly affect its mobilization level.

From Mobilization to Collective Action

Collective action is joint action in pursuit of common ends. Up to this point, I have argued that the extent of a group's collective action is a function of (1) the extent of its shared *interests* (advantages and disadvantages likely to result from interactions with other groups), (2) the intensity of its *organization* (the extent of common identity and unifying structure among its members) and (3) its *mobilization* (the amount of resources under its collective control). Soon I will add repression, power, and opportunity/threat to those determinants of a group's collective action. In this general statement, the argument is not very controversial. It rejects Durkheimian theories which trace routine collective action back to society's integration and which trace non-routine collective action back to society's disintegration. Still a great many Weberian, Marxian, and Millian analyses will fit, with a bit of shoving, into the boxes defined by interests, organization, and mobilization.

The Detection and Measurement of Collective Action

When trying to study joint action in pursuit of common ends, we face the practical problems of detecting the action, and then determining how joint it is and how common its ends. If we confine our attention to clear-cut examples, such as strikes, elections, petitions, and attacks on poorhouses, we still face the practical problems of gauging their magnitudes—especially if we want to say "how much" collective action one group or another engaged in over some period of time. As with the measurement of mobilization, we commonly have the choice between (a) indicators of collective action which come to us in a more or less quantitative form, but are too narrow or too remote to represent adequately the range of action we have in mind, or (b) indicators derived from qualitative descriptions, which are usually discontinuous, which often vary in coverage from one group or period to another, and which are always hard to convert reliably into meaningful numbers.

Let us concentrate on collective violence within a population under the control of a single government. Let us agree to pay attention to war, to full-fledged games, to individual violence, and to highly discontinuous interactions. We are then still free to examine events in which the damage was only incidental to the aims of most of those involved. In our own investigations, my research group has discovered that we can, without huge uncertainty, single out events occurring within a particular national state in which at least one group above some minimum size (commonly twenty or fifty persons) seizes or damages someone or something from another group. We use newspapers, archival sources, and historical works for the purpose. As the minimum size goes down, collective violence begins to fade into banditry, brawling, vandalism, terrorism, and a wide variety of threatening nonviolent events, so far as our ability to distinguish them on the basis of the historical record is concerned.

We use the community-population-day as an elementary unit. On a particular day, did this segment of the population of this community engage in collective violence, as just defined? If so, we have the elementary unit of a violent event. Did an overlapping set of people carry on the action in an adjacent community? If so, both communities were involved in the same event.

Did an overlapping set of people continue the action the following day? If so, the incident lasted at least two days. Introduce a break in time, space, or personnel, and we are dealing with two or more distinct events. The result of this modular reasoning is both to greatly simplify the problem of bounding the "same" incident and to fragment into many separate incidents series of interactions (such as the Spanish Civil War as a whole) which many analysts have been willing to treat as a single unit.

For some purposes, like the comparative study of revolutions, a broader criterion may serve better. Still other investigations will require more stringent standards—more participants, a certain duration, someone killed, a particular minimum of property damage. But the general reasoning of such choices would be the same: identify *all* the events above a certain magnitude, or at least a representative sample of them, before trying to sort them out in terms of legitimacy or in terms of the aims of the participants.

Repression and Facilitation

Contention for power always involves at least two parties. The behavior of the second party runs along a range from repression to facilitation. Let us recall the definitions: *repression* is any action by another group which raises the contender's cost of collective action. An action which lowers the group's cost of collective action is a form of *facilitation*. (We call repression or facilitation *political* if the other party is a government.) A group bent on repressing or facilitating another group's action has the choice of working on the target group's mobilization or directly on its collective action. For example, a government can raise a group's mobilization costs (and thereby raise its costs of collective action) by disrupting its organization, by making communications difficult or inaccessible, by freezing necessary resources such as guns and manpower. Standard repressive measures such as suspending newspapers, drafting strikers, forbidding assemblies, and arresting leaders illustrate the antimobilization avenue. Or a government can operate directly on the costs of collective action by raising the penalties, making the targets of the action inaccessible, or inducing a waste of the mobilized resources; the *agent provocateur*, the barricades around the city hall, the establishment of military tribunals for insurgents fall familiarly into the strategy of moving directly against collective action. Facilitation likewise has two faces, both familiar: promobilization activities such as giving a group publicity, legalizing membership in it, and simply paying it off; activities directly reducing the group's costs of collective action, such as lending information or strategic expertise, keeping the group's enemies out of the action, or simply sending forces to help the action along.

Governmental repression is the best-known case. For example, the United States government's outlawing of the Communist Party during the Cold War essentially guaranteed that the party would lose leaders to jail when it acted together in any visible way. That is a high cost to pay for collective action. The law also raised the party's cost of mobilization by penalizing individuals who dared to contribute time, money, or moral support to its work. From a government's point of view, raising the costs of mobilization is a more reliable repressive strategy than raising the costs of collective action alone. The antimobilization strategy neutralizes the actor as well as the action, and makes it less likely that the actor will be able to act rapidly when the government suddenly becomes vulnerable, a new coalition partner arises, or something else quickly shifts the probable costs and benefits of collective action. Raising the costs of collective action alters the pattern of effective demand from mobilized groups, while raising the costs of mobilization reduces demand across the board.

Governmental repression is uniquely important because governments specialize in the control of mobilization and collective action: police for crowd control, troops to back them, spies and informers for infiltration, licensing to keep potential actors visible and tame.

Selectivity by type of collective action shows up in the very rules of the game, and in their changes; at a given time, it may be legal to petition, associate, vote as a bloc, acquire a patron in the legislature, and assemble as a formally constituted community, but not to demonstrate, strike, boycott, form militias, or invade the legislature. The repression and facilitation reside in the government's action to alter the relative costs of different forms of collective action. Legality matters because laws state the costs and benefits which governments are prepared (or at least empowered) to apply to one form of action or another.

E. P. Thompson's analysis of the background of the Black Act of 1723 is a case in point. The Black Act set the death penalty for no fewer than fifty offenses, especially armed and disguised hunting, poaching, rick burning and other attacks on rural property. Thompson shows that it was essentially class legislation; it was engineered by Sir Robert Walpole and his friends to consolidate their exclusive enjoyment of their estates over the resistance of the small farmers nearby.

The nineteenth-century case is particularly interesting because of the great professionalization of policing which occurred in most western countries as the century moved on. Some of the apparently huge expansion of police forces in the nineteenth century resulted from the bureaucratization of volunteer and part-time policing. In France, the regular national forces rose from about 5,000 policemen and 16,000 gendarmes (for a combined rate of 57 police per 100,000 population) in 1848 to about 16,000 policemen and 21,000 gendarmes (for a combined rate of 97 per 100,000 population) in 1897. But a significant part of the increase in policemen consisted of the incorporation of irregular local forces into the national police (see Tilly, Levett, Lodhi, and Munger 1975). In the United States, no national police emerged, but parallel changes in policing occurred. There we see the shift from "entrepreneurial" to "bureaucratic" police forces (Levett 1974). In the entrepreneurial stage, three kinds of forces shared the responsibility: (1) citizen forces; they were called such things as posse and deputies when the government did not authorize them; (2) regular troops; (3) constables and similar officers, often short-term or part-time, often given little or no regular remuneration, often drawing most of their police income from fees: fines, a share of recovered property, rewards posted for the apprehension of major criminals, and so on. These forces had little incentive to carry on comprehensive patrols, to deal with routine public order offenses, or to protect the poor. The third group were "entrepreneurial" in that they made their livings by competing for the available fees. With a growing, increasingly segregated and increasingly foreign-born working class gathering in nineteenth-century cities, however, American political officials became increasingly interested in forming regular police forces which would patrol the entire city, deal with victimless offenses such as public drunkenness, and contain major threats of hostile collective action. Thus they organized bureaucratized, salaried, uniformed full-time forces.

The same general change took place in England.

The alteration of the relative attractiveness of different forms of collective action by repression and facilitation is easy to illustrate and hard to establish as a general rule. The "channeling" of collective action by governments shows up in the nineteenth-century preference for mutual-aid societies over trade unions. Western governments generally discouraged the banding together of workers who sought to control production. They diverted workers into presumably safer organizations oriented to consumption. The tactic worked in the short run; until they became legal, trade unions attracted few members. At first, Friendly Societies and *sociétés de secours mutuels* busied themselves with problems of welfare away from work. In the longer run, however, they became the nuclei of action against employers and against the state. The lower-cost alternative eventually became a very effective one.

That repression makes a difference does not mean that it always accomplishes what the repressors had in mind.

Power and Polity Membership

Contention for power links the mobilization model to the polity model. Contention for power consists of the application of resources to influence other groups, and power itself consists of a group's making its interests prevail over others with which they are in conflict. Contention for *political* power involves applying resources to a particular kind of organization: a government. A government is simply the organization, if any, which controls the principal concentrated means of coercion within some population. The contenders for power within a given population include all groups which are collectively applying resources to influence the government.

Within the modern world, however, governments are so likely to claim the right to regulate and to extract resources from any mobilizing group that mobilization usually propels a group into contention for power over one government or another—at least into an effort to secure guarantees of its basic rights to exist, assemble, accumulate resources, and carry on its valued activities. Eric Wolf's (1969) analysis of the involvement of peasant communities in revolutions, for instance, shows how regularly they mobilize and then contend for power not because they initially want a change in government, but in self-defense.

Wolf's analysis also tells us how crucial to the success of the contention for power are the coalitions peasant communities make with other groups outside. No coalition = lost revolution. In a great many situations, a single contender does not have enough resources—enough committed people, enough guns, enough trained lawyers, enough cash—to influence the government by itself. A coalition with another contender which has overlapping or complementary designs on the government will then increase the joint power of the contenders to accomplish those designs.

Collective Action as a Function of Threats and Opportunities

An asymmetrical response to threat and opportunity is more plausible than a symmetrical response. Assuming equal probabilities of occurrence, a given amount of threat tends to generate more collective action than the "same" amount of opportunity. On the whole, response to opportunity is likely to require more alteration of the group's organization and mobilization pattern than its response to threat; the group can respond to threat via its established routines. European peasant communities relied on their local communication networks and shared understandings in getting together to chase out the unwanted tax collector. They had much more trouble sending a delegation to the capital to demand an alteration of the tax burden. Furthermore, groups generally inflate the value of those things they already possess, when someone else is seeking to take them away. For equal probabilities, the loss of the existing village common land counts more than the gain of the same amount of common land. Finally, threats generalize more readily than opportunities do. A group is more likely to see a threat to a particular interest as a sign of threats to a wide range of its interests than it is to see an opportunity for enhancement of one of its interests as a sign of opportunity for a wide range of its interests.

The asymmetry, I believe, produces a deep conservatism in every polity. Members of the polity resist changes which would threaten their current realization of their interests even more than they seek changes which would enhance their interests. They fight tenaciously against loss of power, and especially against expulsion from the polity. They work against admission to the polity of groups whose interests conflict significantly with their own.

Changing Forms of Collective Action

The Forms of Contention

Real people do not get together and Act Collectively. They meet to petition Parliament, organize telephone campaigns, demonstrate outside of city hall attack powerlooms, go on strike. The abstract mobilization model we have been using has many virtues, but it tends to obscure two fundamental facts. First, collective action generally involves interaction with specific other groups, including governments. Collective action rarely consists of solitary performances. People do not ordinarily act to influence abstract structures such as polities and markets; they try to get particular other people to do particular things. As a consequence, explanations of collective action which concentrate on the capacities and inclinations of one participant at a time—or the average capacities and inclinations of all participants—will leave us disappointed.

Second, collective action usually takes well-defined forms already familiar to the participants, in the same sense that most of an era's art takes on a small number of established forms. Because of that, neither the search for universal forms (such as those sometimes proposed for crowds or revolutions) nor the assumption of an infinity of means to group ends will take us very far. Because of that, the study of the concrete forms of collective action immediately draws us into thinking about the cultural settings in which more forms appear. Much of the pleasure and adventure in the historical study of collective action comes from the rich complexity of the material: having to learn how and why the Parisians of 1789 paraded severed heads on pikes, how and why the young people of Berkeley, California occupied a makeshift park in 1969.

Putting the two themes together opens the way to a first rough classification of forms of collective action. The classification stresses the nature of the interaction between other groups and the group whose action we are classifying. More precisely, it depends on the claims the collective actors are asserting in their action: *competitive* claims, *reactive* claims, or *proactive* claims. The classification leaves out pursuit of common ends which involve no claims on other groups: pure recreation, contemplation, escape. In fact, it applies most easily where the claims express a conflict of interest among the parties. I have worked out the categories in studying the evolution of forms of conflict in western Europe, and will illustrate them from European experience.

Competitive actions lay claim to resources also claimed by other groups which the actor defines as rivals, competitors, or at least as participants in the same contest.

Some features of collective competition, such as the ritualized mockery, carried over into the second major category: *reactive* collective actions. (We can also call them collective reactions.) They consist of group efforts to reassert established claims when someone else challenges or violates them. Speaking of peasant land invasions in contemporary Peru, E. J. Hobsbawm points out that they take three forms: squatting on land to which no one (or only the government) has a clear title, expropriating land to which the invaders have not previously enjoyed a claim and to which someone else has, repossessing land from which the invaders have themselves been expropriated (Hobsbawm 1974: 120–121).

The third variant is the clear reactive case: the dispossessed react. That sort of land reoccupation characterized the first stages of Zapata's rebellion during the Mexican Revolution, recurred through much of southern Italy during the massive nineteenth-century concentration of land in bourgeois and noble hands, and marked the consolidation of bourgeois landownership wherever it developed in the presence of solidary peasant communities. In a standard European scenario, a group of villagers who had long pastured their cattle, gathered firewood, and gleaned in common fields, found a landlord or a local official (or, more likely, the two in collaboration) fencing the fields by newly acquired or newly asserted right of property. The villagers commonly warned against the fencing. If the warning went unheeded, they attacked the fences and the fencers. They acted in the name of rights they still considered valid.

Proactive collective actions assert group claims which have not previously been exercised.... The strike for higher wages or better working conditions provides an everyday illustration.

In Europe of the last few hundred years, the three forms of collective action have waxed and waned in sequence. In the fifteenth and sixteenth centuries, competitive actions seem to have predominated. From the seventeenth into the nineteenth century, the reactive forms became much more widespread, while the competitive forms remained steady or perhaps declined. With the nineteenth and twentieth centuries, collective proaction began to predominate, the reactive forms dwindled, while new forms of competition came into existence. If I read the record aright, seventeenth- and eighteenth-century Europeans took collective action in defense of threatened rights much more than their predecessors had, while twentieth-century Europeans became exceptionally prone to act in support of claims they had not previously exercised.

The reasons for the successive changes are, I think, twofold: (1) During the period from 1600 to 1850, more so than before and after, the agents of international markets and of national states were pressing their new (and proactive) claims on resources which had up to then been under the control of innumerable households, communities, brotherhoods, and other small-scale organizations. The small-scale organizations reacted repeatedly, fighting against taxation, conscription, the consolidation of landed property, and numerous other threats to their organizational well-being. Eventually the big structures won, the battle died down, the reactive forms diminished. (2) Increasingly, the pools of resources necessary to group survival came under the control of large organizations, especially governments, which only redistributed them under the pressure of new claims.

Repertoires of Collective Action

At any point in time, the repertoire of collective actions available to a population is surprisingly limited. Surprisingly, given the innumerable ways in which people could, in principle, deploy their resources in pursuit of common ends. Surprisingly, given the many ways real groups have pursued their own common ends at one time or another.

Most twentieth-century Americans, for example, know how to demonstrate. They know that a group with a claim to make assemblies in a public place, identifies itself and its demands or complaints in a visible way, orients its common action to the persons, properties, or symbols of some other group it is seeking to influence. Within those general rules, most Americans know how to carry on several different forms of demonstration: the massed march, the assembly with speechmaking, the temporary occupation of premises. Moreover, there are some specifiable circumstances in which most Americans would actually apply their knowledge by joining a real demonstration. Americans who have not learned this complicated set of actions through personal participation have nonetheless witnessed demonstrations directly, read about them, watched them on television. Various forms of demonstration belong to the *repertoire* of twentieth-century Americans—not to mention twentieth-century Canadians, Japanese, Greeks, Brazilians, and many others. The repertoire also includes several varieties of strikes, petitioning, the organization of pressure groups, and a few other ways of articulating grievances and demands.

Few Americans, on the other hand, know how to organize the hijacking of an airplane, despite the publicity hijackings have received in recent years; even fewer would seriously consider hijacking as a way of accomplishing their collective objectives. Hijacking belongs to the repertoire of only a few groups anywhere. Machine breaking, once a frequent occurrence, has dropped out of the repertoire. So have the charivari and the serenade. So has the regular inter-village fight; only football remains to remind us of that old form of bloodletting.

Hijacking, mutiny, machine breaking, charivaris, village fights, tax rebellions, foot riots, collective self-immolation, lynching, vendetta have all belonged to the standard collective-action repertoire of some group at some time. In one setting or another, people have known routinely how to initiate every one of them. People have at sometime recognized every one of them as a legitimate, feasible way of acting on an unsatisfied grievance or aspiration. Most of these forms of action are technically feasible in contemporary America. Yet they occur rarely, or not at all. More important, no substantial American group with a pressing grievance or aspiration considers any of them to be a genuine alternative to demonstrating, striking, petitioning, or forming a pressure group. They do not belong to the contemporary American repertoire of collective action.

The means of collective action alter and spread from one group to another. For instance, in the Italy of 1919 sit-down strikes were rather a novelty. But by August 1920 half a million workers were occupying their factories. Given such events, we can gauge the importance of repertoires by comparing the successive choices of similar groups and by observing innovation and diffusion in the means of action.

A population's repertoire of collective action generally includes only a handful of alternatives. It generally changes slowly, seems obvious and natural to the people involved. It resembles an elementary language: familiar as the day to its users, for all its possible quaintness or incomprehensibility to an outsider.

Prior experience also counts. The relevant experience includes both the contender's own successes or failures and the contender's observations of other similar groups. We see that blend of previous practice and observation in the rich street theater which grew up in the American colonies from the Stamp Act crisis of 1765 to the Revolution. Mock trials, parading of effigies, ritualized attacks on the homes and offices of royal officials, tarring and feathering of Loyalists accompanied petitions, declarations, and solemn assemblies. Within weeks of Boston's first display of a boot containing a devil as a symbol of Stamp Act promoter-Lord Bute, the boot and devil had become standard participants in urban gatherings to oppose the Stamp Act up and down the American coast. The particular form and content of these gatherings were new. But all their principal elements were already well-established ways of dealing with declared enemies of the people. The prior experience of urban sailors, artisans, and merchants shaped the revolutionary repertoire of collective action.

Repression likewise affects the repertoire. Repression makes a large difference in the short run because other powerful groups affect the relative costs and probable returns of different forms of action theoretically available to a particular group. It also matters in the long run because that sort of cost setting tends to eliminate some forms of action as it channels behavior into others. The widespread legalization of the strike in the 1860s and 1870s so increased its attractiveness relative to direct attacks on employers and on industrial property that the latter virtually disappeared from the workers' repertoire. All these changes, however, occur with a lag. The forms of collective action which worked during the last crisis have a special appeal during this one as well. Thus the successes and failures of contention for power produce changes in the repertoire of collective action, but only within the limits set by the actors own daily routines and conceptions of justice.

The idea of a standard repertoire of collective actions, if correct, simplifies the study of variations in collective action from one place, time, and population to another. It simplifies by breaking the problem into two parts: (1) how the population in question came to have its particular repertoire, and (2) the population selected a particular form of action (or no action at all) from that repertoire. The analysis of innovation in collective action—for example, the invention and diffusion of the sit-in as a way of pressing for equal rights in public accommodations—breaks neatly into the same two parts.

The idea of a standard repertoire also provides insight into "contagion" and "spontaneity" in collective action. It raises the possibility that when a particular form of riot or demonstration spreads rapidly, what diffuses is not the model of the behavior itself, but the information—correct or not—that the costs and benefits associated with the action have suddenly changed. The news that the authorities are (or are not) cracking down on demonstrators in city A filters rapidly to city B, and influences the estimates of potential demonstrators in city B as to the probable consequences of demonstrating. In that regard the grouches who argue that governmental "permissiveness" will encourage more agitation are often right. It is clear, likewise, that an action can be "spontaneous" in the sense of not having been planned in advance by any of the participants, and yet be highly organized, even ritualized. There the grouches are usually wrong; the grouchy inclination is to attribute sustained, concerted action to some sort of conspiracy.

A Case in Point: The Strike

Over the last century or so, the most visible alteration of the working-class repertoire of collective action in western countries has been the rise of the strike. Some form of concerted work stoppage goes far back in time. What is more, the idea must have been invented independently many times; the disparate words for the strike which emerged in various European languages suggest multiple origins: sciopero, turnout, Streik, grève, zabastovka, huelga. Nevertheless, strikes were rare events at the beginning of the nineteenth century. By 1900, they were routine facts of working-class life. They were generally illegal, and frequently prosecuted, in 1800. A century later, they were generally legal, and rarely prosecuted. What is more, in most western countries the intensity of strike activity continued to rise past the middle of the twentieth century (see Hibbs 1976). In the process, strikes routinized: settled down to a few standard formats, acquired their own jurisprudence, became objects of official statistics. By "routinized," I do not mean "calmed down." Despite the complex, standard rules according to which they are played, professional hockey matches are often angry, bone-crunching affairs. The same is true of strikes.

How and why did strikes enter the repertoire? In multiple ways, proletarianization created the strike. By definition, proletarianization created the worker who exercised little or no discretionary control over the means of production and who was dependent for survival on the sale of his or her labor power. That proletarian and the worker threatened with becoming that proletarian have long been the chief participants in strikes. (The word "proletarian" has, alas, recently lost some of the precision Marx gave it in *Das Kapital*. In Marx's analysis the central elements were separation from the means of production + wage labor. Agricultural workers were, in fact, the chief historical case Marx discussed. He certainly did not concentrate on unskilled factory workers.) Of all workers, the proletarian most clearly had interests opposing him directly to his employer. The proletarian had the most to gain through the withholding of labor power, and the least to gain by other means.

Now, the pace of proletarianization increased greatly during the nineteenth century. My own minimum guess is that in Europe as a whole from 1800 to 1900, while the total population rose from about 190 million to 500 million, the proletarian population increased from about 90 million to 300 million. If that is true, the very kinds of workers who were the prime candidates for strike activity were multiplying. Furthermore, many strikes were *about* proletarianization. Whether the immediate issue was wages, hours, or working conditions, the underlying struggle commonly turned about the employer's effort to exercise greater and greater control over the disposition of the means of production, and therefore over the worker's own use of his labor.

The word "socialism" itself originally represented the vision of a *social* order in which producers would control their own fates. The strike grew up as one of the primary means by which artisans threatened with proletarianization and semiproletarians threatened with complete loss of control over the disposition of their labor fought back.

If my analysis is correct, the strike entered the collective-action repertoires of European workers as a reactive means, but later became a primary means of collective proaction. In the process, the strike routinized. One sign is its legalization. Most western countries legalized some form of strike activity during the latter half of the nineteenth century; Great Britain led the way in 1824. Saxony followed in 1861, France in 1864, Belgium in 1866, Prussia in 1869, Austria in 1870. Another sign is the advent of regular statistical reporting: the 1880s and 1890s saw the launching of annual strike statistics in many western countries, including the United States. A third sign is the growth of professional bureaucracies devoted to monitoring, regulating, reporting, and, on occasion, settling strikes. These officials, employers, and organized workers hammered out standard definitions of strikes and lockouts. They worked out rules concerning the proper behavior of the parties to a strike. They developed means of registering and publicizing a strike's end and outcome. They, the courts, police, and other public officials were fixing the precise place of the strike in the day's repertoire of collective action. To be sure, the rules remained uncertain in important regards, the rules changed as the balance of power changed, and most of the rule making occurred as a by-product of bitter struggle. That is the way repertoires of collective action usually change.

In Britain, organized labor, despite the Labor Party, never developed the continuous, intimate, and reliable tie to the government that the long incumbency of the Social Democrats afforded to Swedish labor; in Sweden, the stronger labor became the easier it was to settle disputes through means other than the strike: negotiation, legislation, governmental pressure on the employers. As labor entered the British polity, multiple trade unions retained a good deal of autonomy; no central labor organization acquired the power to negotiate for all its members or to force those members to abide by the terms of their contracts. In Sweden, a highly centralized federation acquired great power both as a negotiator and as an enforcer. Under these circumstances, polity membership encouraged strikes in Britain and made routine political pressure a more attractive alternative to strikes in Sweden.

Elections, Demonstrations, and Political Systems

The lesson is more general. The simple model of the polity laid out earlier provides a useful starting point, but it misses the importance of political coalitions and of the means of actions built into the existing political organization. The use of elections to do public business is a major case in point. Political scientists have long since noticed that the establishment of binding national elections promotes the growth of political parties—not only because governments tend to legalize elections and parties at the same time but because electoral competition gives such a patent advantage of interests which are organized in parties. I think the effect of electoral systems on the pattern of collective action is even more general. A comparison of the histories of contentious collective action in Italy, Germany, France, and England (Tilly, Tilly, and Tilly 1975) suggests a close connection between the institution of national elections and the use of formal associations of all sorts as vehicles for collective action. The great proliferation of clubs, circles, and sodalities in the French, German, and Italian revolutions of 1848 (in which expanding the electorate and increasing the political significance of elections were standard parts of the revolutionary program) illustrates the connection. The experience of those same countries also makes plausible the hypothesis that the growth of elections promotes the crystallization and spread of the demonstration as a form of collective action.

Why? Because of an umbrella effect: the legal umbrella raised to protect the electoral process, and to keep it huddled in the center away from the rain, has a ragged edge. There is shelter for others at its margins. The grant of legality to an electoral association or an electoral assembly provides a claim to legality for associations and assemblies which are not quite electoral, not *only* electoral or not *now* electoral. The grant of legality lowers the group's costs of mobilization and collective action. It also provides a prestigious, accessible model for action in general. In the United States of the 1960s we find a grudging grant of legitimacy to the Black Panther Party, the Mississippi Freedom Democratic Party, the Peace and Freedom Party.

The demonstration we know entered the standard repertoire of collective actions in most western countries during the nineteenth century. In England and America, nevertheless, we can see its form crystallizing before 1800. For several centuries, Englishmen had gathered in large numbers on certain standard holidays, such as Guy Fawkes' Day. During the festivities they often expressed their collective opinions of the day's heroes, villains, and fools. They paraded effigies, floats, charades, and placards. Hangings, funerals, exits from prison, royal birthdays, announcements of military victories drew crowds and, sometimes, concerted expressions of demands, sympathies, or complaints. In all these cases, the authorities provided the occasion and, to some degree, the sanction for the assemblies in question. Contested elections fell easily into the same pattern, and the assemblies of supporters of different candidates acquired a degree of protection.

During these same years the demonstration was becoming a standard way of doing public business in Britain's North American colonies. Like the contemporaneous battles over Wilkes in England, the American resistance to the Stamp Act of 1765 helped separate the demonstration from the sanctioned assembly, helped establish its importance as a routine instrument for the application of political pressure. On the fourteenth of August two effigies appeared, suspended from a great tree on a strategic street into Boston; one represented the tax-stamp distributor, Andrew Oliver, the other, a large boot containing a devil. The crowd which gathered refused to let the effigies be taken down.

> Towards evening some men cut down the effigy of the stamp-master and placed it on a bier, which was carried through the town accompanied by a cheering and huzzaing multitude: "Liberty and property forever," "No stamps," "No Placemen." In this concourse, "some of the highest Reputation" were walking "in the greatest order," "and in solemn manner." At the head of the procession "Forty or fifty tradesmen, decently dressed, preceded; and some thousands of the mob followed ..." The concourse, amidst the acclamations of large numbers of people lining the street, went down Main Street, turned into King Street and stopped under the town house where Governor and Council were assembled. The multitude, well knowing this, "gave three huzzas by Way of Defiance, and pass'd on"
>
> (Hoerder 1971: 153)

The great elm which held the effigies later became famous as the Liberty Tree. It was the model for thousands of liberty trees consecrated, and struggled over, in America. Later the Liberty Tree became a prime symbol in Revolutionary France. In many histories the resistance to the Stamp Act counts as the beginning of the American Revolution. The demonstration took an important and durable place in the American repertoire of collective actions as that revolutionary movement swelled.

The case of the demonstration teaches a general lesson. The forms, frequencies and personnel of collective action depend intimately on the existing structure of government and politics. When we begin refining the simple model of government, polity and contenders with which we started, we must pay attention to the specific rules of polity membership, the existing pattern of repression and facilitation, the rights claimed by different contenders. Our elementary model does little more than specify in what connections each of these variables should be significant.

On the question of political rights, for instance, the argument unfolded so far favors a view of the right to vote, to petition, to assemble, to publish, and so on as (a) consisting not of a general principle, but of a specific claim of a defined contender on a certain government, (b) coming into being as the result of struggles among mobilized contenders and governments. Thus the common idea that a standard set of political rights gradually extended from a small elite to the general population is misleading. Not wrong, because on the whole the share of the population having enforceable claims on various national governments with respect to voting, petitioning, assembling, and publishing has expanded enormously over the last two centuries, has increased in distinct steps from elites to ordinary people, has not contracted drastically once it has grown. Nevertheless misleading, because the similar claims ordinary people have had on other governments (especially local governments) have generally dwindled in the same process, and because each step of the expansion has usually occurred in response to the demand of some well-defined contender or coalition of contenders.

The fact that the rights consist of enforceable claims on the government by particular groups makes it less puzzling that such elementary rights as assembly and petition should be so easily denied to challengers (prostitutes, millennialists, Fascists, homosexuals) whose personal characteristics, objectives, or activities are unacceptable to most other groups. The denial of rights to a challenger only threatens the rights of existing members of the polity when the challenger's characteristics, organization, objectives, or activities resemble those of some members, or when a coalition between challenger and member has formed.

All our inquiries into the forms and frequencies of collective action eventually lead us back to questions of power. A close look at competitive, reactive and proactive forms of action dissolves the common distinction between "pre-political" and "political" protest. A careful exploration of the context of strike activity challenges the separation of "economic" and "political" conflicts from each other. A thoughtful reflection on the demonstration, the charivari, and the food riot raises fundamental doubts about any effort to single out a class of spontaneous, expressive, impulsive, evanescent crowd actions—although it confirms the importance of creativity, innovation, drama, and symbolism within the limits set by the existing repertoire of collective action and the existing structure of power.

References

Hibbs, Douglas, A., Jr. 1976. "Industrial Conflict in Advanced Industrial Societies." *American Political Science Review* 70: 1033–1058.

Hobsbawn, E. J. 1974. "Peasant Land Occupations." *Past and Present* 62: 120–152.

Hoerder, Dirk. 1971. *People and Mobs: Crowd Action in Massachusetts during the American Revolution, 1765–1780*. Berlin: privately published.

Levett, Allan. 1974. "Centralization of City Police in the Nineteenth Century United States." Unpublished Ph.D. Dissertation in Sociology, University of Michigan.

Tilly, Charles, Allan Levett, A.Q. Lodhi and Frank Munger. 1975. "How Policing Affected the Visibility of Crime in Nineteenth-Century Europe and America." Working Paper 115, Center for Research on Social Organization, University of Michigan.

Tilly, Charles; Louise Tilly; and Richard Tilly. 1975. *The Rebellious Century, 1830–1930.* Cambridge: Harvard University Press.

Wolf, Eric. 1969. *Peasant Wars of the Twentieth Century.* New York: Harper & Row.

Contentious Performances

5

Charles Tilly

From Campaign to Campaign

In his panorama of Mexican popular collective action between 1968 and the 1990s, Sergio Tamayo shows how one national campaign shaped the next. The transformation of popular contention, he concludes,

> was a cumulative process of citizens' actions that during the first five years of the 1990s reached a level of extensive participation, using every sort of resource, as much legal and formal as informal and violent ... As for Mexico City, the citizenry appeared with great strength, certainly a result of the city's special character as capital of the republic and urban center where regardless of its origin the national political debate concentrated.
>
> (Tamayo 1999: 353)

That "continuous process" produced a mutation, Tamayo tells us, from a turbulent 1968 in which students and workers alike agitated for various forms of socialism to a wide range of demands for citizen power during the 1990s. To some extent, violent visions of class confrontation gave way to democratic debate.

Tamayo sees five elements that transformed Mexican popular politics: 1) the Zapatista rising of 1994 and thereafter signaled a new phase of action at the national scale, 2) demonstrations, strikes, and union filing of complaints justifying strikes (*aplazamientos a huelga*) multiplied as vehicles of popular voice, 3) the contested elections of 1988 and 1994 weakened the hegemonic party, PRI, 4) civil society grew larger, more vocal, and more fragmented, and 5) old forms of participation—"performances" in this book's terms— used by the local citizens' committees of 1988 gave way to the national and international actions pioneered by the Zapatistas: "We can add that precisely because of the way that the [elections of 1988] ended, a cycle of participation and social movement development could close in Mexico, and with the Zapatista movement a new cycle could open" (Tamayo 1999: 355).

The (possibly fraudulent) loss of populist presidential candidate Cuauhtémoc Cárdenas to Carlos Salinas de Gortari in 1988 first stirred enormous protests. But that mobilization's failure, Tamayo observes, sounded the death knell for the time-honored performances of Mexican populist politics. A new kind of political campaign took shape.

Tamayo's rich account of popular contention in Mexico thus raises a question of general importance for the study of contentious politics: under what circumstances, to what extent, and how do claim-making campaigns transform the character of contention itself? At a smaller scale, how does one campaign influence what happens in the next campaign? Without a clear understanding of that influence, any account of repertoire change remains woefully incomplete. This chapter attempts to clarify our understanding of the impact of claim-making campaigns on subsequent claim-making campaigns.

A campaign is a sustained, coordinated series of episodes involving similar claims on similar or identical targets. In 1968, leftist students initiated a campaign for democratic rights on the eve of the Mexico City Olympic Games and suffered severe repression by the government of Gustavo Diaz Ordaz. As Tamayo says, the Zapatista campaign for indigenous rights launched in 1994 took a fundamentally different tack: guerrilla mobilization in the Chiapas backlands, control of ostensibly liberated zones, national and international broadcasts of critiques, and eventually peaceful mass marches from the jungle to the national capital.

Here a campaign transforms political opportunity structure (POS), changes the array of available models for contentious performances, and alters connections among potential actors. Among other ways, a campaign sometimes alters POS by bringing new actors into a regime, changing a regime's repressive policy, or establishing new alliances between challengers and established holders of power; all three happened in Mexico after 1968. Such alterations in POS almost inevitably alter the repertoire of subsequent campaigns.

A campaign sometimes produces changes in available models of performances, most directly by innovating as the Zapatistas did in 1994 and thereafter. Old models generally retain prestige and predictability, but at least occasionally repertoire change occurs because of innovative campaigns. Once an innovation has occurred and produced results for the innovators, others frequently try it. Tamayo tells us that the Zapatistas' national and international performances produced just such a change.

Finally, a campaign sometimes alters connections among potential actors. Tamayo describes new alliances within civil society as occurring in response to the crises of 1968 and, especially, 1988. New alliances brought about the possibility of broad citizens' fronts on behalf of democracy. Often the most durable impact of a relatively successful campaign appears less in POS and repertoire than in altered connections among actors who collaborate in subsequent campaigns.

To be sure, between campaigns POS, models, and connections interact. Shifts in POS affect the viability of different performances, new models foster fresh connections among potential claimants, and newly elaborated connections sometimes alter POS itself. In the case of Mexico, the Zapatista rising caused all three to happen at once, as international activists who supported the Zapatistas allied with domestic activists, promoted their models of claim making, and intervened with unprecedented force in the Mexican structure of power.

Examined closely, to be sure, the effects of opportunity and threat are asymmetrical and somewhat more subtle. For example, rising threats to collective survival tend to incite increases in collective action by well-connected groups, at least in the short run (Davenport 2007, Goldstone and Tilly 2001). For the moment, however, it matters most that campaigns often affect all six features of POS: openness of the regime, coherence of its elite, stability of political alignments, availability of allies for potential actors, repression or facilitation, and pace of change. In the case of Mexico from 1968 to the 1990s, Tamayo provides evidence that the radical and populist campaigns of the 1970s and 1980s increased the opportunity for new challenges. They did so by increasing divisions within the elite, promoting instability, and helping install new allies for challengers.

What about change in available models of performances? Tamayo provides rich documentation concerning this set of effects. The Zapatistas offer the most dramatic examples. Their guerrilla activity actually followed extensive models from elsewhere in rural Mexico from the 1960s through the 1980s (Turbiville 1997). But after initial bloody encounters with the Mexican army, they shifted their focus from clandestine attacks on government forces to ingenious publicity for their demands, extensive outreach to potential allies both within and outside of Mexico, and public displays of

WUNC through rallies and marches (Olesen 2005). Clifford Bob describes one Zapatista performance:

> Shifts in opportunity = Changes in the environment of political actors (in this case, an idealized single challenger) that signal shifts in likely consequences of different interactions with other actors
>
> This also applies cross-sectionally: if regime A is more open, its elites more divided, more generally unstable, richer in potential allies, and less repressive than regime B, similar challengers will contend more extensively and effectively in regime A.
>
> On March 11, 2001, 24 leaders of Mexico's Zapatista Army of National Liberation (EZLN) trooped into the Zócalo, Mexico City's huge central square. Seven years after their armed uprising, the Zapatistas arrived with government blessing, the group's spokesman, Subcomandante Marcos, proclaiming "We are here" to an audience of more than 100,000. Days later, Comandanta Esther addressed the Mexican Congress, urging adoption of a law granting significant new rights to the country's indigenous population. Throughout the Zapatistas' multiweek stay in the capital and their triumphal bus journey from remote bases in the southern state of Chiapas, foreign supporters accompanied the rebels. Conspicuous among them, dressed in white overalls and acting incongruously as security guards, strode dozens of monos blancos, or white monkeys, Italian activists prominent at European antiglobalization protests. In the Zócalo to greet the Zapatistas stood a host of left-wing luminaries: France's ex-first lady Danielle Mitterrand, film producer Oliver Stone, and McDonald's "dismantler" José Bové. Around the world, thousands of Zapatista followers monitored the March for Indigenous Dignity, the "Zapatour," on the Internet. To pay for the event, the Zapatistas solicited donations from national and transnational civil society and opened a bank account accessible to depositors around the world.
>
> (Bob 2005: 117)

Obviously, the Zapatistas had gone far beyond the Ché Guevara-style focus of the 1960s.

Just as obviously, our third element—change in connection among potential actors—was occurring in Mexico, and strongly affecting the new round of campaigns. Thomas Olesen distinguishes three levels of organization in the Zapatista mobilization: the Zapatista organization (EZLN) as such, the transnational solidarity network that grew up in immediate support of

Category	Increasing Opportunity	Increasing Threat
Openness of regime	Regime becoming increasingly open	Regime closing down
Coherence of elite	Increasing divisions within elite	Increasing solidarity of elite
Stability of political alignments	Rising instability	Increasing stability
Availability of allies	New allies in regime available to challengers	Potential allies disappear or lose power
Repression/ facilitation	Increasing facilitation, declining repression	Decreasing facilitation, rising repression
Pace of change	Acceleration in any of the above	Deceleration in any of the above

Figure 5.1 Political Opportunity, Political Threat, and Their Impacts on Contention

the Zapatistas, and the "transnational justice and solidarity network" that dealt with a wide variety of leftist causes, including the Zapatistas. The third level, according to Olesen,

> barely existed at the time of the EZLN uprising in 1994, when the left was still finding its feet after the end of the Cold War. It began to take shape in the second half of the 1990s, and made its first strong impression in Seattle in November 1999. The EZLN, and especially the intercontinental encounters in Chiapas in 1996, have played an important role in this development. The prospects for the left have, accordingly, undergone significant change during the 1990s, and the EZLN has seen many of its political ideas and visions echoed in the activities of the transnational justice and solidarity movement.
>
> (Olesen 2005: 209)

The EZLN, Olesen speculates, may be fading from the international scene, but leaving behind it crucial transnational connections among activists. From the late 1990s, those connections shaped the transnational politics of anti-globalization.

Parallel processes occurred within Mexican politics. Tamayo stresses how Mexican feminists allied themselves with activists on other issues than women's rights:

> Feminist activists who were also political party militants added a major component to internal party dynamics between electoral campaigns. It might be surprising but appears clearly that after the elections of July 1988 and with the new emergence of a movement against electoral fraud women participated actively and collectively ... Thus as the period of transition closed various women's organizations called for the National Assembly to combat institutionalized electoral fraud, creating the Benita Galeana Women's Alliance with working class clusters, political parties, activists, and nongovernmental organizations.
>
> (Tamayo 1999: 320)

A major double transition was occurring in Mexican popular politics: from clients of populist leaders to self-starting activists, from single-issue mobilizations to broad coalitions for democratic reform. Claim-making campaigns themselves played major parts in the two transitions. They did so by altering POS, available models, and connections among potential actors.

Mexico was not unique. On the contrary, Mexico from 1968 to the 1990s illustrates two extremely general patterns in contentious politics. First, much of the change in performances and repertoires that occurs anywhere results from the influence of one campaign—successful or not—on the next. Second, that influence operates through interacting alterations in three channels: POS, available models, and connections among potential actors.

Here we begin to see clearly the analytic advantages of treating collective claim making as a series of learned performances that group into repertoires. The three elements—POS, available models, and connections—identify three different aspects of the situations faced by potential makers of claims. POS identifies the likely political outcomes of different collective actions claimants might undertake together. Available models identify the known routines among which claimants can choose. And connections indicate who is likely to participate, as well as how. The three together produce a matrix of choice for potential participants in contention. But they also produce a matrix of explanation for us observers of contentious politics.

Political Opportunity Structure

When Great Britain defeated France in the Seven Years' War (1756–1763), it added Québec's large Catholic population to its already restive Catholics of Scotland, England, and especially Ireland. In the Québec Act of 1774, Québec's Catholics received more extensive political rights in the colony than their co-religionists enjoyed in the British Isles. During the 1770s, war with the thirteen colonies south of Québec made the British government eager to solicit support among Catholics and to recruit Catholic soldiers (previously barred from service by the requirement that they abjure the Pope). Parliament made modest concessions to Catholic rights in the Catholic Relief Act of 1778. John Wilkes, for one, saw those concessions as minor and acceptable (Rogers 1998: 157). Nevertheless, the government's proposal to extend those concessions to Scotland excited a vigorous anti-Catholic mobilization.

Anti-Catholicism had attracted plenty of support—and Catholics had suffered serious restrictions of their political rights—in Great Britain since the Glorious Revolution of 1688–1689 had dethroned a Catholic king. But the Protestant Association, formed in 1779, produced something new. It gave anti-Catholicism an organizational base and a mass following on the model of Wilkes's supporters. Unlike the reform associations that were starting to spring up across Great Britain, it adopted "radical forms to press for appeal, holding monthly general meetings, distributing handbills, advocating instructions to MPs, and embarking on mass petitioning" (Rogers 1998: 158). All of these innovations built on precedents supplied by the Wilkes campaign. Scottish Lord George Gordon's speeches against the Catholic Relief Act and its extension to Scotland catapulted Gordon into the presidency of the London-based Association. In bringing the Association's campaign to Parliament the following year, Gordon precipitated one of Britain's bloodiest domestic struggles in decades.

Models of Action

Innovation by claimants, especially successful claimants, makes new models of performances available to other potential actors. Most such innovation occurs incrementally and on the small scale, but it occurs. During the 1820s and 1830s, Great Britain experienced a great many performance innovations that stuck. A comparison of two overlapping campaigns in the 1820s will make the point. Seen from the pinnacle of parliamentary politics, repeal of the Test and Corporation Acts (1828) and passage of Catholic Emancipation

(1829) look like feats of elite maneuvering that then transformed public opinion. As John Stuart Mill summed it up in a letter to Gustave d'Eichthal in March 1829: "The alteration of so important and so old a law as that which excludes Catholics from political privileges, has given a shake to men's minds which has weakened all old prejudices, and will render them far more accessible to new ideas and to rational innovations on all other parts of our institutions" (Hinde 1992: 187).

Seen from the valleys of popular politics, however, these abolitions of religious restrictions on political participation rested on extensive contention. What's more, they fortified models of performance that shook the British establishment over the next few years. They contributed significantly to the forms of activism that developed during the great parliamentary reform campaign of 1830–1832.

In the move from religious rights to parliamentary reform, political opportunity structure, available models of performances, and connections among potential political actors changed continuously, in constant connection with each other. They did, in any case, transmit the influence of one contentious campaign to the next.

References

Bob, Clifford. 2005. *The Marketing of Rebellion: Insurgents, Media, and International Activism*. Cambridge: Cambridge University Press.

Davenport, Christian. 2007. *State Repression and the Domestic Democratic Peace*. Cambridge: Cambridge University Press.

Goldstone, Jack and Charles Tilly. 2001. "Threat (and Opportunity): Popular Action and State Response in the Dynamics of Contentious Action" in Ronald Aminzade *et al.*, *Silence and Voice in Contentious Politics*. Cambridge: Cambridge University Press.

Hinde, Wendy. 1992. *Catholic Emancipation: A Shake to Men's Minds*. Oxford: Blackwell.

Olesen, Thomas. 2005. *International Zapatismo: The Construction of Solidarity in the Age of Globalization*. London: Zed.

Rogers, Nicholas. 1998. *Crowds, Culture, and Politics in Georgian Britain*. Oxford: Clarendon Press.

Tamayo, Sergio. 1999. *Los veinte octubres mexicanos: La transición a la modernización y la democracia, 1968–1988*. Mexico City: Universidad Autónoma Metropolitana-Azcapotzalco.

Turbiville, Graham H. 1997. "Mexico's Other Insurgents," *Military Review* 77 (May–June), online version: www-cgsc.army.mil/milrev/milrvweb/html/mayne/tur.html.

Pernicious Postulates   **6**

Charles Tilly

False Principles

The nineteenth century's legacy to twentieth century social scientists re-sembles an old house inherited from a rich aunt: worn, over-decorated, cluttered, but probably salvageable. Appraising the old structure, we will want to save the belief in intelligible patterns of social interaction, the hope that disciplined observation will make those patterns more intelligible, the search for fundamental structures and processes, the attempt to reconstruct the processes that created our contemporary ways of life, and the organiza-tion of these inquiries as a cumulative, collective enterprise. We will want to retain a few specific theories, such as Marx's theory of capital accumulation. But we will also want to throw out and strip down.

To reduce the clutter, false general principles derived from the bourgeois reaction to nineteenth-century changes should be the first to go. Let us dis-card the ideas of society as a thing apart and of societies as overarching enti-ties; of social behavior as the consequence of individual mental events shaped by society and of those mental events as the links between persons and soci-eties; of social change as a single coherent phenomenon; of standard stages through which societies develop; of differentiation as the dominant, inevita-ble logic of social change; of a contest between differentiation and integration as the source of order and disorder; of disorder itself as a general phenomenon resulting from the strain of rapid social change; of sharp separation between legitimate and illegitimate forms of coercion, conflict, and expropriation.

In recent years, the eight pernicious postulates have lost some of their hold. The encounters of European and American social scientists with the

Third World, with social scientists based in the Third World, and with critics of their own governments' involvements in the Third World have shaken all the postulates to some degree.

Some postulates have lost more ground than others. The ideas of society and societies have come under strong attack from advocates of world-system analysis, but no theory or practice dispensing with them has really taken hold. Much social analysis still takes individual mental events, rather than social relationships, as the center of social life. Except among Marxist theoreticians, it has become unfashionable to fashion general statements about social change as such. Stage theories have lost much of their glitter, partly as a result of the move away from general theories of social change. Differentiation still captures the imagination of many social analysts, especially those who worry about fragmentation of everyday existence. The balder theories pitting differentiation against integration have given way to explanations of the same presumably "disorderly" phenomena as organized, interest-oriented behavior.

At the same time, scholars have become much more skeptical about the sequence rapid change/strain/disorder. Yet no comparable decline has struck the notion of two separate processes underlying "illegitimate" and "legitimate" coercion, conflict, and expropriation. In varying degrees of health, the eight pernicious postulates still live. Let us take them up in turn, giving more attention to those that currently play an important part in social scientists' theories of large-scale structure and process.

Society Is a Thing Apart

Sociology's greatest victory as an academic discipline brought its greatest defeat as an intellectual enterprise. Persuading others that a distinct realm called "society" and distinct entities called "societies" existed freed sociologists to justify their studies. Those premises justified sociology as at once essential and independent of philosophy, psychology, or biology. Although human beings created society, once in existence society had its own laws. Such presociological thinkers as Montesquieu had long since established the practices of comparing "societies" and of distinguishing between formal organizations (especially states) and the social structures, or societies, shaping and sustaining them. Comte, Spencer, Durkheim, and other nineteenth-century greats consolidated those practices into a discipline called sociology. That discipline promised to explain social variation and to develop means of repairing rents in the social fabric. On the basis of those promises its promoters built a method, an organization, and a cluster of concepts: society, norm, role, status, collective belief, and so on.

In the same process, a division of labor emerged. Sociology investigated the internal structure of rich, powerful societies. Anthropology, for its part, received a double duty: to account for large variations among societies and to analyze the internal structures of societies outside the charmed circle of power and wealth.

That accomplishment, nevertheless, gave sociologists and anthropologists a terrible burden; the task of delineating structures and processes of fictitious entities. As a practical matter, sociologists usually began with existing national states and defined society residually. Society was everything else but the state, or everything but the organization of production, the structure of distribution, and the state.

Anthropologists have customarily dealt with the problem of delineating societies either by starting with a local community and assuming that the definitions of identity with others stated by members of that community delineated a larger "society" or by accepting the political entities—"tribes," "peoples," "kingdoms," and so forth—encountered by westerners in the course of commercial and imperial expansion. They, too, have run into doubts. Many anthropologists who lean toward statistical analysis, for example, worry about "Galton's problem": the likelihood that as a result of diffusion of cultural traits adjacent "societies" fail to qualify as the independent cases one needs for crisp analyses of cultural covariation...

Ethnographers who have observed the coexistence and interpenetration of distinctly different cultural identities, furthermore, despair of bundling the world up neatly into separate societies. Those separate, autonomous entities are fictitious.

All of the standard procedures for delineating societies run into severe trouble when the time comes either to check the clarity and stability of the social boundaries thus produced or to describe the coherent structures and processes presumably contained within those boundaries. How? In many variants, all the troubles return to two fundamental difficulties: **first**, how to make boundaries of the "same" unit consistent in time, space, and personnel; **second**, how to determine whether the proposed boundaries do, in fact, delimit a distinct and coherent social entity.

In the first case, each of the criteria—national state boundaries, local-community statements, westerners' politically derived definitions—groups heterogeneous populations, produces conflicting delineations of the terrains and populations involved, and/or encounters changes in the apparently relevant boundaries. What bounds, for example, should we place around "German society" at the moment in which Europe contained dozens of states whose populations were mainly German-speaking, in which the courtiers of those same states affected French, and in which the Habsburg empire included not only a substantial block of German-speaking subjects, but also millions of people speaking Czech, Rumanian, Serbian, Turkish, and twenty other languages?

What about German society at the moment in which Napoleon's troops had conquered substantial German-speaking populations and laid down the French state's administrative apparatus in important parts of Central Europe? German society at the moment in which Prussia and a number of other mainly German-speaking states formed a customs union, while emigrants from their territories had established numerous German-speaking communities in the Americas? German society in the days of the Federal Republic, the Democratic Republic, Berlin, and the Austrian Republic—not to mention German-speaking enclaves in Czechoslovakia, France, Switzerland, Italy, Hungary, and elsewhere?

No consistent set of boundaries will contain all these multifarious entities, or even their cores. No continuous German Society underwent all these permutations. German society, as such, did not exist. The second problem is to delineate coherent, distinct social entities. Without some coherence and distinctiveness, one cannot reasonably treat a "society" as a self-sustaining entity with dominant norms, values, beliefs, and mechanisms of control. Yet we have no a priori guarantee that current national-state boundaries, local-community statements, or westerners' conquest-derived delineations—to return to the three standard means of identifying societies in sociology and anthropology—mark the limits of interpersonal networks, shared beliefs, mutual obligations, systems of production, or any of the other presumed components of a "society."

In principle, to be sure, we face an empirical question: To what extent do the boundaries of different kinds of social relations coincide? Certainly some geographic divisions separate a wide range of social life; consider the lines separating West Berlin from East Berlin, Haiti from the Dominican Republic, Hong Kong from the Chinese People's Republic. Surely national states control migration, trade, and many other flows across their frontiers. Unquestionably people on either side of the Hungarian-Austrian border see a boundary that bounds genuine differences.

Yet these politically reinforced frontiers do not contain all social life. Economic geographers enjoy demonstrating how different in scale and contour are the units defined by different activities or social relations: ties of credit versus ties of marriage, trips to buy food versus trips to sell computers, and so on. Economic geographers also delight in showing the enormous, even worldwide, extension of some sorts of interdependence: intercontinental migration chains, huge circuits of trade, far-flung professional structures, international flows of capital. Both demonstrations challenge any notion of neatly packaged social units.

Savor, for example, a geographer's final word on the notion of region:

> In summary, regions do exist, they do have meaning, and we can delineate them. However, they are not clear-cut areas in which activities are confined. Rather, regions are useful more as a system of classification; they are imperfect generalizations of the underlying spatial complex, which itself can be better described as the connections of countless individuals, farms, plants, and businesses.
>
> (Morrill 1970: 186)

The point applies as well to regions at the scale of the national state or the continent as it does to smaller territories.

Although activities and populations have orderly spatial distributions, they typically lack sharp boundaries. Such boundaries as exist for one activity or population almost never coincide with the boundaries defined by another activity or population. (Anyone who tries to separate the area called "Canada" from the area called "United States" by means of communications flows, markets, personal acquaintance, and other criteria of interaction soon discovers how much social life spans the legal frontier. See Bourne and Simmons 1983: 45.)

If we insist on clinging to the idea of societies as spatial clusters, we have only a few choices: (1) to turn the existence of large, bounded, comprehensive, coherent social groups—of societies—from a general presumption to an empirical question: to what extent, and under what conditions, do such groups ever form?; (2) to choose a single activity or relationship—citizenship, language, market—as the criterion of a society's boundaries and leave the relationship of that phenomenon to the boundaries of other phenomena open to empirical inquiry; (3) to admit that social relations form continuous fields and to block out "societies" more or less arbitrarily within those fields.

Unless the world does, however, fall into neatly bounded complexes of friendship, kinship, production, consumption, power, belief, and language, any of the three procedures compromises the effort to erect within the boundaries of a "society" the norms, roles, beliefs, values, hierarchies, controls, and self-sustaining activities about which we presume to theorize.

Even if every aspect of social life had its own sharp boundaries, that would not be enough. If boundaries of different sorts of action do not **coincide**, the idea of a society as an autonomous, organized, interdependent system loses its plausibility. Not all interdependent systems, to be sure, have sharp boundaries. But an interdependent system that is at once distinct from adjacent systems and organized around enforced rules requires such boundaries.

If a spatial criterion does not delineate societies, other criteria work even less well. We are therefore better off in abandoning the notion of "society" and "societies" as autonomous systems. We are better off in adopting the alternative idea of multiple social relationships, some quite localized, and some worldwide in scale.

In recent years, advocates of world-system analysis have been offering a similar critique of the notion of society, but concluding that the remedy is to consider the entire world a single unit of analysis. Easy in principle, hard in practice. So far, world-system analysts have had more success in pursuing the remedy theoretically and conceptually than methodologically.

The most serious difficulty, in my opinion, lies in the shift to observation of **interactions** rather than the behavior of individual units. There is no inconsistency among conceiving of the world as a connected whole, testing whether the hypothesized connections exist, and examining numerous interactions to see whether they correspond to the expectations we derive from our models of that connected whole. But there we confront the legacy of the nineteenth century: Both existing evidence and ingrained habits of thought depend on the fragmentation of interactions into characteristics of individuals and of societies.

Paradoxically, the belief in societies as overarching social structures with their own logic dovetails neatly with the belief in the socially conditioned mental event as the prime link between person and society. A mind, in the simplest model, internalizes society and directs behavior in conformity with that internalization. Undesirable behavior then results from imperfect internalization or from a bad fit between what the mind internalizes and the immediate situation of the troubled individual.

Mental Events Cause Social Behavior

It is easy and convenient to think of individual mental events as (1) products of social life, (2) determinants of social behavior, (3) links between persons and societies. With that postulate, we can readily sum individual consciousnesses into a global mentality.

Social researchers have built a good deal of their twentieth-century technique on the assumption that individual mental events are their basic social units. The survey, our own time's dominant means of amassing evidence on social life, involves a direct attempt to stimulate and record individual mental events for aggregation into social structure. If we include censuses—the largest of all social surveys—individual interviews and questionnaires provide the great bulk of the hard evidence that social scientists analyze.

By and large, our techniques for deriving group structure from individual observations remain feeble and artificial. Standard techniques of computing and statistical analysis in the social sciences assume that the evidence refers to independent individual events; data-analysis routines work best when the evidence comes in uniform, separate individual packets; statistical models compare an observed distribution of individuals with the distribution of individual events produced by random processes or by an ideal type such as perfect equality or complete segregation. The practice of social scientists depends on a close analogy between the social behavior under study and the operation of an idealized market.

Yet just as real markets consist of shifting, constructed social relations among limited numbers of actors, other social structures begin with interactions among persons (see White 1981). When we discover that some of these interactions recur in approximately the same form, we can reasonably begin to speak of social structure. Rather than individual orientations, social ties. Rather than social atoms, social networks.

Let me state this delicate point with care. Individual human beings exist. No one can see, hear, smell, taste, or feel a social relationship in the same sense that he can identify another human being. Social relationships, indeed, are merely abstractions from multiple interactions among individual human beings. But that brings us to the point: We abstract not from individual behaviors, but from sets of individual behaviors involving two or more persons at a time.

If the point seems strange, consider two problems. First, how do we know that an individual encountered at several separate times is the "same" individual? Organisms, to be sure, persist form birth to death. Willfully scientific identifications of individuals depend on lasting features of the organism such as height, skin color, scars, fingerprints, dental structure, and facial configuration. Yet what we normally experience as sameness ultimately depends on the reckoning of relationships. Al remains Al as the son of Bill, the lover of Cathy, the father of Dorothy, the employer of Ed.

What do a firm, a household, a patron-client chain, a lineage, a football team, and a community have in common? Surely not that they consist of some precise set of individuals, but that they amount to very different ways of organizing relationships among individuals. A player leaves, the team continues.

The point is not new. Forty years ago, Pitirim Sorokin was inveighing against the search for the "simplest social unit," and especially against the acceptance of the individual as the basic social unit. "The most generic model of any sociocultural phenomenon," wrote Sorokin, "is the meaningful interaction of two or more human individuals" (Sorokin 1947: 40).

Following an approach sketched long ago by Georg Simmel but strangely neglected by subsequent sociologists, Harrison White has fashioned this insight into a simple, effective instrument of social analysis. White begins with populations of two or more individuals and distinguishes a pair of elements: categories and networks. A population forms a **category** to the extent that its members share a characteristic distinguishing them from others. (White restricts his attention to characteristics that the persons themselves recognize as shared with the others, but his formulation adapts readily to common characteristics identified by outside observers.) All Welshmen, all coal miners, and all viola players are examples of populations qualifying as categories.

A population forms a **network** to the extent that its members are connected by the same social tie.

A population forms a **catnet** (category x network), finally, to the extent that both conditions—common characteristics and linking ties—apply. A catnet, thus described, comes close to the intuitive meaning of the word "group." Nuclear families, households, firms, voluntary associations, churches, states, armies, and parties, among other sets of persons, commonly meet the criteria for a catnet. Whether those entities we refer to indecisively as communities, institutions, classes, movements, ethnic groups, and neighborhoods correspond to genuine catnets remains an empirical question: Some do, some don't. Societies, cultures, civilizations, peoples, publics, and masses, as analysts ordinarily use these words, almost never qualify as catnets. Indeed, in most cases the words do not even designate bounded populations, categories, or networks.

The elementary units of categories, networks, and catnets are not individual mental events, but relationships: relationships established by the sharing of social characteristics on the one hand and by the presence of social ties on the other. By specifying the character and intensity of the social characteristics and/or social ties in question, we can accomplish three fundamental tasks of social description:

1   establish workable taxonomies of social structures for particular analytical purposes;

2   convert absolute distinctions such as community/noncommunity into
    empirically distinguishable continua;
3   locate observable sequences of human behavior within the taxonomies
    thereby established.

Thus we may identify a specified population as a household to the **extent
that** its members share a distinct dwelling and food supply, and collaborate
in the maintenance and use of the dwelling and food supply.

Such a definition immediately brings out similarities and differences between a household and a barracks, a prison, a hospital, a hotel, or a picnic
ground. It also allows variation as to the degree of distinctiveness in dwelling and food supply or the extent of collaboration among household members. With the elementary apparatus of population, relationship, category,
and network, the basic tasks of social description become manageable.

In eschewing socially conditioned mental events as the prime ties of individuals to societies, must we also abandon rational-action models of social
behavior? No, we need not jettison the life preserver with the ballast. In many
fields of social inquiry, models of social behavior as rational choice offer our
best hope of escape from the tyranny of societal determinism. What we
need, however, is better means of moving from the action of a single person
or group taken in isolation, to rational interaction among two or more actors.

Take the study of social movements as a case in point. In understanding contemporary social movements, rational-action models of the kind
proposed by William Gamson have much greater explanatory power than
the society-driven irrationalism that so long dominated the study of crowds,
protests, and movements. To use rational-action models, we have no need to
assume that all collective action is fundamentally calculated, willed, desirable, feasible, and efficacious. We need only assume, provisionally, a coherent set of relationships among the interests, organization, shared beliefs, and
actions of the actors. Rational-action models of social movements generally
assume a single actor—a movement, organization, an aggrieved group, or
something of the sort—provide accounts of that actor's behavior, and sometimes state the effects of that behavior.

Furthermore, real social movements always involve a symbolically
constrained conversation among multiple actors, in which the ability to
deploy symbols and idioms significantly affects the outcome of the interaction. Existing theories and models do not provide useful accounts of that
interaction.

Game theory will not suffice. Eventually we must find the means of placing relationships rather than individuals at the very center of the analysis.

Many of the relationships that constitute and constrain social life have so small a component of strategic interaction as to require other sorts of analysis. Communication networks, routine relations between bosses and workers, flows of tax money, spread of diseases, movements of capital, chain migrations, and promotion ladders all certainly involve strategic interaction at one time or another. But their crystallization into durable structures requires a specifically structural analysis. So, for that matter, does their incessant change.

"Social Change" Is a Coherent Phenomenon

It would be astounding to discover that a single recurrent social process governed all large-scale social change. Perhaps the hope of becoming the Newton of social process tempts social scientists into their repeated, fruitless efforts at discovering that philosopher's stone. Newton, however, had some concrete regularities to explain: the acceleration of falling bodies, the behavior of celestial objects, and many others. Social scientists are not so lucky. At Newton's level of empirical generality—that of the world or the universe as a whole—they have no significant and well-established uniformities to explain.

Somehow the absence of an explicandum has not kept social scientists from elaborating general models of social change. Nor has it kept them from using social change in general as a cause of other phenomena: social movements, emotional distress, crime, suicide, divorce.

Their quest is idle. There is no such thing as social change in general. Many large-scale processes of change exist; urbanization, industrialization, proletarianization, population growth, capitalization, bureaucratization all occur in definable, coherent ways. Social change does not.

The worst version of the belief in social change as a coherent general phenomenon, from the viewpoint of practical effects, is its implicit version, the version built into standard methods without requiring any reflection of their users. Three variants come to mind. The first is the use of comparison among a large number of units—most often national states—at the same point in time as the means of drawing conclusions about sequences: for instance, drawing conclusions about "political development" by arraying a hundred countries all observed in 1960 to 1970 along a scale established by means of a multiple regression of numerous variables for each of those countries. There is no logical connection between the sequence of change in those variables followed by individual countries and the differences that show up in a cross-section. Worse yet, there is no logical justification for the scale itself; although multiple regression and similar techniques will, indeed, show which characteristics covary in linear fashion, that covariation is as likely to result from diffusion or from common structural position in a worldwide system as from any internal logic of development.

A cross section provides no substitute for a time-series.

The second variant compounds this difficulty. It consists of using factor analysis or similar techniques to take many, many characteristics of separate "societies" and reduce them to a few "dimensions" of variation.

The third variant is, alas, the most common. It consists of estimating relationships among variables all aggregated to a national level, but actually representing observations on a wide variety of social units: presence or absence of a bicameral legislature (observed directly for national state), urbanization (aggregated from local populations), Gross National Product (aggregated from market transactions), median age (aggregated from individuals), proportion of labor force in agriculture (aggregated in peculiar ways from households and/or firms), and so on. Leave aside the great faith in the quality and comparability of the data such a procedure entails. To have any confidence in estimated relationships among such diverse variables requires tremendous confidence either in the integrity of the national state as a coherent aggregate or in the generality and coherence of social change.

In the last analysis, all three variants of methodological naiveté result from the same basic problem. The available analytical procedures—from simple cross-tabulation to factor analysis—assume variation (1) among well-defined independent units in (2) independently observed characteristics of those units along (3) dimensions that are analogous to those built into the procedures. They also typically assume (4) that their user is estimating a well-specified model rather than exploring for statistical relationships. Rare is the study of large-scale structural change that meets even two of these assumptions halfway. The belief in social change as a coherent general phenomenon compromises the four crucial assumptions.

Stage Theories

Social scientists once used stage models of social change as freely as blacksmiths use their hammers; they banged away at almost every object that came into their hands. Models of economic or political development normally specified the stages through which every developing society had to pass, explained the movement of societies from stage to stage, and sorted the world's contemporary states into the postulated stages.

Stage theories of economic growth or of political modernization had many attractions. They were easier to construct, understand, and apply than were continuous multivariate models. When illustrated with existing states, they had a concrete realism that abstract models of change lacked. They provided a splendid organizing principle for comparative economic or political history. One could even imagine using a valid stage model to guide public policy toward countries at different phases of a common process. An all-purpose hammer, indeed.

During the last few decades, nonetheless, social scientists have packed away that well-worn tool. The general abandonment of optimistic development theories in the face of political criticism, of empirical disconfirmation, and of the elaboration of counter-theories featuring dependency and/or world-economic processes hastened the discarding of stage theories. So did the difficulty of forcing real national states, with their cantankerous complexity, into a single stage of development: What did one do with a Kuwait, oil-rich and dominated by a single lineage? With a South Africa, riven by division between poor blacks and prosperous whites? With a Turkey, a large share of whose workers were off earning money in Germany or Switzerland?

Four More Pernicious Postulates

Differentiation Is a Progressive Master Process

No doubt the marked successes of evolutionary models in natural history encouraged nineteenth-century social theorists to adopt differentiation as a master principle of social change. The specialization of work, the subdivision of governments, the extension of commodity markets, and the proliferation of associations all seemed to exemplify rampant differentiation. The invention of the simple, undifferentiated, "primitive" society as a model of the small, poor populations Europeans encountered in the course of their mercantile and colonial expansion articulated neatly with the same scheme. All societies fell on the same continuum from simple to complex, differentiation drove societies toward greater and greater complexity, and complexity created strength, wealth, and suppleness. The fittest—the most differentiated—survived.

To be sure, differentiation always had rivals. Auguste Comte placed the advance of knowledge at the base of long-term social change; mankind progressed from Theological to Metaphysical to Positive society through the accumulation of sure, disciplined, and comprehensive scientific understanding. Karl Marx saw changes in the organization of production, broadly defined, beneath the carapace of politics and culture. Nevertheless, within the disciplines of the social sciences, two nineteenth-century hypotheses hardened into twentieth-century dogmas: first, that increasing differentiation was the dominant, nearly inexorable logic of large-scale change; second, that over the long run differentiation leads to advancement.

After World War II, theories of "modernization" and "development" epitomized the social-scientific concern with differentiation as the fundamental large-scale social process. All such theories took the world's rich and powerful countries to be more differentiated than other countries, considered that differentiation to constitute a significant part of their advantage over other countries, and held out the creation of new, specialized structures as a major means by which poorer and less powerful countries could come to share the comforts of the rich and powerful. These theories connected closely with an improving program, a program of deliberately inducing development. Both theories and program, in their turn, rested on an optimistic ideology.

The ideology, as F. X. Sutton has reminded us, involved three central tenets: "(1) the capacity of governments as agents and guides to development; (2) the efficacy of education and training; and (3) the possibility of mutually beneficent cooperation between rich and poor countries in an equitable international order" (Sutton 1982: 53). Early United Nations programs of aid to poor countries embodied the ideology and promoted the spread of the associated theories; for all their cantankerous variation, academic specialists in development shared a certain confidence in the three tenets. They took on the mission of building theories that would simultaneously explain and guide the development of one country after another.

All such theories established a continuum of societies having rich Western countries at one end; they were, obviously, "modern" and "developed." Economists had the easiest time of it. For many of them, development came to mean increasing national income, or income per capita. Whatever one could say about the difficulties of measuring national income accurately and in comparable terms, as a criterion of development national income had splendid virtues:

1 Properly measured, it provided a principle on which all countries could be ranked with little ambiguity.
2 Those countries which economists generally regarded as most advanced unquestionably stood at the top of the scale.
3 Countries in all parts of the world were moving up the scale with few important reversals.
4 Position on the scale clearly (if imperfectly) correlated with international power, material well-being, and a great deal more.

With that imperfect correlation, however, the troubles began. For political scientists, sociologists, anthropologists, and others took on the job of specifying, measuring, explaining, and even promoting the other changes that presumably accompanied rising national income. Political development, communications development, educational development, and a dozen other forms of development came into being. A new vocabulary proliferated: developing countries, underdevelopment, late developers, and so on.

Whatever other virtues these multifarious criteria of development had, none of them matched national income in simplicity or efficacy: International rankings remained quite arguable, odd countries kept showing up near the tops of the relevant scales, the continuous drift of the world's countries in the same direction was hard to establish, and the correlations among different presumed forms of development left something to be desired. Yet the nagging correlations persisted. It was somehow true, on the average, that richer countries had higher life expectancy, larger shares of their population in cities, greater literacy, smaller completed family sizes, more durable institutions of parliamentary government, and so on, through a long list of national characteristics not deducible by definition from national income.

In the course of his forty years as a theorist, Talcott Parsons carried on a love/hate affair with the analysis of differentiation. He began the very first page of his vast *Structure of Social Action* with a quotation from Crane Brinton: "Who now reads Spencer? . . . We have evolved beyond Spencer" (Parsons 1937: 1). In 1937, Parsons thought that Spencerian ideas, with their unilinear evolution, their utilitarianism, and their positivism, were dead; they had expired in the crossfire from Pareto, Durkheim, Weber, and other contributors to the Action Frame of Reference.

Late in his career, nevertheless, Parsons began to use analogies with organic evolution quite explicitly. In 1966, Parsons wrote that "a major feature of the evolutionary process is that progressively greater differentiation increasingly frees the cybernetically higher factors from the narrow specifics of the lower-order conditioning factors, thus enabling the basic patterns of the cultural system to become more generalized, objectified, and stabilized (Parsons 1966: 114).

Much of this is nineteenth-century evolutionary thinking in a new garb. And it is wrong. Not that differentiation is an unimportant feature of social processes. Many significant social processes do involve differentiation. But many social processes also involve dedifferentiation: Linguistic standardization, the development of mass consumption, and the agglomeration of petty sovereignties into national states provide clear examples. Futhermore, differentiation matters little to other important social processes such as capital concentration and the diffusion of world religions. Indeed, we have no warrant for thinking of differentiation in itself as a coherent, general, lawlike social process.

In any case, summing up these massive changes in terms of differentiation or dedifferentiation distorts their fundamental character. After several centuries in which manufacturing grew—and grew substantially—through the multiplication of small, dispersed units linked by merchant capitalists, the nineteenth century brought a great movement of capital concentration. Capitalists accumulated capital as never before; converted it from variable to fixed by building or buying such expensive items as factories, steam engines, and locomotives; gained control of the labor process, established time- and work-discipline within spaces they controlled, extended wage-labor as the principal condition for involvement of workers in production; and concentrated their workers at a limited number of production sites.

From a geographic point of view, Europe felt an enormous **implosion** of production into a few intensely industrial regions, as capital, labor, and trade drained from the rest of the continent. Karl Marx, witnessing these changes, saw that employers used differentiation of tasks as one of their techniques for increasing their own control over production and undermining the power of workers. But he also saw that the fundamental process involved concentration rather than differentiation.

My point is not that concentration of capital, or concentration in general, is the fundamental social process. One could equally make the case for connection, or communication, or control of energy. Here is the point: In this abstract sense, no process is fundamental. In a given era, specific historical processes dominate the changes occurring in a given population or region. Over the last few hundred years, the growth of national states and the development of capitalism in property and production have dominated the changes occurring in increasing parts of the world. More generally, alterations in the organization of production and of coercion have set the great historical rhythms.

In other eras, the creation or decline of empires and the establishment or destruction of command economies have dominated all other changes. Those historically specific changes in the organization of production and coercion, rather than abstractly specified processes such as differentiation or concentration, mark out the limits for intelligible analysis of social processes.

Differentiation Versus Integration

A belief in differentiation as the master process of social change clamps neatly to a nearby postulate: that the state of social order depends on the balance between processes of differentiation and processes of integration or control, with rapid or excessive differentiation producing disorder. Rapid or excessive differentiation, in this view, produces disorder. Differentiation can take the form of industrialization, urbanization, immigration of people from alien cultures, and any number of other changes. In essence, any change that increases the variety of social forms having durable connections to each other qualifies as differentiation.

Integration (alias social control, hegemony, and solidarity in different versions of the theory) can occur through repression, socialization, mutual obligation, or consensus. Disorder sometimes appears in this formulation as crime, as war, as emotional disturbance, as rebellion, as alienation, as family instability, as violence. Order, in most statements of the argument, amounts simply to the absence of disorder.

Change, Strain, Disorder

Another false postulate: the equivalence of different forms of disorder. Generations of social scientists clung to the nineteenth-century equation of crime, violence, family instability, rebellion, social movements, and other forms of disapproved behavior. The equation made them all into disorder, disorganization, maladaptation. Various disapproved behaviors became equivalent in several senses: (1) as direct evidence of the malfunctioning of individual and society, (2) as consequences of rapid and/or excessive social change, (3) as alternative expressions of the same tensions, (4) as "social problems" to be solved in collaboration by powerholders and social scientists. These equations coincided in an extended version of the differentiation versus integration argument in which rapid or excessive structural change built up a variety of strains, and those strains expressed themselves in a range of disorders.

In the heyday of developmental theories, many theorists considered these various forms of disorder to be unavoidable costs of development.

Fortunately, students of development often launched empirical inquiries in presumably disorganized areas. Those students sometimes included natives of the areas under analysis. Now and then they came to identify themselves politically and morally with the people whose behavior was being explained. Under these circumstances, evidence began to arrive concerning the various forms of order hidden in all that presumed disorder. Studies of African and Latin American rural immigrants, for example, showed repeatedly the creation of rural outposts in cities through chain migration, rather than the atomization, culture shock, and consequent social disorganization the breakdown theories required.

Joan Nelson evaluated the "theory of the disruptive migrants" on the basis of the accumulating evidence from throughout the Third World. Here is what she found:

> In sum, the more dramatic and dire predictions about migrants' social assimilation are wide of the mark. The social mechanisms of family and home-place circles, sometimes supplemented by ethnic-group or voluntary associations or both, ease the transition and provide continuing social support for most migrants. That some are isolated, disappointed, desperate, is undeniable and should not be ignored. That others live as "urban villagers" in tight enclaves that turn their backs upon the city is also true, although much of what has been interpreted as evidence of "urban rurality" may be the result of superficial observation or misinterpretation. But the bulk of migrants in the cities of Africa, Asia, and Latin America are not isolated, disappointed, or desperate, nor are they urban villagers. Much of their lives, their aspirations, and their problems are shaped more by the pressures and the opportunities of the city than by their migrant status, and these pressures and opportunities are shared with urban natives of similar economic and educational background.
>
> (Nelson 1979: 108)

Illegitimate Versus Legitimate Force

All the pernicious postulates assume sharp separation between the worlds of order and disorder. The most explicitly political application of that assumption separates illegitimate and legitimate forces from each other. Illegitimate conflict, coercion, and expropriation, in this mystification, include riot, rebellion, assault, protection rackets, robbery, and fraud; they result from processes of change and disorder. Legitimate conflict, coercion, and expropriation, then, include war, crowd control, capital punishment, imprisonment, taxation, and seizure of property for debt; all of them presumably result from processes of integration and control. The very same acts, indeed, switch from illegitimate to legitimate if a constituted authority performs them. Killing appears in both columns, but with very different values. The values depend on whether the killer is a soldier, a policeman, an executioner, or a private person.

In the realm of politics, the distinction between illegitimate and legitimate uses of force is absolutely crucial. I don't deny its political necessity or the likelihood that I will call the police if someone steals my wallet or assaults my child. Nevertheless the sharp distinction should never have entered the world of systematic explanation. It is at once impractical and obfuscating.

The distinction is **impractical** because nearly identical actions fall on both sides of the line, and only a political judgment separates them. Recent attempts to build systematic theories of terrorism, for example, have foundered repeatedly over a simple fact: one person's terror is another person's resistance movement. Martha Crenshaw, who attempts to build from a neutral definition of terrorism, despairs of Conor Cruise O'Brien's normative approach: "He defines terrorism," comments Crenshaw,

> in terms of the political context in which it occurs, seeing terrorism as unjustified violence against a democratic state that permits effective and peaceful forms of opposition. Thus a black activist who bombs a police station in South Africa is not a terrorist; the Provisional Irish Republican Army (IRA) bomber of a British military barracks is. Identical acts performed in different situations do not fall under the same definition.
>
> (Crenshaw 1983: 1–2)

For theoretical purposes, such a criterion is impractical indeed.

The distinction between illegitimate and legitimate force is **obfuscating** because it reinforces the idea of a struggle between differentiation and integration and it separates phenomena that have much in common and spring from similar conditions. A small example comes from the study of collective violence: In the examinations of "riots" that proliferated with the great ghetto conflicts of the United States in the 1960s, it became customary to gauge the intensity of the event, among other ways, by the number of killed and wounded, to focus the analysis on explaining the participation of civilians in those riots, and to seek the explanation of variations in "riot intensity" in relationships among local social structure, selective participation of certain types of ghetto-dwellers, and the forms of action of the "rioters." In short, observers built their explanations as though the use of "illegitimate" force were a self-contained phenomenon, explicable through the character and circumstances of the people who used it and quite independent of the "legitimate" force deployed to stop it.

Small wonder, then, that no satisfactory explanations emerged: In fact, the events in question typically began with contested actions of police, the conflict consisted mainly of interactions between armed authorities and civilians, the armed authorities did most of the killing and wounding, and the extent of killing and wounding depended at least as much on the tactics of police and troops as it did on the number of people in the streets or the amount of property seized and destroyed.

Part of the confusion resulted from the use of the term **riot** itself. Like the words disturbance, mob, and rabble, the word belongs exclusively to authorities and hostile observers. Unlike demonstrators, participants in social movements, and vigilantes, people whom others call rioters never use the term for themselves. In Anglo-Saxon law, the term riot has long had legal standing. It denotes an assembly which frightens the public and, in the eyes of the authorities, displays the intention to break the law. After due warning and a decent interval for voluntary compliance, to declare an assembly riotous justifies the use of public force to disperse it. As a legal device, one can see why authorities find it useful. As an analytic term, however, it cuts through the very middle of the social interaction constituting the event to be explained.

A large example comes from the close analogy, rarely noticed, between racketeering and routine government. Both depend on the establishment of a near-monopoly of force in a given area and its use to coerce people to pay for goods or services offered by suppliers allied with the wielders of force and to exclude other suppliers of those goods and services from the market. To the extent that a government manufactures external threats to justify the military protection it provides and the taxes it collects for that purpose, it operates a protection racket.

Government is that racket which has managed to establish control over the most concentrated means of coercion in an area and to command the acquiescence of most of the population to its use of those means throughout that area.

I don't insist on the strong word **racket** and certainly don't claim that the monopolization of coercion and the extraction of various forms of tribute exhaust the activities of governments. Nevertheless, notice how the analogy with racketeering clarifies the actions of governments we regard as illegitimate and the process by which new governments or quasi-governments arise.

Anyone who has looked closely at the formation of national states in Europe has seen elements of the process over and over:

- the early uncertainty as to the location of the government in the midst of great lords and private armies;
- the intense campaigns of kings and ministers to tear down castle walls, disarm the lords, diminish the private use of armed force in such forms as dueling and banditry, disband the private armies, incorporate all troops into forces under royal control, and turn nobles into royal military officers;
- the creation of distinct government-controlled police forces;
- the use of that growing monopoly of force to collect taxes, conscript soldiers, force the sale of salt, define and discourage smuggling, seize control of criminal and civilian justice, subject the population at large to registration and surveillance, regulate all other organizations.

Those processes **created** the distinctions between legitimate and illegitimate, legal and illegal, that exist today. Those distinctions and their origins are important objects of study. But as analytical distinctions, they do little but obscure the understanding.

Let that stand as an epitaph for all eight of the pernicious postulates the social sciences inherited from the nineteenth century. Without exception, they call attention to important processes, processes that frightened our nineteenth-century forebears, processes that remain influential today. Without exception, they construe those processes in such a way as to hinder their systematic analysis. We must hold on to the nineteenth-century problems, but let go of the nineteenth-century intellectual apparatus.

References

Bourne, Larry S. and Simmons, James. 1983. "The Canadian Urban System." In *Urbanization and Settlement Systems*, by L. S. Bourne *et al*. Oxford: Oxford University Press.

Crenshaw, Martha (ed), 1983. *Terrorism, Legitimacy, and Power: The Consequences of Political Violence*. Middletown, CT: Wesleyan University Press.

Morrill, Richard L. 1970. *The Spatial Organization of Society*. Belmont, CA: Duxbury Press.

Nelson, Joan. 1979. *Access to Power: Politics and the Urban Poor in Developing Nations*. Princeton, NJ: Princeton University Press.

Parsons, Talcott. 1937. *The Structure of Social Action*. New York: McGraw-Hill.

Parsons, Talcott. 1966. *Societies: Evolutionary and Comparative Perspectives*. Englewood Cliffs, NJ: Prentice-Hall.

Sorokin, Pitirim A. 1947. *Society, Culture and Personality*. New York: Harper & Row.

Sutton, Francis X. 1982. "Rationality, Development, and Scholarship." *Social Science Research Council Items* 36: 49–57.

White, Harrison. 1981. "Production Markets as Induced Role Structures." In *Sociological Methodology*. San Francisco, CA: Jossey-Bass.

State Making

II

War Making and State Making as Organized Crime

7

Charles Tilly

If protection rackets represent organized crime at its smoothest, then war making and state making—quintessential protection rackets with the advantage of legitimacy—qualify as our largest examples of organized crime. Without branding all generals and statesmen as murderers or thieves, I want to urge the value of that analogy. At least for the European experience of the past few centuries, a portrait of war makers and state makers as coercive and self-seeking entrepreneurs bears a far greater resemblance to the facts than do its chief alternatives: the idea of a social contract, the idea of an open market in which operators of armies and states offer services to willing consumers, the idea of a society whose shared norms and expectations call forth a certain kind of government.

The reflections that follow merely illustrate the analogy of war making and state making with organized crime from a few hundred years of European experience and offer tentative arguments concerning principles of change and variation underlying the experience. My reflections grow from contemporary concerns: worries about the increasing destructiveness of war, the expanding role of great powers as suppliers of arms and military organization to poor countries, and the growing importance of military rule in those same countries. They spring from the hope that the European experience, properly understood, will help us to grasp what is happening today, perhaps even to do something about it.

The Third World of the twentieth century does not greatly resemble Europe of the sixteenth or seventeenth century. In no simple sense can we read the future of Third World countries from the pasts of European countries. Yet a thoughtful exploration of European experience will serve us well. It will show us that coercive exploitation played a large part in the creation of the European states. It will show us that popular resistance to coercive exploitation forced would-be power holders to concede protection and constraints on their own action. It will therefore help us to eliminate faulty implicit comparisons between today's Third World and yesterday's Europe.

This essay, then, concerns the place of organized means of violence in the growth and change of those peculiar forms of government we call national states: relatively centralized, differentiated organizations the officials of which more or less successfully claim control over the chief concentrated means of violence within a population inhabiting a large, contiguous territory.

War makes states, I shall claim. Banditry, piracy, gangland rivalry, policing, and war making all belong on the same continuum—that I shall claim as well. For the historically limited period in which national states were becoming the dominant organizations in Western countries, I shall also claim that mercantile capitalism and state making reinforced each other.

Double-Edged Protection

In contemporary American parlance, the word "protection" sounds two contrasting tones. One is comforting, the other ominous. With one tone, "protection" calls up images of the shelter against danger provided by a powerful friend, a large insurance policy, or a sturdy roof. With the other, it evokes the racket in which a local strong man forces merchants to pay tribute in order to avoid damage—damage the strong man himself threatens to deliver. The difference, to be sure, is a matter of degree: A hell-and-damnation priest is likely to collect contributions from his parishioners only to the extent that they believe his predictions of brimstone for infidels; our neighborhood mobster may actually be, as he claims to be, a brothel's best guarantee of operation free of police interference.

Which image the word "protection" brings to mind depends mainly on our assessment of the reality and externality of the threat. Someone who produces both the danger and, at a price, the shield against it is a racketeer. Someone who provides a needed shield but has little control over the danger's appearance qualifies as a legitimate protector, especially if his price is no higher than his competitors'. Someone who supplies reliable, low-priced shielding both from local racketeers and from outside marauders makes the best offer of all.

Apologists for particular governments and for government in general commonly argue, precisely, that they offer protection from local and external violence. They claim that the prices they charge barely cover the costs of protection. They call people who complain about the price of protection "anarchists," "subversives," or both at once. But consider the definition of a racketeer as someone who creates a threat and then charges for its reduction. Government's provision of protection, by this standard, often qualifies as racketeering. To the extent that the threats against which a given government protects its citizens are imaginary or are consequences of its own activities, the government has organized a protection racket. Since governments themselves commonly simulate, stimulate, or even fabricate threats of external war and since the repressive and extractive activities of governments often constitute the largest current threats to the livelihoods of their own citizens, many governments operate in essentially the same ways as racketeers. There is, of course, a difference: Racketeers, by the conventional definition, operate without the sanctity of governments.

How do racketeer governments themselves acquire authority? As a question of fact and of ethics, that is one of the oldest conundrums of political analysis. Back to Machiavelli and Hobbes, nevertheless, political observers have recognized that, whatever else they do, governments organize and, wherever possible, monopolize violence. It matters little whether we take violence in a narrow sense, such as damage to persons and objects, or in a broad sense, such as violation of people's desires and interests; by either criterion, governments stand out from other organizations by their tendency to monopolize the concentrated means of violence. The distinction between "legitimate" and "illegitimate" force, furthermore, makes no difference to the fact. If we take legitimacy to depend on conformity to an abstract principle or on the assent of the governed (or both at once), these conditions may serve to justify, perhaps even to explain, the tendency to monopolize force; they do not contradict the fact.

Legitimacy is the probability that other authorities will act to confirm the decisions of a given authority. Other authorities are much more likely to confirm the decisions of a challenged authority that controls substantial force; not only fear of retaliation, but also desire to maintain a stable environment recommend that general rule. The rule underscores the importance of the authority's monopoly of force. A tendency to monopolize the means of violence makes a government's claim to provide protection, in either the comforting or the ominous sense of the word, more credible and more difficult to resist.

Frank recognition of the central place of force in governmental activity does not require us to believe that governmental authority rests "only" or "ultimately" on the threat of violence. Nor does it entail the assumption that a government's only service is protection. Even when a government's use of force imposes a large cost some people may well decide that the government's other services outbalance the costs of acceding to its monopoly of violence. Recognition of the centrality of force opens the way to an understanding of the growth and change of governmental forms. Here is a preview of the most general argument: Power holders' pursuit of war involved them willy-nilly in the extraction of resources for war making from the populations over which they had control and in the promotion of capital accumulation by those who could help them borrow and buy. War making, extraction, and capital accumulation interacted to shape European state making. Power holders did not undertake those three momentous activities with the intention of creating national states—centralized, differentiated, autonomous, extensive political organizations. Nor did they ordinarily foresee that national states would emerge from war making, extraction, and capital accumulation.

Instead, the people who controlled European states and states in the making warred in order to check or overcome their competitors and thus to enjoy the advantages of power within a secure or expanding territory. To make more effective war, they attempted to locate more capital. In the short run, they might acquire that capital by conquest, by selling off their assets, or by coercing or dispossessing accumulators of capital. In the long run, the quest inevitably involved them in establishing regular access to capitalists who could supply and arrange credit and in imposing one form of regular taxation or another on the people and activities within their spheres of control.

As the process continued, state makers developed a durable interest in promoting the accumulation of capital, sometimes in the guise of direct return to their own enterprises. Variations in the difficulty of collecting taxes, in the expense of the particular kind of armed force adopted, in the amount of war making required to hold off competitors, and so on resulted in the principal variations in the forms of European states. It all began with the effort to monopolize the means of violence within a delimited territory adjacent to a power holder's base.

Violence and Government

What distinguished the violence produced by states from the violence delivered by anyone else? In the long run, enough to make the division between "legitimate" and "illegitimate" force credible. Eventually, the personnel of states purveyed violence on a larger scale, more effectively, more efficiently, with wider assent from their subject populations, and with readier collaboration from neighboring authorities than did the personnel of other organizations. But it took a long time for that series of distinctions to become established. Early in the state-making process, many parties shared the right to use violence, the practice of using it routinely to accomplish their ends, or both at once. The continuum ran from bandits and pirates to kings via tax collectors, regional power holders, and professional soldiers.

The uncertain, elastic line between "legitimate" and "illegitimate" violence appeared in the upper reaches of power. The long love-hate affair between aspiring state makers and pirates or bandits illustrates the division. "Behind piracy on the seas acted cities and city-states ... Behind banditry ... appeared the continual aid of lords," writes Fernand Braudel (1966: 88–89) of the sixteenth century. In times of war, indeed, the managers of full-fledged states often commissioned privateers, hired sometime bandits to raid their enemies, and encouraged their regular troops to take booty. In royal service, soldiers and sailors were often expected to provide for themselves by preying on the civilian population: commandeering, raping, looting, taking prizes. When demobilized, they commonly continued the same practices, but without the same royal protection; demobilized ships became pirate vessels, demobilized troops bandits.

It also worked the other way: A king's best source of armed supporters was sometimes the world of outlaws. Robin Hood's conversion to royal archer may be a myth, but the myth records a practice. The distinctions between "legitimate" and "illegitimate" users of violence came clear only very slowly, in the process during which the state's armed forces became relatively unified and permanent.

Up to that point, as Braudel says, maritime cities and terrestrial lords commonly offered protection, or even sponsorship, to freebooters. Many lords who did not pretend to be kings, furthermore, successfully claimed the right to levy troops and maintain their own armed retainers. Without calling on some of those lords to bring their armies with them, no king could fight a war; yet the same armed lords constituted the king's rivals and opponents, his enemies' potential allies. For that reason, before the seventeenth century, regencies for child sovereigns reliably produced civil wars. For the same reason, disarming the great [lords] stood high on the agenda of every would-be state maker.

Tudor demilitarization of the great lords entailed four complementary campaigns: eliminating their great personal bands of armed retainers, razing their fortresses, taming their habitual resort to violence for the settlement of disputes, and discouraging the cooperation of their dependents and tenants. [Those] who kept armies and castles along the border, threatened the Crown but also provided a buffer against Scottish invaders. Yet they, too, eventually fell into line.

In France, Richelieu began the great disarmament in the 1620s. With Richelieu's advice, Louis XIII systematically destroyed the castles of the great rebel lords, Protestant and Catholic, against whom his forces battled incessantly. He began to condemn dueling, the carrying of lethal weapons, and the maintenance of private armies. By the later 1620s, Richelieu was declaring the royal monopoly of force as doctrine.

By the later eighteenth century, through most of Europe, monarchs controlled permanent, professional military forces that rivaled those of their neighbors and far exceeded any other organized armed force within their own territories. The state's monopoly of large-scale violence was turning from theory to reality.

The elimination of local rivals, however, posed a serious problem. Beyond the scale of a small city-state, no monarch could govern a population with his armed force alone, nor could any monarch afford to create a professional staff large and strong enough to reach from him to the ordinary citizen. Before quite recently, no European government approached the completeness of articulation from top to bottom achieved by imperial China. Even the Roman Empire did not come close. In one way or another, every European government before the French Revolution relied on indirect rule via local magnates. The magnates collaborated with the government without becoming officials in any strong sense of the term, had some access to government-backed force, and exercised wide discretion within their own territories: junkers, justices of the peace, lords. Yet the same magnates were potential rivals, possible allies of a rebellious people.

Eventually, European governments reduced their reliance on indirect rule by means of two expensive but effective strategies: (a) extending their officialdom to the local community and (b) encouraging the creation of police forces that were subordinate to the government rather than to individual patrons, distinct from war-making forces, and therefore less useful as the tools of dissident magnates. In between, however, the builders of national power all played a mixed strategy: eliminating, subjugating, dividing, conquering, cajoling, buying as the occasions presented themselves. The buying manifested itself in exemptions from taxation, creations of honorific offices, the establishment of claims on the national treasury, and a variety of other devices that made a magnate's welfare dependent on the maintenance of the existing structure of power. In the long run, it all came down to massive pacification and monopolization of the means of coercion.

Protection as Business

In retrospect, the pacification, cooptation, or elimination of fractious rivals to the sovereign seems an awesome, noble, prescient enterprise, destined to bring peace to a people; yet it followed almost ineluctably from the logic of expanding power. If a power holder was to gain from the provision of protection, his competitors had to yield. As economic historian Frederic Lane put it twenty-five years ago, governments are in the business of selling protection … whether people want it or not. Lane argued that the very activity of producing and controlling violence favored monopoly, because competition within that realm generally raised costs, instead of lowering them. The production of violence, he suggested, enjoyed large economies of scale.

Working from there, Lane distinguished between (a) the monopoly profit, or *tribute,* coming to owners of the means of producing violence as a result of the difference between production costs and the price exacted from "customers" and (b) the *protection rent* accruing to those customers—for example, merchants—who drew effective protection against outside competitors. Lane, a superbly attentive historian of Venice, allowed specifically for the case of a government that generates protection rents for its merchants by deliberately attacking their competitors. In their adaptation of Lane's scheme, furthermore, Edward Ames and Richard Rapp (1977) substitute the apt word "extortion" for Lane's "tribute." In this model, predation, coercion, piracy, banditry, and racketeering share a home with their upright cousins in responsible government.

This is how Lane's model worked: If a prince could create a sufficient armed force to hold off his and his subjects' external enemies and to keep the subjects in line for 50 megapounds but was able to extract 75 megapounds in taxes from those subjects for that purpose, he gained a tribute of 25 megapounds [...]

If citizens in general exercised effective ownership of the government—O distant ideal!—we might expect the managers to minimize protection costs and tribute, thus maximizing protection rent. A single self-interested monarch, in contrast, would maximize tribute, set costs so as to accomplish that maximization of tribute, and be indifferent to the level of protection rent. If the managers owned the government, they would tend to keep costs high by maximizing their own wages, to maximize tribute over and above those costs by exacting a high price from their subjects, and likewise to be indifferent to the level of protection rent. The first model approximates a Jeffersonian democracy, the second a petty despotism, and the third a military junta.

Lane did not discuss the obvious fourth category of owner: a dominant class. If he had, his scheme would have yielded interesting empirical criteria for evaluating claims that a given government was "relatively autonomous" or strictly subordinate to the interests of a dominant class. Presumably, a subordinate government would tend to maximize monopoly profits— returns to the dominant class resulting from the difference between the costs of protection and the price received for it—as well as tuning protection rents nicely to the economic interests of the dominant class. An autonomous government, in contrast, would tend to maximize managers' wages and its own size as well and would be indifferent to protection rents. Lane's analysis immediately suggests fresh propositions and ways of testing them.

Lane also speculated that the logic of the situation produced four successive stages in the general history of capitalism:

1   A period of anarchy and plunder
2   A stage in which tribute takers attracted customers and established their monopolies by struggling to create exclusive, substantial states
3   A stage in which merchants and landlords began to gain more from protection rents than governors did from tribute
4   A period (fairly recent) in which technological changes surpassed protection rents as source of profit for entrepreneurs

Unfortunately, Lane did not take full advantage of his own insight. Wanting to contain his analysis neatly within the neoclassical theory of industrial organization, Lane cramped his treatment of protection: treating all taxpayers as "customers" for the "service" provided by protection-manufacturing governments, brushing aside the objections to the idea of a forced sale by insisting that the "customer" always had the choice of not paying and taking the consequences of nonpayment, minimizing the problems of divisibility created by the public-goods character of protection, and deliberately neglecting the distinction between the costs of producing the means of violence in general and the costs of giving "customers" protection by means of that violence. Lane's ideas suffocate inside the neoclassical box and breathe easily outside it. Nevertheless, inside or outside, they properly draw the economic analysis of government back to the chief activities that real governments have carried on historically: war, repression, protection, adjudication.

More recently, Richard Bean has applied a similar logic to the rise of European national states between 1400 and 1600. He appeals to economies of scale in the production of effective force, counteracted by diseconomies of scale in command and control. He then claims that the improvement of artillery in the fifteenth century (cannon made small medieval forts much more vulnerable to an organized force) shifted the curve of economies and diseconomies to make larger armies, standing armies, and centralized governments advantageous to their masters. Hence, according to Bean, military innovation promoted the creation of large, expensive, well-armed national states.

History Talks

The arrival of effective artillery came too late to have *caused* the increase in the viable size of states. (However, the increased cost of fortifications to defend against artillery did give an advantage to states enjoying larger fiscal bases.)

Stripped of its technological determinism, nevertheless, Bean's logic provides a useful complement to Lane's, for different military formats do cost substantially different amounts to produce and do provide substantially different ranges of control over opponents, domestic and foreign. After 1400 the European pursuit of larger, more permanent, and more costly varieties of military organization did, in fact, drive spectacular increases in princely budgets, taxes, and staffs. After 1500 or so, princes who managed to create the costly varieties of military organization were, indeed, able to conquer new chunks of territory.

The word "territory" should not mislead us. Until the eighteenth century, the greatest powers were maritime states, and naval warfare remained crucial to international position. Consider Fernand Braudel's roll call of successive hegemonic powers within the capitalist world: Venice and its empire, Genoa and its empire, Antwerp–Spain, Amsterdam–Holland, London–England, New York–the United States. Although Brandenburg–Prussia offers a partial exception, only in our own time have such essentially landbound states as Russia and China achieved preponderant positions in the world's system of states. Naval warfare was by no means the only reason for that bias toward the sea. Before the later nineteenth century, land transportation was so expensive everywhere in Europe that no country could afford to supply a large army or a big city with grain and other heavy goods without having efficient water transport. Rulers fed major inland centers such as Berlin and Madrid only at great effort and at considerable cost to their hinterlands. The exceptional efficiency of water-ways in the Netherlands undoubtedly gave the Dutch great advantages at peace and at war.

Access to water mattered in another important way. Those metropolises on Braudel's list were all major ports, great centers of commerce, and outstanding mobilizers of capital. Both the trade and the capital served the purposes of ambitious rulers. By a circuitous route, that observation brings us back to the arguments of Lane and Bean. Considering that both of them wrote as economic historians, the greatest weakness in their analyses comes as a surprise: Both of them understate the importance of capital accumulation to military expansion. As Jan de Vries says of the period after 1600:

> Looking back, one cannot help but be struck by the seemingly symbiotic relationship existing between the state, military power, and the private economy's efficiency in the age of absolutism. Behind every successful dynasty stood an array of opulent banking families. Access to such bourgeois resources princes' state-building and centralizing policies.

Great capitalists played crucial parts on both sides of the transaction: as the principal sources of royal credit, especially in the short term, and as the most important contractors in the risky but lucrative business of collecting royal taxes.

(The government's failure to pay those *rentes*, incidentally, helped align the Parisian bourgeoisie against the Crown during the Fronde, some twelve decades later.) By 1595, the national debt had risen to 300 million francs; despite governmental bankruptcies, currency manipulations, and the monumental rise in taxes, by Louis XIV's death in 1715 war-induced borrowing had inflated the total to about 3 billion francs, the equivalent of about eighteen years in royal revenues (Hamilton 1950:247, 249). War, state apparatus, taxation, and borrowing advanced in tight cadence.

Although France was precocious, it was by no means alone. "Even more than in the case of France," reports the ever-useful Earl J. Hamilton,

> the national debt of England originated and has grown during major wars. Except for an insignificant carry-over from the Stuarts, the debt

began in 1689 with the reign of William and Mary. In the words of Adam Smith, "it was in the war which began in 1688, and was concluded by the treaty of Ryswick in 1697, that the foundation of the present enormous debt of Great Britain was first laid."

(Hamilton 1950:254)

Hamilton, it is true, goes on to quote the mercantilist Charles Davenant, who complained in 1698 that the high interest rates promoted by government borrowing were cramping English trade. Davenant's complaint suggests, however, that England was already entering Frederic Lane's third stage of state-capital relations, when merchants and landowners receive more of the surplus than do the suppliers of protection.

Until the sixteenth century, the English expected their kings to live on revenues from their own property and to levy taxes only for war. G. R. Elton marks the great innovation at Thomas Cromwell's drafting of Henry VIII's subsidy bills for 1534 and 1540: "1540 was very careful to continue the real innovation of 1534, namely that extraordinary contributions could be levied for reasons other than war" (Elton 1975:42). After that point as before, however, war making provided the main stimulus to increases in the level of taxation as well as of debt. Rarely did debt and taxes recede. What A. T. Peacock and J. Wiseman call a "displacement effect" (and others sometimes call a "ratchet effect") occurred: When public revenues and expenditures rose abruptly during war, they set a new, higher floor beneath which peacetime revenues and expenditures did not sink. During the Napoleonic Wars, British taxes rose from 15 to 24 percent of national income and to almost three times the French level of taxation (Mathias 1979:122).

True, Britain had the double advantage of relying less on expensive land forces than its Continental rivals and of drawing more of its tax revenues from customs and excise—taxes that were, despite evasion, significantly cheaper to collect than land taxes, property taxes, and poll taxes. Nevertheless, in England as well as elsewhere, both debt and taxes rose enormously from the seventeenth century onward. They rose mainly as a function of the increasing cost of war making.

What Do States Do?

As should now be clear, Lane's analysis of protection fails to distinguish among several different uses of state-controlled violence. Under the general heading of organized violence, the agents of states characteristically carry on four different activities:

1. War making: Eliminating or neutralizing their own rivals outside the territories in which they have clear and continuous priority as wielders of force
2. State making: Eliminating or neutralizing their rivals inside those territories
3. Protection: Eliminating or neutralizing the enemies of their clients
4. Extraction: Acquiring the means of carrying out the first three activities—war making, state making, and protection

The third item corresponds to protection as analyzed by Lane, but the other three also involve the application of force. They overlap incompletely and to various degrees; for example, war making against the commercial rivals of the local bourgeoisie delivers protection to that bourgeoisie. To the extent that a population is divided into enemy classes and the state extends its favors partially to one class or another, state making actually reduces the protection given some classes.

War making, state making, protection, and extraction each take a number of forms. Extraction, for instance, ranges from outright plunder to regular tribute to bureaucratized taxation. Yet all four depend on the state's tendency to monopolize the concentrated means of coercion. From the perspectives of those who dominate the state, each of them—if carried on effectively—generally reinforces the others. Thus, a state that successfully eradicates its internal rivals strengthens its ability to extract resources, to wage war, and to protect its chief supporters. In the earlier European experience, broadly speaking, those supporters were typically landlords, armed retainers of the monarch, and churchmen.

Each of the major uses of violence produced characteristic forms of organization. War making yielded armies, navies, and supporting services. State making produced durable instruments of surveillance and control within the territory. Protection relied on the organization of war making and state making but added to it an apparatus by which the protected called forth the protection that was their due, notably through courts and representative assemblies. Extraction brought fiscal and accounting structures into being. The organization and deployment of violence themselves account for much of the characteristic structure of European states.

The general rule seems to have operated like this: The more costly the activity, all other things being equal, the greater was the organizational residue. To the extent, for example, that a given government invested in large standing armies—a very costly, if effective, means of war making—the bureaucracy created to service the army was likely to become bulky. Furthermore, a government building a standing army while controlling a small population was likely to incur greater costs, and therefore to build a bulkier structure, than a government within a populous country. Brandenburg–Prussia was the classic case of high cost for available resources. The Prussian effort to build an army matching those of its larger Continental neighbors created an immense structure; it militarized and bureaucratized much of German social life.

With respect to state making (in the narrow sense of eliminating or neutralizing the local rivals of the people who controlled the state), a territory populated by great landlords or by distinct religious groups generally imposed larger costs on a conqueror than one of fragmented power or homogeneous culture. This time, fragmented and homogeneous Sweden, with its relatively small but effective apparatus of control, illustrates the corollary.

Finally, the cost of protection (in the sense of eliminating or neutralizing the enemies of the state makers' clients) mounted with the range over which that protection extended. Portugal's effort to bar the Mediterranean to its merchants' competitors in the spice trade provides a textbook case of an unsuccessful protection effort that nonetheless built up a massive structure.

Thus, the sheer size of the government varied directly with the effort devoted to extraction, state making, protection, and, especially, war making but inversely with the commercialization of the economy and the extent of the resource base. What is more, the relative bulk of different features of the government varied with the cost/resource ratios of extraction, state making, protection, and war making. In Spain we see hypertrophy of Court and courts as the outcome of centuries of effort at subduing internal enemies, whereas in Holland we are amazed to see how small a fiscal apparatus grows up with high taxes within a rich, commercialized economy.

Clearly, war making, extraction, state making, and protection were interdependent. Speaking very, very generally, the classic European state-making experience followed this causal pattern:

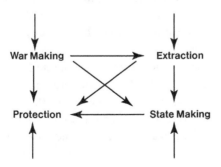

In an idealized sequence, a great lord made war so effectively as to become dominant in a substantial territory, but that war making led to increased extraction of the means of war—men, arms, food, lodging, transportation, supplies, and/or the money to buy them—from the population within that territory. The building up of war-making capacity likewise increased the capacity to extract. The very activity of extraction, if successful, entailed the elimination, neutralization, or cooptation of the great lord's local rivals; thus, it led to state making. As a by-product, it created organization in the form of tax-collection agencies, police forces, courts, exchequers, account keepers; thus it again led to state making. To a lesser extent, war making likewise led to state making through the expansion of military organization itself, as a standing army, war industries, supporting bureaucracies, and (rather later) schools grew up within the state apparatus. All of these structures checked potential rivals and opponents. In the course of making war, extracting resources, and building up the state apparatus, the managers of states formed alliances with specific social classes. The members of those classes loaned resources, provided technical services, or helped ensure the compliance of the rest of the population, all in return for a measure of protection against their own rivals and enemies. As a result of these multiple strategic choices, a distinctive state apparatus grew up within each major section of Europe.

How States Formed

This analysis, if correct, has two strong implications for the development of national states. First, popular resistance to war making and state making made a difference. When ordinary people resisted vigorously, authorities made concessions: guarantees of rights, representative institutions, courts of appeal. Those concessions, in their turn, constrained the later paths of war making and state making. To be sure, alliances with fragments of the ruling class greatly increased the effects of popular action; the broad mobilization of gentry against Charles I helped give the English Revolution of 1640 a far greater impact on political institutions than did any of the multiple rebellions during the Tudor era.

Second, the relative balance among war making, protection, extraction, and state making significantly affected the organization of the states that emerged from the four activities. To the extent that war making went on with relatively little extraction, protection, and state making, for example, military forces ended up playing a larger and more autonomous part in national politics. Spain is perhaps the best European example. To the extent that protection, as in Venice or Holland, prevailed over war making, extraction, and state making, oligarchies of the protected classes tended to dominate subsequent national politics. From the relative predominance of state making sprang the disproportionate elaboration of policing and surveillance; the Papal States illustrate that extreme. Before the twentieth century ... any state that failed to put considerable effort into war making was likely to disappear. As the twentieth century wore on, however, it became increasingly common for one state to lend, give, or sell war-making means to another; in those cases, the recipient state could put a disproportionate effort into extraction, protection, and/or state making and yet survive.

This simplified model, however, neglects the external relations that shaped every national state. Early in the process, the distinction between "internal" and "external" remained as unclear as the distinction between state power and the power accruing to lords allied with the state. Later, three interlocking influences connected any given national state to the European network of states. First, there were the flows of resources in the form of loans and supplies, especially loans and supplies devoted to war making. Second, there was the competition among states for hegemony in disputed territories, which stimulated war making and temporarily erased the distinctions among war making, state making, and extraction. Third, there was the intermittent creation of coalitions of states that temporarily combined their efforts to force a given state into a certain form and position within the international network. The war-making coalition is one example, but the peace-making coalition played an even more crucial part: From 1648, if not before, at the ends of wars all effective European states coalesced temporarily to bargain over the boundaries and rulers of the recent belligerents. From that point on, periods of major reorganization of the European state system came in spurts, at the settlement of widespread wars. From each large war, in general, emerged fewer national states than had entered it.

War as International Relations

Early in the process, external and internal rivals overlapped to a large degree. Only the establishment of large perimeters of control within which great lords had checked their rivals sharpened the line between internal and external.

If we allow that fragile distinction between "internal" and "external" state-making processes, then we might schematize the history of European state making as three stages: (*a*) The differential success of some power holders in "external" struggles establishes the difference between an "internal" and an "external" arena for the deployment of force; (b) "external" competition generates "internal" state making; (c) "external" compacts among states influence the form and locus of particular states ever more powerfully. In this perspective, state-certifying organizations such as the League of Nations and the United Nations simply extended the European-based process to the world as a whole. Whether forced or voluntary, bloody or peaceful, decolonization simply completed that process by which existing states leagued to create new ones.

The extension of the Europe-based state-making process to the rest of the world, however, did not result in the creation of states in the strict European image. Broadly speaking, internal struggles such as the checking of great regional lords and the imposition of taxation on peasant villages produced important organizational features of European states: the relative subordination of military power to civilian control, the extensive bureaucracy of fiscal surveillance, the representation of wronged interests via petition and parliament. On the whole, states elsewhere developed differently. The most telling feature of that difference appears in military organization. European states built up their military apparatuses through sustained struggles with their subject populations and by means of selective extension of protection to different classes within those populations. The agreements on protection constrained the rulers themselves, making them vulnerable to courts, to assemblies, to withdrawals of credit, services, and expertise.

To a larger degree, states that have come into being recently through decolonization or through reallocations of territory by dominant states have acquired their military organization from outside, without the same internal forging of mutual constraints between rulers and ruled. To the extent that outside states continue to supply military goods and expertise in return for commodities, military alliance or both, the new states harbor powerful, unconstrained organizations that easily overshadow all other organization within their territories. To the extent that outside states guarantee their boundaries, the managers of those military organizations exercise extraordinary power within them. The advantages of military power become enormous, the incentives to seize power over the state as a whole by means of that advantage very strong. Despite the great place that war making occupied in the making of European states, the old national states of Europe almost never experienced the great disproportion between military organization and all other forms of organization that seems the fate of client states throughout the contemporary world. A century ago, Europeans might have congratulated themselves on the spread of civil government throughout the world. In our own time, the analogy between war making and state making, on the one hand, and organized crime, on the other, is becoming tragically apt.

References

Ames, Edward, and Richard T. Rapp. 1977. "The Birth and Death of Taxes: A Hypothesis." *Journal of Economic History* 37: 161–78.

Braudel, Fernand. 1966. *La Méditerranée et le monde méditerranéen à l'époque de Philippe II.* 2d ed. 2 vols. Paris: Armand Colin.

———— 1979. *Civilisation materielle, économie, et capitalisme, XVe–XVIIIe siècle.* 3 vols. Paris: Armand Colin.

Elton, G. R. 1975. "Taxation for War and Peace in Early-Tudor England." In *War and Economic Development: Essays in Memory of David Joslin,* edited by J. M. Winter. Cambridge: Cambridge University Press.

Hamilton, Earl J. 1950. "Origin and Growth of the National Debt in France and England." In *Studi in onore di Gino Luzzato,* vol. 2. Milan: Giuffre.

Mathias, Peter. 1979. "Taxation and Industrialization in Britain, 1700–1870." In *The Transformation of England: Essays in the Economic and Social History of England in the Eighteenth Century,* edited by Peter Mathias. New York: Oxford University Press.

Coercion, Capital, and European States, A.D. 990–1990

8

Charles Tilly

How Wars Began

A system wrought by war shaped the conditions under which its members went to war. The conditions under which states went to war changed significantly—and more than once—during the long period we are examining. With significant modulations as a function of a state's chief rivals, the character of its dominant classes, and the sort of protective activity undertaken on its dominant classes' behalf, conditions changed as a function of a now-familiar constant logic that continued to operate under shifting circumstances: rulers normally tried to establish both a secure area within which they could enjoy the returns from coercion and a fortified buffer zone to protect the secure area. When the effort worked well, the buffer zone became a secure area, which encouraged the wielder of coercion to acquire a new buffer zone surrounding the old. So long as adjacent powers were pursuing the same logic, war resulted. In Europe, once the Roman Empire collapsed, thousands of warlords engaged in the same exercise. Hence unceasing and widespread, if chiefly regional, warfare. The later enlargement of state territories, the substitution of compact national states for multiple territories and the securing of borders through international agreements greatly reduced the length of vulnerable borders, but did not eliminate the war-promoting logic.

Other conditions, however, altered drastically. During the era of *patrimonialism* (up to 1400 in much of Europe), the groups that controlled substantial coercive means were typically either kin groups, neighbors, sworn

communities of warriors, or combinations of the three. Ducal lineages exemplify the first, crusading orders the second, and feudal aristocracies their
combination. Groups that controlled substantial coercive means generally
sought to maximize the tribute they could extract from surrounding populations, by force if necessary, and to assure the future availability of tribute for
their offspring and followers. By intermarrying, creating a noble caste, and
(encouraged by a Catholic church that benefited from donations of land and
revenues) establishing widely shared rules of inheritance, the ruling classes
laid the groundwork for dynastic politics in which marriages cemented alliances among states and successions became the object of international attention. At the same time peasant communities, urban militias, groups of
brigands, and other groups having no claims to state authority often warred
on their own. As a result, wars tended to occur when a powerholder showed
signs of weakness vis-à-vis his neighbor, when a disputable succession occurred, and when a new conqueror heaved onto the scene.

For the first half of our millennium, indeed, it is hardly worth asking
when states warred, since most states were warring most of the time. True,
massed armies drew chiefly on militias and feudal levies, which means
that campaigns ordinarily went on during only a few months of each year.
When an international war began, nevertheless, it usually ran for many
campaigns....

From the sixteenth century onward, the situation changed fundamentally. Consolidation of the state system, segregation of military from civilian
life, and disarmament of the civilian population sharpened the distinction
between war and peace. War became more intense and destructive, more
continuous once it began, but a much rarer event. The twentieth century, in
that respect, merely caps a long-term trend.

In the time of *brokerage* (roughly 1400 to 1700 in important parts of the
continent), dynastic ambitions still dominated state policy, but the bulk of
the state apparatus and the scale of war efforts meant that the interests of
the major classes supporting the state seriously limited the possibilities for
war; only with their consent and collaboration could monarchs assemble
the means to fight. The interests of landlords weighed heavily in coercion-
intensive states, the interests of capitalists in capital-intensive states.

... The dominant classes' commercial opportunities and threats became
more frequently occasions for war, states whose economic bases were expanding became much more able to seize opportunities and head off threats,
alliances among states entered the definitions of those opportunities and
threats, such alliances frequently formed to contain the expansion of the currently most powerful state, expanding states fought more often to enlarge

their contiguous territories rather than to accrete new tribute-paying units regardless of their location, and large-scale rebellions incited by rulers' attempts to extract the means of war or to impose a national religion provided more frequent opportunities for intervention by neighboring states. Meanwhile the gradual disarmament of the civilian population reduced the involvement of non-governmental groups as combatants—but not, alas, as victims—in wars. To some extent, the defense of coreligionists displaced dynastic inheritance as the ground of intervention by one state in the affairs of another.

As European states moved into the phase of *nationalization* (especially between 1700 and 1850, with wide variation from one kind of state to another), dynasties lost much of their ability to make war on their own behalf, and something we vaguely call "national interest" came to dominate states' involvement or non-involvement in wars. National interest synthesized the interests of the dominant classes, but compounded them with a much stronger drive to control contiguous territories and populations within Europe, as well as a fiercer competition for land outside of Europe.

Under nationalization, three critical changes affected the conditions for war: the current condition of the entire state system—notably the extent to which a balance of power currently obtained—began to make a major difference in the likelihood and location of war (Levy 1989); increasingly, pairs of states that were approaching equality of power went to war, especially if they occupied adjacent territories (Organski and Kugler 1980, Moul 1988, Houweling and Siccama 1988); total (rather than per capita) national income began limiting the military capacity of states as never before, with the result that large commercial and industrial states began to prevail within the state system. The era of war on the basis of rational expectations of gain and rational minimization of loss came upon Europe and its extensions.... As grounds for intervention, common nationality displaced both dynastic inheritance and shared religion.

During the subsequent period of *specialization*, the conditions for war altered relatively little, except that competition for empire ... played a larger part than ever. After 1945, the standoff between the Soviet Union and the United States almost eliminated war among European states within Europe, but made the points of contact among Soviet, American, and Chinese power outside of Europe critical locations for the pursuit of national interest.

With the nationalization and specialization of armed force, international war developed a reciprocal relationship to revolution, rebellion, and civil war. During the centuries in which dynasties usually controlled states, a weakening in the ruling kin group—for example, the death of a king with an infant heir or none at all—signaled to rivals outside the state an opportunity to attack. When rebellion occurred first, it invited outsiders to intervene on behalf of the challengers. As religious divisions became fundamental matters of state (which means especially between 1520 and 1650), the incentives to intervene became even more compelling. Both the effort of a ruler to extract greatly increased means of war from a reluctant population and the weakening of a state through losses in war sometimes incited rebellions and civil wars. If the rebel coalition won its battle with the rulers, displaced them, and undertook a social transformation, a full-scale revolution resulted.

All of Europe's great revolutions, and many of its lesser ones, began with the strains imposed by war. The English Revolution began with the efforts of Charles I to bypass Parliament in acquiring revenues for war on the continent and in Scotland and Ireland. The debt accumulated by the French monarchy during the Seven Years' War and the War of American Independence precipitated the struggles of the French Revolution. Russian losses in World War I discredited tsarist rule, encouraged military defections, and made the state's vulnerability patent; the revolutions of 1917 followed.

State formation also affected the rhythms and character of popular collective action short of revolution. During the phases of brokerage and nationalization, episodic but massively increasing demands for money and men repeatedly stimulated resistance at the level of the village or the region. Local people ran out the tax collector, attacked the house of the tax farmer, hid their young men from recruiters, petitioned the king for relief, asked patrons to intercede for them, and fought efforts to inventory their wealth. They aimed especially at local people who were linked to the state, either as state officials or as agents of indirect rule. With the later stages of nationalization and the movement to specialization, popular collective action itself nationalized and became more autonomous; as the national state's policies and demands came to bear more and more directly on their fates, workers, peasants, and other ordinary people banded together to make claims on the state—claims for redress, certainly, but also claims for rights they had never previously enjoyed at a national scale (Tilly, Tilly, and Tilly 1975, Tilly 1986). The political party, the special-interest association, the national social movement, and all the rest of popular politics took shape. Thus war drove not only the state system and the formation of individual states, but also the distribution of power over the state. Even with the last few centuries' civilianization of Western governments, war has remained the defining activity of national states.

Soldiers and States in 1990

Political Misdevelopment

As recent colonies of various Western powers, a majority of newly independent states began their careers with formal organizations traced on Western lines and incorporating significant parts of the colonial apparatus. Western-educated state leaders sought self-consciously to install administrations, parliaments, parties, armies, and public services of Western inspiration. What is more, they said so; Third World leaders declared that they would modernize their countries, develop them politically. Major Western powers assisted them actively, lending experts, models, training programs, and funds. So long as Japan was reeling from its losses in World War II and China was consumed with its internal struggles, no other models were obviously available. The choices seemed to run from Soviet-type socialism to American-style capitalism, with no viable paths of state formation beyond either extreme.

... We have seen how widely the trajectories of European state formation varied as a function of the geography of coercion and capital, the organization of major powerholders, and pressure from other states. We have examined how a long series of unequal struggles among rulers, other powerholders, and ordinary people created specific state institutions and claims on the state. We have noticed how much the eventual organizational convergence of European states resulted from competition among them, both within Europe and in the rest of the world. We have witnessed the profound impact of war, and preparation for war, on other features of state structure. All these observations lead to the conclusions—vague but helpful—that Third World state formation should be distinctively different, and that the changed relations between coercion and capital should provide clues as to the nature of that difference.

In what ways should contemporary experience differ from that of the European past? After centuries of divergences among capital-intensive, coercion-intensive, and capitalized-coercion paths of state formation, European states began to converge a few centuries ago; war and mutual influence caused the convergence. Although shared colonial experience imposed common properties on many Third World states, however, no great homogenization has so far occurred among them. On the contrary. Any student of European state formation can hardly help noticing the variety of today's Third World states. Variety marks any category that includes both immense, ancient China and tiny, brand-new Vanuatu.... Not all the states of the Third World, furthermore, are "new" states, by any stretch of the imagination. China and Japan stand among the world's oldest continuously existing states, Siam/Thailand is centuries old, and most Latin American states acquired formal independence during the Napoleonic Wars....

Look more closely, however: exactly what is heterogeneous about Third World states? Not so much their organizational structures as relations between citizens and states. Formal organizational characteristics of the world's states have, in fact, converged dramatically over the last century or so; the adoption of one Western model or another has become a virtual prerequisite for recognition by prior members of the state system. The present 160-odd recognized states cover a much narrower organizational range than the 200-odd European states of 1500, which included city-states, city-empires, federations, kingdoms, territorial empires, and more. Except for relatively centralized federations and quite attenuated kingdoms, those once-abundant political forms have all but disappeared. After 1500, both the pressures of large-scale warmaking and the negotiations of large-scale peacemaking drove all European states toward a new organizational form: the national state. The drift from "internal" to "external" state formation which prevailed in Europe has continued into our own time, and imposed a common definition on states in very diverse parts of the world. Contemporary state structures, in the narrow sense, resemble each other in featuring courts, legislatures, central bureaucracies, field administrations, standing armies, specialized police forces, and a panoply of public services; even the differences among socialist, capitalist, and mixed economies fail to override these common properties.

Yet such formally similar organizations do not work at all in the same manner.... In the European experience, states took forms that mediated between the exigencies of external war and the claims of the subject population; to some degree, each state's organization adapted to local social and economic conditions. As existing national states sculptured newcomers in their own image, local adaptation occurred instead in relations between citizens and states. These days the difference between coercion-intensive, capital-intensive, and capitalized-coercion settings affects the formal structure of states much less than it used to, but affects relations between citizens and states even more. In that regard, the contemporary world remains extremely diverse.

Does the Third World exist? Certainly Latin American, Middle Eastern, and East Asian states differ greatly with respect both to internal organization and to position within the world system of states. The justification for beginning with such a crude, composite category rests on the fact that states in lower-income regions of the world have long endured under the formal control of Europe and its extensions, have commonly adopted European or American models of formal organization, find themselves caught in super-power struggles over which they can exert little control, and constitute an uneasy but recurrent pool for alliances with newcomers to the state system (Ayoob 1989). In extending to the non-European world, the state system did not simply remain the same; the entrance of scores of independent states from Asia, Africa, and Latin America transformed the system in ways that a comparison with previous European experience can illuminate.

We still have something to gain, then, from the comparison of contemporary Third World experience with that of national states for which a long record is already available. At a minimum, that comparison will help us take two useful steps: (1) to discard ideas about state formation that have already proven themselves faulty before wasting time applying them to contemporary experience; (2) to sharpen our sense of what is distinctive, and what familiar, in the processes of state formation, transformation, and deformation now occurring in the poorer parts of the world.

Reflecting on European experience, what might we expect to find happening in the contemporary world? Given the diversity of state formation within Europe, we have no reason to anticipate a single trajectory of change. But we might [...] improve considerably on the old notion that Third World states would somehow recapitulate the idealized experience of the most effective Western national states.

The Impact and Heritage of World War II

What, then, distinguishes state formation in the contemporary world from its counterparts in the past? Although twentieth-century war takes a deadlier toll than ever, war has changed significantly in character. Large-scale civil wars, often aided and abetted by great powers, have become much more common in the world since 1945 than they were in European experience. The threat of nuclear arms and other technical menaces has compounded the likely costs of a major war....

World War II transformed the state system and the states within it. As citizens of belligerent states, as inhabitants of battle zones, or both, most of the world's people felt the war's impact. The war broke all records for killing, for destruction of property, and for displacement of populations. By dropping atomic bombs on Hiroshima and Nagasaki, the United States introduced into warfare the first weapons in history with the potential to annihilate all humanity in a few days.

We can reasonably place the start of World War II in 1938 (when Japan and Russia began to fight while Germany annexed Poland and dismembered Czechoslovakia) or in 1939 (when Germany invaded Poland and then the rest of Czechoslovakia). In either case, Japan's surrender in 1945 marks a relatively neat end to the war. Perhaps fifteen million deaths in battle and another twenty-five million as a direct result of war made World War II by far the most destructive belligerency in human history. Powers sustaining at least a thousand battle deaths included Bulgaria, the United Kingdom, Australia, Canada, Ethiopia, Poland, USA, USSR, Belgium, Brazil, China, Yugoslavia, the Netherlands, Rumania, Italy, New Zealand, France, South Africa, Greece, Norway, Mongolia, Japan, Germany, Hungary, and Finland (Small and Singer 1982: 91). The war left Japan, important parts of China, and much of Europe devastated.

As the war ended, two states towered over all the rest: the USA and the USSR. The United States had suffered relatively light losses (408 thousand battle deaths as compared, for instance, with Germany's 3.5 million) during World War II but had mobilized enormous industrial capacity after a debilitating depression. It is not surprising that the United States, an industrial colossus grown even more muscular in war, seized a dominant position in the world system of states. The rise of the Soviet Union is the greater puzzle. The USSR had endured terrible privations in the war (7.5 million battle deaths, perhaps 20 million in total fatalities, and 60 percent of industrial capacity lost) but had built up a formidable state organization in the process (Rice 1988). No doubt that enhanced state capacity, and the extension of Soviet control to other eastern European states, helps account for the other pole of the bipolar world. Almost immediately the former allies turned to an enmity that blocked a general peace settlement for the first time in four centuries. As a result, losers of the war such as Japan and Germany long endured the victors' military occupation, and only slowly regained membership in the state system. In fact, the victors and the vanquished only settled the war piecemeal, in occupations, provisional international agreements, partial treaties, and *de facto* recognitions. The war's complexity and scale, plus its bipolar outcome, overwhelmed the capacity of the international system to produce the sort of general settlement that had ended major European wars since 1503.

The postwar process of state formation distinguished itself from its predecessors especially in the wholesale transformation of Western colonies into formally independent states. The situation favored European withdrawal: the USSR had no colonies in the major areas of European colonization, and the United States had few, while the European powers were preoccupied with recovery from the ravages of war. At a dizzying pace, dependencies demanded and won recognition as autonomous entities. In 1960 alone the Belgian Congo (now Zaïre), Benin, Cameroon, the Central African Republic, Chad, the Congo, Cyprus, Gabon, Côte d'Ivoire, Madagascar, Mali, Niger, Nigeria, Senegal, Somalia, Togo and Upper Volta (now Burkina Faso) all joined the United Nations shortly after receiving recognition as independent states.

At the same time the Soviet Union and, especially, the United States, extended the networks of their military bases, military assistance programs, and intelligence facilities throughout the world (Eden 1988). In East Asia, for example, the United States substituted its own military power for that of a demilitarized Japan, reorganized and ran the South Korean military, and subsidized China's KMT forces both in their losing mainland battles and in their retreat to control of Taiwan (Cumings 1988, Dower 1988, Levine 1988). Between 1945 and 1984, furthermore, the United States pumped $13 billion of military-economic aid into South Korea and another $5.6 billion into Taiwan, as compared with a total for all Africa of $6.89 billion and all Latin America of $14.8 billion (Cumings 1984: 24).

For the most part, European powers relinquished their overlordships with remarkably little travail. With the exception of the Algerian struggle for independence and the early stages of the Indochinese conflicts, the bitterest battles occurred where more than one group claimed the right to rule the new state, where a segment of the liberated population demanded its own state, and where the division among the claimants incited extensive great power intervention; China, Palestine, Malaya, Kenya, Cyprus, Aden, Borneo, Korea, Vietnam, the Philippines, Ruanda, Angola, and Mozambique provide the obvious examples. The United Nations undertook to register and manage the entry of new members into the international system of states.

The new entrants, on the average, were following coercion-intensive paths to statehood. The departing colonial powers left little accumulated capital behind them, but bequeathed to their successor states military forces drawn from and modeled on the repressive forces they had previously established to maintain their own local administrations. Relatively well equipped and trained armed forces then specialized in control of civilian populations and in combat against insurgents rather than interstate war. Once Europeans dismantled their own governmental apparatus, the armed forces, the churches, and Western corporations were frequently the most effective organizations operating in the state's territory. The armed forces, furthermore, had some distinctive characteristics: their senior ranks filled rapidly with men who had previously occupied subordinate positions in colonial armies. Often, continuing a pattern of recruitment established by colonial powers, they drew disproportionately on one linguistic, religious, and/or regional population, and therefore became the instrument or the site of sharp ethnic rivalries.

Except where charismatic national leaders deliberately held them in check, Third World armies commonly resisted civilian control. Senior officers frequently felt, and said, that they knew better than mere politicians what the country's destiny required, and how to maintain order on the way to fulfilling that destiny. To the extent that their states generated revenues by selling commodities on the international market, bought arms overseas, and received military aid from great powers, furthermore, the armed forces enjoyed insulation from reliance on taxation and conscription authorized by civilian governments.

How far the military of exporting countries were able to maintain autonomy, however, depended on the alliances they formed (or failed to form) with major elements of the ruling class, and on the success of the export program. In Bolivia, the encapsulation of tin tycoons, who lived handsomely on export income and established few strong ties within the country, made them vulnerable to military seizure of state power and of tin revenues (Gallo 1985).

Civil wars that occurred after 1945 sometimes arose from general struggles among classes for state power. More often they sprang from the claims of particular religious, linguistic, and territorial groups for autonomy or for control of an existing state. In this limited sense, nationalism has become more salient in wars as the world as a whole has settled into a complete map of stable, mutually-exclusive state territories; the powerholders of excluded nationalities see their chances slipping away from them. At the same time, great powers have intervened increasingly in civil wars, seeking alignment and cooperation of those who control the state by assuring that the sympathetic faction wins....

With a few significant exceptions, military conquest across borders has ended, states have ceased fighting each other over disputed territory, and border forces have shifted their efforts from defense against direct attack toward control of infiltration. Armies (and, for that matter, navies and air forces) concentrate increasingly on repression of civilian populations, combat of insurgents, and seizures of power. As a consequence, governments become more unstable as their borders become more secure. Because those who control states define whole populations as their enemies, wars generate refugees at a huge rate (conventional estimates set the number of refugees in the world at 8 million toward 1970 and 10.5 million toward 1980: Zolberg 1981: 21).

Today's Military in Historical Perspective

Starting in the sixteenth century and ending only very recently, Western states incorporated the rest of the world into their system through colonization, elaboration of commercial ties, and direct negotiation. Most recent entrants joined the system as independent actors through decolonization, and therefore arrived with administrative structures, fiscal systems, and armed forces designed on Western lines; titles, perquisites, and uniforms of the former colonies reflect those national influences. Yet reproducing a table of organization provides no guarantee that the new state will behave like the old. Nowhere is that clearer than in the behavior of the Third World's military. The armies of poor countries resemble those of rich countries in many regards. But on the whole they intervene in domestic political life far more directly and frequently, and with more obviously damaging consequences for rights of citizens. Why should that be?

Think back to the central paradox of European state formation: that the pursuit of war and military capacity, after having created national states as a sort of by-product, led to a civilianization of government and domestic politics. That happened, I have argued, for five main reasons: because the effort to build and sustain military forces led agents of states to build bulky extractive apparatuses staffed by civilians, and those extractive apparatuses came to contain and constrain the military forces; because agents of states bargained with civilian groups that controlled the resources required for effective warmaking, and in bargaining gave the civilian groups enforceable claims on the state that further constrained the military; because the expansion of state capacity in wartime gave those states that had not suffered great losses in war expanded capacity at the ends of wars, and agents of those states took advantage of the situation by taking on new activities, or continuing activities they had started as emergency measures; because participants in the war effort, including military personnel, acquired claims on the state that they deferred during the war in response to repression or mutual consent but which they reactivated at demobilization; and finally because wartime borrowing led to great increases in national debts, which in turn generated service bureaucracies and encouraged greater state intervention in national economies.

In a cartoon history of Europe, the story would appear in four panels. In the first panel, the king wears armor and carries a sword, recruiting and commanding his own army and navy, which maintain personal loyalty to his service. In the second, the king bears glorified military garb, but contracts with a *condottiere* for the hire of mercenaries to fight his battles. In the third panel, the king, fitted out in a grand costume utterly unsuitable for fighting wars, consults with generals and ministers of war who find their places in a complex, civilian-dominated structure. In the last scene we see a king (who may now be a president or prime minister in disguise) sporting a business suit and negotiating not only with his staff but also with duly constituted representatives of major civilian interests and of the population at large. (The four panels bear the familiar subtitles Patrimonialism, Brokerage, Nationalization, and Specialization.) To be sure, the comic-book version of civilianization describes different national experiences with varying verisimilitude; it fits German experience better than Dutch or Russian. But it will do as a schematic summary of civilianization in European states.

Another general feature of European state formation deserves our attention. Relations with other states played a significant part in the formation of any particular state, if only because wars and war settlements significantly affected the state's structure and boundaries. Nevertheless, the organizational structures of the first national states to form took shape mainly as a consequence of struggles between would-be rulers and the people they were trying to rule. As the European state system solidified, however, whole sets of states began to decide the outcomes of wars, and therefore the organizational structures of states that emerged from the wars. Thus Napoleon's forces drastically reorganized states as they conquered, and the Congress of Vienna redrew the map to include a previously nonexistent kingdom of the Netherlands plus a greatly-reshaped Prussia, Sardinia, Bavaria, Baden, and Austria. Europe moved from relatively "internal" to relatively "external" processes of state formation. That shift toward the external continued into the twentieth century. Only a glance at twentieth-century processes of state formation reveals that they are triply external: many new national states formed as colonial possessions of other states, especially European states; many built their governing institutions under the influence of another, much greater, power; and concerts of nations—the United Nations being their latest embodiment—have ratified and to some extent sustained their existence as separate members of the international state system. One consequence is a decreasing flexibility of state boundaries in the twentieth century. Except as a part of a general peace settlement negotiated by many states, it becomes decreasingly likely that conquest will lead to a major redrawing of any state's perimeter. These days Guatemala claims all of Belize and Venezuela claims some of Guyana, but other states of the Americas will not tolerate a territorial grab in either case. Although wars, guerrilla and otherwise, continue to occur quite frequently, many states face no serious external military threat. That means many armies have little prospect of going to war. They specialize in internal control.

Third World militaries have drawn specifically on European or American models, aid, and training to a far larger degree than European states intervened in the formation of each other's armies. In Latin America, for example, before World War II France and Germany trained many of the officers of Argentina, Bolivia, Brazil, Chile, and Peru. After the war, the United States took over the task (Nunn 1971). This external intervention gave Latin American militaries exceptional maneuverability vis-à-vis their potential rivals and chosen enemies. In Europe, the external imposition of state forms occurred without obvious impact on the stability of regimes. Most of the states formed out of the ruins of the Ottoman and Austro-Hungarian empires had, it is true, unsteadier holds on stable democracy than their northern neighbors, and one might argue a connection between late national state formation and vulnerability to fascism in Germany and Italy. But in northern Europe, the late independence of Finland, Norway, and the Baltic republics did not stop them from establishing relatively durable regimes (see Alapuro 1988).

In the world since 1945, however, the relationship between external imposition and instability seems to have increased. Where the ability of rulers to draw revenues from commodity exports or from great-power military aid has allowed them to bypass bargaining with their subject populations, large state edifices have grown up in the absence of significant consent or support from citizens. Lacking strong ties between particular state institutions and major social classes within the population, those states have become more vulnerable to forcible seizures of power and abrupt changes in the form of government.

How Did the Military Gain Power?

Libya followed yet another path to military rule (Anderson 1986: 251–69). Italian imperialism made a single territory of hostile and distinctly different Tripolitania and Cyrenaica. Sanusi leader Idris, who became king at independence in 1951, drew support chiefly from Cyrenaica; his cooperation in the Allied effort to oust Italy from North Africa gave him a decisive political advantage over his Tripolitanian rivals. No well-defined national state emerged in independent Libya. Instead, overlapping extended families governed through patronage. Oil revenues enriched them, allowed the construction of a measure of infrastructure, and permitted the king and his satraps to rule without building a substantial central bureaucracy. The small Royal Libyan Army formed from units that had fought with the British in World War II, but were overshadowed by provincial security forces drawn from tribal populations and by the presence of American and British military bases. Despite the Anglo-American presence, captain Mu'ammar al-Qaddafi led a successful coup d'état in 1969. Indeed, control over oil revenues made it possible for Qaddafi to expel the British and Americans, root out most of the old rulers, Islamize and Arabize the state, undertake a program of assistance to nascent revolutionary regimes elsewhere, and yet to continue his predecessor's avoidance of bulky central structure. The transformed state gingerly began a courtship with the Soviet Union and a campaign of opposition to American power. A kind of nationalism, then, bolstered a fragile state and justified military rule.

In South Korea, an American occupation directly shaped the postwar state. In Brazil, changing American orientations toward Latin American militaries conditioned political shifts but by no means governed the history of military power. Libya moved to a military regime despite an American military presence. Conditions and consequences of military power obviously vary significantly from one part of the Third World to another. Great power competition and intervention play no more than supporting parts in any particular coup and in the maintenance of any particular military regime. But alterations in relations of Third World states to great powers and to each other seem to have contributed importantly to changes in the overall rhythms of military control in the world as a whole. To that extent, the state system as such has made a difference.

If great power confrontation and intervention in national militaries has the influence this analysis gives it, one path toward civilianization seems clear. It has two branches: either a reduction in the great power competition to build up the military strength of the Third World states or an insulation of the target states from that competition. It involves the promotion of bargaining between the state's civilian institutions and the bulk of its citizens. The creation of regular systems of taxation, equitably administered and responsive to the citizenry, would probably speed the process. So would the opening of viable career alternatives to military service....

References

Alapuro, Risto. 1988. *State and Revolution in Finland*. Berkeley, California: University of California Press.

Anderson, Lisa. 1986. *The State and Social Transformation in Tunisia and Libya, 1830–1980*. Princeton, New Jersey: Princeton University Press.

Ayoob, Mohammed. 1989. "The Third World in the System of States: Acute Schizophrenia or Growing Pains?" *International Studies Quarterly* 33: 67–79.

Cumings, Bruce. 1984. "The Origins and Development of the Northeast Asian Political Economy: Industrial Sectors, Product Cycle, and Political Consequences," *International Organization* 38: 1–40.

——— 1988. "Korea and the War Settlement in Northeast Asia," Working Paper 65, Center for Studies of Social Change, New School for Social Research.

Dower, John W. 1988. "Japan: Legacies of a Lost War," Working Paper 66, Center for Studies of Social Change, New School for Social Research.

Eden, Lynn. 1988. "World War II and American Politics," Working Paper 68, Center for Studies of Social Change, New School for Social Research.

Gallo, Carmenza. 1985. "The State in an Enclave Economy: Political Instability in Bolivia from 1900 to 1950," Unpublished doctoral dissertation in sociology, Boston University.

Houweling, Henk and Jan G. Siccama. 1988. "Power Transitions as a Cause of War," *Journal of Conflict Resolution* 32: 87–102.

Levine, Steven. 1988. "War Settlement and State Structure: The Case of China and the Termination of World War II," Working Paper 62, *Center for Studies of Social Change*, New School for Social Research.

Levy, Jack. 1989. "The Causes of War: A Review of Theories and Evidence," in Philip E. Tetlock *et al.*, eds., *Behavior, Society, and Nuclear War*. New York: Oxford University Press.

Moul, William Brian. 1988. "Balances of Power and the Escalation to War of Serious Disputes among the European Great Powers, 1815–1939: Some Evidence," *American Journal of Political Science* 32: 241–75.

Nunn, Frederick M. 1971. "The Latin American Military Establishment: Some Thoughts on the Origins of its Socio-Political Role and an Illustrative Bibliographical Essay," *The Americas* 28: 135–51.

Organski, A.F.K., and Jacek Kugler. 1980. *The War Ledger*. Chicago, IL: University of Chicago Press.

Rice, Condoleezza. 1988. "The Impact of World War II on Soviet State and Society," Working Paper 69, Center for Studies of Social Change, New School for Social Research.

Small, Melvin and J. David Singer. 1982. *Resort to Arms. International and Civil Wars, 1816–1980*. Beverly Hills, CA: Sage.

Tilly, Charles. 1986. *The Contentious French*. Cambridge: Belknap.

Tilly, Charles, Louise A. Tilly and Richard Tilly. 1975. *The Rebellious Century, 1830–1930*. Cambridge: Harvard University Press.

Zolberg, Aristide. 1981. "International Migrations in Political Perspective," in Mary M. Kritz, Charles B. Keely, and Silvano M. Tomasi, eds., *Global Trends in Migration. Theory and Research on International Population Movements*. Staten Island, New York: Center for Migration Studies.

Democracy

Democracy Is a Lake   9

Charles Tilly

Once theorists thought vibrant, viable democracy emerged from centuries of struggle or maturation. In such formulations as Barrington Moore's, class and politics interacted over hundreds of years to create democracy or its alternatives (Moore, 1966). Disillusioned by the failure of various revolutionary programs during the previous two decades, bemused by the cold war's ending, and enticed by the opportunity to prescribe programs of political change for Eastern Europe, Latin America, or Africa, recent theorists of democracy have moved away from the populism and revolutionism of the 1960s toward a remarkable elitism: suppositions that the masses have little to do with the making of democracy, that (however regrettably) presidents, priests, political patrons, planters, police chiefs, paratroop commanders, and plutocrats perform the essential operations producing durable democratic institutions.

Not all the change resulted from disillusion. Impressed by the rapid displacement of authoritarian regimes set in place by Franco, Salazar, or Brazilian generals, and pressed to formulate futures for Eastern Europe, Latin America, and Africa, recent theorists have accelerated the tempo so that at times the transition to democracy looks almost instantaneous: put the pact in gear and go. After decades of bottom-up, deterministic, long-term theories, we now see top-down models, instrumental and constructivist approaches to democratization, and short-run analyses beginning to prevail. Top-down models specify what rulers and leaders must do to promote democracy, instrumental ideas make democratization seem a matter of social engineering (whoever serves as engineer), constructivist approaches assert that democracy depends on certain kinds of social beliefs, and short-run analyses say how politics move toward democracy today, this month, or this year rather than at a scale of centuries.

Timescale matters both theoretically and practically.

People actually *construct* democracy, however, in two different senses of the word. First, they create a set of political arrangements the effects of which are democratic, however we define democracy. This sense of *construct* has the misleading connotation of blueprints and carpenters, when over the last few hundred years, the actual formation and deformation of democratic regimes has more often resembled the erratic evolution of a whole city than the purposeful building of a single mansion. Still, the first sense draws our attention to the ways that human agency, however consciously, produces and destroys the objective conditions for democracy.

The second sense of *construction* refers to the shared understandings, the culture, that people create for themselves. Extreme versions of linguistic skepticism reduce all social reality to construction in this sense, on an argument that conflates epistemology and ontology: if social existence can only be known through language, it does not exist independently of language. Short of that extreme, however, even hard-nosed realists recognize that people do construct shared understandings concerning their political arrangements. Indeed, shared understandings affect how those arrangements work. In the case of democracy, as Robert Dahl points out repeatedly, much depends on the readiness of political actors who lose in the current round of struggle to believe that they will get another reasonably fair chance to win later on. Adam Przeworski makes just such an institutionalization of uncertainty the hallmark of democracy (1986, 1989). That shared belief is a social product.

More generally, ideas of justice, of due process, of official propriety, of efficiency, of collective interest, of property, of rights, and of history pervade every set of political arrangements, including those of democracy. No system of parliamentary democracy, for example, can survive the generalization of a belief (however false) that its elections are fraudulent and its officials powerless. The real questions are: (1) how such beliefs and their democracy-sustaining antitheses form, wax, or wane; (2) exactly what relation they bear to the political system's operation, routine or otherwise.

In short, an emphasis on the social construction of democracy does not resolve, theoretically or empirically, the choice among timescales for its analysis.

Meanwhile, a historical puzzle arises. Broad-based democracy on a large scale first took shape in Western Europe. In the past, durable democratic institutions emerged out of repeated, long-term struggles in which workers, peasants, and other ordinary people were much involved, even where the crucial maneuvers involved an elite's conspiring in small concessions to avoid large ones. Revolutions, rebellions, and mass mobilizations made a significant difference to the extent of democracy in one country or another....

To Conceptualize Democracies

... In order to get to democracy, we must work our way down a chain including state, polity, rights, and citizenship. Here is the chain:

State: an organization controlling the principal concentrated means of coercion within a delimited territory and exercising priority in some respects over all other organizations within the same territory.
Polity: the set of relations among agents of the state and all major political actors within the delimited territory.
Rights: enforceable claims, the reciprocal of *obligations*.
Citizenship: rights and mutual obligations binding state agents and a category of persons defined exclusively by their legal attachment to the same state.

With that conceptual chain in place, we can begin hauling up an idea of democracy as a particular form of citizenship. Democracy combines *broad and relatively equal citizenship with (a) binding consultation of citizens in regard to state personnel and policies as well as (b) protection of citizens from arbitrary state action.*

This definition stands between those emphasizing ideal outcomes and those stipulating institutional arrangements. Robert Dahl speaks of "a political system in which the members regard one another as political equals, are collectively sovereign, and possess all the capacities, resources, and institutions they need in order to govern themselves" (Dahl, 1991:1). As Dahl himself stresses, such a definition is not only problematic in detail (do children, convicts, and students from other countries, for instance, all qualify as "members"?), but also empirically empty (no large state has ever met its requirements). Yet it states a standard against which we can array real political arrangements.

Rueschemeyer, Stephens, and Stephens, on the other hand, offer an eminently institutional definition of democracy:

It entails, first, regular, free and fair elections of representatives with universal and equal suffrage, second, responsibility of the state apparatus to the elected parliament (possibly complemented by direct election of the head of the executive), and third, the freedoms of expression and association as well as the protection of individual rights against arbitrary state action.

(Rueschemeyer, Stephens, and Stephens, 1992: 43)

For some questions (for example, what political arrangements are worth sacrificing for?), the ideal definition serves best, while for others (for example, what sort of government should we now organize in our new country?), the institutional definition makes much more sense. My definition lies between the two.

An intermediate definition, on the one hand, makes problematic the relationship between institutions and their consequences or correlates, whereas it facilitates, on the other hand, the linking of theories of democratization with theories of nationalism, citizenship, revolution, political conflict, and change in state structure. I claim that different institutional arrangements—town meetings in some settings, secret ballots for party-nominated candidates in others, and so on—promote democracy within different sorts of social structure, hence that strictly institutional criteria of democracy yield misleading conclusions on a large scale. To repeat, democracy consists of *broad and relatively equal citizenship with (a) binding consultation of citizens in regard to state personnel and policies as well as (b) protection of citizens from arbitrary state action.*

Notice what this conception does *not* do. It does not make general equality of means or opportunity a criterion of democracy; equality only refers to claims on and from the state in a person's capacity as citizen. As much as it invites a search for institutions guaranteeing democratic outcomes, it does not stipulate any particular political institutions as defining features of democracy. It ignores the unequal treatment of noncitizens, disregarding any disabilities they suffer with respect to binding consultation and protection from arbitrary state action. It certainly does not require intelligent communication, patriotism, legitimacy, happiness, or prosperity. It leaves theoretically and empirically open the relationship of democracy to general economic equality, care for noncitizens, social justice, communication, and innumerable other features that people sometimes consider inseparable from democracy. It excludes many connotations of the word *democracy* on the ground that including them all would bar any effective theoretical or empirical investigation of the subject.

The proposed conception of democracy *does,* on the other hand, declare that a polity is undemocratic to the degree that citizens' political rights and obligations vary by gender, race, religion, national origin, wealth, or any other general set of categories, that it is likewise undemocratic to the extent that large numbers of people subject to the state's jurisdiction lack access to citizenship. It makes binding consultation and protection from arbitrary state action, furthermore, matters of degree—recognizing, for example, that in large democratic states, the sheer existence of parliaments limits consultation and state agents sometimes commit injustices. Even breadth and equality, after all, have their limits; when Paul Peterson (1992) proposes "that all citizens, even our youngest, should cast votes or have their votes cast for them by their parents or guardians," even he must concede that the infants his proposal would enfranchise generally lack the reasoned political self-interest his argument requires; hence the extra votes his scheme entrusts to parents and guardians. The definition, in short, simply allows us to designate polities as democratic *insofar* as they embody broad, equal citizenship that gives its beneficiaries binding consultation and protection from arbitrary state action.

In European experience, at least, citizenship in the sense of rights and mutual obligations binding state agents and a category of persons defined by their legal attachment to the same state only became a widespread phenomenon during the nineteenth century. Before then, small units such as the city-states of the Low Countries, the Rhineland, and Italy had sometimes sustained participates of the rich and powerful; with respect to the state, these narrow segments of the total population had enjoyed relative equality, binding consultation, and protection from arbitrary action. But large states all ruled indirectly until the eighteenth or nineteenth century; they relied for troops, revenues, and compliance with state directives chiefly on regional power holders who maintained substantial autonomy and dealt with populations having distinctive traditions, cultures, and rights.

In these circumstances, neither citizenship nor democracy existed at a national scale in any strong sense of the words. At most, nobles and priests constituted a semicitizenry in countries such as England (but not Great Britain or, even less, the British Isles) where a skeletal administrative structure and a unitary state church intertwined. The greatest exception appeared in Sweden, where the articulation of a domestically recruited army, a state church, and direct peasant representation vis-à-vis the Crown produced quasi citizenship as early as the seventeenth century (Artéus, Olsson, and Stromberg-Back 1981; Böhme, 1983; Lindegren 1985; Nilsson 1988). Given its great inequality and its limits to binding consultation, however, Sweden's polity remained far from democracy until the twentieth century. Extensive democracy awaited strong pressure from organized workers allied with fragments of the bourgeoisie and the popular movements that proliferated during the nineteenth century (Alestalo and Kuhnle 1984; Hemes 1988; Lundqvist 1977; Öhngren 1974).

For centuries, to be sure, many Europeans had exercised something like citizenship and even democracy in smaller units such as villages and municipalities. There, heads of propertied households commonly governed collectively or at least shared power with priests and nobles; they frequently led burgher militias as well. In very small states, the government of the capital city thereby established a narrow quasi citizenship at a national scale. With its cantonal structure, Switzerland federated a set of partial democracies in this style beginning with the sixteenth century (Brady 1985). In such countries as the Dutch Republic, eighteenth-century revolutionary movements commonly took that municipal experience as a model for political transformation (Prak 1991; Te Brake 1989, 1990).

After the middle of the eighteenth century, and especially during the nineteenth, the abandonment of intermittent mercenary armies in favor of large standing armies drawn from, and supported by, national populations engaged rulers in vast struggles with their reluctant subjects. The settlements of those struggles, in their turn, created the rudiments of citizenship. In large states, the French Revolution and the wars of 1792–1815 marked the crucial break. The revolutionary and conquering French provided a model of citizenship, a stimulus to military mobilization, and—in their areas of conquest—a compulsion to reorganize on the French model. Thus citizenship went from being rare and chiefly local in Europe to being a predominant model of political organization.

With citizenship, limited democracy did not by any means become a necessity; plenty of European states developed political arrangements more closely approximating oligarchy or paternalism with some trappings of representation. Democracy did, however, become an option and a persistent program for reformers and revolutionaries. All over Europe, they began to demand equal, broad citizenship with binding consultation and protection for citizens from arbitrary state action. They began to demand democracy. Some even had their way.

European experience suggests strong hypotheses concerning the social bases of democracy's components:

1 *Protection from arbitrary state action* depends on (a) subordination of the military to civilian control, (b) class coalitions in which old power holders ally with relatively powerless but large segments of the population (for example, bourgeois and workers), thus extending old privileges and protections.

2 *Binding consultation* depends on (a) subordination of the military to civilian control, (b) extensive domestic taxation (as opposed, for example, to state revenues drawn directly from exports), (c) representation with respect to the assessment and collection of taxes.

3 *Equal citizenship* depends on (a) broad class coalitions including power holders, (b) creation and expansion of electoral systems.

4 *Broad citizenship* depends on (a) extensive domestic taxation, (b) broad class coalitions, (c) direct recruitment of large military services from the domestic population.

We might reasonably hypothesize that the relative strength of these factors prior to democratization also affects the kind of democracy that emerges, for example, that systems growing up chiefly through subordination of the military via defeat in war, military occupation, or some other cause will emphasize protection and breadth more than equality or binding consultation, while domestic taxation alone will promote binding consultation and breadth of citizenship while leaving equality and protection more uncertain. As Hanspeter Kriesi (1990) has pointed out, democracy operates quite differently in Switzerland and the Netherlands as a result of the contrast between Switzerland's federal coalescence and the transformation of the Dutch state under French conquest in the 1790s. The Dutch creation of a centralized bureaucracy and a subordinated military promoted a greater emphasis on breadth and equality of citizenship, which in turn led to the incorporation of the population's competing segments by means of "pillarization" in parallel organizations rather than the creation of multiple local niches for different kinds of politics. The Swiss system operates quite differently, tolerating considerable inequality among geographically segregated niches (Mathias and O'Brien 1988, 1989; Lindert and Williamson 1983).

Democracy and Citizenship in Great Britain

In a telling simplification, T. H. Marshall (1950) described the whole process of democratization as a movement from civic to political to social rights. Marshall's formulation misleads us in two important ways: by substituting a neat succession for a tangled intertwining of civic, political, and social rights, and by erasing many curtailments of rights, for example, the massive repression of 1795–1799 and the defeat of Chartism in the 1840s. Nevertheless, Marshall's scheme rightly calls attention to the alternation among relative emphases on the breadth of citizenship, its equality, its protections against arbitrary state action, and control of citizens over state personnel and policy. British history of the last two centuries illustrates the truism that changes in the character of the state and of citizenship entail alterations in the extent and character of democracy.

Once we recognize the importance of military activity to the British state's transformation, British history takes on a delightful irony. In the world as a whole, autonomous militaries generally inhibit democracy, even when they seize power in the name of democratic programs. They regularly inhibit democracy by diminishing the protections of citizens against arbitrary state action and often by blocking the definitiveness of popular consultation—annulling or falsifying elections, bypassing or intimidating parliaments, evading public surveillance of their activities. Yet in Britain, militarization of the state indirectly fostered democratization. It did so through the struggle and bargaining it generated, which fortified citizenship and subordinated military activity to parliamentary control.

The process began in the sixteenth century with Tudor checking of great lords' private armies and fortified castles. It ended, for practical purposes, in the nineteenth century with the elimination of press gangs. An aristocratically led military continued to draw a major share of the state budget, retained great freedom of action in Ireland and the colonies, and enjoyed great prestige at home, yet as such, never wielded autonomous power in domestic politics after 1660. The reliance of the British military on Parliament for finance and supply—still an acute issue in the struggles that led up to the revolution of 1640—eventually subordinated the army and navy to civilian, parliamentary control. In retrospect, we can see the crucial importance of that subordination to the later creation of British democracy.

Democracy Resembles a Lake

The exploration of tautologically necessary conditions for democracy—states and citizens—clears the way for thinking about contingent causes and concomitants of democracy. No one has so far succeeded in separating common correlates of democratic arrangements from nontautologically necessary, sufficient, or contingently causal conditions.

The problem resists solution because democracy does not resemble an oil field or a garden, but a lake. A lake—a large inland body of water—can come into being because a mountain stream feeds into a naturally existing basin, because someone or something dams up the outlet of a large river, because a glacier melts, because an earthquake isolates a segment of the ocean from the main body of water, because people deliberately dig an enormous hole and channel nearby watersheds into it, or for a number of other reasons. Once it exists, nevertheless, a lake nurtures characteristic ecosystems and maintains characteristic relations with its surroundings, so much so that limnologists have built a scientific specialty around the study of those regularities. Democracy behaves like a lake: although it has distinguishing properties and a logic of its own, it forms in a variety of ways, each of which retains traces of its singular history in the details of its current operation.

Quick! Let's abandon the simile before it drowns us! Here is the point: we have absolutely no a priori reason to believe that only one set of circumstances produces and sustains democracy, even if during the last few hundred years' experience, particular circumstances have often nurtured democracy. The most we can reasonably hope to get from scrutinizing historical cases of democratization is a map of alternative paths by which the process has occurred, an indication of sufficient—not necessary—conditions for that transformation, and a specification of general mechanisms that play a part in producing or sustaining democratic institutions when they form.

From their outstanding comparative study of democratization within four sets of states (Western and Central Europe, British settler states, mainland Latin America, and Central America/Caribbean), Rueschemeyer, Stephens, and Stephens draw important conclusions. They confirm Barrington Moore's assertion that the political power of labor-controlling landlords inhibited democratization while denying Moore's association of democratization with a politically strong bourgeoisie. Instead, they show, workers allied with others (who were often bourgeois) and pushed much more reliably for democracy, sometimes over the resistance of bourgeois who preferred more limited forms of political participation.

Rueschemeyer *et al.* conclude that in general capitalism does, as often alleged, promote democracy, but not because capitalists prefer democratic government; all other things equal and enemies such as landlords absent, capitalists prefer something like oligarchies of wealth. Such oligarchies allow them to use state power to control workers. But capitalism generates both working classes and the conditions under which they are likely to mobilize; working classes then press for enlargements of citizens' rights and full inclusion of workers among citizens. Given powerful allies, they often succeed....

As my tale of Great Britain suggests, Rueschemeyer *et al.* (1992: 279) find that mass military mobilization empowers the classes supplying the bulk of military manpower, both in Europe and elsewhere:

> In the United States, soldiers' demands for suffrage rights at the time of the wars against Britain accelerated the broadening of suffrage. Over one hundred years later, the presence of black soldiers in the armed forces during World War II and afterward contributed to the movement which eventually resulted in the extension of suffrage to southern blacks. In Canada, the mass mobilization for World War I was critically implicated in the institution of universal suffrage there. In nineteenth century Latin America, on the other hand, repeated involvement in wars led to a buildup of the military and increased the political weight of the military.

The formula does not run, then: war, hence democracy. If it did, every state in bellicose Europe would have democratized by the sixteenth or seventeenth century.

Even in a smoothly operating democracy, a lost war, or a deep depression, the formation of an authoritarian mass movement, economic dependency on an outside power, or the acquisition of autonomy by military forces sometimes undermines that expectation rapidly, as the experiences of Italy and Germany after World War I illustrate vividly. Expectations, however much based on realistic observation, depend heavily on social construction and remain subject to social deconstruction. That is why democracy, once formed, does not stay in place forever. That is why sites of democracy always display the sign Under Construction.

References

Alestalo, Matti and Stein Kuhnle. 1984. "The Scandinavian Route: Economic, Social, and Political Developments in Denmark, Finland, Norway, and Sweden." Research Report no. 31, *Research Group for Comparative Sociology*, University of Helsinki.

Artéus, Gunnar, Ulf Olsson, and Kerstin Stromberg-Back. 1981. "The Influence of the Armed Forces on the Transformation of Society in Sweden, 1600–1945," in Kungl, ed., *Krigsvetenskaps akademins Bihafte—Militarhistorisk Tidskrift*: 133–144.

Böhme, Klaus-Richard. 1983. "Schwedische Finanzbürokratie und Kriegsführung 1611 bis 1721," in Goran Rystad, ed., *Europe and Scandinavia: Aspects of the Process of Integration in the 17th Century*. Lund: Esselte Studium.

Brady, Thomas A. 1985. *Turning Swiss: Cities and Empire, 1450–1550*. Cambridge: Cambridge University Press.

Dahl, Robert. 1991. *Democracy and Its Critics*, New Haven: Yale University Press.

Hemes, Helga. 1988. "Scandinavian Citizenship," *Acta Sociologica* 31: 199–215.

Kriesi, Hanspeter. 1990. "Federalism and Pillarization: The Netherlands and Switzerland Compared," *Acta Politica* 25: 433–450.

Lindegren, Jan. 1985. "The Swedish 'Military State,' 1560–1720," *Scandinavian Journal of History* 10: 305–336.

Lindert, Peter H. and Jeffrey G. Williamson. 1983. "English Workers' Living Standards during the Industrial Revolutions: A New Look," *Economic History Review* 36: 1–2.

Lundqvist, Sven. 1977. *Folkrörelserna i det svenska samhället, 1850–1920*. Stockholm: Almqvist & Wiksell.

Marshall, T. H. 1950. *Citizenship and Social Class*. Cambridge: Cambridge University Press.

Mathias, Peter and Patrick K. O'Brien. 1988. "Taxation in Britain and France: 1715–1810. A Comparison of the Social and Economic Incidence of Taxes Collected for the Central Governments." *Journal of European Economic History* 5.3: 601.

——— 1989. "The Impact of Revolutionary and Napoleonic Wars, 1973–1815, on the Long-Run Growth of the British Economy," *Economic History Review* 12 (1989): 335–395.

Moore, Jr., Barrington. 1966. *Social Orders of Dictatorship and Democracy.* Boston: Beacon Press.

Nilsson, Sven A. 1988. "Imperial Sweden: Nation-Building, War, and Social Change," in Sven A. Nilsson *et al., The Age of New Sweden.* Stockholm: Livrustkammaren.

O'Brien, Patrick K. 1988. "The Political Economy of British Taxation, 1660–1815," *Economic History Review* 41: 1–32.

Öhngren, Bo. 1974. Folk irörelse: Samhällsutveckling, flyttningsmonster och folkrörelser i Eskilstuna, 1870–1900. Uppsala. *Studia Historica Upsaliensia 55.*

Peterson, Paul E. 1992. "An Immodest Proposal," *Daedalus* 121, no. 4: 151–174.

Prak, Maarten. 1991. "Citizen Radicalism and Democracy in the Dutch Republic: The Patriot Movement of the 1780s," *Theory and Society* 20: 73–102.

Przeworski, Adam. 1986. "Some Problems in the Study of the Transition to Democracy," in Guillermo O'Donnell, Philippe C. Schmitter, and Laurence Whitehead, eds., *Transitions from Authority Rule: Comparative Perspectives.* Baltimore: Johns Hopkins University Press.

———— 1989. "Some Problems" Robert A. Dahl. *Democracy and Its Critics.* New Haven, CT: Yale University Press.

Rueschemeyer, Dietrich, John Stephens, and Evelyn Huber Stephens. 1992. *Capitalist Development and Democracy.* Chicago: University of Chicago Press.

Te Brake, Wayne. 1989. *Regents and Rebels: The Revolutionary World of the 18th Century Dutch City.* Oxford: Blackwell.

———— 1990. "How Much in How Little? Dutch Revolution in Comparative Perspective," *Tijdschrift voor Sociale Geschiedenis* 16: 349–363.

Where Do Rights Come From?

10

Charles Tilly

Where do rights come from? We could ground this grand question in analytic philosophy *à la* Rawls, metaphysics *à la* Rousseau, or rational action *à la* Riker. I want instead to ground it in European political history. In this, I take my lead from Barrington Moore's *Social Origins of Dictatorship and Democracy*, which repeatedly treats rights as historical products, outcomes of struggle. In particular, *Social Origins* argues that the creation of democracy—checking of arbitrary rulers, establishment of just, rational political rules, and influence of the "underlying population" in the making of such rules—entailed the making of rights (Moore 1966:414).

In that book, Moore grounded the crucial rights in Western European feudalism. "For our purposes," he argued, "the most important aspect was the growth of the notion of the immunity of certain groups and persons from the power of the ruler, along with the conception of the right of resistance to unjust authority. Together with the conception of contract as a mutual engagement freely undertaken by free persons, derived from the feudal relation of vassalage, this complex of ideas and practices constitutes a crucial legacy from European medieval society to modern Western conceptions of a free society" (Moore 1966:415). Despite this passage's whiff of idealism, Moore's comparative history portrayed those crucial rights as coming to fruition by means of revolution and class struggle; he gave his opening chapter, after all, the title "England and the Contributions of Violence to Gradualism." My argument will diverge from Moore's in three directions: doubting the centrality of feudalism, downgrading the relative importance of ideas, and considering the crucial events to have occurred after the general dissolution of feudalism. It will nevertheless agree with Moore in two fundamental ways: by emphasizing resistance and struggle, by grounding rights in the specific histories of different European regions.

Grounded historically, the question about origins of rights becomes a naturalistic one: How have European people acquired enforceable claims on the states to which they were subject? More narrowly, how have rights of citizenship come into being? How did authorities come to owe goods, services, and protections to people merely on the ground of their belonging to a category, the category of people in the political community attached to a state? How did that political community expand to include most people, or at least most households, in the population at large?

Even more surprising, how did ordinary people get the power to enforce such weighty obligations? Vying in vain in a national arena, did Europeans instead wrest rights from local authorities and then see them eventually extended to a national scale? Or did benevolent despots first grant these rights to a small number of companions, and then, as enlightenment spread among rulers and ruled, extend them gradually to the rest of the population? Or did they emerge from struggle at a national scale? My answer hews to the third alternative: struggle at a national scale. Rights, in this formulation, resemble what Amartya Sen (1981) calls entitlements, enforceable claims on the delivery of goods, services, or protections by specific others. Rights exist when one party can effectively insist that another deliver goods, services, or protections, and third parties will act to reinforce (or at least not to hinder) their delivery. Such entitlements become *citizenship* rights when the object of claims is a state or its agent and the successful claimant qualifies by simple membership in a broad category of persons subject to the state's jurisdiction. Citizenship rights came into being because relatively organized members of the general population bargained with state authorities for several centuries, bargained first over the means of war, then over enforceable claims that would serve their interests outside of war. This bargaining enlarged the obligations of states to their citizens, broadening the range of enforceable claims citizens could make on states even more than it expanded the population who held rights of citizenship.

From previous work on state transformation comes recognition of the extractive, repressive relationship of states to subject populations through most of history, leaving us to wonder that they should ever concede extensive citizens' claims. From previous work on collective action comes a two fold model of struggle: (1) struggle over demands made by states on their subjects, by subjects on states, or by subjects on each other; and (2) struggle by specific groups of subjects to enter the polity (the set of persons and groups having routine, enforceable claims on the state), to help others enter the polity, to defend certain polity memberships, or to exclude others from the polity. In caricature, the argument says that rights of citizenship formed as the bargains struck in the course of both sorts of struggle, first chiefly in defense against invasive state demands for the means of war, later in the pursuit of a much wider range of collective action and state intervention.

This way of explaining rights is at once empiricist, speculative, and cynical. It is empiricist because it infers regularities from diverse experiences of Europeans over the last thousand years of state formation and transformation. It is speculative because no one has assembled the mass of comparative evidence required for definitive verification or falsification. It is cynical because it assumes that whatever enforceable claims on states people acquired, however wrong they may now appear to be, constituted rights.

Citizenship rights belong in principle (if not always in practice) to everyone who qualifies as a full-fledged member of a given state; membership in the category suffices to qualify a person for the enforceable claims. Although all systems of citizenship establish more than one category of eligibility (even today's democratic states exclude children, prisoners, and certified incompetents from some citizenship rights), the major dividing line separates noncitizens from native-born and naturalized citizens. These days, citizens of European states typically have rights to vote in national and local elections, to engage in a wide range of collective action outside of elections, to receive a considerable number of governmental benefits and services, to move freely within the frontiers of their states, and even to receive the protection of their states when they travel or reside outside their frontiers; citizens can lose these rights only through a formal process of degradation, such as a criminal sentence or commitment to a psychiatric hospital; with respect to the same states, otherwise identical noncitizen neighbors do not generally share these rights.

Expansion of Rights, Creation of Citizenship

T. H. Marshall's classic formulation distinguished three elements of citizenship: civil, political, and social.[1] Civil rights comprised those elements protecting individual freedom; political rights, those elements guaranteeing participation in the exercise of political power; and social rights, those providing access to material and cultural satisfactions. Thinking of England, Marshall (1965) assigned the definitive acquisition of civil rights to the eighteenth century, of political rights to the nineteenth, and of social rights to the twentieth.... Marshall conceived of the rights' extension as the almost Hegelian realization of a principle in history....

Although at times he recognized that labor fought capital and the state for its social rights, Marshall explicitly rejected the line of argument I have taken: "Rights are not," he declared, "a proper matter for bargaining" (Marshall 1965:122). Despite recognizing that civil rights (protections of individual freedom) provided the frame for political and social rights, he did not see how the struggle for one kind of right prepared claimants to struggle for the next kind. No doubt he resisted that line of argument because in 1946, when he wrote, it would have made the struggle for social rights a matter of *rapport des forces* at a time when he sought to prepare his audience for intervention in the order of social classes and to justify that intervention as a matter of unavoidable principle. However that may be, his otherwise perceptive analysis suffered acutely from historical foreshortening. We can place it in more adequate perspective by attempting to place the gain and loss of rights more firmly into history than Marshall did.

Citizens of European states now enjoy *ipso facto* rights to education, housing, health care, income, and a wide variety of political participation. Some resident noncitizens also have legal access to many of these benefits, but the enforceability of their claims remains limited and contested. If France and other EU members grant the local vote to *ressortissants* of other states, the distinction will start to blur. When distinctions of this sort disappear, we have two linguistic choices: we can say that the rights attached to citizenship have diminished, or we can say that states have begun to equate citizenship with authorized long-term residence. In the case of Europe, a third choice may also apply: that citizenship rights have devolved to the European Union. The test will come with the treatment of nationals from outside the Union. In the meantime, citizenship makes a significant difference to the claims on a state any individual can enforce.

As the European Union's scope expands, one of the thorniest issues its members face grows on precisely that flowering bush: To what extent, in what ways, and with what sort of enforcement will citizenship rights become vested in the Union as a whole rather than in any particular state? To what extent will they become uniform and transferable among states? Instead of rebels and runaways, what about refugees? If one European state recognizes a set of people as political refugees who have high priority for citizenship, must all other members of the Union recognize those rights? Will the right of a newly unemployed worker to income, job placement, and retraining apply in the state to which he has migrated? Who will pay the benefits? When rights vary from state to state, will the lowest common denominator prevail throughout Europe? The average? The highest value anywhere? Similar questions face the rebuilders of political life in Latin America and Eastern Europe, as the decline of authoritarian regimes brings a new era of constitution making. The question of citizenship has become newly salient.

It has, in fact, remained prominent in Europe for about three hundred years, since the time when larger European states began building big standing armies drawn largely from their own populations—armies (and often navies) supported by regular taxation and state-funded debt. To be sure, long before the seventeenth century, expatriate European merchants formed "nations" in metropolises such as Constantinople and Rome, gaining a measure of self-government and of protection from their home states in return for policing their own members, assuring their own food supplies in times of subsistence, and bearing negotiated shares of citywide expenses. No doubt the generalization of resident diplomatic missions in later fifteenth-century Europe entailed a certain mutual recognition of citizenship. For the burghers of city-states such as Florence and federations of city-states such as the Dutch Republic, membership in the financial elites and political councils of their own cities qualified them for claims on their states as well, long before the seventeenth century; in that limited sense, as Max Weber half-understood, Bürgerschaft anticipated citizenship.

Most European states and their subjects, however, did not begin bargaining out the rights and obligations of citizenship on a relatively large scale until the seventeenth and eighteenth centuries. Before then, unwritten constitutions frequently bound rulers to members of their ruling classes, but not to the ordinary population. Then rulers turned away from the episodic use of militias and mercenary forces for warfare, trying instead to staff standing armies from their own populations and to force the civilians in their own populations to pay for the armies routinely and well. Large populous states thus gained the advantage over small rich states, as a Venice or a Dutch Republic lost tire ability simply to rent an army of poor foreigners and thereby to vanquish its neighbors.

From Indirect to Direct Rule

The attempts to establish standing armies raised a critical problem: the transition from indirect to direct rule. Until the creation of mass national armies, all larger European states ruled indirectly, counting on the cooptation of various sorts of magnates who acted for the state and guaranteed the delivery of resources to it, but who also retained a large measure of autonomy within their own reserved zones. Even France, that Tocquevillian model of centralization, relied heavily on hereditary governors, provincial estates, and privileged municipalities until Richelieu (pressed for funds to join the widening European wars of the 1620s) improvised intendants to bypass stubborn regional magnates. Mazarin and Colbert regularized intendants into direct and more or less subordinated regional executors of royal will. Even then the intendants spent much of their time negotiating with estates, *parlements,* military governors, and other regional power holders who had the power to block the crown's demands and sometimes to incite massive resistance against royal policy.

The dilemma bore sharp horns. Reliance on coopted power holders guaranteed a certain level of compliance so long as the crown limited its demands and respected the power holders' privileges, but it reinforced the central authority's chief domestic rivals and most dangerous enemies. The installation of direct, centralized rule, however, was a costly, risky, time-consuming operation that often exploded in rebellion.

The expansion of armed forces impelled high officials of European states to undertake the cost, the risk, and the effort. In large states such as Prussia and Russia, reliance on powerful, partly autonomous intermediaries set a severe limit on the portion of national resources to which the central state could gain access, even if up to that limit it made the amassing of resources easier. Two of war's many unfortunate features are that (1) it really is a zero-sum game at best, and a negative-sum game much of the time—if one party wins, another definitely loses, often incurring penalties greater than the putative winner's gains, (2) within the limits imposed by declining efficacy as a function of the time and space separating antagonists, the party with the most effective armed force sets the terms—a state having small, very efficient armed forces sometimes loses wars against a state having large, inefficient ones, and usually loses to a state having large, fairly efficient ones. As a consequence of these principles, the most effectively armed European states set the military terms for all the rest.

For several centuries before about 1750, the most effectively armed European states were those that could rent the most mercenary troops.

Mercenaries had the great advantage of being available rapidly for whoever had the necessary funds or credit. But they had dramatic disadvantages: they were expensive, unruly, unreliable if not paid, and a great nuisance if not deported once a war had ended; unemployed mercenaries often became bandits, pirates, or the equivalent on a larger scale: warlords.

The old European alternatives to nationally recruited mercenaries had been urban militias, private armies of great lords, and various sorts of feudal levies—the three overlapped. From the perspective of rulers, these forces had the advantages of being cheap and disposable. But they were available only in limited numbers, for limited terms, in service whose conditions themselves generally had well-specified limits; what is more, their leaders and patrons had minds, interests, and ambitions of their own. Only the invention of mass national armies recruited directly from the subject population by the state and operated under control of the state's own officers overcame the clear disadvantages of mercenaries and of the older levies.

The creation of a large, durable national army recruited from the domestic population, however, posed one of those problems of consent beloved of political philosophers. Supporting any army required large resources continuously over long periods: food, uniforms, weapons, transport, wages, and more. In the seventeenth century, most states that hired mercenaries borrowed money from local capitalists in the short run, bought the requisites on well-organized markets in which state functionaries and capitalists collaborated, then taxed the general population in various ways to repay their capitalist creditors. A national army had the added disadvantage of withdrawing able-bodied workers from households that relied on them for support. These workers would disappear from their households for years, possibly returning useless or not at all, and remitting no income in the meantime. Entrepreneurs who knew how to deliver freely hired mercenaries did not necessarily know how to pry unwilling recruits from reluctant households. Furthermore, standing armies required substantial increases in taxation.

How to gain consent? All army-building states turned to some combination of reliance on coopted entrepreneurs, aggressive recruitment, impressment, and conscription. Even so, they faced widespread resistance to the increased burden of taxation and to the seizure of young men for the military. They bargained. They bargained in different ways: by sending in troops to recruit troops and collect taxes, by negotiating quotas for troops and taxes with the headmen of regions and local communities, by confirming the rights of existing assemblies (Parliament in England, Estates in France, Cortes in Castile, Corts in Catalonia, States-General in the Dutch Republic) to legislate contributions to military budgets. Even bloody repression of rebellions typically involved bargaining. Authorities punished a few offenders spectacularly while pardoning others who agreed to comply with the state's demands. Further-more, the settlement of a rebellion would generally state the grounds and procedures for legitimate future remonstrance. White-hot bargaining forged rights and obligations of citizenship.

The error lies in conceiving of the process as one of gradual enlightenment rather than continuous struggle, and in imagining that the same sequence of inclusion appeared everywhere that enlightenment spread. The implicit strategy of rulers was to grant national rights to the minimum set of persons that would guarantee the delivery of militarily essential resources to the state, and to collaborate with citizens so privileged in exploiting and repressing the rest. Women and male servants, for example, only escaped from that collusion very recently. Indirect rule operated reasonably well with a small number of people having rights of citizenship—so few that in some cases the phrase "indirect rule" is more misleading than helpful.

Contrasting Experiences

The shift to direct rule did not immediately eliminate such distinctions. With whom rulers bargained varied according to their strategies for enlarging military force, which in turn depended on the social structures of the regions in which they based their states. Where rulers could coopt well-established regional power holders such as landlords who would guarantee a supply of troops and taxes to the state, nobilities and gentries flourished, distinctions actually increased, and citizenship in relation to the national state was slow to expand.

Where rulers' agents bargained directly for resources with commercially active burghers or village elders, they had little choice but to concede claims on the state to large numbers of people, even if the consequence of those concessions was to reinforce the positions of those local elites within their own communities. Holland and Sweden followed different variants of that path.

In the process of building nationally based military forces and citizenship, indeed, Sweden was precocious. Sweden, poor in funds but rich in peasants, had recruited relatively large armies from its own population during its warlike sixteenth-century expansion.

Despite its deserved reputation as a sea power, the Dutch Republic built substantial armies in the seventeenth century, and maintained about 5.3 percent of its population under arms in 1700. Holland and its neighbors built their great seventeenth-century military force by means of a peculiar federal state in which mercantile municipalities held decisive power.

Prussia and Russia likewise turned toward their own populations for troops in the seventeenth century. Unlike Sweden, however, both states relied for recruitment and command on state-serving landlords who exercised great discretion within their own fiefs. Those great lords held the power to block excessive demands from the state. Thus Prussia and Russia rebuilt indirect rule and the obstacles it set to centralized control.

...In Sweden, peasants acquired direct political representation on a national scale, even to the extent of having their own formally constituted estates. In Holland and the other Dutch provinces, citizenship remained vested in municipal ruling classes until a series of struggles in the eighteenth century and the French conquest of 1798. In Prussia and Russia, peasants had practically no access to the national state except through the same landlords whose short-run interests lay in oppressing and exploiting them. Although no one should exaggerate the power of Swedish peasants or forget their subjection to clergy and bureaucrats, seventeenth-century Sweden had conceded a minimum set of citizenship rights to the population at large—or at least to the propertied classes—while its neighbors had granted none. On the contrary, as they built military power Prussia and Russia abridged the autonomies of merchants and villagers alike. The manner of recruiting soldiers made a large difference.

The French Revolution and Its Aftermath

Nevertheless, the decisive move to a model of mass national armies, direct rule, and extensive citizens' rights on a national scale came with the French Revolution.

Consider the importance of military changes in their own right: the crucial defection of French Guards in the Parisian revolution; the institution of citizen militias, a nearly universal feature of the local revolutionary activity of 1789; the search for weapons to arm the new Parisian militia, which was the immediate incentive for breaking into the Bastille; the strong ties between the military recruitment of 1791 or 1792, and the support for the Revolution in general; the sale of church and émigré property to finance the state's military efforts; the crucial place of military conscription in the widespread counter-revolutionary movements of 1793; the enactment of most instruments of the Terror in reaction to the double military threat from external enemies and domestic rebels; and the organization in the larger cities of so-called Revolutionary Armies whose chief business was bending the people of their hinterlands (including peasants who were reluctant to deliver food) to patriotic action.

Consider furthermore that it was precisely the fiscal crisis stemming from the American war—a crisis set in motion, not by the general inability of the French economy to absorb the cost, but by the fiscal limits intrinsic to the French system of indirect rule—that led to the momentous convocation of the Estates General in 1789.

Repeatedly, nevertheless, the effort to reorganize, enlarge and finance the state's military activity led to bargaining with major sectors of the population, and thereby to the establishment or confirmation of enforceable claims such as the right to elected representation. Complaints about taxation—less its sheer bulk than the equity of its distribution—dominated parish, Third Estate, and noble *cahiers de doléances* prepared for the Estates General of 1789. What is more, the *cahiers* often linked citizenship directly to the payment of taxes (Markoff 1990).

During the French Revolution, from the Declaration of the Rights of Man (August 26, 1789) onward, bargaining that established citizenship rights took place right out in the open. The first revolutionary constitution (1790) installed a sharp distinction between active citizens (who paid the equivalent of three or more days' wages in taxes, and had the right to vote) and passive citizens (who paid fewer taxes or none at all and could not vote). It also set up a secondary distinction of second-degree active citizens (who paid ten or more days' wages in taxes and could not only vote but also serve as electors and hold office). This latter group was a reasonable representation of the independent and propertied population who had dominated the Third Estate of 1789. But before the elections of fall 1792, in the shadow of general war, the National Assembly decreed that almost all males twenty-five and over could vote, with the exception of servants and other presumed dependents. Advocates of the expanded electorate argued specifically that men who could fight for the *patrie* should also be able to vote for its governors. Unwilling conscripts of March 1793 often turned the argument around, declaring that they would be ready to serve if the government also drafted the officeholders who were receiving military exemptions.

On June 23, 1793—in the midst of war, insurrection, and bitter struggles over the food supply—the Convention abrogated martial law (including the Le Chapelier law forbidding private associations such as guilds) yet authorized severe price controls. The next day it voted on a new constitution as well as on the recently drafted Declaration of the Rights of Man and the Citizen. While outlawing slavery (black insurgents of Saint-Domingue had finally received a hearing), they guaranteed not only manhood suffrage, but also rights to rebellion, to education, to public welfare, to property, and to subsistence. True, legislatures of Thermidor and thereafter abridged citizens' rights dramatically; manhood suffrage did not reappear in France until the Revolution of 1848. But by 1793 the French had clearly established the category of citizen as well as the principle and practice of negotiating the rights and obligations attached to that category in elected national assemblies. Their military conquests and their example spread category, principle, and practice to much of Europe. The citizenship that emerged from the French Revolution and Napoleonic Wars remained exiguous by today's standards, although from an eighteenth-century perspective it was thick indeed. It consisted of property-restricted rights to vote for legislative assemblies, veterans' benefits, limited protection for political associations, relative freedom of movement within national boundaries, a measure of religious toleration, and little more. The array obviously varied from country to country within Europe; Russia in 1815 was far from granting anything resembling national citizenship, while in Great Britain even ambitious rulers did not dare to abridge the prerogatives of a Parliament chosen by an amalgam of electors, the general right of religious association (political and economic association remained much more fragile but never nonexistent), freedom to assemble for peaceful purposes (although which purposes were peaceful likewise remained open to negotiation and official interpretation), or the right to petition national authorities. Nevertheless through much of Europe it meant that the capitalists who were so crucial to state finance, had obtained political positions and freedom of action they had not enjoyed in most places during the eighteenth century.

What Happened, Again?

In a long, uneven first phase, the creation of mass national armies created the rudiments of national citizenship in European states. Then between the eighteenth century and the recent past, the rights attached to membership in the national category of citizen expanded dramatically. Why and how? It happened in two further phases: the second, a bourgeois-led drive for civil and political rights, and the third, a phase in which workers, petits bourgeois, and peasants bargained more autonomously with the state.

In the second phase, negotiation over the making of war continued to play a central role. General war among European powers diminished for a century after 1815, but Europeans maintained nationally recruited standing armies and exported war to the rest of the world in the form of imperial conquest. Greatly increased military budgets empowered the bourgeois- and landlord-dominated legislatures that had taken shape during the French wars and never quite disappeared after they had ended; they now became the loci of struggle over government expenditure, the gateways through which ministers and kings had to pass on their way to military expansion. But to balance their aristocratic counterparts in the legislature, fragments of the national bourgeoisie commonly formed coalitions, implicit or explicit, with unenfranchised but increasingly organized workers and petty bourgeois. Within limits, the same civil rights that advanced the bourgeois position supported the organization of workers and petty bourgeois. As they pushed for freedom of association, freedom of assembly, freedom of the press, and related liberties, they willy-nilly promoted the mobilization of poorer, less powerful members of their commercial world.

No exaggeration, please! The British Reform Act of 1832 slammed shut in the faces of organized workers a door they and the bourgeois who benefited from the Act had battered open together. Workers' consequent sense of betrayal helped motivate the great Chartist Movement that followed almost immediately. Its relation to the coalition-breaking of 1832, and the recognition of political advantages that industrial masters drew from it, explains to a considerable degree the surprisingly political program of Chartism. One might have expected impoverished and browbeaten workers to emphasize wages, employment, and working conditions rather than annual meetings of Parliament, but not until 1867 did substantial numbers of British workers begin to vote in national elections. European bourgeois of the post-Napoleonic period found themselves in an ambivalent position, enjoying the sharp political distinction between themselves and workers or shopkeepers, and yet wanting those workers and shopkeepers to act as counterweights against their powerful political rivals. Nevertheless, the net effect of their action was to enlarge the zone of civil rights and to make the state more vulnerable to workers', shopkeepers', and peasants' demands for political rights.

In the third phase, promoted by the bourgeois-worker-peasant coalitions of 1848 revolutions, the chief beneficiaries of expanded civil, political, and social rights began to mobilize and act more autonomously than before. If Marshall was right to name the twentieth century as the great age for social rights, the nineteenth century laid the foundations in two important ways: by providing workers, shopkeepers, and peasants with the space to organize legally and state their demands forcefully, and by initiating a three-way process of negotiation among workers, capitalists, and the state over state-enforced limits on exploitation and over the minimum material benefits to which all citizens were entitled. Under Bismarck, the newly formed German state preempted the negotiation by installing a remarkable social contract top down (Steinmetz 1993). But to some degree most European states found themselves intervening in the organization of production and distribution under pressure from increasingly organized workers and consumers.

With the later nineteenth century came an age in which military expenditure and debt service for past military expenditure no longer dominated European state budgets, as they had ever since distinct budgets had started to form in the sixteenth century. Wars began to matter chiefly as times when state powers and budgets expanded, and ends of wars began to matter as crucial times of political mobilization; the widespread adoption of female suffrage after World War I illustrates those effects. But much more than suffrage was at stake. Social rights to public services—education, health, and welfare—became major businesses of government. Many European states became welfare states, states committed to providing services and guaranteeing income to large categories of their citizenry.

The chronology itself requires enormous qualifications: formally designated serfs, for example, still existed in the Russia of 1860 but had disappeared from England and the Netherlands four or five centuries earlier; even today, rights of free speech vary enormously from Albania and Turkey to Norway and Finland. Most European states have found it expedient at some times in the twentieth century to define some putative citizens—communists, fascists, Gypsies, Jews, homosexuals, collaborators—as undeserving of their rights. A full theory of citizenship rights would account for these variations as well as broad trends over the whole continent. Please treat my account

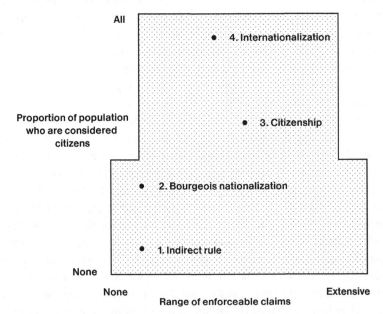

Figure 10.1 Hypothetical Trajectory of National Citizenship in Europe

exactly as it deserves: as a provocative, historically grounded, theoretical sketch that invites confirmation, refutation, modification, and extension.

Extensions and Applications

The model says in general that rights—enforceable claims—arise from the repeated making of similar claims under certain conditions: (1) the claimant and the object of claims each can reward or punish the other in some significant way; (2) the two are in fact bargaining over those rewards and punishments; (3) one or both also bargain with third parties who have an interest in the claims being made, and will act to enforce future granting of the claims in question; and (4) the three or more parties to the claims thus constituted have durable identities and relations with each other.

The model also suggests how rights disappear. If any of the four founding conditions—claimant and object controlling relevant rewards and punishments, actual bargaining, interested third parties, durable identities and social relations—weakens significantly, so will rights.

When the bargaining model is used to inform historical and comparative analysis, it helps make sense both of where rights come from and when they can disappear. This model of rights as the product of interest-driven bargaining looks at least as plausible as the common notions that rights derive from mentalities, Zeitgeisten, general theories, or the sheer logic of social life (Coleman 1990).

Note

1   For explications and critiques of Marshall's analysis, see J. M. Barbalet, *Citizenship* (Minneapolis; University of Minnesota Press, 1988); Margaret R. Somers, "Citizenship and the Place of the Public Sphere: Law, Community, and Political Culture in the Transition to Democracy," *American Sociological Review* 58 (1993): 587–620; Bryan S. Turner, ed., *Citizenship and Social Theory* (Newbury Park: Sage, 1993).

References

Barrington Moore, Jr. 1966. *Social Origins of Dictatorship and Democracy.* Boston: Beacon Press.

Coleman, James S. 1990. *Foundations of Social Theory.* Cambridge: Harvard University Press, Belknap Press.

Markoff, John. 1990. "Peasants Protest: The Claims of Lord, Church, and State in the *Cahiers de doléances* of 1789," *Comparative Studies in Society and History* 32: 413–54.

Marshall, T. H. 1965. *Class, Citizenship, and Social Development.* Garden City: Doubleday.

Sen, Amartya. 1981. *Poverty and Famines: An Essay on Entitlement and Deprivation.* Oxford: Clarendon Press.

Steinmetz, George. 1993. *Regulating the Social: The Welfare State and Local Politics in Imperial Germany.* Princeton: Princeton University Press.

Democratization and **11**
De-democratization
Charles Tilly

What Is Democracy?

To take democracy seriously, we must know what we are talking about. Developing a precise definition of democracy is particularly important when trying—as we are here—to describe and explain variation and change in the extent and character of democracy.

Observers of democracy and democratization generally choose, implicitly or explicitly, among four main types of definitions: constitutional, substantive, procedural, and process-oriented (Andrews and Chapman 1995; Collier and Levitsky 1997; Held 1996; Inkeles 1991; O'Donnell 1999; Ortega Ortiz 2001; Schmitter and Karl 1991). A *constitutional approach* concentrates on laws a regime enacts concerning political activity. Thus we can look across history and recognize differences among oligarchies, monarchies, republics, and a number of other types by means of contrasting legal arrangements. Within democracies, furthermore, we can distinguish between constitutional monarchies, presidential systems, and parliament-centered arrangements, not to mention such variations as federal versus unitary structures. For large historical comparisons, constitutional criteria have many advantages, especially the relative visibility of constitutional forms. As the cases of Kazakhstan and Jamaica show, however, large discrepancies between announced principles and daily practices often make constitutions misleading.

Substantive approaches focus on the conditions of life and politics a given regime promotes: Does this regime promote human welfare, individual freedom, security, equity, social equality, public deliberation, and peaceful conflict resolution? If so, we might be inclined to call it democratic regardless of how its constitution reads. Two troubles follow immediately, however, from any such definitional strategy. First, how do we handle tradeoffs among these estimable principles? If a given regime is desperately poor but its citizens enjoy rough equality, should we think of it as more democratic than a fairly prosperous but fiercely unequal regime?

Second, focusing on the possible outcomes of politics undercuts any effort to learn whether some political arrangements—including democracy— promote more desirable substantive outcomes than other political arrangements. What if we actually want to know under what conditions and how regimes promote human welfare, individual freedom, security, equity, social equality, public deliberation, and peaceful conflict resolution? Later we will discuss in depth how whether a regime is democratic affects the quality of public and private life.

Advocates of *procedural definitions* single out a narrow range of governmental practices to determine whether a regime qualifies as democratic. Most procedural observers center their attention on elections, asking whether genuinely competitive elections engaging large numbers of citizens regularly produce changes in governmental personnel and policy. If elections remain a non-competitive sham and an occasion for smashing governmental opponents as in Kazakhstan, procedural analysts reject them as criteria for democracy.

Process-oriented approaches to democracy differ significantly from constitutional, substantive, and procedural accounts. They identify some minimum set of processes that must be continuously in motion for a situation to qualify as democratic. In a classic statement, Robert Dahl stipulates five process-oriented criteria for democracy. Speaking first of how they might work in a voluntary association, he proposes:

Effective participation. Before a policy is adopted by the association, all the members must have equal and effective opportunities for making their views known to the other members as to what the policy should be.

Voting equality. When the moment arrives at which the decision about the policy will finally be made, every member must have an equal and effective opportunity to vote, and all votes must be counted as equal.

Enlightened understanding. Within reasonable limits as to time, each member must have equal and effective opportunities for learning about the relevant alternative policies and their likely consequences.

Control of the agenda. The members must have the exclusive opportunity to decide how and, if they choose, what matters are to be placed on the agenda. Thus the democratic process required by the three preceding criteria is never closed. The policies of the association are always open to change by the members, if they so choose.

Inclusion of adults. All, or at any rate most, adult permanent residents should have the full rights of citizens that are implied by the first four criteria. Before the twentieth century this criterion was unacceptable to most advocates of democracy. (Dahl 1998: 37–38)

The final standard—inclusion of adults—ironically rules out many cases that political philosophers have regularly taken as great historical models for democracy: Greek and Roman polities, Viking crews, village assemblies, and some city-states. All of them built their political deliberations by means of massive exclusion, most notably of women, slaves, and paupers. Inclusion of all (or almost all) adults basically restricts political democracy to the last few centuries.

When Dahl moves from local associations to national regimes, he holds on to his process-oriented insights, but shifts to talk of institutions. Institutions, for Dahl, consist of practices that endure. The sort of regime that Dahl calls a "polyarchal democracy" installs six distinctive institutions: elected officials; free, fair, and frequent elections; freedom of expression; alternative sources of information; associational autonomy; and inclusive citizenship (Dahl 1998: 85; Dahl 2005: 188–189). Once again, the procedure of voting appears on the list. But taken together Dahl's criteria for polyarchal democracy describe a working process, a series of regularized interactions among citizens and officials. These go far beyond the usual procedural standards.

Yet there is a catch. Basically, Dahl provides us with a static yes-no checklist; if a regime operates all six institutions, it counts as a democracy. If it lacks any of them, or some of them aren't really working, it doesn't count as a democracy. For an annual count of which regimes are in or out, such an approach can do the job even if critics raise questions about whether elections in such places as Jamaica are free and fair. Suppose, however, that we want to use process-oriented standards more ambitiously. We do not want merely to count the democratic house at a single point in time. Instead, we want to do two more demanding things: first, to compare regimes with regard to how democratic they are; second, to follow individual regimes through time, observing when and how they become more or less democratic.

Furthermore, the autonomy of powerful elitist, racist, sexist, or hate-mongering associations regularly undermines the inclusiveness of citizen-ship. Should a democracy let well-financed pressure groups drive punitive anti-immigrant legislation through the legislature? To enter fully into comparison and explanation, we will have to improve on Dahl's criteria while remaining faithful to their process-oriented spirit.

Elements of Democracy, Democratization, and De-democratization

How can we move ahead? Before identifying process-oriented criteria for democracy, democratization, and de-democratization, let us clarify what we have to explain. In order to do so, it will help to simplify radically. Later we can return to complications that our first take on the problem ignores. Let us adopt three simple ideas.

First, we start with a state, an organization that controls the major concentration of coercive means within a substantial territory, exercises priority in some regards over all other organizations operating within the same territory, and receives acknowledgment of that priority from other organizations, including states, outside the territory. You begin to see the complications: what about federal systems, civil wars, warlord-dominated enclaves, and rival factions within the state? For the time being, nevertheless, we can pose the problem of democracy more clearly by assuming a single, fairly unitary state.

Second, we lump everyone who lives under that state's jurisdiction into a catchall category: citizens. Again complications immediately come to mind: what about tourists, transnational corporations, members of the underground economy, and expatriates? Soon I will point out that most historical regimes have lacked full-fledged citizenship, which plays a crucial part in democracy. But for a start, calling everyone who lives under a given state's jurisdiction a citizen of that state will clarify what we have to explain. Democracy will then turn out to be a certain class of relations between states and citizens, and democratization and de-democratization will consist of changes in those sorts of relations.

Dahl's principles already imply such a step; even associational autonomy, for example, depends on state backing of associations' right to exist rather than the sheer presence of many, many associations.

Some of public politics consists of *consulting* citizens about their opinions, needs, and demands. Consultation includes any public means by which citizens voice their collective preferences concerning state personnel and policies. In relatively democratic regimes, competitive elections certainly give citizens a voice, but so do lobbying, petitioning, referenda, social movements, and opinion polling. This time the missing complications are obvious: bribes, patron-client chains, favors to constituents and followers, kinship connections among officials, and similar phenomena blur the boundary between public and private politics. What is more, we will soon discover that we can't make sense of public politics by focusing on citizen-state interactions alone, but must examine coalitions, rivalries, and confrontations among major political actors outside of the state as well.

In this simplified perspective, *a regime is democratic to the degree that political relations between the state and its citizens feature broad, equal, protected and mutually binding consultation.* Democratization means net movement toward broader, more equal, more protected, and more binding consultation. De-democratization, obviously, then means net movement toward narrower, more unequal, less protected, and less binding consultation.

State Capacity and Regime Variation

So far I have purposely omitted an important feature of regimes: the state's capacity to enforce its political decisions. No democracy can work if the state lacks the capacity to supervise democratic decision making and put its results into practice. This is most obvious for protection. A very weak state may proclaim the principle of shielding citizens from harassment by state agents, but can do little about harassment when it occurs. Very high-capacity states run the opposite risk: that decision making by state agents acquires enough weight to overwhelm mutually binding consultation between government and citizens.

State capacity means the extent to which interventions of state agents in existing non-state resources, activities, and interpersonal connections alter existing distributions of those resources, activities, and interpersonal connections as well as relations among those distributions. (State-directed redistribution of wealth, for example, almost inevitably involves not only a redistribution of resources across the population but also a change in the connection between the geographic distributions of wealth and population.) In a high-capacity regime, by this standard, whenever state agents act, their actions affect citizens' resources, activities, and interpersonal connections significantly. In a low-capacity regime, state agents have much narrower effects no matter how hard they try to change things.

The great bulk of historical regimes have fallen into the low-capacity undemocratic sector. Many of the biggest and most powerful, however, have dwelt in the high-capacity undemocratic sector. High-capacity democratic regimes have been rare and mostly recent. Low-capacity democratic regimes have remained few and far between.

Over the long run of human history, then, the vast majority of regimes have been undemocratic; democratic regimes are rare, contingent, recent creations. Partial democracies have, it is true, formed intermittently at a local scale, for example in villages ruled by councils incorporating most heads of household. At the scale of a city-state, a warlord's domain, or a regional federation, forms of government have run from dynastic hegemony to oligarchy, with narrow, unequal citizenship or none at all; little or no binding consultation; and uncertain protection from arbitrary governmental action.

Before the nineteenth century, furthermore, large states and empires generally managed by means of indirect rule: systems in which the central power received tribute, cooperation, and guarantees of compliance on the part of subject populations from regional power holders who enjoyed great autonomy within their own domains. Even in supposedly absolutist France, for example, great nobles only started to lose their regional power during the later seventeenth century, when Louis XIV undertook a sustained (and ultimately successful) effort to replace them with government-appointed and removable regional administrators. Before then, great lords ran their domains like princes and often took up arms against the French crown itself.

Seen from the bottom, such systems often imposed tyranny on ordinary people. Seen from the top, however, they lacked capacity; the intermediaries supplied soldiers, goods, and money to rulers, but their autonomous privileges also set stringent limits to rulers' ability to govern or transform the world within their presumed jurisdictions.

Only the nineteenth century brought widespread adoption of direct rule: creation of structures extending governmental communication and control continuously from central institutions to individual localities or even to households, and back again. Creation of direct rule commonly included such measures as uniform tax codes, large-scale postal services, professional civil services, and national military conscription. Even then, direct rule ranged from the unitary hierarchies of centralized monarchy to the segmentation of federalism. On a large scale, direct rule made substantial citizenship, and therefore democracy, possible. Possible, but not likely, much less inevitable: instruments of direct rule have sustained many oligarchies, some autocracies, a number of party- and army-controlled states, and a few fascist tyrannies. Even in the era of direct rule most regimes have remained far from democratic.

After putting more preliminaries into place, the book organizes its main explanations of democratization and de-democratization around three central clusters of changes:

1　Increase or decrease of integration between interpersonal networks of trust (e.g. kinship, religious membership, and relationships within trades) and public politics
2　Increase or decrease in the insulation from public politics of the major categorical inequalities (e.g. gender, race, ethnicity, religion, class, caste) around which citizens organize their daily lives
3　Increase or decrease in the autonomy of major power centers (especially those wielding significant coercive means) such as warlords, patron-client chains, armies, and religious institutions with respect to public politics

The fundamental processes promoting democratization in all times and places, the argument runs, consist of increasing integration of trust networks into public politics, increasing insulation of public politics from categorical inequality, and decreasing autonomy of major power centers from public politics.

French Democratization and De-democratization, 1600–2006

Even during its recent history, democracy has been a precarious and reversible form of rule. To see the recency, precariousness, and reversibility of democracy, we might inspect the history of France since 1600. Here I can draw on a lifetime's work in French political history (especially Shorter and Tilly 1974; Tilly 1964, 1986, 1993, chapter 5, 2004, chapter 4). France offers a fascinating challenge to common explanations of democratization and de-democratization. It emphatically refutes any notion of democratization as a gradual, deliberated, irreversible process or as a handy set of political inventions a people simply locks into place when it is ready. On the contrary, it displays the crucial importance of struggle and shock for both democracy and its reversals.

Following the North American and Dutch revolutions of the previous two decades, the early French Revolution (1789–1793) established one of history's most influential models of national democratic government. In an Athenian gesture that Machiavelli might well have deplored, the early revolutionaries replaced the sovereign king and his council with a parliament elected by citizens at large. Only through vast experimentation and struggle, including civil wars, did they work their way back to a central executive, with Napoleon's rise to power from 1799 onward its culmination (Woloch 1970, 1994). Under Napoleon's rule, moreover, democracy declined as state capacity rose.

By no means did Napoleon's authoritarian regime bring the end of struggles and reversals. (For compact summaries of French constitutional regimes and elections, see Caramani 2000: 292–373, 2003: 146–148.) During the nineteenth century, France not only returned to the (more or less constitutional) Restoration and July monarchies from 1815 to 1848, but then underwent another democratic revolution before moving back into an authoritarian regime (1851–1870) under Louis Napoleon Bonaparte. A relatively peaceful and relatively democratic revolution (1870) preceded a year of struggle with and within the Communes of Paris and other major cities.

The Communes bring us only to the halfway point between the great revolution of the 1790s and the French regime we know today. A long-lived Third Republic (relatively democratic except for the exclusion of women) took shape during the 1870s and lasted until the Nazi occupation of 1940. Not until the conclusion of major postwar struggles (1944–1947), however, did contemporary France's more or less continuously democratic regime lock into place. Finally (1945) women acquired the rights to vote and hold elective office in France. (Even then we might consider the fierce Algerian civil war of 1954–1962 and Charles de Gaulle's war-induced return to power in 1958 to count as a democratic recession, and think of the vast mobilizations against de Gaulle in 1968 as yet another crisis of democracy.) Depending on how we count lesser reversals, between 1789 and the present, France underwent at least four substantial periods of democratization, but also at least three substantial periods of de-democratization.

Let us return to our capacity-democracy regime space for greater clarity. By *democracy*, we still mean the extent to which the regime features broad, equal, protected, binding consultation of citizens with respect to state actions. By *state capacity,* we still mean the extent to which interventions of state agents in existing non-state resources, activities, and interpersonal connections alter existing distributions of those resources, activities, and interpersonal connections as well as relations among those distributions. In these terms, Figure 11.1 traces France's complex trajectory from 1600 to the present. Despite its many turns, the graph actually simplifies greatly, in ways that bear on the rest of our analysis. Take, for example, the middle of the seventeenth century. At 1600 the graph properly portrays France at a low point of both democracy and state capacity as it emerged shattered from the sixteenth century's titanic Wars of Religion. Precious little breadth, equality, protection, mutually binding consultation, or state capacity existed in the battered kingdom. Capacity then recovered somewhat under aggressive kings, with no move toward anything faintly resembling democracy for the bulk of French people.

The period from 1648 to 1653 brought a France that had partly recovered from anarchy under kings Henry IV and Louis XIII back into the same anarchic zone of low capacity and minimal democracy. The civil wars of the Fronde split France repeatedly. The young Louis XIV and his advisors only started to regain control of vast regions during the mid-1650s, and managed

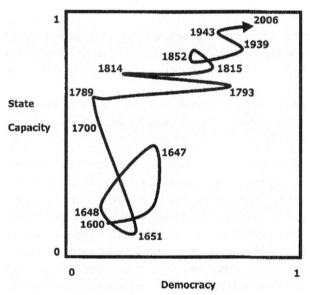

Figure 11.1 Trajectory of French National Regimes, 1600–2006

to subdue large areas of Protestant autonomy within the self-declared Catholic state beginning in the 1680s.

It will not help us much to follow every squiggle and turn of French political history from 1600 to the present. Here are the main messages to draw from the diagram:

- Over the first half of the seventeenth century the French regime stayed entirely out of democratic territory but gained and lost capacity at a dizzying pace.
- Only when the king and his close allies were able to subdue or buy off their largely autonomous rivals within the country did state capacity increase significantly; rebellions and demands led by regional magnates repeatedly reversed the growth of capacity.
- During the second half of the same century the consolidating rule of Louis XIV built up capacity enormously, at the expense of an even greater retreat from anything resembling democracy; regional power holders and enclaves lost autonomy massively.
- No major change of direction occurred until the Revolution of 1789, when France began an extraordinary experiment with democratic forms.
- Soon, however, revolutionaries' efforts to combat both domestic and foreign enemies led to a new buildup of capacity at the expense of democracy.
- From the end of the Napoleonic Wars (1814) to the end of World War II, the country veered constantly between spurts of democratization and de-democratization; state capacity usually headed upward in either phase.
- During the postwar period, France built a high-capacity democratic state that (at least so far) does not seem to be reversing its direction significantly.

Nonetheless, fully revolutionary situations continued into the eighteenth century and accelerated during the nineteenth. The country did not escape massive, if intermittent, fragmentation of state control over its people, resources, and territory until the end of World War II. If we extend the count of revolutionary situations from Metropolitan France to overseas territories, the Algerian and Vietnamese wars would greatly extend the period of threatened revolutionary disruption. Even more than the capacity-democracy diagram, the chronology (Box 11.1) shows to what extent French democratization resulted from revolutionary struggle.

BOX 11.1 Revolutionary Situations within Metropolitan France, 1648–2006

1648–1653	The Fronde
1655–1657	Tardanizat Rebellion (Guyenne)
1658	Sabotiers Rebellion (Sologne)
1661–1662	Bénauge Rebellion (Guyenne)
1662	Lustucru Rebellion (Boulonnais)
1663	Audijos Rebellion (Gascony)
1663–1672	Angelets guerrilla warfare (Roussillon)
1675	Papier Timbre, Bonnets Rouges (or Torrében) rebellions (Brittany)
1702–1706	Camisard rebellions of Cévennes and Languedoc
1768–1769	Corsican Rebellion
1789–1799	Multiple French revolutions and counter-revolutions
1815	Hundred Days
1830	July Revolution
1848	French Revolution
1851	Louis Napoleon *coup d'état*, insurrection
1870	State collapse, German occupation, republican revolutions
1870–1871	Multiple Communes
1944–1945	Resistance and Liberation

Democratization and De-democratization

Since independence in 1947, India has occupied a position somewhere within the high-capacity, high-democracy quadrant of our capacity-democracy space. Both capacity and democracy have fluctuated somewhat over the sixty years, but in general India's national regime has resembled that of

Canada, say, more than that of Jamaica or Kazakhstan. This country of 1.1 billion inhabitants nevertheless poses problems for any analysis of de-mocratization and de-democratization. Those problems arise in a number of different ways:

- Despite extensive poverty and inequality among its people, the Indian economy is becoming one of the world's great makeweights.
- Its 25 states—many of them larger and more populous than most European states—vary enormously in wealth, social composition, and political character.
- Its public politics regularly features vivid displays of religiously tinged ritual.
- Hindu, Muslim, Sikh, and other religious militants all intermittently massacre one another and attack one another's sacred symbols.
- Around the country's edges (for example, in Kashmir and in the ethnically fragmented northeast) separatist groups regularly use armed force to attack government personnel and state security personnel regularly employ brutal repression.
- In the country's central regions Maoist guerrillas (commonly called Naxalites), who have some political presence in about a quarter of all Indian political districts, likewise use lethal means to massacre government forces and uncooperative villagers.

Signs of Democratization and De-democratization

The formidable case of India thus brings us back to this book's general mission. In broadest terms, we are trying to describe and explain variation and change in the extent to which the state behaves according to its citizens' expressed demands. To make the description manageable, it helps to break our inquiry into four components: how wide a range of citizens' expressed demands come into play, how equally different groups of citizens experience a translation of their demands into state behavior, to what extent the expression of demands itself receives the state's political protection, and how much the process of translation commits both sides, citizens and state. These four components lead directly to our working definition: A regime is democratic to the degree that political relations between the state and its citizens feature broad, equal, protected, mutually binding consultation. Democratization then means net movement toward broader, more equal, more protected, and more mutually binding consultation and de-democratization means net movement toward narrower, more unequal, less protected, and less mutually binding consultation.

But how can we know that such changes are actually happening? The problem breaks into two parts: principles of detection and available evidence that would allow us to apply those principles. Let us leave aside the second question—available evidence—for a moment in order to concentrate on principles. In a world of unlimited information, how would we go about detecting democratization and de-democratization according to these principles? Box 11.2 presents a summary of the guidelines discussed for detecting these processes.

My earlier analyses of France, post-socialist regimes, and India all applied these principles, however informally. The organizing ideas are simple: start with citizen-state interactions; concentrate on dynamics rather than static comparisons; average the changes in breadth, equality, protection, and mutually binding consultation; specify the range of cases within which you are working; standardize changes on that range; and let deviations from close correlation among changes signal important explanatory problems. In the case of India, for example, these principles call particular attention to the democratic crises of 1975 to 1977 and 1991 to 1994.

Let me not, however, raise your expectations too high. None of the analyses in the rest of the book reach the ambitious standard of measurement set by the examples in Box 11.2. Often I will propose an analytically informed narrative in the style of my accounts for France and India, keeping the Box 11.2 principles in mind but without setting out numbers or even precise comparisons with other regimes. Repeatedly (as in the case of India) I will rely on annual Freedom House ratings of a regime's political rights and civil liberties, with political rights scores standing as rough proxies for breadth, equality, and mutually binding consultation while civil liberties stand in for protection. These measures fall far short of the precision it would take to verify—or falsify—this book's arguments. But they concretize my claims about particular regimes and thus open my analyses to confirmation, revision, or refutation by specialists.

Choice of comparison cases will obviously affect our understanding of the low to high democracy range. Suppose, for example ... Adam Przeworski and his collaborators, who studied the performances of 141 independent regimes between 1950 and 1990 (Przeworski *et al.* 2000: 18–36). ... Over the four decades studied, the great bulk of these regimes turned out to conduct formal elections, however fraudulent. Two conclusions follow. First, in the 1950 to 1990 study, the range runs essentially from sham elections to fully competitive electoral systems but involves no further distinctions beyond those limits...

BOX 11.2 Principles for Description of Democracy, Democratization, and De-democratization

1. Concentrate on observations of interactions between citizens and states; for example, observe what happens when groups of citizens make claims on state officials and when state officials seek to repress their enemies or rivals.

2. Invent or adopt measures that aggregate over many citizen-state interactions and/or sample a wide range of interactions; for example, analyze correspondence and meetings between officials and ordinary citizens.

3. Look for changes in breadth, equality, protection, and mutually binding consultation of state-citizen consultation; for example, analyze shifts in the frequency with which officials detain dissidents in the absence of due process.

4. Average those changes, on the assumption that alterations in breadth, equality, protection, and mutually binding consultation make equal contributions to democratization and de-democratization. For example, derive separate summary scores for changes in breadth, equality, protection, and mutually binding consultation before combining them into overall scores for democratization or de-democratization.

5. If the changes are distinctly heterogeneous (one element changes in the opposite direction, or one shifts far more or far less than the others), tag them for special attention. For example, if breadth, equality, and protection all increase while mutually binding consultation declines, investigate the possibility of a move toward benevolent despotism.

6. Set a clear range of comparison cases arrayed from least to most democratic, with the comparison cases ranging from all regimes that have ever existed to a quite narrow array, depending on your analytical purposes. For example, for an investigation of World War I's impact on democracy, compare all eventual belligerents year by year from 1915 to 1925.

7. Standardize changes in the case at hand on the range developed; for example, when looking at Germany from 1915 to 1925, score its degree of democracy relative to the highest (1) and lowest (0) democracy scores any of the war-affected regimes reached during the period.

8. Complement that comparison among regimes with detection of changes in the extent to which the state implemented the results of state-citizen consultation. For example, year by year from 1915 to 1925, compare German state performance with demands articulated by voting and social movement activity.

9. If this analysis reveals changes in implementation, investigate whether shifts in state capacity caused those changes. For example, determine whether postwar reparations, inflation, and reconstruction reduced the German state's ability to respond to citizen demands.

Astonishing Switzerland

Let us see, for example, whether we can convert the unruly political history of Switzerland into something like a disciplined set of observations on democratization and de-democratization. We close in on Switzerland as a relatively unknown experimenter with both democratization and de-democratization. A close look at Swiss history between the late eighteenth century and the middle of the nineteenth century allows us to clarify the questions that have been emerging in this chapter so far: how we can trace movement along the democracy-undemocracy dimension, whether regimes that have entered the zone of possibility for democracy then become more liable to both democratization and de-democratization, and whether democratization and de-democratization typically occur at different tempos and with different forms of opposition between state and citizen power.

Swiss experience provides some surprises in all these regards, both because of the common assumption that the Swiss simply refashioned ancient Alpine local democracy into a national regime and because of Switzerland's reputation as a calm, smug, orderly country. In fact, the Swiss path to democracy led the country close to utter fragmentation and passed through nearly two decades of civil war.

The French Revolution shook Switzerland's economic and political ties to France while exposing Swiss people to new French models and doctrines. From 1789 onward, revolutionary movements formed in several parts of Switzerland. In 1793, Geneva (not a federation member, but closely tied to Switzerland) underwent a revolution on the French model. As the threat of French invasion mounted in early 1798, Basel, Vaud, Lucerne, Zurich, and other Swiss regions followed the revolutionary path. Basel, for example, turned from a constitution in which only citizens of the capital chose their canton's senators to another giving urban and rural populations equal representation.

In 1798, an expansive France conquered Switzerland in collaboration with Swiss revolutionaries. Under French supervision, the Swiss regime then adopted a much more centralized form of government with significantly expanded citizenship. The new regime incorporated the territories of cantons St. Gallen, Grisons, Thurgau, Ticino, Aargau, and Vaud on equal terms with the older cantons, but followed French revolutionary practice by reducing the cantons to administrative and electoral units. The central government remained fragile, however; four coups occurred between 1800 and 1802, alone. At the withdrawal of French troops in 1802, multiple rebellions broke out. Switzerland then rushed to the brink of civil war. Only Napoleon's intervention and the imposition of a new constitution in 1803 kept the country together.

The 1803 regime, known in Swiss history as the Mediation, restored considerable power to the cantons, but by no means reestablished the Old Regime. Switzerland's recast federation operated with a national assembly, official multilingualism, relative equality among cantons, and freedom for citizens to move from canton to canton. Despite some territorial adjustments, a weak central legislature, judiciary, and executive survived Napoleon's defeat. Survival only occurred, however, after another close brush with civil war, this time averted by Great Power intervention during 1813 to 1815.

In the war settlement of 1815, Austria, France, Great Britain, Portugal, Prussia, Russia, Spain, and Sweden accepted a treaty among 22 cantons (with the addition of Valais, Neuchâtel, and Geneva) called the Federal Pact as they guaranteed Switzerland's perpetual neutrality and the inviolability of its frontiers. As compared with the period of French hegemony, however, the Federal Pact greatly reduced the central state's capacity; Switzerland of the Federal Pact operated without a permanent bureaucracy, a standing army, common coinage, standard measures, or a national flag. It had to struggle with multiple internal customs barriers, a rotating capital, and incessant bickering among cantonal representatives who had no right to deviate from their home constituents' instructions. At the national scale, the Swiss lived with a system better disposed to vetoes than to concerted change.

At France's July 1830 revolution, anticlericalism became more salient in Swiss radicalism. Historians of Switzerland in the 1830s speak of a regeneration movement pursued by means of "publicity, clubs, and mass marches"

(Nabholz *et al.* 1938 II, 406). A great spurt of new periodicals and pamphlets accompanied the political turmoil of 1830 to 1831 (Andrey 1986: 551–552). Within individual cantons, empowered liberals began enacting standard nineteenth-century reforms such as limitation of child labor and expansion of public schools. Nevertheless, the new cantonal constitutions installed during that mobilization stressed liberty and fraternity much more than they did equality.

Between 1830 and 1848, Switzerland underwent a contradictory set of political processes. Although the era's struggles unquestionably activated many convinced democrats, they pitted competing conceptions of democracy against each other. On one side, broadly speaking, we see the defenders of highland liberty: each village, city, and canton—or at least its property-holding adult males—should be free to control their collective destinies. On the other side we find the advocates of representative democracy at a national scale, who rejected the highland view in favor of greatly enlarged state capacity, equality across Switzerland as a whole, protection provided by federal authorities, and national consultation that would bind all parts of the country.

Behind the divisions between the two sides lay further divisions of religion, class, and integration into capitalist organization. The country's richer, more Protestant cantons struggled their way toward democracy. Those cantons installed representative institutions instead of the direct democracy of male citizens that had long prevailed in highland communities and cantons. Activists based in reformed cantons then used armed force to drive their unreformed neighbors toward representative democracy. They did so first in raids across cantonal boundaries, then in open, if short-lived, civil war.

The political problem became acute because national alignments of the mid-1840s pitted twelve richer and predominantly liberal-Protestant cantons against ten poorer, predominantly conservative-Catholic cantons in a diet in which each canton had a single vote. Ironically, the highland cantons that most prided themselves on direct democracy, Swiss style, dug in most fiercely against democratization that would involve population-based representation at a national scale. Thus liberals deployed the rhetoric of national patriotism and majority rule while conservatives countered with cantonal rights and defense of religious traditions. Three levels of citizenship—municipal, cantonal, and national—competed with one another.

Contention occurred incessantly, and often with vitriolic violence, from 1830 to 1848. Reform movements were already under way in Vaud and Ticino as 1830 began—indeed, Ticino preceded France by adopting a new constitution on July 4th, 1830 (Sauter 1972). Nevertheless, France's July Revolution of

1830 and its Belgian echo later in the year encouraged Swiss reformers and revolutionaries. As the French and Belgian revolutions rolled on, smaller-scale revolutions took place in the Swiss towns and cantons of Aargau, Lucerne, St. Gallen, Schaffhausen, Solothurn, Thurgau, Vaud, and Zurich. Thereafter, republicans and radicals repeatedly formed military bands and attempted to take over particular cantonal capitals by force of arms. Such bands failed in Lucerne (1841) but succeeded in bringing new administrations to power in Lausanne (1847), Geneva (1847), and Neuchâtel (1848).

The largest military engagement took place in 1847. Switzerland's federal Diet ordered dissolution of the mutual defense league (Sonderbund) formed by Catholic cantons two years earlier; when the Catholic cantons refused, the Diet sent an army to Fribourg and Zug (whose forces capitulated without serious fighting), then Lucerne (where a short battle occurred). The Sonderbund had about 79,000 men under arms, the federation some 99,000.

The Sonderbund War itself produced fewer casualties than the smaller-scale struggles that preceded it. Historian Joachim Remak titled his book on the subject *A Very Civil War* (1993). The war ended with 33 dead among Catholic forces and 60 dead among the attackers. Their defeat consolidated the dominance of liberals in Switzerland as a whole and led to the adoption of a cautiously liberal constitution, based on something like an American model, in 1848. The long negotiations of the peace settlement benefited greatly from two external factors: the distraction of Europe's major powers by their own 1848 revolutions and the unwillingness of Austria, Prussia, and France to let either of its rival powers gain political advantage in Switzerland.

The subsequent period resembled America's Reconstruction, the troubled time that followed the United States' own Civil War—grudging coexistence, persistent testing, but no more approaches to a definitive split. The "patriots" of 1848 led the country for years. General Guillaume Dufour, who led the federal troops that defeated the Sonderbund (and who had once taught Louis Napoleon at the Thun military school), for example, commanded the Swiss army for much of the first postwar decade. Between 1849 and 1870, all Swiss cantons terminated their profitable centuries-old export of mercenary units for military service outside of Switzerland. Thereafter, only papal guards and a few ceremonial military units represented Swiss soldiery outside of Switzerland itself. From that point onward, the image of tidy villages and orderly cities displaced the memory of incessant, bitter military strife.

Switzerland's complex history between 1790 and 1848 poses a serious challenge for the representation of democratization and de-democratization.

Our capacity-democracy space helps to meet that challenge. Figure 11.2 traces Switzerland's astonishing trajectory from 1790 to 1848. Despite direct adult male democracy in a number of villages and highland cantons, the regime as a whole started its itinerary with low state capacity and little democracy. French intervention from 1798 onward boosted both capacity and democracy somewhat, but not permanently. At the 1815 peace settlement the Swiss regime both de-democratized and lost capacity. The energetic mobilizations of the 1830s restored some democracy to the regime as a whole without expanding the central state's capacity.

Soon Switzerland's divisions splintered first into civil wars at the cantonal and inter-cantonal levels before consolidating into the national civil war of the Sonderbund. By 1847 Switzerland had receded to its lowest levels of state capacity and democracy over the entire period. But with the military defeat of autonomist and conservative forces, the peace settlement of 1848 established a national regime of unprecedented democracy and state capacity. To be sure, late-nineteenth-century Switzerland never came close to neighboring France, Prussia, or Austria with regard to central capacity. But it became a European model for decentralized democracy.

Before 1798, Switzerland had never come close to substantial capacity or democracy at a national scale. The French conquest of that year simultaneously imposed a much more centralized national government and connected Switzerland's advocates of national representative government with powerful French allies. At that point, Switzerland switched into a long phase of rapid, and often violent, alternation between democratization and de-democratization. Precisely because of the regime's decentralized structure, variety, and sharp divisions, Swiss experience between 1798 and 1848 makes it difficult to divide national politics neatly into "state" and "citizens."

Swiss activists fought over that division for half a century. Yet a pair of generalizations that have been building up over other cases we have examined apply here as well: on the whole, Swiss de-democratization occurred more rapidly and violently than Swiss democratization, and in general, privileged elites backed de-democratization against the expressed will of most citizens. Formation of the Catholic-conservative Sonderbund (1845) and its engagement in outright civil war against liberal forces (1847) brought Switzerland's crisis of elite reaction. In Switzerland, as elsewhere, democratization and de-democratization turn out to have been asymmetrical processes.

Let me draw a methodological conclusion. As pleasant as it would be to manipulate quantitative measures of democratization, de-democratization, increase in state capacity, and decrease of state capacity, in the present state

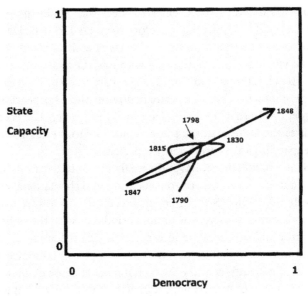

Figure 11.2 Fluctuations in Swiss National Regimes, 1790–1848

of knowledge, detailed analytical narratives of the kind we have just reviewed for Switzerland promise more for general explanations of democratization and de-democratization. They promise more because they allow us to match detailed changes in relations among political actors to alterations in their presumed causes. Although I will rely repeatedly on ratings such as those provided by Freedom House in chapters to come, the crucial matching of arguments and evidence will come in the form of analytical narratives.

What Next?

It is therefore time to move toward explanation of democratization and de-democratization. Almost inadvertently, we have accumulated a series of pressing explanatory questions. Answers to any of these questions, if correct, will provide major payoffs for today's studies of democracy. (If you yearn for fame and influence, and not necessarily fortune, as an analyst of democracy, answer one or more of these questions definitively.) Although I have phrased the questions in broadly historical terms, most students of the recent past are actually pursuing their own versions of the same questions. Box 11.3 summarizes the significant questions we have encountered so far.

BOX 11.3 Payoff Questions in the Study of Democratization and De-democratization

1. In what ways did the truncated democratic institutions of city-states, warrior bands, peasant communities, merchant oligarchies, religious sects, and revolutionary movements provide models for more extensive forms of democracy? Given their availability, why did they never become direct templates for democracy at a national scale?

2. Why did Western Europe lead the way toward democratization, followed closely by the Americas?

3. How did (and do) such countries as France move from absolute immunity against national democratic institutions to frequent alternations between democratization and de-democratization?

4. Why, in general, did (and do) surges of de-democratization occur more rapidly than surges of democratization?

5. How do we explain the asymmetrical patterns of support for and involvement in democratization and de-democratization?

6. Why does democratization typically occur in waves, rather than in each regime separately at its own pace?

7. What explains the spread of democratization and de-democratization during the nineteenth and (especially) twentieth centuries from its Western European starting points to the rest of the world?

8. Why (with the partial exceptions of Egypt and Japan) did democratization only start to occur in Asia and Africa well after World War II?

9. How can we account for the dramatically different experiences of post-socialist states with democratization and de-democratization?

10. Under what conditions, to what extent, and how does the growth of state capacity promote a regime's availability for democratization and de-democratization?

11. To what extent and how do an undemocratic regime's interactions with democratic regimes promote democratization in that regime?

12. How do the forms and sources of a state's sustaining resources (e.g. agriculture, minerals, or trade) affect its regime's susceptibility to democratization and de-democratization?

13. Do any necessary or sufficient conditions exist for democratization and de-democratization, or (on the contrary) do favorable conditions vary significantly by era, region, and type of regime?

Trust networks are ramified interpersonal connections, consisting mainly of strong ties, within which people set valued, consequential, long-term resources and enterprises at risk to the malfeasance, mistakes, or failures of others. Trading diasporas, kinship groups, religious sects, revolutionary conspiracies, and credit circles often comprise trust networks. Throughout most of history, participants in trust networks have carefully shielded themselves from involvement in political regimes, for justified fear that rulers would either seize their precious resources or subordinate them to the state's programs.

So long as they remain entirely segregated from regimes, however, trust networks constitute obstacles to democratization; their segregation blocks members' commitment to democratic collective enterprises. Democratization becomes possible when trust networks integrate significantly into regimes, and thus motivate their members to engage in mutually binding consultation—the contingent consent of citizens to programs proposed or enacted by the state (Tilly 2005). Two large processes affecting trust networks therefore underlie democratization: 1) dissolution or integration of segregated trust networks and 2) creation of politically connected trust networks. In Switzerland, the violent struggles of 1830 to 1847 and the peace settlement of 1848 promoted both processes (Tilly 2004: 187–190).

Within the two processes appear a series of recurrent mechanisms, for example:

- Disintegration of existing segregated trust networks (e.g. decay of patrons' ability to provide their clients with goods and protection promotes withdrawal of clients from patron-client ties)
- Expansion of population categories lacking access to effective trust networks for their major long-term risky enterprises (e.g. growth of landless wage-workers in agrarian regions increases population without effective patronage and/or relations of mutual aid)
- Appearance of new long-term risky opportunities and threats that existing trust networks cannot handle (e.g. substantial increases in war, famine, disease, and/or banditry visibly overwhelm protective capacity of patrons, diasporas, and local solidarities)

In Switzerland, all three of these mechanisms reshaped trust networks between 1750 and 1848. Intensive growth of cottage textile production preceded nineteenth-century re-concentration in lowland cities, including Zürich. That two-stage industrial transformation swelled Switzerland's proletarian population as it shook the patronage-cum-control of landlords and parish priests (Braun 1960, 1965; Gruner 1968; Gschwind 1977; Joris 1994; Joris and Witzig 1992; Rosenband 1999). Successive French invasions, the 1815 great power settlement, and the struggles of 1830 through 1847 themselves had dual effects: They shook old relations between trust networks and public politics at the cantonal level, but—at least for Protestants and secular liberals-created new connections between interpersonal trust networks and the new half-regime that was emerging at a national scale within the Protestant-liberal coalition.

Each of the three mechanisms just listed promotes the dissolution of segregated trust networks and the creation of politically connected trust networks. The next chapter takes a detailed look at processes and mechanisms affecting trust networks' segregation from and integration into public politics.

What of categorical inequality? The term means organization of social life around boundaries separating whole sets of people who differ collectively in their life chances, as is commonly the case with categories of gender, race, caste, ethnicity, nationality, and religion and is sometimes the case with categories of social class. To the extent that such inequalities translate directly into categorical differences in political rights and obligations, democratization remains impossible. Any democratization process depends not necessarily on diminution of categorical inequality but on insulation of public politics from categorical inequality. Two main processes contribute to that insulation: equalization of the categories themselves in some regards and buffering of politics from the operation of those categories.

Here are the sorts of mechanisms that operate within the broader processes of equalization and buffering:

- Equalization of assets and/or well-being across categories within the population at large (e.g. booming demand for the products of peasant agriculture expands middle peasants)
- Reduction or governmental containment of privately controlled armed force (e.g. disbanding of magnates' personal armies weakens noble control over commoners, thereby diminishing nobles' capacity to translate noble-commoner differences directly into public politics)
- Adoption of devices that insulate public politics from categorical inequalities (e.g. secret ballots; payment of officeholders; and free, equal access of candidates to media forward the formation of cross-category coalitions)

These and similar mechanisms figured prominently in the Swiss history we have reviewed. In Switzerland, the regime that formed in 1848 established effective barriers between public politics and the categorical inequalities over which Swiss activists killed each other during the previous 17 years.

These arguments center on a core idea. Democratization never occurs without at least partial realization of three large processes: integration of interpersonal trust networks into public politics; insulation of public politics from categorical inequalities; and elimination or neutralization of autonomous, coercion-controlling power centers in ways that augment the influence of ordinary people over public politics and increase the control of public politics over state performance. Substantial withdrawal of trust networks from public politics, increasing insertion of categorical inequalities into public politics, and rising autonomy of coercive power centers all promote de-democratization. Although delays occur in the effects of these processes as a function of institutions set in place in the past, the three large processes and their reversals always dominate moves toward and away from democracy.

References

Andrews, George Reid and Herrick Chapman, eds. 1995. *The Social Construction of Democracy, 1870–1990.* New York: New York University Press.

Andrey, Georges. 1986. "La Quête d'un État National." In *Nouvelle Histoire de la Suisse et des Suisses,* edited by Jean-Claude Fayez. Lausanne, Switzerland: Payot.

Braun, Rudolf. 1960. *Industrialisierung und Volksleben.* Zurich, Switzerland: Rentsch.

———. 1965. *Sozialer und Kultureller Wandel in Einem Ländlichen Industriegebiet.* Zurich, Switzerland: Rentsch.

Caramani, Daniele. 2000. *The Societies of Europe: Elections in Western Europe since 1815. Electoral Results by Constituencies.* London: Macmillan.

———. 2003. *The Formation of National Electorates and Party Systems in Europe.* Cambridge: Cambridge University Press.

Collier, David and Steven Levitsky. 1997. "Democracy with Adjectives: Conceptual Innovation in Comparative Research." *World Politics* 49: 430–451.

Dahl, Robert A. 1998. *On Democracy.* New Haven, CT: Yale University Press.

———. 2005. "What Political Institutions Does Large-Scale Democracy Require?" *Political Science Quarterly* 120: 187–197.

Gruner, Eric. 1968. *Die Arbeiter in der Schweiz im 19. Jahrhundert.* Bern, Switzerland: Francke.

Gschwind, Franz. 1977. *Bevölkerungsentwicklung und Wirtschaftsstruktur der Landschaft Basel im 18. Jahrhundert.* Liestal, Switzerland: Kantonale Drucksachen-und Materialzentrale.

Held, David. 1996. *Models of Democracy.* 2nd ed. Stanford, CA: Stanford University Press.

Inkeles, Alex, ed. 1991. *On Measuring Democracy: Its Consequences and Concomitants.* New Brunswick, NJ: Transaction.

Joris, Elisabeth. 1994. "Auswirkungen der Industrialisierung auf Alltag und Lebenszusammenhänge von Frauen im Zürcher Oberland (1820–1940)." In *Historias Regionales-Historia Nacional: La Confederación Helvetica,* edited by Joseba Agirreazkuenaga and Mikel Urquijo. Bilbao, Spain: Servicio Editorial, Universidad del País Vasco.

Joris, Elisabeth and Heidi Witzig. 1992. *Brave Frauen, Aufmüpfige Weiber. Wie Sich die Industrialisierung auf Alltag und Lebenszusammenhänge von Frauen Auswirkte (1820–1940)*: Zurich, Switzerland: Chronos.

Nabholz, Hans, Leonhard von Muralt, Richard Feller, and Edgar Bonjour. 1938. *Geschichte der Schweiz*. 2 vols. Zurich, Switzerland: Schultheiss and Co.

O'Donnell, Guillermo. 1999. *Counterpoints: Selected Essays on Authoritarianism and Democratization*. Notre Dame, IN: University of Notre Dame Press.

Ortega Ortiz, Reynaldo Yunuen, ed. 2001. *Caminos a la Democracia*. Ciudad de México: El Colegio de México.

Przeworski, Adam, Michael Alvarez, José Antonio Cheibub, and Fernando Limongi. 2000. *Democracy and Development: Political Institutions and Well-Being in the World, 1950–1990*. Cambridge: Cambridge University Press.

Remak, Joachim. 1993. *A Very Civil War: The Swiss Sonderbund War of 1847*. Boulder, CO: Westview.

Rosenband, Leonard N. 1999. "Social Capital in the Early Industrial Revolution." *Journal of Interdisciplinary History* 29: 435–458.

Sauter, Beat Walter. 1972. *Herkunft und Entstehung der Tessiner Kantonsverfassung von 1830*. Zurich, Switzerland: Schulthess.

Schmitter, Phillipe C. and Terry Lynn Karl. 1991. "What Democracy Is...and Is Not." *Journal of Democracy* 2: 77–88.

Shorter, Edward and Charles Tilly. 1974. *Strikes in France, 1830–1968*. Cambridge: Cambridge University Press.

Tilly, Charles. 1964. *The Vendée*. Cambridge, MA: Harvard University Press.

———. 1986. *The Contentious French*. Cambridge, MA: Harvard University Press.

———. 1993. *European Revolutions, 1492–1992*. Oxford: Blackwell.

———. 2004. *Contention and Democracy in Europe, 1650–2000*. Cambridge: Cambridge University Press.

———. 2005. *Trust and Rule*. Cambridge: Cambridge University Press.

Woloch, Isser. 1970. *Jacobin Legacy: The Democratic Movement under the Directory*. Princeton, NJ: Princeton University Press.

———. 1994. *The New Regime: Transformations of the French Civic Order, 1789–1820s*. New York: Norton.

Trust and Democratic Rule   **12**

Charles Tilly

Democratization means movement toward greater breadth, equality, consultation, and protection of mutual rights and obligations between citizens and governmental agents. De-democratization means movement away from breadth, equality, consultation, and protection. By these standards, Ireland was a very undemocratic place at the start of the nineteenth century, and had democratized significantly by the 1920s. Ireland's democratization occurred through mighty, bloody struggle (Tilly 2004: 136–164).

How do trust networks figure in this turbulent history? We have little direct evidence on Irish trust networks as such, but we do know something about configurations of kin groups, religious congregations, fraternal orders, sporting clubs, and militant nationalist organizations. Close studies of local conflict, furthermore, provide graphic evidence concerning the involvement of these sorts of organizations in public politics.[1] In his superb close study of Cork between 1916 and 1923, for example, Peter Hart shows how the Irish Republican Army drew on previously existing youth networks, and took on their forms:

> I.R.A. units were a natural extension of this youth subculture and its body of unspoken assumptions and bonds. Usually benign events and practices became vehicles for political mobilization, and customs such as 'strawing' became part of the political struggle. The family resemblance between the majority of I.R.A. 'operations' and the actions of the Straw Boys is close and clear: the same use of masks or blackened and painted faces, often the same 'queer clothes,' the same-sized gangs of young bachelors acting anonymously under a 'captain,' the same pseudo-military posturing, and the same nocturnal raiding and petty intimidation.
>
> (Hart 1998: 180)

Let us therefore make two strong assumptions: that the visible forms of popular connection contained trust networks, and that their overall segregation from or integration into systems of rule tells us about trust and rule in Ireland.

On that assumption, each of the critical dates—1829, 1869, 1884, and 1919–1923—created new ties between Catholics' trust networks and the ruling regime. Each transition shook earlier control of the regime by elite Protestant networks.

A Dutch ethnographer's remarkable study of an Irish rural area during the later 1960s provides evidence for brokered integration of local trust networks into national politics. In the (unnamed) region where Mart Bax lived, political parties did not represent distinct class or sectoral interests, but assiduously aggregated local interests. Both county and national legislators fought for their positions by using their governmental connections to do concrete favors for their actual or prospective constituents. As much as possible, they undercut the ability of their competitors to do similar favors.

A successful Irish politician, Bax tells us, used and created multiple ties of friendship, kinship, and voluntary association membership with constituents. He (the vast majority were male) also maintained a cadre of local brokers, most frequently within his party's clubs. Students of politics elsewhere will recognize some standard patterns of patronage systems (see e.g. Auyero 2000, Fox 1994, Willerton 1992). Irish patronage, in Bax's account, provided many of the most important connections between citizens and government. Only so long as a politician delivered governmental goods to local trust networks did he maintain his following.

Trust in Democracy

How do such connections affect democracy? Robert Putnam's work on Italy and the United States puts the connections between trust and democracy prominently on the agenda of democratic theory without actually stating a clear argument concerning the causal chain between trust and democracy.... On the side of governmental institutions, Putnam drifts into interpreting more effective institutions as more democratic. On the side of civic engagement, Putnam begins to treat organizational networks, social capital, norms of reciprocity, and fabrics of trust as an indissoluble block. This double glissando leads to his book's final sentence: "Building social capital will not be easy, but it is the key to making democracy work" (Putnam 1993: 185).

Politics, for Warren, combines conflicts over goods, pressures to associate for collective action, and attempts to produce collectively binding decisions (Warren 1999: 311). All these processes—goods conflicts, collective action, and bids for collectively binding decisions—occur more widely in the public politics of democracies. But precisely those processes threaten naturally accumulated trust: goods conflicts generate dissension, collective action brings us-them boundaries into play, and collectively binding decisions mean unequal realization of individual and group interests. Thus democracies require greater trust—at least with regard to outcomes of political struggle—than other sorts of regimes. We might call Warren's formulation *the democratic dilemma of trust*.

My argument likewise addresses the democratic dilemma, but radically recasts it and proposes a fourth solution. By now, readers who have traveled with me this far should find the recasting and resolution familiar. They consist of:

- treating trust as a relationship in which at least one party places valued enterprises at risk to the errors, failures, or malfeasance of another party
- recognizing that such relationships cluster in distinctive networks, especially as the duration and stakes of the valued enterprises increase
- further recognizing that although historically most trust networks have grown up outside of public politics, sometimes they originate within major political actors (e.g. trade unions) or in government itself (e.g. veterans' pension systems)
- denying that associations as such hold the key to democratic participation
- asserting instead that relations between trust networks and public politics matter deeply
- reinterpreting the democratic dilemma as how to connect those valued enterprises and the networks that sustain them to public politics without damaging either trust networks or public politics
- deducing that the connection will only work well with contingent consent on the part of trust network members
- arguing that a governmental shift away from coercion toward combinations of capital and commitment promotes contingent consent
- noting that the trajectory of democratization therefore differs greatly depending on whether the previous relationships between trust networks and rulers are those of authoritarianism, theocracy, patronage, brokered autonomy, evasive conformity, or particularistic ties

As an exit from authoritarianism, for example, democratization depends on movement away from coercion and relaxation of governmental controls over visible trust networks. From a starting point of patronage, in contrast, democratization depends on weakening of patrons' mediation and on more direct integration of trust networks into public politics.

Of breadth, equality, consultation, and protection, integration of trust networks into public politics most directly affects consultation. To the extent that people integrate their trust networks into public politics, they come to rely on governmental performance for maintenance of those networks. They also gain power, individual and collective, through the connections to government those networks mediate. They acquire an unbreakable interest in governmental performance. The political stakes matter. Paying taxes, buying governmental securities, yielding private information to officials, depending on government for benefits, and releasing network members for military service cement that interest and promote active bargaining over the terms of its fulfillment.

Interested citizens participate more actively, on the average, in elections, referenda, lobbying, interest group membership, social movement mobilization, and direct contact with politicians—that is, in consultation. Conversely, segments of the population that withdraw their trust networks from public politics for whatever reasons weaken their own interest in governmental performance, hence their zeal to participate in democratic public politics. To the extent that rich, powerful people can buy public officials or capture those pieces of government bearing most directly on their interests, furthermore, they weaken public politics doubly: by withdrawing their own trust networks and by undermining the effectiveness of less fortunate citizens' consultation.

Three main processes, all of them by now quite familiar, integrate trust networks into public politics: dissolution of segregated trust networks, integration of previously segregated trust networks, and new creation of politically connected trust networks. These processes qualify, I argue, as necessary conditions for democratization. They are necessary because without them citizens lack incentives to face the adversities of democratic politics and can easily exit from public politics when things go against them. In Albert Hirschman's terms, integrated trust networks encourage citizens to choose voice and loyalty over exit (Hirschman 1970).

Integration of trust networks into public politics is not, however, a *sufficient* condition for democratization; authoritarian regimes and theocracies, after all, likewise integrate trust networks. For a full explanation of democratization, we also have to consider two other clusters of processes: 1) insulation of categorical inequalities (for example, by class, gender, and race) from public politics and 2) transformation of public politics itself through a) broadening of political participation, b) equalization of political participation,

c) enhancement of collective control over government, and d) inhibition of arbitrary power by political actors, including agents of government (Tilly 2004: 15–23). Together, these transformations of public politics, insulation of categorical inequalities, and integration of trust networks produce the broad, equal, binding, and protective relations between citizens and governmental agents that characterize democracy.

Ireland certainly experienced the requisite transformations of public politics after the 1820s: step-by-step political participation broadened and equalized, binding consultation of citizens increased dramatically as the country moved away from tight British control, and protections for citizens expanded significantly along the way. Insulation of public politics from categorical inequality likewise increased greatly as both gender distinctions and the Protestant-Catholic divide lost their formal presence in political rights and obligations. But here we focus on shifts in relations between trust networks and public politics. In the case of Ireland—always excluding the North—we witness some dissolution of trust networks as old solidarities of kinship and religion disintegrate. We see substantial integration of existing trust networks into public politics, notably as Catholics become organized political actors. We notice creation of new politically connected trust networks as the Irish state takes on the sorts of social security programs widely adopted by Western states during the twentieth century.

Although the evidence at hand falls short of clinching the case, it looks as though integration of Irish networks in public politics played a significant part in advancing Irish democracy. Let us see whether the same framework helps make sense of a very different history: that of Mexico.

Mexican Democratization

Like Ireland, Mexico fought its way to a relatively democratic regime through constant struggle, occasional civil war, and many a reversal (McAdam, Tarrow, and Tilly 2001: 290–302). Repeatedly, popular mobilizations challenged the state only to succumb under a wicked synthesis of repression and co-optation. Mexico's experience with trust networks and public politics matched the complexity of Ireland's, but followed a very different trajectory. Most dramatically, successive Mexican regimes dispossessed, sidelined, or at least contained the Roman Catholic Church. With the revolution of 1910, Catholic activists began to form Catholic Workers' Circles and even formed a National Catholic Party. But by 1914 revolutionaries were actively attacking the church and seizing its properties (Bailey 1974: 17–26).

Despite small accommodations during the following years, the election of revolutionary general Plutarco Elías Calles to the presidency in 1924 reinforced the government's anticlericalism and drove the church out of national politics:

> [T]he post-revolutionary state broke with the Church in the 1920s, as it implanted itself in the countryside, provoking a wave of violent uprisings throughout the south and centre of the country in which peasants and clergy rose up to demand land and the reopening of the Churches. The repression was brutal, and although a sweeping land reform was implemented in the early 1930s and the Churches were allowed to reopen, for fifty years Mexican governments behaved outwardly as if the Church did not exist. The Church for its part, confined firmly to civil society, has avoided the crises brought about by commitment to social and political causes, and has lived comfortably with a popular religious practice embedded in the daily life of the people.
>
> (Lehmann 1990: 145)

Much more broadly, the revolution of 1910 to 1919 fostered popular mobilization, both urban and rural, that Calles and his allies finally contained. In Veracruz, for example, a remarkable tenants' movement formed after stevedore and labor organizer Rafael Garcia became the city's mayor in 1921. Until Calles' election of 1924, tenants' organizations played central parts in Veracruz politics. But soon after Calles' inauguration, federal officials arrested tenant leader and anarchist Herón Proal; Proal's imprisonment brought the beginning of the end (Wood 2001, Chapters 4–8). Tenants, dockers, and other workers continued to struggle in municipal politics, but lost their connections with the national level of public politics. Even more so than with regard to Ireland, any analysis of Mexican democratization must distinguish sharply between the national and local levels.

Nationally, Mexico installed some of the conventional democratic apparatus, such as formally competitive elections, political parties, and manhood suffrage, about the same time as many of its European counterparts (Caramani 2000, 2004; Tilly 2004: 213–217). Civil wars, rebellions, coups, and authoritarian regimes repeatedly curtailed democratic rights at a national scale, only to be reversed with surprising rapidity and followed by periods of renewed democratization. At the local and regional scales, however, much of Mexico experienced only highly selective integration into national politics, much less into democratic rights and obligations, before the last few decades of the twentieth century. In particular, the surviving indigenous population—about a tenth of the national total at the twentieth century's end—remained largely excluded from national public politics.

Table 12.1 lays out a rough chronology of national events affecting Mexican democratization and de-democratization from 1848 to 2000. Despite omitting many an insurrection and smaller-scale civil war, the chronology portrays a century and a half of tumultuous politics. My task here is not to provide a complete description and explanation of Mexican democratization and de-democratization, but to ask whether the segregation and integration of trust networks played the parts assigned to them in my causal account. Answer: a plausible connection exists. Before the revolution that began in 1910, the Mexican regime operated from the top down almost entirely through patron-client ties. For half a century after the revolution, the government provoked resistance repeatedly, but successfully insulated it from national politics. More so than in Ireland, sharp disjunctions developed between national and local politics. As a result, the state looked much more powerful from the top than from the bottom. During the twentieth century's final decades, however, workers, peasants, and indigenous people began to escape from patronage, brokered autonomy, and evasive conformity into direct involvement with national politics.

Despite the relatively early establishment of manhood suffrage (1857), before the revolution Mexico's national politics revolved around competition among warlords who backed their claims to power—and their control over

Table 12.1   Democratization and De-democratization in Mexico, 1848–2000

1848	as part of war settlement, Mexico cedes California, Arizona, and New Mexico plus parts of Utah, Nevada, and Colorado to the United States
1855–1861	period of liberal reforms under caudillo Juan Alvarez and minister, then president Benito Juárez; universal male suffrage (1857), nationalization of church property, separation of church and state (1859)
1861–1864	French invasion, conquest, installation of Maximilian as emperor, followed by his defeat and execution
1884–1910	dictatorship of Porfirio Díaz, liberalization of economy, dispossession and extermination of Indians

1910–1919 insurrection against Díaz begins revolution and civil war, radical constitution (1917), universal primary education, right to strike, return of peasant lands, oil declared national property

1926–1929 prochurch Cristero rebellion crushed, subordination of Catholic Church

1928–1929 assassination of president Alvaro Obregón, insurrections, settlement with church and labor

1934–1940 Lazaro Cárdenas president, land expropriations, redistribution to peasants as collective property, emergence of organized labor movement, nationalization of U.S. and British oil properties, formation of Party of the Mexican Revolution, predecessor of PRI

1946–1952 consolidation of PRI power, repression of labor and peasant organizations

1953 female suffrage

1958–1959 suppression of nationwide strike, jailing of labor leaders

1968 army puts down student demonstrations for democracy, kills 500, arrests more than 1500; widening of guerrilla activity

1976 landless peasants seize land in Sonora, president López Portillo grants peasants 250,000 acres

1982 nationalization of fifty-nine Mexican banks

1988 dubiously elected Carlos Salinas de Gortari undertakes neoliberal privatization program

1989 opposition parties PAN (liberal) and PRD (left) make gains in regional elections

1992 NAFTA signed with Canada and the United States (implemented January 1994)

1993 Zapatistas seize four towns in Chiapas, begin international campaign

1994 further PAN gains in regional elections

1999 PRI holds first presidential primary after Ernesto Zedillo ends practice of president's naming successor

2000 PAN candidate Vicente Fox Quesada wins presidency, but PRI keeps control of legislature

electoral processes—with military might. Between 1910 and 1930, regionally organized workers and peasants united repeatedly behind populist leaders, both clerical and anticlerical, but no firm integration of their trust networks into national public politics occurred. From the 1930s onward, however, Lazaro Cárdenas and his successors performed the organizational miracle of building selective patron-client chains into a hegemonic national party, first known as the Party of the Mexican Revolution. Under Cárdenas, the government initiated a long-term practice of nationalizing large estates and redistributing them to compliant peasants as agricultural cooperatives, or *ejidos*. During the postwar years the Party of the Revolution mutated into the significantly named *institutional* revolutionary party (*Partido Revolucionario Institucional*), or PRI.

The party eventually commanded electoral support from important segments of the peasantry and organized workers by means of a brokered distributional network. From that point to the 1960s, except at the very summit the Mexican regime ran largely as a patron-client system, with indigenous communities connected to the regime only through evasive conformity, particularistic ties to rulers, or (more rarely) brokered autonomy. Meanwhile, breakaway segments of the PRI, organized students, fragments of organized workers, and some peasant groups intermittently tried to contest PRI-dominated public politics, but with little success.

Depending on employment opportunities in the United States, Mexican peasants alternated between migration north, movement into the edges of major cities, and patronized seizures of agricultural land (Sanderson 1984). Although landless peasants who seized land in northern Mexico did get substantial concessions from outgoing President Luis Echeverría in 1976, in general the government met public claim making that bypassed PRI's patrons with armed repression. Historian Enrique Krauze speaks of a 1971 massacre of students that he witnessed personally from a Mexico City rooftop where he had fled for shelter:

> Although there were fewer killings that day than there were at Tlatelolco in 1968, Mexico's most notorious student massacre, in many ways it was a repeat performance: the government had violently suppressed students. President Luis Echeverría spoke that night on television, promising to open an investigation 'no matter who is found guilty.' A few days later, he fired two officials and the promised inquiry was never begun. Years later, the weekly news magazine Processo explained why: Mr. Echeverría had orchestrated the killings himself.
>
> (Krauze 2004: A21)

By 2004, anti-PRI President Vicente Fox was filing charges of genocide against ex-President Echeverría for that incident and calling for a truth commission to investigate PRI's abuses while in office (Thompson 2004). PRI had not, however, relied on repression alone. The party grew adept at absorbing protest groups that had gained enough organizational strength to threaten party control. It did so through judicious combinations of patronage and governmental repression.

Nevertheless, a series of social changes undermined PRI hegemony from the 1960s onward. Booming oil exports supported economic expansion, creation of an independent bourgeoisie, migration to cities, and new demands for technocratic public administration. Peasant migration to the United States created opportunities and connections outside of existing patron-client chains through remittances, flows of information, and political activity on the part of emigrants. Greater involvement of Mexico in the international economy accelerated the same processes, but also promoted domestic liberalization and increased responsiveness to international scrutiny of electoral politics; the initiation of the North American Free Trade Agreement (NAFTA, 1994) simply reinforced Mexico's neoliberal forces. Under these conditions, the once dominant government response to challenge—co-opt and repress—became less and less feasible. Opposition parties of left and right began to make significant inroads on PRI support during the 1980s. In 2000, the neoliberal PAN (Party of National Action) finally won the Mexican presidency, even if it could not capture control of the legislature.

Trust Networks in Mexico

What evidence do we have concerning connections between trust networks and Mexico's public politics over the long run of 1848 to 2000? Not much. Still, Carlos Forment has assembled a catalog of 2,291 named voluntary groups that were active in Mexico at one time or another during the nineteenth century. They include groups devoted to development, fraternal orders, mutual aid, patriotic causes, artisans, ethnic protection, education, literary and scientific causes, professional privilege, charity and welfare, religion (both Catholic and heterodox), leisure, hobbies, holidays, credit, and savings. Forment's analysis reveals an impressively vigorous nineteenth-century civic life in Mexico's cities and towns. A number of the groups participated actively in local politics, and even came to power at the municipal level. But, Forment insists, they stayed out of national politics,

"We have centralized public life," declared Manuel Rejón, a Mexico City activist, in 1846,

> and have been forced to deposit our sovereignty in a single place with-
> out allowing citizens to divide it among different locales... This has
> left the nation cold, inert and in a state of complete paralysis. Our
> country is vast. The state cannot attend to our interests without also
> extinguishing all our energies. In any case, the administrators they
> have sent to manage our local affairs are uninterested in them. This
> is the cause for all the rebellions that have taken place in the country.
> Citizens now regard the government as a foreign power.
>
> (Forment 2003: 163)

Forment argues that such nineteenth-century activists created municipal democracy, but shielded it as much as possible from national intervention. That description seems to hold for most of Mexico well into the twentieth century. Not only civic associations, but trust networks as well, remained segregated from the regime except for the selective integration of patron-client chains headed by major political figures. In Mexico's federal system, furthermore, the pattern repeated itself at regional and local levels: warlords eventually gave way to political bosses, but patron-client politics operated in most states and municipalities (Cornelius 2001).

During the twentieth century's final decades, however, Mexico's eco-nomic expansion and international integration produced a powerful new combination of changes:

- increasing proportions of the population felt the pressure of market ex-pansion without sharing in its gains
- the capacity of PRI-backed regional bosses to contain those populations declined
- governmental programs designed to continue the decades-old strategy for co-optation of newly mobilized populations failed to incorporate all their targets and actually provided bases for new organization
- trust networks built into peasant cooperatives and indigenous commu-nities connected increasingly with regional and even national political actors outside of patron-client networks and PRI

In his close study of Mexican food policy and its political ramifica-tions, Jonathan Fox gives the example of the largely indigenous highland Montaña region in Guerrero, the Pacific Coast state south of Mexico City. A national program of food distribution initiated in 1980 connected there with a decade-old peasant movement (led in part by radical school-teachers) that had been gaining strength in municipal politics. By 1984 leaders of local food councils had formed a Production Consultation Committee coordinating local activities in about a third of the region's communities (Fox 1992: 188). Among other things, they distributed government-subsidized maize through their own local food stores, thus using national political means to serve local ends.

Mobilization and organization went even farther in the central valleys of adjacent Oaxaca. There, old local trust networks provided the basis for effective organization:

> Behind this traditional defense of local autonomy is a complex web of communitarian institutions. The still widespread *tequio* system of unpaid obligatory community labor, for example, was often used to build the village stores themselves. The roles of rural food committee and store managers also often fit smoothly into the traditional civil-religious authority system known as *cargos*, which organized essential village services such as water, agrarian matters, and parent-teacher associations as well as religious festivals. The cargo system ran parallel to the formal municipal authorities, whose main task was to settle local disputes and to represent the community to outside institutions.
>
> (Fox 1992: 199; more generally, see Fox 1994)

In 1984, the coordinating committee of Oaxaca food councils hosted the first national meeting of the National Union of Autonomous Regional Peasant Organizations. They were thereby integrating themselves into public politics via a newly formed national political actor. Contrary to its PRI-based authors' intentions, the national program of food distribution provided means and incentives for regionally based political entrepreneurs to enter the national scene.

Elsewhere in Oaxaca, Jeffrey Rubin has documented a parallel process in the predominantly Zapotec city of Juchitán. In that city, a largely indigenous Coalition of Workers, Peasants, and Students of the Isthmus (COCEI) came to power in 1989. After widespread protests of workers and peasants from the late 1960s onward, PRI sought to reassert control in Juchitán by imposing political boss Mario Bustillo. Mobilization against Bustillo began characteristically not in Oaxaca but with the Mexico City activities of an Association of Juchiteco Students. Lower-income students from the region gained influence in the association, pressing programs of Zapotec identity and collective self-improvement in place of the integration and personal advancement pursued by their middle-class predecessors. They began to win association elections in 1973. By the end of that year, the student association was allying with local activists in Juchitán as it organized to oust a hospital director and create new health programs there (Rubin 1997: 105–107). COCEI emerged from that citywide mobilization.

The *Coalición* (as participants called it) worked opportunistically, identifying groups of aggrieved peasants or workers and supporting their demands for recognition and redress. Although it straddled the boundary between legal and illegal making of claims, COCEI retained the support of local moderates:

> COCEI's militant and at times illegal approaches were potentially acceptable to moderates in Juchitán in light of the failure of earlier reform efforts, and, equally important, because of their local origin and their embeddedness in Zapotec language and cultural forms. COCEI was seen as a genuine response on the part of the pueblo to the economic and political exploitation that the moderates themselves had exposed. As a result, faced with a local world at odds with their convictions, moderates discussed and rethought their positions on basic political issues, such as democracy, opposition, and violence. Their willingness to support a radical grassroots movement, even as most middle-class and elite Juchitecos fiercely opposed radical politics and tacitly supported ongoing repression, strengthened COCEI at key moments in its development, bringing votes, degrees of local tolerance, and support from some officials in Mexico City.
>
> (Rubin 1997: 110)

In Juchitán, we watch indigenous groups of peasants and workers exiting from patronage, brokered autonomy, and evasive conformity toward democracy through unexpected alliances with university students and local moderates. We watch durable connections forming between indigenous trust networks and national public politics.

Distrust and De-democratization

If integration of trust networks into public politics promotes democratization, their withdrawal from public politics weakens democracy. Withdrawal can occur either voluntarily or involuntarily. Voluntarily, groups of citizens can sever their commitments to public politics at large by creating their own alternatives to government services or acquiring private control over differ-ent pieces of government. White segregationists that created private school systems during the American civil rights era did the first, whereas regulated industries that co-opt their regulators do the second. Involuntarily, previ-ously connected groups can suffer categorical exclusion or termination of the institutions that previously tied them to the regime. Japanese-Americans endured the first fate during World War II, while wholesale contraction of welfare programs probably had a similar effect on low-income American families during the 1990s.

De-democratization occurs more frequently than democratic theorists generally allow. In most theories of democracy, democratization is hard to achieve, but also difficult to reverse.

Threats to Democracy

Plausible, perhaps, but certainly not proven. In the twentieth-century histo-ries of Ireland, Mexico, and Spain we discover not certainties, but a prom-ising research program. The next round of inquiries into democratization should take seriously the segregation and integration of trust networks into public politics. Even if my analyses of how segregation and integration work contain serious errors, at least they establish the interest and importance of such connections. Surely connections between interpersonal trust networks and public politics strongly affect the viability of democratic institutions. But how strongly and how remain open to investigation.

Suppose, however, that I have it right. Two worrisome conclusions loom. First, even in rich, powerful countries democracy remains vulner-able to withdrawal of trust networks from public politics, especially if the networks that withdraw have subjected the rich and powerful to the give and take of contention. Private and home schooling, exclusive clubs and religious sects, gated communities, and capture of governmental agencies or offices for private profit all provide means for elites to secure their own advantages without subjecting themselves to the costs and constraints of public politics.

Second, to the extent that members of trust networks in relatively un-democratic countries manage either to subordinate government to those networks or to maintain themselves without integration into public politics, prospects for democracy will remain dim in those countries. In those coun-tries, totalitarianism, theocracy, and patron-client politics seem more likely futures than democracy.

Note

1   Broeker 1970, Bryan 2000, Clark and Donnelly 1983, Conley 1999a, 1999b, Farrell
    2000, Jarman 1997, Jupp and Magennis 2000, O'Neill 2001, Palmer 1988.

References

Auyero, Javier. 2000. *Poor People's Politics: Peronist Survival Networks and the Legacy of Evita.* Durham, NC: Duke University Press.

Bailey, David C. 1974. *Viva Cristo Rey! The Cristero Rebellion and the Church-State Conflict in Mexico.* Austin: University of Texas Press.

Broeker, Galen. 1970. *Rural Disorder and Police Reform in Ireland, 1812–36.* London: Routledge & Kegan Paul.

Bryan, Dominic. 2000. *Orange Parades: The Politics of Ritual, Tradition and Control.* London: Pluto Press.

Caramani, Daniele. 2000. *The Societies of Europe. Elections in Western Europe since 1815: Electoral Results by Constituencies.* New York: Grove's Dictionaries.

———. 2004. *The Nationalization of Politics: The Formation of National Electorates and Party Systems in Western Europe.* Cambridge: Cambridge University Press.

Clark, Samuel and James S. Donnelly, Jr., eds. 1983. *Irish Peasants: Violence and Political Unrest, 1780–1914.* Madison: University of Wisconsin Press.

Conley, Carolyn A. 1999a. *Melancholy Accidents: The Meaning of Violence in Post-Famine Ireland.* Lanham, MD: Lexington Books.

———. 1999b. "The Agreeable Recreation of Fighting," *Journal of Social History 33*: 58–72.

Cornelius, Wayne. 2001. "Huecos en la democratización: la política subnacional como un obstáculo en la transición Mexicana" in Reynaldo Yunuen Ortega Ortiz, ed., *Caminos a la democracia.* Mexico City: El Colegio de México, pp. 241–266.

Farrell, Sean. 2000. *Rituals and Riots: Sectarian Violence and Political Culture in Ulster, 1784–1886.* Lexington: University Press of Kentucky.

Forment, Carlos A. 2003. *Democracy in Latin America 1760–1900. Volume I: Civic Selfhood and Public Life in Mexico and Peru.* Chicago: University of Chicago Press.

Fox, Jonathan. 1992. *The Politics of Food in Mexico: State Power and Social Mobilization.* Ithaca, NY: Cornell University Press.

Fox, Jonathan. 1994. "The Difficult Transition from Clientelism to Citizenship: Lessons from Mexico," *World Politics 46*: 151–184.

Hart, Peter. 1998. *The I.R.A. & its Enemies: Violence and Community in Cork, 1916–1923.* Oxford: Clarendon Press.

Hirschman, Albert O. 1970. *Exit, Voice, and Loyalty: Responses to Decline in Firms, Organizations, and States.* Cambridge, MA: Harvard University Press.

Jarman, Neil. 1997. *Material Conflicts: Parades and Visual Displays in Northern Ireland.* Oxford: Berg.

Jupp, Peter and Eoin Magennis, eds. 2000. *Crowds in Ireland c. 1720–1920.* London: Macmillan.

Krauze, Enrique. 2004. "Past Wrongs, Future Rights," *New York Times*, August 10, A21.

Lehmann, David. 1990. *Democracy and Development in Latin America: Economics, Politics and Religion in the Post-War Period*. Philadelphia: Temple University Press.

McAdam, Doug, Sidney Tarrow, and Charles Tilly. 2001. *Dynamics of Contention*. Cambridge: Cambridge University Press.

O'Neill, Joseph. 2001. *Blood-Dark Track. A Family History*. London: Granta.

Palmer, Stanley H. 1988. *Police and Protest in England and Ireland 1780–1850*. Cambridge: Cambridge University Press.

Putnam, Robert D. 1993. *Making Democracy Work: Civic Traditions in Modern Italy*. Princeton, NJ: Princeton University Press.

Rubin, Jeffrey W. 1997. *Decentering the Regime: Ethnicity, Radicalism, and Democracy in Juchitán, Mexico*. Durham, NC: Duke University Press.

Sanderson, Susan R. Walsh. 1984. *Land Reform in Mexico, 1910–1980*. Orlando, FL: Academic Press.

Thompson, Ginger. 2004. "Mexico's Leader to Pursue Genocide Case," *New York Times*, September 1, A10.

Tilly, Charles. 2004. *Contention and Democracy in Europe, 1650–2000*. Cambridge: Cambridge University Press.

Warren, Mark E., ed. 1999. *Democracy and Trust*. Cambridge: Cambridge University Press.

Willerton, John P. 1992. *Patronage and Politics in the USSR*. Cambridge: Cambridge University Press.

Wood, Andrew Grant. 2001. *Revolution in the Street: Women, Workers, and Urban Protest in Veracruz, 1870–1927*. Wilmington, DE: Scholarly Resources.

Durable Inequality   IV

Durable Inequality　　**13**

Charles Tilly

We could reasonably call James Gillray (1757–1815) Britain's first professional cartoonist (George 1967: 57; Hill 1976). He left us unforgettable images of public and private affairs under George III. Very few handsome people figure in Gillray's caricatures. In the savage portrayals of British life he drew, etched, and colored toward 1800, beefy, red-faced aristocrats commonly tower over other people, while paupers almost invariably appear as small, gaunt, and gnarled. If Gillray painted his compatriots with malice, however, he also observed them acutely.

Take the matter of height. Let us consider fourteen-year-old entrants to the Royal Military Academy at Sandhurst to represent the healthier portion of the aristocracy and gentry, and fourteen-year-old recruits for naval service via London's Marine Society to represent the healthier portion of the city's jobless poor. At the nineteenth century's start, poor boys of fourteen averaged only 4 feet 3 inches tall, while aristocrats and gentry of the same age averaged about 5 feet 1 inch (Floud, Wachter, and Gregory 1990: 197; for the history of the Marine Society as an aristocratic benefaction, see Colley 1992: 91–93). An average beginning military cadet stood some 10 inches taller than a newly recruited mariner. Because poor youths then matured later than rich ones, their heights converged an inch or two by adulthood. Nevertheless we can imagine their counterparts in the army: aristocratic officers glowering down half a foot or more at their plebeian troops. Such an image vivifies the phrases "high and mighty," "haughty," and "look down on someone."

Poor people have few good times. But the years around 1800 brought Britain's low-income families especially bad times. In the short run, massive diversion of resources and labor power to French Revolutionary and

Napoleonic wars depleted domestic production as it drove up consumer prices. Over the longer run, the urbanization, industrialization, and sharpened inequality promoted by capitalist expansion were then aggravating the hardships faced by Western Europe's poorer households. As poor people ceased producing their own food faster than agricultural productivity rose, hardship extended to their daily bread.

... Toward the end of the eighteenth century, from 3 to 10 percent of the English and French work forces had too little food to sustain any effective work at all, while a full fifth of the population commanded too little for more than a few hours of light work per day (Fogel 1994: 371–374). At those low nutritional levels, furthermore, English and French workers were extremely vulnerable to chronic disease, hence liable to work lives disrupted by illness and early death. Fogel speculates that malnutrition itself thereby accounted for the stunning proportion of beggars—up to 20 percent of the entire population—reported in various regions of eighteenth-century Europe.

Over population categories, regions, and countries, as Fogel and other researchers have recently established, material well-being and stature vary in strong relation to each other (Floud, Wachter, and Gregory 1990; Fogel 1993, 1994; Fogel and Costa 1997; Komlos 1987, 1990, 1994). Richard Steckel sums up:

> Stature adeptly measures inequality in the form of nutritional deprivation; average height in the past century is sensitive not only to the level of income but to the distribution of income and the consumption of basic necessities by the poor. Unlike conventional measures of living standards based on output, stature is a measure of consumption that incorporates or adjusts for individual nutritional needs; it is a net measure that captures not only the supply of inputs to health but demands on those inputs.
>
> (Steckel 1995: 1903)

Well-being and height link through food consumption; victuals invigorate. Although genes set variable limits to height distributions in human populations, childhood nutrition strongly affects the degree to which any individual approaches her or his genetic limit. Low birth weight, which typically results from a mother's illness and malnutrition, predicts reliably to a child's health problems, diminished life expectancy, and smaller adult size.

Within a given population, furthermore, short stature itself generally predicts to higher levels of morbidity and mortality—most likely not because of height's inherent advantages but because, on the whole, short stature correlates with unfavorable childhood health experiences and lesser body strength. Rising height across an entire population therefore provides one of our clearest signs that the well-being of that population is increasing, and marked adult height differentials by social category within the male or female population provide a strong indicator of durable inequality.

That average heights of adults in Western countries have typically risen 6 inches or so over the past century and a half reflects a significant rise in living standards. That even in egalitarian Sweden recent studies reveal lower birth weights for the newborn of less-educated women (in this case, most likely a joint outcome of smoking and nutrition) tells us that material inequalities persist into prosperity (*Dagens Nyheter* 1996). That at my modest altitude I easily see over the heads of many adult males with whom I travel on New York subways—especially those speaking languages other than English—signals that in capitalist countries we still have profound inequalities of life experience to identify and explain.

Since sexual dimorphism prevails among primates and since humans commonly live in mixed-sex households whose members share food, one might suppose that female/male height differences, unlike class inequalities, derive almost entirely from genetic predisposition. Not quite. Nature and nurture are disentangled with difficulty when it comes to such matters as sex differences in body size. As James Tanner puts it:

> Variation between the heights of *individuals* within a subpopulation is indeed largely dependent on differences in their genetic endowment; but the variation between the means of groups of individuals (at least within an ethnically homogeneous population) reflects the cumulative nutritional, hygienic, disease, and stress experience of each of the groups. In the language of analysis of variance, most of the within-group variation is due to heredity, and most of the between-group variation is due to childhood environment.
>
> (Tanner 1994: 1)

What counts, however, as a subpopulation, or group? Surely not any cohabiting population, regardless of social divisions within it. For "group," read "category" to recognize that class, gender, race, ethnicity, and similar socially organized systems of distinction clearly qualify. (I will follow current conventions by speaking of "sex" in reference to X and Y chromosome–linked biological differences, "gender" in reference to social categories.) In each of these cases, differences in "nutritional, hygienic, disease, and stress experience" contribute to differences in adult stature. Researchers in the field have so far done much more with class differences, national differences, and change over time than with male/female differences.

Still, gender likewise marks distinctive childhood experiences, even when it comes to nutrition. When children in pastoral and agricultural economies begin serious work in their household enterprises, they almost always take on gender-differentiated tasks. That means their daily routines give boys and girls unequal access to food. Most of the time girls get less, and their food is of lower quality. Where men fish or hunt while females till and gather, however, the division of labor often attaches girls and women to the more reliable and continuous sources of calories. Thus in some circumstances females may actually get better nourishment than males.

The fundamental fact, then, is gender differentiation in nutrition, with the usual but not universal condition being inferior nutrition for females. We have enough episodic documentation concerning gender discrimination with respect to health care, feeding, infanticide, and general nurture, as well as slivers of evidence suggesting gender-differential patterns of improvement or decline in nutrition under the influence of broad economic fluctuations, to support hypotheses of widespread unequal treatment of males and females, of inequality in their resulting life chances, hence of a social contribution to gender differences in weight and height as well.

Such socially organized differences in well-being illustrate this book's main subject: the causes, uses, structures, and effects of categorical inequality. The book does not ask what causes human inequality in general. Instead it addresses these questions: How, why, and with what consequences do long-lasting, systematic inequalities in life chances distinguish members of different socially defined categories of persons? How do categorical inequalities form, change, and disappear? Since all social relations involve fleeting, fluctuating inequalities, let us concentrate on *durable* inequalities, those that last from one social interaction to the next, with special attention to those that persist over whole careers, lifetimes, and organizational histories.

Let us concentrate, furthermore, on distinctly bounded pairs such as female/male, aristocrat/plebeian, citizen/foreigner, and more complex classifications based on religious affiliation, ethnic origin, or race. We focus on *categories* rather than on continua such as [rich/poor, tall/short], and so on. Bounded categories deserve special attention because they provide clearer evidence for the operation of durable inequality, because their boundaries do crucial organizational work, and because categorical differences actually account for much of what ordinary observers take to be results of variation in individual talent or effort.

As Max Weber noted almost a century ago, the creation of what he called "social closure" advances efforts by the powerful to exclude less powerful people from the full benefits of joint enterprises, while facilitating efforts by underdogs to organize for the seizure of benefits denied (Weber 1968, 1:43–46, 1:341–348; Parkin 1979: 44–116). A relationship is likely to be closed, Weber remarked,

> in the following type of situation: a social relationship may provide the parties to it with opportunities for the satisfaction of spiritual or material interests. If the participants expect that the admission of others will lead to an improvement of their situation, an improvement in degree, in kind, in the security or the value of the satisfaction, their interest will be in keeping the relationship open. If, on the other hand, their expectations are of improving their position by monopolistic tactics, their interest is in a closed relationship.
>
> (Weber 1968, 1:43)

Organizations such as firms and clans use closure by drawing complete boundaries around themselves and then monitoring flows across those boundaries with care. Contrary to Weber, however, I argue that at a scale larger than a single organization completely bounded categories are rare and difficult to maintain, that most categorical inequality relies on establishment of a partial frontier and defined social relations across that frontier, with much less control in regions distant from the frontier. Yet in other regards my analysis resonates with Weber's discussion. It builds a bridge from Max Weber, on social closure to Karl Marx on exploitation, and back. Crossing that bridge repeatedly, this book concerns social mechanisms—recurrent causal sequences of general scope—that actually lock categorical inequality into place. The central argument runs like this: Large, significant inequalities in advantages among human beings correspond mainly to categorical differences such as black/white, male/female, citizen/foreigner, or Muslim/Jew rather than to individual differences in attributes, propensities, or performances. In actual operation, more complex categorical systems involving multiple religions or various races typically resolve into bounded pairs relating just two categories at a time, as when the coexistence of Muslims, Jews, and Christians resolves into the sets Muslim/Jew, Muslim/Christian, and Jew/Christian, with each pair having its own distinct set of boundary relations.

Even where they employ ostensibly biological markers, such categories always depend on extensive social organization, belief, and enforcement. Durable inequality among categories arises because people who control access to value-producing resources solve pressing organizational problems by means of categorical distinctions. Inadvertently or otherwise, those people set up systems of social closure, exclusion, and control. Multiple parties—not all of them powerful, some of them even victims of exploitation—then acquire stakes in those solutions. Variation in the form and durability of inequality therefore depends chiefly on the nature of the resources involved, the previous social locations of the categories, the character of the organizational problems, and the configurations of interested parties.

Through all these variations, we discover and rediscover paired, recognized, organized, unequal categories such as black/white, male/female, married/unmarried, and citizen/noncitizen. The dividing line between such categories usually remains incomplete in two regards: first, some people (persons of mixed race, transsexuals, certified refugees, and so on) do not fit clearly on one side of the line or the other; and, second, in many situations the distinction between the members of any particular pair does not matter. Where they apply, however, paired and unequal categories do crucial organizational work, producing marked, durable differences in access to valued resources. Durable inequality depends heavily on the institutionalization of categorical pairs.

Roots of Categorical Inequality

How and why does the institutionalization of categorical pairs occur? ... The list will serve as a preliminary map of the wilderness this book will explore:

1   Paired and unequal categories, consisting of asymmetrical relations across a socially recognized (and usually incomplete) dividing line between interpersonal networks, recur in a wide variety of situations, with the usual effect being the unequal exclusion of each network from resources controlled by the other.

2   Two mechanisms we may label *exploitation* and *opportunity hoarding* cause durable inequality when their agents incorporate paired and unequal categories at crucial organizational boundaries.

3   Two further mechanisms we may title *emulation* and *adaptation* reinforce the effectiveness of categorical distinctions.

4   Local categorical distinctions gain strength and operate at lower cost when matched with widely available paired and unequal categories.

5   When many organizations adopt the same categorical distinctions, those distinctions become more pervasive and decisive in social life at large.

6   Experience within categorically differentiated settings gives participants systematically different and unequal preparation for performance in new organizations.

7   Much of what observers ordinarily interpret as individual differences that create inequality is actually the consequence of categorical organization.

8   For these reasons, inequalities by race, gender, ethnicity, class, age, citizenship, educational level, and other apparently contradictory principles of differentiation form through similar social processes and are to an important degree organizationally interchangeable.

People establish systems of categorical inequality, however inadvertently, chiefly by means of these two causal mechanisms:

- *Exploitation* which operates when powerful, connected people command resources from which they draw significantly increased returns by coordinating the effort of outsiders whom they exclude from the full value added by that effort.
- *Opportunity hoarding,* which operates when members of a categorically bounded network acquire access to a resource that is valuable, renewable, subject to monopoly supportive of network activities, and enhanced by the network's modus operandi.

The two mechanisms obviously parallel each other, but people who lack great power can pursue the second if encouraged, tolerated, or ignored by the powerful. Often the two parties gain complementary, if unequal, benefits from jointly excluding others.

Two further mechanisms cement such arrangements in place: *emulation,* the copying of established organizational models and/or the transplanting of existing social relations from one setting to another; and *adaptation,* the elaboration of daily routines such as mutual aid, political influence, courtship, and information gathering on the basis of categorically unequal structures. Exploitation and opportunity hoarding favor the installation of categorical inequality, while emulation and adaptation generalize its influence.

A certain kind of inequality therefore becomes prevalent over a large population in two complementary ways. Either the categorical pair in question—male/female, legitimate/illegitimate, black/white, citizen/non-citizen, and so on—operates in organizations that control major resources affecting welfare, and its effects spread from there; or the categorical pair repeats in a great many similar organizations, regardless of their power.

The basic mechanisms that generate inequality operate in a similar fashion over a wide variety of organizational settings as well as over a great range of unequal outcomes: income, wealth, power, deference, fame, privilege, and more.

People who create or sustain categorical inequality by means of the four basic mechanisms rarely set out to manufacture inequality as such. Instead they solve other organizational problems by establishing categorically unequal access to valued outcomes. More than anything else, they seek to secure rewards from sequestered resources. Both exploitation and opportunity hoarding provide a means of doing so. But, once undertaken, exploitation and opportunity hoarding pose their own organizational problems: how to maintain distinctions between insiders and outsiders; how to ensure solidarity; loyalty, control, and succession; how to monopolize knowledge that favors profitable use of sequestered resources. The installation of explicitly categorical boundaries helps to solve such organizational problems, especially if the boundaries in question incorporate forms of inequality that are already well established in the surrounding world. Emulation and adaptation lock such distinctions into place, making them habitual and sometimes even essential to exploiters and exploited alike.

To be sure, widely applicable categories accumulate their own histories and relations to other social structures: male/female distinctions have acquired enormous, slow-moving cultural carapaces yet reappear within almost all social structures of any scale, whereas in the United States the distinction Hispanic/white remains a disputed, politically driven division of uncertain cultural content. Such categorical pairs therefore operate with characteristic differences when imported into new settings. The distinction citizen/foreigner, for instance, does a variety of organizational work— separating temporary from long-term employees, differentiating access to public benefits, managing rights to intervene in political processes, and so on—but everywhere and always its existence and effectiveness depend on the present capacity of a relatively centralized government. The power of a differentiator based on membership or nonmembership in a political party (notable cases being communist parties in state socialist regimes) similarly depends on the existence of a hegemonic party exercising extensive state power and controlling a wide variety of valued resources.

Again, the founder of a small manufacturing firm, following models already established in the trade, divides the firm's work into clusters of jobs viewed as distinct in character and qualifications and then recruits workers for those jobs within well-marked categories. As turnover occurs and the firm expands, established workers pass word of available jobs among friends and relatives, collaborating with and supporting them, once they join the work force. Those new workers therefore prove more reliable and effective than others hired off the street, and all concerned come to associate job with category, so much so that owner and workers come to believe in the superior fitness of that category's members for the particular line of work.

Another case in point. Householders in an urban neighborhood build up a precarious system of trust on the basis of common backgrounds and shared relations to third parties, live with persons and property at risk to that system of trust, and then react violently when newcomers whom they cannot easily integrate into the same networks threaten to occupy part of the territory. In the process, members of the two groups elaborate compelling stories about each other's perfidy and utter incompatibility.

Members of an immigrant stream, finally, peddle craft goods from their home region on big-city streets, and some of them set up businesses as suppliers, manufacturers, or retail merchants. New immigrants find work in the expanding trade, and not only an immigrant niche but an ethnically specific international connection provides exclusive opportunities for the next generation. In all these cases, organizational improvisations lead to durable categorical inequality. In all these cases, but with variable weight, exploitation and opportunity hoarding favor the installation of categorical inequality, while emulation and adaptation generalize its influence.

When it comes to the determinants of durable inequality, are these special cases or the general rule? This book gives reasons for thinking that categorical inequality in general results from varying intersections of exploitation, opportunity hoarding, emulation, and adaptation. It goes farther, claiming that much of the inequality that seems to result from individual or group differences in ability actually stems from the same causes:

- Authoritatively organized categorical differences in current performance (e.g. categorically differentiated cooperation or sabotage by fellow workers, subordinates, and supervisors)
- Authoritatively organized categorical differences in *rewards* for performance (e.g. systematically lower pay for blacks than for whites doing similar work)
- Authoritatively organized differences in the acquisition of *capacities* for performance (e.g. categorically segregated and unequal schools)

It also argues that the social mechanisms which generate inequality with respect to a wide range of advantages—wealth, income, esteem, protection, power, and more—are similar. Although historical accumulations of institutions, social relations, and shared understandings produce differences in the day-to-day operation of various sorts of categories (gender, race, citizenship, and so on) as well as differences in various sorts of outcomes (e.g. landed wealth versus cash income), ultimately interactions of exploitation, opportunity hoarding, emulation, and adaptation explain them all.

Nutrition turns out to provide a useful general model for categorical inequality, since in most settings feeding differs with categorical membership, and since in many cases the cumulative effects of feeding elsewhere help to explain categorical differences in performance in the current case. In direct parallel, the information and social ties that individuals and groups can currently acquire differ categorically, but previous categorical experience also strongly affects the information and social ties these individuals and groups already have at their disposal, not to mention the means they have of acquiring new information and social ties.

Feelings of identity, on one side, and intergroup hostility, on the other, may well accompany, promote, or result from the use of categorical differences to solve organizational problems. But the relative prevalence of such attitudes plays a secondary part in inequality's extent and form. Mistaken beliefs reinforce exploitation, opportunity hoarding, emulation, and adaptation but exercise little independent influence on their initiation—or so I will argue. It follows that the reduction or intensification of racist, sexist, or xenophobic attitudes will have relatively little impact on durable inequality, whereas the introduction of certain new organizational forms—for example, installing different categories or changing the relation between categories and rewards—will have great impact.

If so, the identification of such organizational forms becomes a significant challenge for social scientists. It also follows that similar organizational problems generate parallel solutions in very different settings, in articulation with very different sets of categories. Thus matches of positions with categories, and the justifications for such matches, vary much more than recurrent structural arrangements—for example, when similar clusters of jobs acquire contrasting racial, ethnic, or gender identifications in different labor markets. Causal mechanisms resemble each other greatly, while outcomes differ dramatically, thus inviting very different rationalizations or condemnations after the fact. Social scientists dealing with such durable forms of inequality must hack through dense ideological overgrowth to reach structural roots.

Relational analysis, as we shall see in detail, typically treats categories as problem-solving social inventions and/or by-products of social interaction (Elster 1983: 25–88). Relational analysts characteristically conceive of culture as shared understandings that intertwine closely with social relations, serving as their tools and constraints instead of constituting an autonomous sphere. Strongly relational analysis remains a minority movement in social science as a whole; individualisms and holisms continue to reign. In the choice between essences and bonds, nevertheless, I want to hold high the banner of bonds. I claim that an account of how transactions clump into social ties, social ties concatenate into networks, and existing networks constrain solutions of organizational problems clarifies the creation, maintenance, and change of categorical inequality.

Elements of Inequality

Before undertaking the necessary reconstruction, however, let us think about inequality as such. Human inequality in general consists of the uneven distribution of attributes among a set of social units such as individuals, categories, groups, or regions. Social scientists concern themselves especially with the uneven distribution of costs and benefits—that is, *goods,* broadly defined. Relevant goods include not only wealth and income but also such various benefits and costs as control of land, exposure to illness, respect from other people, liability to military service, risk of homicide, possession of tools, and availability of sexual partners. Students of social inequality have paid little attention to the uneven distribution of other attributes such as genetic traits and musical tastes except as they correlate with the uneven distribution of goods in this broad sense.

Goods vary in the extent to which they are *autonomous* (observable without reference to outside units, as in accumulations of food) or *relative* (observable only in relation to other units, as in prestige). Wealth, income, and health exemplify autonomous goods, while prestige, power, and clientele exemplify relative goods. (Some analysts prefer to call relative goods "positional," on the grounds that they attach to positions rather than to persons, but that usage draws attention away from their relational character.) On the whole, inequalities with respect to autonomous goods reach greater extremes than inequalities with respect to relative goods.

Analysis of exploitation by the elite, opportunity hoarding by the nonelite, emulation, and adaptation makes it clear that autonomous and relative goods depend intimately on each other. Although people come to value them for their own sakes, relative goods generally occupy a subordinate, derivative position: they serve as a means of creating or maintaining categorical inequality with respect to autonomous goods. Possession of prestige, power, clientele, and status-marking goods then justifies the superior position of favored categories ex post facto, just as the perquisites of favored categories give autonomous goods such as well-built housing, luxurious automobiles, comfortable workspaces, fine foods, good liquor, or rich entertainment the patina of relative goods as well. The chief reversals in the priority of autonomous over relative goods occur in such public displays as potlatch, charitable donations, and ostentatious weddings, where wealthy or powerful people incur great expenditures in the short run to mark their superiority over other people. Even there, successful displays—for example, magnates parading great clienteles in the public rituals of Renaissance Florence—characteristically enhance the longer-run advantages of those who mount them (Paige and Paige 1981; Trexler 1981).

I certainly did not discover the interaction between autonomous and relative goods. Pierre Bourdieu has spent much of his career exploring it, with his analytic division among economic, cultural, and social capitals representing the interdependence of autonomous goods narrowly conceived, valued information, and the social ties that provide differential access to those goods and information (Bourdieu 1979; Bourdieu and Wacquant 1992: 118–119; Buchmann 1989: 31–42). When ever-relational Karl Marx traced back relative goods (not his term!) to origins in relations of production, he likewise portrayed prestige, power, clientele, and possession of status-marking goods as instruments and products of categorically based exploitation. Categorical inequality with respect to autonomous goods gains strength from and generates parallel differences in relative goods.

Since the late nineteenth century, individualistic models of inequality have crowded out categorical models. From Adam Smith to Karl Marx, classical economists generally analyzed categories and relations among them: chiefly land, labor, and capital for Smith, capital and labor alone for Marx. They examined returns to these factors considered collectively and situated socially rather than returns to individual effort. Discussing returns to labor, for example, Smith reasoned:

> What are the common wages of labour, depends everywhere upon the contract usually made between those two parties, whose interests are by no means the same. The workmen desire to get as much, the masters to give as little as possible. The former are disposed to combine in order to raise, the latter in order to lower the wages of labour. It is not, however, difficult to foresee which of the two parties must, upon all ordinary occasions, have the advantage in the dispute, and force the other into a compliance with their terms. The masters, being fewer in

number, can combine much more easily; and the law, besides, autho-
rises, or at least does not prohibit their combinations, while it prohibits
those of the workmen.

(Smith 1910 [1776], 1: 58–59)

Although Smith certainly saw market conditions—in this case, especially
rates of growth in demand for labor—as crucial to the advantage of one
party or the other, he reasoned about categories, groups, institutions, and
ties. Those ties emphatically included collective, categorical, unequal power.

The neoclassical revolution, however, diverted economic attention from
categories to individuals and markets.

Human-capital theory offers a closely related individualistic account of
inequality, with the additional twist of radical depersonalization. In strict
human-capital models, neither the worker nor the worker's effort earns the
rewards of work; instead, previous investments in the quality of workers
command current returns. Again Stinchcombe's remark applies: such analyses rule out ties among workers or between bosses and workers as independent causes of inequality. They rely on an almost magical belief in the
market's ability to sort out capacities for work.

Still, individualistic analyses of inequality have all the attractions of neoclassical economics: nicely simplified geometric analogies, reassuring references
to individual decision-making, insistence on efficiency avoidance of inconve-
nient complications such as beliefs, passions, culture, and history. They lend
themselves nicely to retroactive rationalization; confronted with unequal outcomes, their user searches the past for individual differences in skill, knowledge, determination, or moral worth that must explain differences in rewards.
These analyses fail, however, to the extent that essential causal business takes
place not inside individual heads but within social relations among persons
and sets of persons. That extent is, I claim, very large. If so, we have no choice
but to undertake relational analyses of inequality—whether or not we finally
couple them with individualistic elements of relevant decision processes.

Two disclaimers on that very point. First, I consider persons to possess as
many identities as the number of social relations they maintain, one identity
per relation, and to acquire their individuality through interactions among
genetic capabilities and social experiences.

[Second] extension of relational analyses within the study of social inequality does not deny the existence of individuals or individual-level effects. It does, however, place individualistic processes in their organizational
context. It does, finally, challenge any ontology that reduces all social processes to the sentient actions of individual persons.

From Transactions to Structures

Viviana Zelizer identifies a momentous irony in the American federal government's generally successful attempt to monopolize production of legal tender across the United States: the more government action reduced the rights of states, municipalities, and firms to issue legally circulating money, the more ordinary Americans and organizations proliferated private monies in the forms of tokens, symbolic objects, and earmarked official currency (Zelizer 1994b). Americans multiplied monies, Zelizer shows, because they were pursuing serious relational business with their monetary transactions. Symbolically and physically, for example, they segregated money destined for their children, servants, and local merchants. They were not only getting, spending, and saving but also distinguishing different categories of social relations. Disagreeing vigorously with social thinkers who suppose that the monetization of social exchanges inexorably rationalizes these exchanges and thins their contents, Zelizer demonstrates that people reshape monetary transactions to support meaningful, differentiated interpersonal relations.

Zelizer categorizes payments as follows:

- *Gifts*, which are transfers of money at the current possessor's discretion, without a prior stipulation of the recipient's consequent obligations
- *Entitlements*, which are payments due the recipient by contractual right, enforceable by appeal to authoritative third parties
- *Compensation*, which is a monetary exchange for goods and services, based on prior agreement concerning the relation between price and a mix of quality and quantity

Contrary to analysts who assume that ultimately all monetary transfers amount to quid pro quo exchanges, Zelizer argues that gifts, entitlements, and compensation involve contrasting rationales, meanings, and social relations. They rely on characteristically different means of enforcement. To mark them off from each other, people invent segregated currencies and visibly different payment routines.

When people make such distinctions, they embed cultural forms in analyses—usually implicit—of social relations. We watch Mary hand Harry a ten-dollar bill. How can we know whether the monetary transfer is a tip, a bribe, a heartfelt gift, regular compensation for goods or services, fulfillment of an entitlement such as an allowance, or some other sort of payment? We can determine this only by ascertaining the relation between Mary and Harry: apartment dweller and doorman, driver and traffic cop, sister and brother, mother and son, householder and handyman, and so on through a wide variety of possible pairs (Zelizer 1998).

Building Blocks

Provisional nominees for the basic set include the chain, the hierarchy, the triad, the organization, and the categorical pair:

- A *chain* consists of two or more similar and connected ties between social sites (persons, groups, identities, networks, or something else).
- A *hierarchy* is a sort of chain in which the connections are asymmetrical and the sites systematically unequal.
- A *triad* consists of three sites having ties to each other that are similar in content, although not necessarily similar in valence.
- An *organization* is a well-bounded set of ties in which at least one site has the right to establish ties across the boundary that can then bind sites connected by internal ties.
- A *categorical pair* consists of a socially significant boundary and at least one tie between sites on either side of it.

I regard these network configurations as social inventions, perhaps developed incrementally by trial and error, no doubt reinvented independently many times, but, when recognized, more or less deliberately installed as a means of coordinating social life.

Scripting and Local Knowledge

In principle, transactions include events in which one actor changes the state of another actor; the term "transaction costs" describes the energy expended in such interchanges. In practice, we concentrate on distinguishable interactions during which at least one actor exhibits a response to the other. Scripts range from the routines involved in such general configurations as triads and paired categories to the specific formulas people adopt to withdraw money from a bank...

Similarly, local knowledge extends, for example, from tacit understandings acquired by long-term residents concerning connections among different locations in a city to the memory of previous conversations that frames today's lunch between two old friends. Scripts provide models for participation in particular classes of social relations, while shared local knowledge provides a means of giving variable content to those social relations. Among the four basic mechanisms that generate durable inequality emulation relies chiefly on scripting, while adaptation relies heavily on accumulation of local knowledge. Actually, however, all four mechanisms—exploitation, opportunity hoarding, emulation, and adaptation—operate through combinations of scripting and local knowledge. Exploitation by means of paired categories, for example, characteristically involves locally constructed variants on widely known differentiations by gender, race, ethnicity, or some other dividing principle.

With little scripting or local knowledge available [...] actors either avoid each other or engage in *shallow improvisations* such as the maneuvers that pedestrians on a crowded sidewalk adopt in order to pass each other with a minimum of bumping and blocking. [...]

Where common knowledge is extensive and scripting slight, we enter the *deep improvisation* of professional jazz, intense sociability, competitive soccer, passionate sexual relations, and playful conversation.

Like learning a language, the establishment of new social relations often follows a zigzag pattern within this space: beginning with a rigidly followed but narrow script, accumulating local knowledge, improvising by means of that knowledge, making mistakes and discovering unanticipated consequences, correcting those mistakes and fixing the consequences until a precarious modus vivendi emerges, moving back to acquire new scripts, and then broadening common knowledge until at times the newcomer participates in the intense rituals of solidarity that assume such common knowledge. By that time, any participant who follows the script rigidly—speaks with schoolbook grammar, observes every formality, works by rule—actually disrupts local social relations, unless she or he does so as a recognizable joke or as an understood way of controlling outsiders. Scripting and common knowledge operate dialectically, modifying each other so that each script not only bends under the weight of local knowledge but also limits the sites that share local knowledge.

By no means do all learning processes complete the arc from shallow improvisation through more extensive scripts to deep improvisation. Staying in a strange city among speakers of an unfamiliar tongue, I have often found myself acquiring rudimentary familiarity with map, public transportation, and crucial phrases while working out a simple set of interaction routines for survival through the day, rehearsing the relevant scripts anxiously in anticipation of the next encounter, and then getting by on that combination of a meager script with dangerously restricted local knowledge. Similarly, many immigrants work up just enough involvement with the world outside their immigrant niche to avoid serious trouble when navigating that world.

Again, the presence of even one important person who lacks familiarity with local language and practices can drive an entire work group or dinner party into the uncomfortable zone of stilted scripting and cramped improvisation.

One of the great secrets of categorical inequality is this: the routines, understandings, and justifications that organizational participants have acquired in other settings are readily available for organizational work. Each durable social setting produces some unique scripts and common knowledge, however trivial, that are available only to its habitués; but it also produces some local variations on the scripts and common knowledge that are attached to widely relevant categorical distinctions according to such principles as age, race, ethnicity, class, locality, and gender.

Our five configurations—chains, hierarchies, triads, organizations, and categorical pairs—provide widely available scripts. They rely on common knowledge, for example, shared understandings of how superiors and inferiors signal their relation to each other. ... Together, familiar scripts and accumulated common knowledge lower the transaction costs of whatever activities an organization carries on. They thereby raise the relative costs of shifting to some other structure of social relations.

Organizations build in educational and class differences, with their established patterns of deference; incorporate existing links among people from common ethnic origins; establish triads defined as "teams" recruited from other organizations; and set up categorical pairs such as physician/nurse or professional/client. Such borrowing of categorical pairs, as later chapters of this book explain, plays a crucial part in durable patterns of inequality.

Managers who borrow structure gain the advantage of low startup costs for new chunks of organization. But they also import meanings, relational routines, and external connections whose features and consequences they cannot always control. Many a store manager has hired a few hard-working immigrants for a particular niche only to discover that part of the store has become a patronage network and he or she an unwitting patron. Many a new lawyer has learned that the road to becoming a partner in the firm is closed because a hidden but powerful hierarchy separates graduates of elite law schools from the rest.

Consider brokers who make their living by mediating between two organizations or populations, equal or not. Such brokers enhance their livelihood by supporting categorical distinctions which ensure that cross-boundary transactions will continue to pass through them instead of knitting together complementary pairs across the boundary. Leaders of ethnic groups often acquire just such an interest in maintaining the distinctions between dominant classes and their own constituencies; they become stronger advocates of bilingual education, distinctive cultural institutions, and installation of legally protected categories than many members of their constituencies (see e.g Hofmevr 1987).

Categories Revisited

We return, then, to categories. Counterintuitively, categories take relational forms. Let us expand the earlier definition. A category consists of a set of actors who share a boundary distinguishing all of them from and relating all of them to at least one set of actors visibly excluded by that boundary. A category simultaneously lumps together actors deemed similar, splits sets of actors considered dissimilar, and defines relations between the two sets (cf. Zerubavel 1996). For obvious examples, consider the following:

Women, a category excluding men
Blacks, a category excluding whites
Slaves, a category excluding masters and other free persons
Muslims, a category generally excluding non-Muslims, but in particular
    locales excluding Jews, Orthodox Christians, Druse, Baha'i, and others

Other important categorical sets include noble/commoner, citizen/foreigner, professional/client, employer/worker, child/adult, prisoner/guard, and any number of ethnic, religious, or racial pairs. Much more rarely, categorical sets also take the form of rank orders such as Indian castes, gradations among military officers, or ladders of academic titles (instructor, assistant professor, associate professor, professor, and so on).

Categories center on boundaries. What causes the location and shape of boundaries? Let us distinguish among three overlapping origins: invention, borrowing, and by-products of network encounters. At one extreme, powerful actors or clusters of actors deliberately manufacture boundaries and accompanying stories, as when nineteenth-century revolutionary conspirators organized secret societies with their cells, hierarchies, and declared enemies, or when nation-building intellectuals constructed histories for their linguistic group that implied they had occupied their territory before speakers of other languages arrived on the scene.

They also generate stories that participants subsequently use to explain and justify their interactions. The stories embody shared understandings of who we are, who they are, what divides us, and what connects us. People create such stories in the context of previously available cultural materials: shared concepts, beliefs, memories, symbols, myths, local knowledge.

Once in place, these stories constrain subsequent interactions across the boundary, modifying only slowly in response to those interactions. Thus, as combinations of solidary and competitive interactions generate ostensibly racial barriers, they also produce genetically framed stories of each group's origins and attributes. Barriers take on racial rather than ethnic or territorial definitions to the extent that in early encounters members of the two populations use phenotypical markers to distinguish each other and resist forming durable sexual unions. If myths or facts of origin distinguish the populations, on the other hand, ethnic categories emerge from their interaction. Different combinations of encounters, barriers, and stories generate definitions of categories as centering on class, citizenship, age, or locality.

Gender boundaries are at once the most general and the most difficult to explain. Although they map to chromosomally driven anatomical differences, they also conform to deep divisions in childhood relations to mothers and others. They correspond approximately to genetically based variations in physiology, yet they incorporate long historical accumulations of belief and practice.

Categories in Action

The most dramatic forms of categorization involve outright stigma. [...] The role of stigma in defining relationships becomes even clearer in the badges that Zurich and other European towns issued to their deserving (as distinguished from undeserving) poor, badges that qualified those persons to receive alms from the citizenry as half-gift, half-entitlement (Jütte 1994: 161). In times of famine, Europe's sixteenth-century cities often used the distinction deserving/undeserving or the related distinction native/alien to draw the line between those paupers who would receive food at municipal expense and those who would be sent away to fend for themselves (Geremek 1994: chapter 3).

Despite such extreme cases, a viable category by no means entails a complete perimeter around all actors on one side of the boundary or the other; on the contrary, complete perimeters require a great deal of management and ordinarily cause more trouble than they save. Nor does a viable category require homogeneity among the actors on a given side. You can be more or less a Muslim, even to the point where other Muslims deny your Muslimness, yet at the boundary with Jews you still fall unmistakably into the Muslim category.

Categorical boundaries certainly need not rely on objectively verifiable characteristics. Social control agencies often use grossly inaccurate indicators to stigmatize a suspect segment of the population, as described here:

> In 1993, the Denver police department compiled a roster of suspected gang members based on "clothing choices," "flashing of gang signals," or associating with known gang members. The list included two-thirds of the city's young black men, of whom only a small percentage were actual gang members.
>
> (Gans 1995: 66–67)

Similarly William Chambliss reports his first-hand observations from regular riding with the Rapid Deployment Unit of the Washington, D.C., Metropolitan Police:

> The RDU patrols the ghetto continuously looking for cars with young black men in them. They are especially attentive to newer-model cars, Isuzu four-wheel-drive vehicles, BMWs and Honda Accords, based on the belief that these are the favorite cars of drug dealers. During our observations, however, the RDU officers came to the conclusion that drug dealers were leaving their fancy cars at home to avoid vehicular stops. It thus became commonplace for RDU officers to stop any car with young black men in it.
>
> (Chambliss 1994: 179)

Categorical work always involves imputing distinctive qualities to actors on either side of boundaries; in the crucial case of paired categories, actors on the two sides engage in mutual labeling. Yet categories rarely pervade life so thoroughly as to forbid crosscutting categorical memberships. Many actors occupy multiple categories without great difficulty, as long as the ties defining one category activate at different times, in different places, and/or in different circumstances than do the ties defining other categories.

Outside of organizations such as firms, governments, parties, and voluntary associations, categories rarely form as deliberate outcomes of planned social action. The most prominent exceptions occur where political entrepreneurs have something to gain by asserting and promoting the existence of a categorical entity that, if recognized, enjoys some sort of collective advantage; claims to speak on behalf of an oppressed, unrecognized, and unorganized nation have this character, as do the demands of social-movement activists to be heard as spokespersons for their unjustly disadvantaged constituencies.

Categories support durable inequality when they combine with hierarchies—ties between social sites in which the connections are asymmetrical and the sites systematically unequal. Each reinforces the other, for a relatively impermeable barrier reduces the likelihood that equalizing relations will form across it, while asymmetrical relations based on unequal resources justify the boundary and render it more visible. Racial inequality seems natural precisely to the extent that all transactions across the boundary occur asymmetrically and dramatize the disparity of resources on either side. Only when inconsistencies occur—privileged members of the ostensibly inferior category, disinherited members of the ostensibly superior category, persons straddling the boundary, open competition for the same positions between members of both categories—do vigorous, violent mobilizations from "above" and "below" become likely (Olzak 1992; cf. Patterson 1995).

References

Bourdieu, Pierre. 1979. *La Distinction: Critique Social du Jugement.* Paris: Editions de Minuit.

Bourdieu and Wacquant. 1992. *Invitation to Reflexive Sociology.* Chicago: University of Chicago Press.

Buchman, Marlis. 1989. *The Script of Life in Modern Society: Entry into Adulthood in a Changing World.* Chicago: University of Chicago Press.

Chambliss, William. 1994. "Policing the Ghetto Underclass: The Politics of Law and Law Enforcement." *Social Problems* 41: 177–194.

Colley, Linda. 1992. *Britons: Forging the Nation 1707–1837.* New Haven: Yale University Press.

Dagens Nyheter. 1996. Storsta studien visar: Lagutbildade far mindre barn. February 13.

Elster, John. 1983. *Explaining Technical Change: A Case Study in the Philosophy of Science.* Cambridge: Cambridge University Press.

Floud, Rodercki, Kenneth Wachter, and Annabel Gregory. 1990. *Height, Health, and History: Nutritional Status in the United Kingdom, 1750–1980.* Cambridge: Cambridge University Press.

Fogel, Robert W. 1993. "New Sources and New Techniques for the Study of Secular Trends in Nutritional Status: Health, Mortality, and the Process of Aging." *Historical Methods* 26: 5–43.

———. 1994. "Economic Growth, Population Theory and Physiology: The Bearing of Long-Term Processes on the Making of Economic Policy." *American Economic Review* 84: 369–395.

———. and Dora L. Costa. 1997. "A Theory of Technophysio Evolution, with Some Implications for Forecasting Population, Health Care Costs and Pension Costs." *Demography* 34: 49–66.

Gans, Herbert J. 1995. *The War Against the Poor: The Underclass and Antipoverty Policy.* New York: Basic Books.

George, M. Dorothy. 1967. *Hogarth to Cruikshank: Social Change in Graphic Satire.* New York: Viking.

Geremek, Bronislaw. 1994. *Poverty: A History.* Oxford: Blackwell.

Hill, Draper, eds. 1976. *The Satirical Etchings of James Gilroy.* New York: Dover.

Hofmevr, Isabel. 1987. "Building a Nation from Words: Africaans Language, Literature, and Ethnic Identity, 1902–1924." In the *Politics of Race, Class, and Nationalism in the Twentieth-Century South Africa,* edited by Shula Marks and Stanley Trapido. London: Longman.

Jutte, Robert. 1994. *Poverty and Deviance in Early Modern Europe.* Cambridge: Cambridge University Press.

Komlos, John. 1987. "The Height and Weight of West Point Cadets: Dietary Change in Antebellum America." *Journal of Economic History* 47: 897–927.

———. 1990. "Height and Social Status in Eighteenth Century Germany." *Journal of Interdisciplinary History* 20: 607–622.

———. 1994. *Stature, Living Standards and Economic Development: Essays in Anthropometric History.* Chicago: University of Chicago Press.

Olzak, Susan. 1992. *The Dynamic of Ethnic Competition and Conflict.* Stanford: Stanford University Press.

Paige, Karen and Jeffrey Paige. 1981. *The Politics of Reproductive Ritual.* Berkeley: University of California Press.

Parkin, Frank. 1979. *Marxism and Class Theory: A Bourgeois Critique.* London: Tavistock.

Patterson, Orlando. 1995. "The Paradox of Integration." *New Republic.* November 6: 24–27.

Smith, Adam. 1910. *The Wealth of Nations,* 2 vols. London: J.M. Dent. First published in 1776.

Steckel, Richard H. 1995. "Stature and the Standard of Living." *Journal of Economic Literature* 33: 1903–1940.

Tanner, James M. 1994. "Introduction: Growth in Height as a Mirror of the Standard of Living." In *States, Living Standards, and Economic Development: Essays in Anthropometric History,* edited by John Komlos. Chicago: University of Chicago Press.

Trexler, Richard C. 1981. *Public Life in Renassaince Florence.* New York: Academic Press.

Weber, Max. 1968. *Economy and Society: An Outline of Interpretive Sociology.* Edited by Guenther Roth and Claude Wittich. 3 vol. New York: Bedminster.

Zelizer, Viviana. 1994. *The Social Meaning of Money.* New York: Basic Books.

———. 1998. "How Do We Know Whether a Monetary Transaction Is a Gift, an Entitlement, or Compensation?" pp. 329–34 in *Economics, Values, and Organization,* edited by A. Ben-Ner and L. Putterman. Cambridge: Cambridge University Press.

Zerubavel, Eviatar. 1996. "Lumping and Splitting: Note on Social Classification." *Sociological Forum* 11: 421–33.

Poverty and the Politics of Exclusion

14

Charles Tilly

Among the many vivid vignettes of poor people's lives recorded in the World Bank's sweeping survey *Voices of the Poor*, listen to one of the more hopeful stories:

> Mahood Rab was destitute when he arrived at the slum of Chittagong City [Bangladesh] with his wife at the age of 18. He left his village after his father died, and his family had become impoverished covering medical expenses. When Mahood arrived in the city, he worked as a rickshaw puller, and his wife took jobs as a maidservant in several homes. Through hard work, and with his own and his wife's savings, he was finally able to buy a rickshaw. Within a year, he owned four. Today, at age 50, Mahood owns eight rickshaws, but does not rely just on this business. He took out a loan from Proshika (a national NGO) and rents five houses he built in another slum area. Mahood shared with the researchers that due to his wealth everyone knows him, and he is among those who are respected and take part in the major decisions of the neighborhood.
>
> (Narayan, Chambers *et al.* 2000:52; see also
> Narayan, Patel *et al.* 2000)

Thirty-two years after Mahood's arrival in Bastuhara, a Chittagong slum, his story reads like a free enterprise morality tale: take risks, work hard, accumulate capital, invest wisely, and you will escape from poverty. According to the Voices of the Poor study of Bastuhara, the slum houses a number of migrants who have moved up through saving, investing, and working hard; new factories and microcredit schemes backed by nongovernmental organizations facilitated their rise (Narayan and Petesch 2002: 124). Mahood Rab's story also appears to illustrate the importance of crucial assets and capabilities of poor people shown on the checklist reproduced in Box 14.1.

Although the tasks of defining and measuring poverty pose perplexing problems for experts, the checklist will serve this chapter's purposes well. "Poor" here means lacking most or all of these assets and capabilities.

As Amartya Sen (1995) puts it, *poverty* means capability deprivation. Relative poverty refers to a comparison with the bulk of a local, regional, or national population, while *absolute poverty* refers to a comparison with a worldwide standard. The once-destitute Mahood Rab, in these terms, left both absolute and relative poverty behind.

The vignette does not tell us to what extent Mahood capitalized on emotional integrity, imagination, information, education, or political representation and accountability. But he clearly benefited from other assets on the checklist. He deployed some of them during his exit from poverty, then enjoyed others as a result of his exit. Even this brief sketch shows him enjoying material assets, respect, dignity, and social belonging.

BOX 14.1 Crucial Assets and Capabilities of Poor People

Material assets

Bodily health

Bodily integrity

Emotional integrity

Respect and dignity

Social belonging

Cultural identity

Imagination, information, and education

Organizational capacity

Political representation and accountability

Source: Narayan and Petesch 2002, 463.

What we don't know, however, is whether he already belonged to some social category that facilitated his exit and whether he used previously existing connections on his way to Chittagong. Most likely he benefited from both social connections and membership in a favorable social category. After all, a landmark study of poverty in the northern Indian village of Palanpur, Uttar Pradesh, indicates that connections and categories matter greatly to South Asian exits from poverty (Lanjouw and Stern 2003). Cultural identities such as gender and caste enormously affect mobility chances in Uttar Pradesh and elsewhere. So do connections with patron-client networks.

A broader look at the case studies in the World Bank's portfolios therefore suggests two qualifications to any straightforward inference from the Mahood Rab story that "virtue × effort = success." First, very few of the poor people surveyed for Voices of the Poor actually accomplished anything like Mahood Rab's spectacular family exit from poverty. In the study's detailed analysis of Bangladesh, for example, some of the "social poor" had connections to draw on, but the "helpless poor" did not, and the "hated poor" clearly belonged to the wrong categories for any such assistance (Narayan and Petesch 2002: 121). Most of the Bangladeshi poor apparently lack favorable categorical memberships and interpersonal connections.

Second, whether or not social connections and membership in a favorably situated social category facilitated Mahood's ascent, in general both of these circumstances affected mobility or immobility a great deal more than did individual pluck or luck. Most of the world's very poor people, it seems likely, lack favorable categorical memberships and helpful connections. If so, their exits from poverty—if they happen at all—would result from either (a) their acquisition of new categorical memberships and/or connections, or (b) political-economic changes that subvert the usual effects of categories and connections. Socially organized patterns of exclusion set formidable barriers to mobility in the way of most poor individuals and households (Munck 2005). The Mahood Rab story, in short, misleads us in two fundamental ways. It suggests that the main thing analysts of poverty reduction must explain is individual-by-individual exits from poverty, and it implies that the main causes of poverty reduction involve individual characteristics and behavior.

On the contrary, the real-life availability of most assets and capabilities on the comprehensive Narayan-Petesch checklist results from economic, organizational, and political processes over which the typical poor individual or household exercises precious little control. Those processes produce and maintain the crucial categorical memberships and social connections. They thereby cause differential exclusion of poor individuals and households. In general discussions of inequality and politics therefore set the backdrop for its narrower treatment of political impacts on escapes from exclusion-induced poverty.

Individualistic Explanations of Inequality

Prevailing views of inequality's production and maintenance make it difficult to grasp the processes by which exclusion generates inequality and inequality causes poverty among excluded populations. In particular, a view of inequality and poverty as outcomes of individual-by-individual competition according to widely shared standards of merit, worthiness, or privilege obscures the significance of organized distinctions and interactions among members of different social categories. Since my main argument concerns categorical distinctions and interactions, it should help to first sketch the common view the argument rejects.

Compare two very different perspectives on the processes that produce inequality: *individual* and *interaction*. In an individual perspective, a person's attributes and behavior locate that person within one or more hierarchies. Individual accounts differ greatly with regard to personal agency: At one extreme, a person's performance determines where he or she ends up within this or that hierarchy. At the other extreme, holders of power decide which attributes to punish or reward, thus placing people with different attributes at different positions within hierarchies (for surveys of competing individual views, see Grusky 2001 and Romero and Margolis 2005).

To be sure, most individual accounts of inequality recognize that previous social experience strongly affects individual attributes and behavior. Still, the perspective's organizing ideas stress that inequality emerges from the sorting of individuals according to their attributes and behavior. In the Mahood Rab story with which we began, Mahood's individual attributes (his "crucial assets and capabilities," in Voices of the Poor terms) and his individual behavior (for example, his extraordinary entrepreneurship) caused his ascent from destitution to wealth.

In the individual perspective, how do hierarchies work? Imagine a rectilinear space with social rank defining its vertical axis, and various social sites along its horizontal axis. In the individual view, inequality consists of differential location within such a space. We can follow current fashion by making the vertical axis represent monetary income or wealth, but nothing in principle keeps us from adding or substituting criteria such as power, fame, prestige, and overall well-being. Any array of social units—individuals, groups, categories, jobs, or other positions—is unequal to the extent that its members occupy different positions along that space's vertical dimension.

The idea lends itself easily to the notion of a single hierarchy within which every individual has a defined place. The hierarchy may, of course, rank individuals according to income, wealth, power, prestige, or some combination of these advantages. The perspective also articulates neatly with the notion of social mobility as movement of individuals from step to step within such a hierarchy. Aggregate inequality thus conceived refers to distributions: in static terms, the extent to which higher-ranking individuals enjoy greater advantages than lower-ranking individuals. In dynamic terms, it concerns the extent to which the average individual and that individual's offspring stay in the same inferior or superior location throughout careers, lifetimes, or generations. A highly unequal system, in these terms, concentrates advantages at its hierarchy's top and fixes individuals or social units at their positions within the hierarchy.

A popular version of the individual perspective portrays the selection process within such hierarchies as a queue. In today's Western analyses of inequality, indeed, queuing images prevail. A queue, in this view, lines up individuals to pass a checkpoint where a monitor scans them; matches their various attributes and performances with well-established templates; and then shunts them into different channels, where they join other people having similar attributes and performances. In a queue, inclusion or exclusion operates one person at a time, even if categorical attributes of individuals such as race, gender, or religion affect an individual's inclusion or exclusion.

The best-known version of the queue employs one main template: human capital. In this scenario, the monitor is a market or its human agents. The monitor scans each individual for human capital, then matches the detected human capital with a position in which it will produce a net return for the market as well as for the individual. In competing versions of the queue, the monitor selects for gender, race, fame, estimated commitment, or other attributes instead of—or in addition to—human capital. Thus the manager of a fast-food restaurant hires, fires, assigns, pays, and promotes counter workers on the basis of a personal preference schedule, but does so in implicit competition with other potential employers of the same workers.

More complex accounts in the same vein allow for additional effects of effort, inheritance, social connections, and learning, with the individual passing multiple checkpoints over a career. Still, the central image shows us one person at a time passing a checkpoint and moving on to differential rewards as a consequence of attributes or performances registered at that checkpoint. Cumulatively, such a process generates distributions of individuals and positions differing significantly in current rewards and accumulations of past rewards as a function of their relationship to criteria built into the monitor. If the process centers on human capital, then the unequal distribution of human capital across the population generates unequal rank and unequal mobility as well.

Inequality-producing queues do exist. Law firms vie vigorously for high-ranking graduates of prestigious law schools, as graduates compete for positions in high-ranking firms. Competitive tryouts for ballet corps, football teams, and Rhodes Scholarships produce sharp divisions between winners and losers. First-past-the-post elections cumulate individual votes into a monitor, having fateful consequences for politicians in parliamentary democracies. A knack for answering questions on ... a "Big Test" ... helped me become the first member of my large, recently immigrated kin network to attend college.

That examination emphatically established a queue—a queue into elite American colleges. The question, then, is not whether inequality, immobility, and mobility ever result from queuing processes, but whether we can reasonably take the queue as a general model for the production of inequality. Later I will give reasons for thinking that, on the contrary, the inequality-generating queue constitutes an exceptional case that only works under special institutional conditions.

Analyses of black-white differentials in wealth and well-being in the United States (e.g. Oliver and Shapiro 1997; Conley 1999) indicate, for example, that even at similar levels of current income, parent-child transfers of wealth give U.S. whites, on average, great advantages over U.S. blacks. Racial endogamy probably reinforces those differences. Social mobility, in interactive perspective, does not consist of individual movement up and down an abstract hierarchy. It involves concrete flows of persons among clusters, especially clusters that differ significantly in dominance.

Long-run changes in inequality, in this view, depend on regrouping of relations among participants. Like their neoclassical counterparts, Marxists emphasize control over productive resources in explaining major shifts in inequality. Classic Marxist explanations differ dramatically from neoclassical formulations, however, in two regards. First, they deny that markets do the crucial adjudicating, insisting instead on the generation of inequality within relations of production. Exploitation—unequal sharing of value added by effort in socially organized production—thus forms unequal social classes.

Second, Marxists differentiate between a medium run and a long run. In the medium run, interaction within modes of production creates changes in the degree, but not the type, of inequality. For the capitalist medium run, Marxist theories predict ever-increasing polarization between capital and labor. In the long run, coercion in the form of conquest, colonization, or revolution creates shifts from one mode of production to another. The two time spans correspond to contrasting styles of interaction: grudging collaboration in the medium run, shouting confrontation in the long run.

At best, the Marxist historical account only explains the evolution of class differences. It lacks a plausible explanation of differences by gender, race, ethnicity, age, nationality, religion, and other categorical principles insofar as those principles operate in partial independence of class. The lack has led a number of Marxist theorists either to argue that inequalities among such nonclass categories ultimately derive from class inequalities or to search for ways in which their existence serves the interests of dominant classes (see, for example, Leiman 1993).

For analysts interested in understanding mobility, then, Box 14.2 provides a convenient checklist of resources that figure prominently in the forms of inequality prevailing in a given community or country.

Once they have identified the fundamental resources involved in the production of inequality, analysts must still figure out how processes based on those resources actually work. Box 14.3 provides an all-purpose questionnaire for identification of the crucial processes.

BOX 14.2 Historically Prominent Inequality-Generating Resources

Coercive means, including weapons, jails, and organized specialists in violence

Labor, especially skilled and/or effectively coordinated labor

Animals, especially domesticated food-producing and/or work animals

Land, including natural resources located in and upon it

Commitment-maintaining institutions such as religious sects, kinship systems, and trade diasporas

Machines, especially machines that convert raw materials, produce goods or services, and transport persons, goods, services, or information

Financial capital—transferable and fungible means of acquiring property rights

Information, especially information that facilitates profitable, safe, or coordinated action

Media that disseminate such information

Scientific-technical knowledge, especially knowledge that facilitates intervention—for good or evil—in human welfare

BOX 14.3 An All-Purpose Questionnaire for Analyzing Escapes from Poverty

What major resources do exploiters control—land, labor, capital, knowledge, something else?

What major resources do opportunity hoarders control?

What boundaries separate exploiters and opportunity hoarders from the rest of the population?

To what extent do those boundaries correspond to other divisions such as gender, caste, religion, ethnicity, or citizenship?

What controls and constraints maintain individual and collective locations on either side of prevailing boundaries?

To what extent and how do beneficiaries of surpluses from exploitation and opportunity hoarding apply those surpluses to reproduce exclusionary boundaries and unequal relations across them?

How frequently do people cross those boundaries in either direction?

To what extent is boundary crossing, when it occurs, individual or collective?

What processes facilitate and inhibit boundary crossing, whether individual or collective?

Through what channels—kinship, religious affiliation, political connections including government employment, underground economies, occupational mobility, or educational achievement—do local people most regularly move out of poverty?

At what pace, and in what ways, are these arrangements changing?

The questionnaire simply translates my earlier arguments into a series of operations applying to any inequality-generating system anywhere. It describes a search for value-producing resources, exploitation, opportunity hoarding, boundaries, and the rest of the apparatus that generates inequality. In so doing, it shifts attention away from conventional concerns with queues, individual mobility, income distributions, and aggregate flows of persons or resources within an economic system. It directs attention toward the processes that produce, reproduce, and transform inequality. It asserts that categorical exclusion from benefits lies at the heart of inequality. It also asserts that categorically organized channels, rather than those that operate at a purely individual level, most often facilitate escapes from poverty when such channels actually form.

Political Underpinnings of Inequality and Its Changes

Our all-purpose questionnaire serves an unexpected purpose. It specifies the pressure points through which political processes affect inequality and its changes. Politics sometimes enters the production, reproduction, and transformation of inequality through all 11 items on the list: control over resources for exploitation and opportunity hoarding, installation of crucial boundaries between controllers of resources and others, correspondence of those boundaries to gender or caste, and so on. Rather than a tedious item-by-item recitation of political influences, let us review them more generally.

Politics includes all exercises of power to which governments are parties, whether primary parties (as in military conscription) or secondary parties (as in legal enforcement of private contracts). Governments specialize in controlling concentrated means of coercion. Indeed, we commonly identify governments by looking for organizations that control the greatest concentrations of coercive means—for example, troops, police, jails, and means of imposing humiliation—within their operating territories. Control of such means gives governments great initial influence over the allocation of other resources.

Governments produce, maintain, and transform inequality both directly and indirectly. Directly, all governments operate systems of exploitation and opportunity hoarding. Via taxation and expropriation, they use their coercive means to organize the production of collective goods, whether or not individual citizens would contribute willingly without coercion. Sometimes they engage in wars—civil or international—that destroy productive resources and thereby increase inequality between the protected few and the damaged many. In the Voices of the Poor study, the impact of Bosnia-Herzegovina's civil war on poverty rivals the impact of Bangladesh's devastating floods (Narayan and Petesch 2002).

Outside of war, governments coordinate exploitation of value-producing resources such as minerals and water so that major categories of the population contributing their effort receive less than the proportionate value they have added. Taxation of wages for governmental projects provides the obvious example, but military conscription and forced nonmilitary labor operate in similar ways (Levi 1997; Tilly 1992). Of course, rulers commonly claim that their coordination of crucial resources adds so much value that everyone benefits in the long run. To say the least, real governments vary enormously in the extent to which they do add value, as opposed to operating essentially as protection rackets or simply seeking rents to benefit rulers (Tilly 1985).

Governments regularly engage in opportunity hoarding. They do so when they monopolize such resources as oil or diamonds and restrict benefits realized from those resources to members of the ruling group. Similarly, in poorer countries, holding governmental office often offers an escape from poverty. Despite meager salaries at all but the highest levels, government jobs offer more secure and remunerative employment than work in the private sector. They also frequently provide opportunities for bribes, service fees, and other payoffs (Bayart 1993; Fatton 1992; Migdal 2004; Roitman 2005; Rotberg 2004; Varese 2000; World Bank 1997).

Much more broadly, all governments provide more protection for their own property rights—for example, rights to armed force, public land, minerals, waterways, and national currencies—than for those of the general population. Distinctions between citizens and noncitizens likewise establish unequal protections for a wide variety of rights, including property rights (Ngai 2004). Those protections, too, involve opportunity hoarding.

Indirectly, but no less powerfully, all governments back up exploitation and opportunity hoarding on the part of their major supporters. To be sure, authoritarian regimes usually concentrate their support on the enterprises of much narrower elites than democracies do. We recognize a democracy precisely by the fact that a large share of the population has some control over how the government behaves and receives a degree of protection for its daily activity, including its pursuit of gain. But all historically known democracies have also favored the property rights, value-producing enterprises, and legal advantages of their dominant classes over those of ordinary people (Bermeo 2003; Tilly 2004).

Well before 19th-century welfare systems came into being, some governments installed protections against famine, disease, and disaster or their worst consequences. Chinese empires worked on authoritarian principles but regularly stockpiled and distributed grain to palliate the effects of famine (Lee and Campbell 1997; Will and Wong 1991; Wong 1997). Until the Black Death struck Europe and the Middle East during the 14th century, England and Egypt roughly equaled each other in wealth and productivity. But Egypt's economy took centuries to recover from the pandemic, while England moved back to its previous economic level quite rapidly. Contrasting systems of rule involving very different forms of land ownership made the difference (Borsch 2005).

Since 1800, most countries have also used some of their top-down power to redistribute income and create some measure of security for vulnerable workers. ... economic expansion has led regularly to formation of redistributive systems for social spending, especially as ordinary workers acquire political voice. Since the 18th century,

> the rise of tax-based social spending has been at the heart of government growth. It was social spending, not national defense, public transportation, or government enterprises, that accounted for most of the rise in governments' taxing and spending as a share of GDP over the last two centuries.
>
> (Lindert 2004, 1:20)

As wage-labor became more central to economies, first in the West and then across the world, redistributive social spending skyrocketed.

Most of that increase has occurred recently. Before the 20th century, social spending never sufficed to maintain poor people in idleness, much less to entice them away from viable employment. Conservative criticisms notwithstanding, Lindert challenges the view that welfare benefits sap initiative. He concludes, indeed, that social spending stabilized the labor force and increased its productive capacity. Because it did so, even very high levels of welfare expenditure occurred at little or no net cost to the whole economy. To that extent, governmental activity (like economic growth in general) produced aggregate exits from poverty. Thus some political initiatives do promote collective escapes from economic exclusion.

Individual passing refers to individual movement across a boundary through a change of identity, for example by acquiring a college degree or suppressing information about ethnic origins. Passing produces no significant transformation of the system. It often reinforces existing inequalities by confirming the value of credentials and committing successful boundary crossers to maintenance of the boundary. To the extent that it drains away potential leaders, indeed, the promotion of individual passing aggravates poverty for remaining members of the impoverished category.

Categorical boundary crossing generally produces more change in the system, partly because movement of a whole category into the territory of privilege sets a visible challenge and precedent for other unprivileged categories, and partly because categorical movement brings new forms of culture and social ties into the privileged zone. The net movement of America's Chinese immigrants from stigmatized labor during the 19th century to entrepreneurship and professional standing during the 20th did not make a new American revolution. But it did change the connection between Chinese migration networks and American centers of wealth (McKeown 2001).

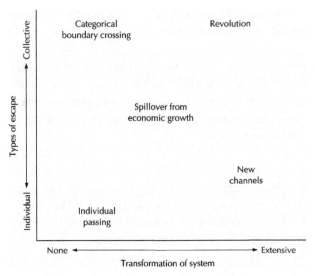

Figure 14.1 A Crude Typology of Escapes from Poverty

Revolutions continue to occur in our own time. In addition to the East European revolutions of 1989, Jeffrey Goodwin's short list of revolutions during the latter half of the 20th century includes Vietnam, China, Bolivia, Cuba, Algeria, Ethiopia, Angola, Mozambique, Cambodia, South Vietnam, Iran, Nicaragua, and Grenada (Goodwin 2001, 4; see also Goodwin 2005). Since they include displacement of a ruling class, revolutions simultaneously transform whole systems of inequality and produce substantial movements across existing boundaries of privilege. (As the painful experience of Russia since 1991 should remind us, however, revolutionary transfers of power do not necessarily reduce poverty across whole populations.)

Formation of *new channels* of mobility in systems of inequality transforms them over the long run by such means as connecting opportunities with new migration streams, moving people from agriculture to manufacturing or services, establishing new patron-client chains, creating new entrepreneurial networks, and destroying barriers that block whole categories of the population from existing mobility channels. If no significant economic growth occurs in the process, however, new channels produce turnover without net exits from poverty. One migrant stream or patron-client network simply displaces another.

Finally, *spillover from economic growth* does generate escapes from poverty to the extent that it opens new economic opportunities for the previously poor and/or involves redistribution of new benefits. Here political change or its absence makes a tremendous difference. On one side (as Lindert's historical comparisons document), redistributive social spending can generate mass exits from poverty as well as further economic growth. On the other side (as the cases of oil-rich authoritarian countries such as Sudan indicate), if a narrow elite hoards the returns from economic growth, poverty often grows more prevalent.

Implications

Despite these hints, no one should read promising poverty-reduction policies directly from my extremely general analysis of poverty and the politics of exclusion. At best, the analysis identifies elements that any worldwide program of poverty reduction must take into account lest it produce perverse consequences. I have not taken the obvious next step: to construct a typology of national inequality regimes that would permit distinctions among different settings requiring differing approaches to policy reduction.

Here are some implications of the analysis that bear on possible policy interventions to facilitate exits from poverty:

1   Although overall investments in economic growth may well produce collective exits from poverty, the social, economic, and political organization of exclusion makes it likely that very poor people will benefit least and last from broad interventions.

2   In the short and medium runs, broad investment programs that succeed will commonly increase inequality and therefore the relative deprivation of the very poor.

3   In particular, membership in stigmatized categories and lack of facilitating interpersonal connections regularly combine to exclude very poor people from mobility opportunities.

4   Existing political arrangements, furthermore, usually reinforce those forms of exclusion.

5   Any wide-ranging and effective intervention to reduce inequality and poverty will therefore harm some existing political interests and will require a political program to attack, subvert, bypass, or buy off those interests.

6   Individual exits from poverty can occur through deliberate facilitation of poor people's crossing of previously effective exclusionary boundaries, especially boundaries separating poor people from those who

control crucial resources and benefit from them by means of exploitation and opportunity hoarding.

7   With greater difficulty but larger consequences for existing political arrangements, collective exits from poverty can also occur through facilitated movement of whole categories across boundaries from exclusion to inclusion.

8   New systems of production in which previously poor people acquire collective control over newly productive resources are likely to benefit whole categories of poor people more directly and rapidly than facilitated crossing of existing boundaries.

All of these changes involve transformation of existing systems of inequality and the political arrangements that support them. All of them together would amount to a quiet revolution across the whole world.

References

Bayart, J. F. 1993. *The State in Africa: The Politics of the Belly.* London: Longman.

Bermeo, N. 2003. *Ordinary People in Extraordinary Times: The Citizenry and the Breakdown of Democracy.* Princeton, NJ: Princeton University Press.

———. 2005. *The Black Death in Egypt and England: A Comparative Study.* Austin: University of Texas Press.

Conley, D. 1999. *Being Black, Living in the Red.* Berkeley: University of California Press.

Fatton, R. 1992. *Predatory Rule: State and Civil Society in Africa.* Boulder, CO: Lynne Rienner.

Goodwin, J. 2001. *No Other Way Out: States and Revolutionary Movements, 1945–1991.* Cambridge: Cambridge University Press.

———. 2005. "Revolutions and Revolutionary Movements." In *Handbook of Political Sociology: States, Civil Societies, and Globalization,* ed. T. Janoski, R. R. Alford, A. M. Hicks, and M. A. Schwartz. Cambridge: Cambridge University Press.

Grusky, D. B., ed. 2001. *Social Stratification: Class, Race, and Gender in Sociological Perspective.*

Lanjouw, P., and N. Stern. 2003. "Opportunities Off the Farm as a Springboard Out of Rural Poverty: Five Decades of Development in an Indian Village." In *Pathways Out of Poverty: Private Firms and Economic Mobility in Developing Countries,* ed. G. S. Fields and G. Pfeffermann. World Bank Publications.

Lee, J. Z., and C. D. Campbell. 1997. *Fate and Fortune in Rural China: Social Organization and Population Behavior in Liaoning, 1774–1873.* Cambridge: Cambridge University Press.

Leiman, M. N. 1993. *The Political Economy of Racism.* London: Pluto Press.

Levi, M. 1997. *Consent, Dissent, and Patriotism.* Cambridge: Cambridge University Press.

Lindert, P. H. 2004. *Growing Public: Social Spending and Economic Growth since the Eighteenth Century.* 2 vols. Cambridge: Cambridge University Press.

McKeown, A. 2001. *Chinese Migrant Networks and Cultural Change: Peru, Chicago, Hawaii, 1900–1936.* Chicago: University of Chicago Press.

Migdal, J. S. 2004. "State Building and the Non-Nation-State." *Journal of International Affairs* 58: 17–46.

Munck, R. 2005. "Social Exclusion: New Inequality Paradigm for the Era of Globalization?" In Romero and Margolis 2005: 31–49.

Narayan, D., R. Chambers, M. K. Shah, and P. Petesch. 2000. *Voices of the Poor: Crying Out for Change.* New York: Oxford University Press for the World Bank.

Narayan, D., and P. Petesch, eds. 2002. *Voices of the Poor: From Many Lands.* New York: Oxford University Press for the World Bank.

Narayan, D., with R. Patel, K. Schafft, A. Rademacher, and S. Koch-Schulte. 2000. *Voices of the Poor: Can Anyone Hear Us?* New York: Oxford University Press for the World Bank.

Ngai, M. M. 2004. *Impossible Subjects: Illegal Aliens and the Making of Modern America.* Princeton, NJ: Princeton University Press.

Oliver, M. L., and T. M. Shapiro. 1997. *Black Wealth/White Wealth: A New Perspective on Racial Inequality.* New York: Routledge.

Roitman, J. 2005. *Fiscal Disobedience: An Anthropology of Economic Regulation in Central Africa.* Princeton, NJ: Princeton University Press.

Romero, M., and E. Margolis, eds. 2005. *The Blackwell Companion to Social Inequalities.* Oxford: Blackwell.

Rotberg, R. I., ed. 2004. *When States Fail: Causes and Consequences.* Princeton, NJ: Princeton University Press.

Sen, A. 1995. "The Political Economy of Targeting." In *Public Spending and the Poor: Theory and Evidence,* ed. D. van de Walle and K. Nead, 11–24. Baltimore: Johns Hopkins University Press.

Tilly, C. 1985. "War Making and State Making as Organized Crime." In *Bringing the State Back In,* ed. P. Evans, D. Rueschemeyer, and T. Skocpol, 169–91. Cambridge: Cambridge University Press.

———. 1992. *Coercion, Capital, and European States, AD 990–1992.* Rev. ed. Oxford: Blackwell.

———. 2004. *Contention and Democracy in Europe, 1650–2000.* Cambridge: Cambridge University Press.

Varese, F. 2000. "Pervasive Corruption." In *Economic Crime in Russia,* ed. A. Ledeneva and M. Kurkchiyan, 99–111. The Hague: Kluwer Law International.

Will, P.-É., and R. B. Wong. 1991. *Nourish the People: The State Civilian Granary System in China, 1650–1850.* Ann Arbor: University of Michigan Press.

Wong, R. B. 1997. *China Transformed: Historical Change and the Limits of European Experience.* Ithaca, NY: Cornell University Press.

World Bank. 1997. *The State in a Changing World: World Development Report 1997.* New York: Oxford University Press.

Political Violence   V

Contentious Conversation

15

Charles Tilly

Ayodhya, India, long sheltered a sixteenth-century mosque, Babri Masjid, named for the first Mughal emperor, Babur. Ayodhya attracted worldwide attention on December 6, 1992, when Hindu militants destroyed Ayodhya's Muslim shrine, began construction of a Hindu temple on the same site, and launched a nationwide series of struggles that eventually produced some twelve hundred deaths (Tambiah 1996: 251; Bose and Jalal 1998: 228). But the campaign behind that newsworthy event began a decade earlier. During the 1980s, militant Hindu groups started demanding destruction of the mosque and erection of a temple to Ram, epic hero of the Ramayana. Just before the 1989 elections, Bharatiya Janata Party (BJP) activists transported what they called holy bricks to Ayodhya and ceremoniously laid a foundation for their temple.

The following year, President Lal Advani of the BJP took his chariot caravan on a pilgrimage *(rath yatra)* across northern India, threatening along the way to start building the Ram temple in Ayodhya. Advani started his pilgrimage in Somnath, fabled site of a great Hindu temple destroyed by Muslim marauders. Advani's followers had fashioned his Toyota van into a simulacrum of legendary hero Arjuna's chariot, an image familiar from Peter Brook's film *Mahabharata*. As the BJP caravan passed through towns and villages, Advani's chariot attracted gifts of flower petals, coconut, burning incense, sandalwood paste, and prayer from local women. Authorities arrested Advani before he could begin the last lap of his journey to Ayodhya, but not before many of his followers had preceded him to the city. When some of them broke through police barricades near the offending mosque, police fired on them, killing "scores" of BJP activists (Kakar 1996: 51).

Both sides represented their actions as virtuous violence—one side as defense of public order, the other side as sacrifice for a holy cause. Hindu activists made a great pageant of cremating the victims' bodies on a nearby river bank, then returning martyrs' ashes to their homes in various parts of India. Soon the fatalities at Ayodhya became themes of widespread Hindu-Muslim-police clashes. Those conflicts intersected with higher caste students' public resistance to the national government's revival of an affirmative action program on behalf of Other Backward Classes (Tambiah 1996: 249). In Hyderabad, reports Sudhir Kakar,

> more than a thousand miles to the south of Ayodhya, the riots began with the killing of Sardar, a Muslim auto-rickshaw driver, by two Hindus. Although the murder was later linked to a land dispute between two rival gangs, at the time of the killing it was framed in the context of rising Hindu-Muslim tensions in the city. Muslims retaliated by stabbing four Hindus in different parts of the walled city. Then Majid Khan, an influential local leader of Subzimandi who lives and flourishes in the shaded space formed by the intersection of crime and politics, was attacked with a sword by some BJP workers and the rumor spread that he had died. Muslim mobs came out into the alleys and streets of the walled city, to be followed by Hindu mobs in their areas of strength, and the 1990 riot was on. It was to last for ten weeks, claim more than three hundred lives and thousands of wounded.
>
> (Kakar 1996: 51)

As his remarkable *Colors of Violence* unfolds, Sudhir Kakar seeks explanations for Hyderabad's 1990 violence by reporting discussions with some of the principals (including Majid Khan, still very much alive), reflecting on the identities involved, and reconstructing the psychological orientations that facilitate lethal violence. He establishes the deep grounding of ostensibly spontaneous intercommunal violence in everyday social relations and in the organization of such groups as the Hindu wrestlers-thugs-activists mobilized by local leaders including Majid Khan.

Instead of choosing between starkly opposed instrumentalist and primordialist accounts, however, students of South Asia's Hindu-Muslim conflicts, of ethnic mobilization, of nationalism, indeed of contentious politics in general can adopt a third alternative: they can recognize the conversational character of contention. They can examine such a conversation's location in continuously negotiated interchanges among specific interlocutors, its constraint and mediation by historically accumulated understandings concerning identities and relations of the parties, its incessant modification of those identities and relations, hence its crucial causal contribution to interactions that instrumentalists explain on the basis of individual or collective interests and primordialists explain on the basis of deeply grounded individual or collective sentiments.

If we regard conversation as continuously negotiated communication and contention as mutual claim-making that bears significantly on the parties' interests—which is how I propose we understand the two terms for present purposes—then the two social phenomena overlap extensively. They overlap in the zone we might call contentious conversation. Conversation is contentious to the extent that it embodies mutual and contradictory claims, claims that, if realized, would significantly alter the longer-term behavior of at least one participant. Contentious conversation certainly activates visceral emotions, neurally processed cognitions, and individual anatomical performances. It also operates within limits set by historically formed conventions, with regard to collectively constituted interests, and in response to stimuli from leaders or bystanders.

Beth Roy's subtle study of ostensibly communal conflict of 1954 in a Pakistani village (Bangladeshi by the time she arrived there in the 1980s) identifies the significance of that causal logic. She shows how a local scuffle among farmers working adjacent fields escalated into a full-scale alignment of self-identified Hindus against self-identified Muslims. At the start, Golam Fakir (categorically Muslim) and Kumar Tarkhania (categorically Hindu) interacted as disputants over the fact that Fakir's untethered cow had eaten Tarkhania's lentils. The series of confrontations did not begin as communal mobilization, but it approximated increasingly to classic models of Hindu/Muslim strife as it grew in geographic scope and mounted the national administrative hierarchy.

Here is the difficulty: humans live in flesh-and-blood bodies; accumulate traces of experiences in their nervous systems; organize current encounters with the world as cognitions, emotions, and intentional actions; and tell stories about themselves in which they acted deliberately and efficaciously or were blocked from doing so by uncontrolled emotion, weakness, malevolent others, bad luck, or recalcitrant nature. They tell similar stories about other people. Humans come to believe in a world full of continuous, neatly bounded, self-propelling individuals whose intentions interact with accidents and natural limits to produce all of social life. In many versions, those "natural limits" feature norms, values, and scripts inculcated and enforced by powerful others—but then internalized by self-propelling individuals. Accounts in this vein adopt phenomenological reductionism. They reduce social life to states of individual consciousness.

Closely observed, however, the same humans turn out to be interacting repeatedly with others, renegotiating who they are, adjusting the boundaries they occupy, modifying their actions in rapid response to other people's reactions, selecting among and altering available scripts, improvising new forms of joint action, speaking sentences no one has ever uttered before, yet responding predictably to their locations within webs of social relations they themselves cannot map in detail. They tell stories about themselves and others that facilitate their social interaction rather than laying out verifiable facts about individual lives. They actually live in deeply relational worlds. If social construction occurs, it happens socially, not in isolated recesses of individual minds.

The problem becomes acute in descriptions and explanations of contentious politics. Political actors typically give individualized accounts of participation in contention, although the "individuals" to which they attribute bounded, unified, continuous self-propulsion are often collective actors such as communities, classes, armies, firms, unions, interest groups, or social movements. They attach moral evaluations and responsibilities to the individuals praising or condemning them for their actions, grading their announced identities from unacceptable (for example, a mob) to laudable (for example, martyrs). Accordingly, strenuous effort in contentious politics goes into contested representations of crucial actors as worthy or unworthy, unified or fragmented, large or small, committed or uncommitted, powerful or weak, well connected or isolated, durable or evanescent, reasonable or irrational, greedy or generous.

Meticulous observation of that same effort, however, eventually tells even a naive observer what almost every combat officer, union leader, or political organizer acknowledges in private—that both public representations of political identities and other forms of participation in struggle proceed through intense coordination; contingent improvisation; tactical maneuvering; responses to signals from other participants; on-the-spot reinterpretations of what is possible, desirable, or efficacious; and strings of unexpected outcomes inciting new improvisations. Interactions among actors with shifting boundaries, internal structures, and identities turn out to permeate what in retrospect or in distant perspective analysts call actor-driven wars, strikes, rebellions, electoral campaigns, or social movements. Hence the difficulty of reconciling individualistic images with interactive realities.

As Hyderabad's bloody contention of 1990 illustrates, furthermore, many confrontations that begin under other definitions eventually activate and receive coding as conventional expressions of communal hostility. We should notice the analogy to family disputes in which available epithets, memories, and lines of fractionation only enter the struggle as it escalates or as third parties enter the fray. Such phenomena provide empirical justification for the "Instrumentalist" accounts of communal conflicts that Sudhir Kakar rightly challenges as sole explanations of the life-threatening interactions he studies. The effective response to instrumental reductionism, however, consists not of turning to phenomenological reductionism but of recognizing the conversational dynamics of such disputes.

The conversational analogy applies to a wide range of political contention. We could pursue it across other instances of ethnic and religious conflict, expressions of nationalism, electoral campaigns, revolutions, parliamentary debates, industrial conflict, and much more. Let us, however, move the discussion onto familiar ground. In his analysis of thousands of demonstrations in Marseille, Nantes, Paris, and other parts of France between 1979 and 1993, Olivier Fillieule identifies the stylized but incessant interchanges that occur among demonstrators, spectators, police, officials, and other persons involved in any demonstration. Although observers, reporters, analysts, and critics often reduce such events to attitudes and actions of the persons who occupy the street with banners, chants, and other dramatizations of their demands, detailed accounts drawn from such sources as police blotters reveal continuous streams of mutual deliberations, taunts, threats, attacks, retreats, delegations, agreements, and much more—usually reported from a single viewpoint, but always reflecting participation in communicative interchange.

Consider the 1986 testimony of an experienced commander of riot police. When asked what would happen if he received contradictory orders from the local police commissioner and his own unit's superiors, he replied that it was unlikely, but added:

> At a moment like that I would probably decide for myself, as I actually once did for our buses. When we were setting ourselves up, the commissioner of the 16th [Parisian] arrondissement asked us, contrary to my view, to reinforce the street barriers with our vehicles. When I saw that the demonstrators were trying to set the barricades on fire, on my own initiative I had the vehicles moved to the middle of the bridge; my buses retreated. The other vehicles of the Parisian police that didn't retreat got burned.
>
> (Fillieule 1997: 257)

Torching buses and moving them back obviously constitutes a crude sort of dialogue. So do deploying shields against stone-throwers, wading into a crowd with flailing clubs, or even receiving delegations from demonstrators at a minister's office. Yet the dialogue involved is real and consequential. It engages two parties, or more. How one party responds to another affects what happens next. The conversation places unceasing improvisation within strongly defined conventions that mark the ongoing interchange as a demonstration rather than, say, a strike, a public meeting, an election rally, routine lobbying, or a coup d'état.

As with all conversation, contentious conversation has a delightfully paradoxical property: improvisation within constraints that produce order. Demonstrators, counterdemonstrators, police, authorities, and other participants in demonstrations improvise incessantly, jockeying for surprise, effect, and strategic advantage. If they simply repeated the routines they had followed during a previous encounter, they would resemble people who utter bromides; they would cede all strategic advantage to their partners and come off as dull automata. Yet as compared with all the actions and interactions of which they are capable, they concentrate their efforts within a narrow range of symbols, utterances, and interactions. Demonstrators often march in ranks, display banners, shout slogans, and present petitions, but rarely carry machine guns, defecate in the street, strip naked, strangle spectators, sing nursery rhymes, stop to buy the day's groceries, or travel in taxis—except, of course, if they appear together in taxi drivers demanding protection from muggers. If participants in contentious conversation did not adopt recognizable idioms, they would undercut their own efforts to coordinate actions, convey messages, and influence objects of their claims.

As in less contentious forms of conversation, contentious conversation produces order by means of improvisation within constraints.

We can capture the theatrical side of contention by speaking of contentious repertoires (Tarrow 1998: chapter 2; Traugott 1995).

Like any other sorts of conversational forms, contentious repertoires embody history and culture. Participants and observers draw on previous experiences, incorporate readily available symbols, make selective references to shared memories, strategize as a function of what happened last time, notice the impact (if any) of their improvisations, compare notes after the fact. Repertoires matter to the course and outcome of contention for several reasons. First, they incorporate scripts that participants know to be performable, in which they know the parts and collaborative routines required, and of whose requisites and possible outcomes they share at least some awareness; all these features facilitate mobilization of participants for a new performance. Second, they draw meaning and effectiveness in part from their connection with previous iterations of the same performances—our opponents' recent meetings or our own, the received history (however mythical) of previous demonstrations, and so on. Third, they eliminate from consideration, and often from consciousness, a vast range of claim-making performances of which participants are technically capable.

Among other things, political identities are at stake. To continue with theatrical metaphors, claim-makers are acting out answers to the question, "Who are you?" When contentious conversation arises in the course of routine social life, the answers are often obvious; we are whoever we were before the contention began, employees of a given company, purchasers in a weekly market, worshippers at a shrine, public officials doing public business, police officers patrolling their beats. Much of the time, however, identities remain unclear until participants dramatize them. All people have multiple identities at their disposal, each one attached to a somewhat different set of social relations: neighbor, spouse, farmer, customer, tenant, schoolmate, lover, or citizen. Some available identities appear in public only intermittently, as is the case with many varieties of party affiliation, association membership, and adhesion to social movements. In these circumstances, participants in contentious conversation regularly make a point of the capacities in which they are interacting, of the identities they are activating.

As in ordinary conversation, some performances actually center on the assertion of identities rather than the making of specific claims. One side says, "Recognize us as significant actors of a certain kind," while the other side accepts or contests that assertion of identity. Social movement activists often initiate performances whose central message declares that the activists and/or the constituency they claim to represent are "WUNC": worthy, united, numerous, and committed.

Whether contentious or otherwise, conversational conventions and the very course of conversation exert significant influence over their participants' behavior. Established identities and their associated social relations, for example, always make a difference to the course of interaction. In the extreme case of Hindu/Muslim massacres, Sudhir Kakar shows that neighbors of one faith often warned members of the other religious category of a coming attack, that in the heat of bloodshed Muslim households sometimes hid Hindus or vice versa, and that bands of killers ordinarily avoided blood-letting within their own neighborhoods; reduction of other people to nothing but their broadest public identities facilitated murder, while the presence of multiple ties and identities inhibited it. In the extreme reduction, extermination squads sorted potential victims by clothing or, for males, the condition of their penises, circumcision signaling Muslim identity, its absence Hindu identity.

Short of such an extreme, conversationally established identities always shape social interaction, including political contention. ...Stories that people create in the course of contentious conversation themselves affect subsequent social interaction, both because they filter collective memory and because they build in commitments to behave consistently with those stories.

Let me state the point more strongly. Conversation in general shapes social life by altering individual and collective understandings, by creating and transforming social ties, by generating cultural materials that are then available for subsequent social interchange, and by establishing, obliterating, or shifting commitments on the part of participants. The same is true of contentious conversation, for the same reasons.

They are conversational in the sense of proceeding through historically situated, culturally constrained, negotiated, consequential interchanges among multiple parties. Whatever else it requires, the explanation of political contention demands that analysts take mere speech acts seriously.

References

Bose, Sugata, and Ayesha Jalal. 1998. *Modern South Asia: History, Culture, Political Economy.* London: Routledge.

Fillieule, Olivier. 1997. *Stratégies de la rue: Les manifestations en France.* Paris: Presses de Sciences Po.

Kakar, Sudhir. 1996. *The Colors of Violence: Cultural Identities, Religion, and Conflict.* Chicago: University of Chicago Press.

Tambiah, Stanley J. 1996. *Leveling Crowds: Ethnonationalist Conflicts and Collective Violence in South Asia.* Berkeley: University of California Press.

Tarrow, Sidney. 1998. *Power in Movement.* Cambridge: Cambridge University Press.

Traugott, Mark, ed. 1995. *Repertoires and Cycles of Collective Action.* Durham: Duke University Press.

The Politics of Collective Violence

16

Charles Tilly

With collective violence we enter the terrain of contentious politics, where people make discontinuous, public, collective claims on each other. By no means all contentious politics generates violence; our problem is precisely to explain when contention takes a violent turn. But all collective violence involves contention of one kind or another.

We can conveniently mark our crossing into contentious politics' territory by noticing when governments—more generally, individuals or organizations that control concentrated means of coercion—become parties to discontinuous, public, collective claims. Governments become parties to contention as claimants, objects of claims, or stakeholders.

Collective violence, then, is a form of contentious politics. It counts as *contentious* because participants are making claims that affect each other's interests. It counts as *politics* because relations of participants to governments are always at stake.

Nevertheless, violence and government maintain a queasy relationship. Where and when governments are very weak, interpersonal violence commonly proliferates in the populations under the nominal jurisdictions of those governments. Where and when governments grow very strong, violence among civilians usually declines. Politicians and political philosophers often advocate good, strong government as a bulwark against violent victimization. But all governments maintain control over concentrated means of violence in the form of arms, troops, guards, and jails. Most governments use those means extensively to maintain what their rulers define as public order.

In all governments, furthermore, some rulers also use violent means to further their own power and material advantage. When large-scale collective violence occurs, government forces of one sort or another almost always play significant parts as attackers, objects of attack, competitors, or intervening agents. International war is simply the extreme case—but, on the whole, the most lethal—of governmental involvement in violence. For these reasons, collective violence and nonviolent politics intersect incessantly.

Rulers, police, philosophers, and historians often distinguish between force and violence. Force, in this view, consists of legitimate short-run damage and seizure—which typically means that the persons who administer damage enjoy legal protection for their actions. Force might therefore include legitimate self-defense but not unprovoked aggression. In such a perspective, violence refers to damage that does not enjoy legal protection.

Will the distinction between force and violence serve our purposes? As citizens, all of us want to make some such distinction; we want to draw lines between right and wrong uses of governmental authority to seize and damage persons or their property. To varying degrees and with competing definitions of propriety, we also want governments to deploy their concentrated coercive means against improper uses of violence. For purposes of explaining violent interactions, however, the distinction between (legitimate) force and (illegitimate) violence faces three insuperable objections.

First, the precise boundary of legitimate force remains a matter of fierce dispute in all political systems. Just think of debates about what does or doesn't constitute proper police behavior in pursuing a suspect, about the rights and wrongs of capital punishment, or about permissible military actions against civilians in wartime. In the very course of initially peaceful demonstrations that turn violent, demonstrators and police are almost always contesting the boundary between legitimate and illegitimate uses of coercive means.

Second, in practical experience a long continuum runs from (1) duly licensed governmental actions whose propriety almost everyone accepts through (2) derelictions by governmental agents to (3) damage wrought with secret support or encouragement from some segment of some government.

A large share of the collective violence in the episodes that people call riots, rebellions, revolutions directly involves governmental agents as purveyors or objects of damage. Without including deaths inflicted or suffered by police and troops, we would have no way of explaining variation in the deadliness of different sorts of collective encounters. In the Paris Commune of 1871, for example, one set of estimates tells us that about 16,000 rebels died in street fighting with French national troops, the conquering national army executed another 3,500 rebels after street fighting ended, and in the process 880 members of the national army died (Chesnais, 1976: 168). In evaluating the Commune's ferocity, we would surely want to include the estimated 16,880 deaths on both sides in street fighting, and might want to include the 3,500 executions as well. For purposes of explanation, it would be odd indeed to call one set of deaths an outcome of violence and another an outcome of legitimate force. If the rebels had won, would their violent acts have converted retroactively to legitimate force?

Not all collective violence, to be sure, consists of confrontations between authorities and citizens. Enough does, however, to require careful examination of authority–citizen interactions. No student of collective violence can afford to exclude actions of governmental authorities or interactions between governmental agents and nongovernmental actors. Indeed, we must eventually explain why regimes differ so greatly with respect to which forms and agents of violence they sponsor, legitimate, tolerate, or forbid.

This chapter identifies the political context for that great variation. After a brief introduction to regimes, it reviews the constitution of political actors, the special place of political entrepreneurs as connectors and organizers of collective violence, and the significance of specialists in violence such as police and bandits.

Any government makes some distinctions between its own agents and polity members, typically putting governmental resources directly at the disposition of agents but requiring polity members to follow established procedures (formal applications, petitions, contracts, hearings, and the like) in order to gain access to similar resources.

Governments also sometimes accept or reinforce boundaries separating challengers from polity members by bargaining out who belongs to them and who has the right to speak for the challengers even while denying them routine access to governmental resources. During early stages of the 1960s civil rights movement for example, U.S. government agents began talking with leaders of civil rights organizations without by any means recognizing them as speaking for African Americans at large. Later, organizations such as the National Association for the Advancement of Colored People acquired a regular place in government-backed discussions of race relations, while the government continued to harass a number of black nationalist groups. Thus the distinctions among governmental agents, polity members, challengers, subjects, and outside political actors acquire legal standing.

Category formation is itself a crucial political process. Category formation creates identities. A social category consists of a set of sites that share a boundary distinguishing all of them from (and relating all of them to) at least one set of sites visibly excluded by the boundary. Category formation occurs by means of three different mechanisms: invention, borrowing, and encounter. *Invention* involves authoritative drawing of a boundary and prescription of relations across that boundary, as when Bosnian Serb leaders decree who in Bosnia-Herzegovina is a Serb and who not, then regulate how Serbs interact with non-Serbs. *Borrowing* involves importation of a boundary *cum* relations package already existing elsewhere and its installation in the local setting, as when rural French Revolutionaries divided along the lines of Patriot versus Aristocrat that had already split Paris and other major French cities. *Encounter* involves initial contact between previously separate (but internally well-connected) networks in the course of which members of one network begin competing for resources with members of the other, interactively generating definitions of the boundary and relations across it.

But categorical boundaries appear within the major clumps of actors as well. Any particular government may, for example, have dealings with different polity members organized as local communities, religious congregations, military units, and categories of property holders. Furthermore, we will soon have to single out two overlapping sorts of political actors that figure prominently in collective violence: (i) political entrepreneurs whose specialty consists of organizing, linking, dividing, and representing constituencies; and (ii) specialists in deployment of violent means such as soldiers, police, thugs, and gang leaders. Distinctions among agents of government, policy members, challengers, subjects, and outside political actors simply start the analysis. They say that a significant divide separates those actors having routine access to government agents and resources from others (e.g. protesting national minorities) lacking that access.

Transactions among agents of government, polity members, challengers, and subjects constitute a *regime*. Public politics within a regime consists of claim-making interactions among agents, polity members, challengers, and outside political actors as well. Public politics includes tax collection, military conscription, individual voting, application for pensions, and many other transactions to which governments are parties.

Contentious politics consists of that (large) subset of public politics in which the claims are collective and would, if realized, affect their objects' interests. Contentious politics therefore excludes routine tax collection, reporting for military service, voting, and application for pensions. But any of these can become continuous if people mount collective resistance to them. In Old Regime Europe, for example, a significant share of all popular rebellions began with royal attempts to impose new or augmented taxes (Tilly 1993).

Some forms of public politics, furthermore, almost always involve collective contention; rebellions, revolutions, social movements, demonstrations, general strikes, and contested electoral campaigns illustrate the irreducibly contentious forms of public politics. Some contentious claim making, finally, takes the form of damage to persons or objects; rebels kill rulers, revolutionaries sack places and son on and such on. That is the subset of contentious politics whose variation we are trying to explain.

Political Actors and Identities

Such actors, however, almost never describe themselves as composite networks. Instead, they offer collective nouns: they call themselves workers, women, residents of X, or United Front Against Y. Such *political identities* offer public, collective answers to the questions "Who are you?", "Who are we?", and "Who are they?" As such, they are subject to constant challenge and negotiation. Who spoke for the Hutu, and who spoke for Rwandans at large, became questions of life and death in 1994

Political identities assemble the following crucial elements:

boundaries separating "us" from "them"—for example, dividing Hutu from Tutsi;
shared *stories* about those boundaries—for example. Hutu stories about distinctive characteristics of Hutu and Tutsi, as well as origins of their differences;
social relations across the boundaries—for example, forms of address governing transactions between Hutu and Tutsi;
social relations *within* the boundaries—for example, signals among Hutu to indicate their common membership.

Political identities serve as springboards for claim making, but they do far more political work than that. To put a complicated process very simply, governmental agents sort political identities into legitimate and illegitimate, recognized and unrecognized.

Political rights come into existence through struggles for recognition (Foweraker & Landman 1997; Tilly 1998).

The rise of nationalism strongly affected the character of such recognition struggles. Before the American and French Revolutions, people rarely demanded rights or claimed that others had obligations to them on the grounds of belonging to a distinct nation. People maintained loyalties to religious and cultural traditions, but in most cases they undertook collective action on behalf of those traditions only when someone else proposed to stamp them out or to take away rights attached to them. From the late eighteenth century, however, nationalism gained importance as a political principle: a nation should have its own independent state, and an independent state should have its own nation.

From this principle flowed two antagonistic versions of nationalism. *Top-down* nationalism claimed the right of existing rulers to impose their preferred definitions of national culture and welfare on subjects of their regimes. *Bottom-up* nationalism claimed the right of distinct nations within heterogeneous states to acquire political independence. Each fed the other; the more rulers tried to impose national cultures and obligations, the more distinct minorities clamored for independence. Because people had often organized networks of trust, trade, sociability, and mutual aid around religious and ethnic ties, top-down nationalism did not simply wound minority self-esteem; it threatened their means of day-to-day survival.

From the American Revolution onward, leaders of powerful states—notably the French Revolutionary and Napoleonic states—used the principle of self-determination to pick apart composite rival powers such as the Habsburg and Ottoman empires. Thus it became advantageous to minorities within all sorts of regimes to designate themselves as nations in the making, to create histories and practices validating that designation, and to ask for outside help in achieving independence. Enterprising ethnic leaders were quick to see that they could gain power by gaining recognition as representatives of valid nations and could easily lose power if someone else got there first. Since World War II, most large-scale violent conflicts across the world have involved some such claims.

Much of what people loosely call "identity politics" consists of struggles over legitimation and recognition. The struggles take place within boundaries, across boundaries, over the placement and character of boundaries, around stories attached to those boundaries, and about relations between people sharing a common answer to the question "Who are you?" on one side and other political actors, including agents of government, on the other (Tilly 2002).

Political Entrepreneurs and Specialists in Violence

The mention of contemporary social movements should remind us of political actors whose voices have remained muted so far. Like their economic counterparts, *political entrepreneurs* engage in various forms of brokerage: creating new connections between previously unconnected social sites. But they do more than link sites. They specialize in activation, connection, coordination, and representation. They specialize in activating (and sometimes deactivating) boundaries, stories, and relations, as when Bosnian Serb leaders sharpened boundaries between Serbs and their Muslim or Croatian neighbors with whom Bosnians of Serbian lineage had long mingled, married, traded, and collaborated. They specialize in connecting (and sometimes disconnecting) distinct groups and networks, as when those same leaders integrated armed Serbian gangs into larger nationalist coalitions. They specialize in coordination, as when those leaders organized joint action on the part of those coalitions.

Political entrepreneurs specialize, finally, in representation, as when Bosnian Serb leaders claimed to speak for all Bosnians of Serbian lineage while demanding aid from Serbia in establishing Serbian political entities within Bosnia. In these ways, political entrepreneurs wield significant influence over the presence, absence, form, loci, and intensity of collective violence. When they promote violence, they do so by activating boundaries, stories, and relations that have already accumulated histories of violence; by connecting already violent actors with previously nonviolent allies; by coordinating destructive campaigns; and by representing their constituencies through threats of violence. After the fact, both participants and observers speak of deeply felt identities and age-old hatreds. But before and during contention, political entrepreneurs play critical parts in activating, connecting, coordinating, and representing participants in violent encounters.

By means of activation, connection, coordination, and representation, political entrepreneurs necessarily engage in inequality-generating opportunity hoarding. They often engage in exploitation as well. They organize opportunity hoarding as they construct or activate us-them boundaries between their networks and outsiders, fend off rival claimants to coordinate and represent some or all of the same networks, draw necessary resources from those networks, and deploy those resources in ways that simultaneously forward collective claims, reproduce the structures they have built, and sustain their own power. Of course they often fail in one regard or another. If that happens, the failure often generates collective violence inside the coalition's boundaries as rival entrepreneurs and their factions battle for control of activation, connection, coordination, and representation.

When political entrepreneurs coordinate the efforts of a large coalition to the advantage of a smaller set within that coalition, their opportunity hoarding becomes a form of exploitation. These well-known risks of contentious politics deserve emphasis because they help explain why political entrepreneurs often promote collective violence when a cool reading of their whole constituency's interest prescribes disbanding, escaping, or lying low. They become specialists in activating boundaries that serve their own readings of collective advantage.

Political entrepreneurs complement and overlap with another significant type of political actor, the *violent specialist*. Every government includes specialists in violence, people who control means of inflicting damage on persons and objects.

Plenty of specialists in violence, however, work outside of government. Some athletes—boxers, gladiators, bullfighters, and rugby players are obvious examples—specialize in doing damage. Armed guards, private police, paramilitary forces, guerrilla warriors, terrorists, thugs, bandits, kidnappers, enforcers, members of fighting gangs, and automobile wreckers sometimes enjoy governmental protection, but usually operate outside of government, even in defiance of government. Before the rise of centralized states on the European model during the seventeenth and eighteenth centuries, indeed, innumerable specialists in violence exercised their trades in at least partial independence of governmental control through most of the world. Even powerful Chinese dynasties lived with warlords and bandits in their midst as well as with armed and predatory nomadic peoples along their edges. In Europe itself, private armies, mercenaries, local militias, bandits, and pirates all competed at some times and collaborated at other times with nominally national armies (Thomson 1994).

Lest we slip into thinking of violent specialists as driven by bloodlust, we should recognize that for most of them most of the time the ideal outcome of a political interaction is to manipulate others without damaging anything. The genuinely effective specialist deploys *threats* of violence so persuasively that others comply before the damage begins (Blok 2001; Cohn 1993). To be sure, an occasional demonstration of ruthlessness solidifies a specialist's reputation, and backing away from visible challenges damages a specialist's credibility. Real-life mafiosi (as distinguished from their cinematic simulacra) know this well; by threatening violence for noncompliance, they provide guarantees for contracts where courts and kin fail to guarantee them, but now and then mafiosi also display the requisite readiness to kill, maim, and steal (Blok 1974, 2001; Gambetta 1993; Varese 2001; Volkov 2002). For government-backed armies, precision parades and displays of weapons produce some of the same effects. Visible ability to inflict damage promotes power over and above anything that damage itself might accomplish.

The category of political entrepreneurs therefore overlaps with the category of violent specialists. At the intersection of the two we find leaders of mercenaries, international weapons merchants, regional warlords, military rulers, and many a political figure who disposes of his or her own armed force. Over the long run of human history, indeed, most important political figures have combined entrepreneurship with control of coercive means. Only during the last few centuries has the unarmed power holder become a common political actor.

Mercenaries such as the ruthlessly efficient South Africa–based Executive Outcomes have intervened with lethal effect in Sierra Leone and elsewhere (Shannon 2002). Yet, as Berkeley says, plenty of predatory violence occurs across Africa. Violent specialists—many of them noncitizens of the countries in which they operate, and some of them European mercenaries or adventurers—join Africa's organized crime syndicates without becoming their obedient servants.

In Latin America as well, specialists in violence have repeatedly seized or tipped the balance of power in whole countries. Central America has suffered especially from the frequent availability of external allies—including drug dealers, arms runners, and the U.S. government—for newly forming armed units, however unsavory. William Stanley describes the terrible year of 1980 in El Salvador, when assassins struck Attorney General Mario Zamora Rivas, Archbishop Oscar Romero, and many other opponents of paramilitary violence. Those killings were only the most visible:

> These deaths were accompanied by almost twelve thousand others. Most were either captured and executed by the death squads or killed in wholesale massacres carried out by government forces in rural areas. With each major demonstration or labor strike, the popular movement lost dozens of supporters and key leaders. In a sense, the repression worked. Demonstrations grew smaller, and fewer people would outwardly identify themselves as being affiliated with leftist organizations. Yet the repressive state paid a high price: though the demonstrations and strikes gradually became smaller, there was a concomitant shift within the leftist opposition toward a military strategy. In May, the left began to move its militants into rural areas to develop a military structure; by September, this process was well advanced, though the groups still lacked arms; and by November, the left, now united as the Farabundo Martí Liberation Front (FMLN) had begun obtaining sufficient weapons to form an army.
>
> (Stanley 1996: 178)

The chilling experience of El Salvador makes several important new points about specialists in violence: they vary systematically in their proximity to (and sponsorship by) governments; they sometimes organize in opposition to existing organizations of violent specialists; and no sharp line separates their politics from those of armed forces belonging to established governments. These points apply in South Asia, Russia, and Africa as well.

All over the world—for example, in Colombia, the Caucasus, Palestine, Liberia, Sri Lanka, and Indonesia—specialists in violence figure importantly in the larger-scale versions of collective violence.

The complex but central position of violent specialists has three major implications for the study of collective violence. First, although it will help to start with distinctions among agents of government, polity members, challengers, and outside political actors, in closer looks at actual regimes and episodes we will have to recognize mobile and intermediate actors— political entrepreneurs and violent specialists prominent among them. No simple distinction between "insurgents" and "forces of order" can possibly capture the complex social interactions that generate collective violence.

Second, specialists in violence do not simply serve the interests of the larger entities (governments, parties, communities, ethnic groups, or others) with which they are currently aligned. They follow dynamics of their own. They regularly engage in exploitation and opportunity hoarding, sometimes at the expense of their own nominal employers or constituencies. At a minimum, any explanation of variations in collective violence will have to account for the acquisition and control of coercive means and skills by those specialists. Regimes differ significantly, furthermore, in the opportunities they offer and the places they assign to specialists in violence. We have no choice but to consider the care and feeding of violent means: recruitment and organization of military forces, supplies of weapons, ties between illicit trades and arms flows, taxation for war, hostage taking as a source of revenue, and employment of violent specialists by established political actors.

Third, the character of relations between governments and specialists in violence strongly affects the extent and locus of collective violence within a regime. Overall, collective violence rises with the extent that organizations specializing in deployment of coercive means—armies, police forces, coordinated banditry, pirate confederations, mercenary enterprises, protection rackets, and the like—increase in size, geographic scope, resources, and coherence. But democratic civilian control over violent specialists mutes those effects. Conversely, collective violence rises to the extent that the specialists escape democratic civilian control.

When it comes to government-led deployment of coercion against challengers, collective violence increases further to the extent that violent specialists' organization offers opportunities for private vengeance and incentives to predation. Where participation in organized violence opens paths to political and economic power, collective violence multiplies. Most notably, power seeking by violent specialists promotes the types of violent interaction I have called coordinated destruction and opportunism. Specialists in violence do not simply deploy damage for the pleasure of it or for the profit it brings them; they use violence and threats of violence to pursue projects of their own.

Over a wide range of collective violence, the interaction of violent specialists and political entrepreneurs with other political actors and with each other therefore deeply affects the extent, character, and objects of damage done. But the places of violent specialists and political entrepreneurs in public politics vary systematically by type of regime.

In all sorts of regimes, a significant share of all collective violence occurs as an outcome of claim making that does not begin with violence; soldiers shoot down peaceful petitioners, nonviolent demonstrators start to break windows, participants in rival religious processions begin to rough each other up, and so on. Hence there is a rough correspondence between the occasions of nonviolent and violent claim making. In high-capacity *undemocratic* regimes, for example, we should expect to find a high proportion of collective violence beginning with forbidden performances. In high-capacity *democratic* regimes, in contrast, we should expect to find most violence originating in tolerated performances.

Salience generally increases when (a) participants in political interaction are themselves specialists in violence, (b) uncertainty about an interaction's outcome increases, (c) stakes of the outcome for the parties increase, and (d) third parties to which the participants have stable relations are absent. Activation and suppression of different political identities (i.e., of bundled boundaries, stories, and social relations) directly affect [these] conditions ... the ease of activation and suppression of various political identities depends in turn on the regime's array of prescribed, tolerated, and forbidden performance.

The *extent of coordination* among violent actors increases as (e) political entrepreneurs create connections among previously independent individuals and groups, (f) authorities control the stakes—both rewards and punishments—of outcomes for participants, (g) categories dividing major blocs of participants (e.g. gender, race, or nationality) figure widely in routine social life, and (h) major participants organize and drill outside of violent encounters. Incorporation and separation strongly affect conditions (e) through (h).

Coordinated Destruction

Destruction as Conquest

Coordinated destruction refers to those varieties of collective violence in which persons or organizations specialized in the deployment of coercive means undertake programs of actions that damage persons and/or objects. It results from combined activation of boundaries, stories, and relations, on one side, and incorporation of multiple social actors and sites, on the other. Together, activation and incorporation produce higher levels of damage, on average, than other forms of collective violence. They also override previously existing relations among participants except in so far as those relations correspond to the activated identities.

Parallel to the distinction between relatively symmetrical and asymmetrical violent rituals, a major distinction within coordinated destruction separates (a) lethal contests, (b) campaigns of annihilation, and (c) conspiratorial terror.

(a) In *lethal contests*, at least two organized groups of specialists in coercion confront each other, each one using harm to reduce or contain the others' capacity to inflict harm. War is the most general label for this class of coordinated destruction, but different variants go by the names civil war, guerrilla, low-intensity conflict, and conquest. Although lethal contests of various sorts stretch back as far as humanity's historical record runs, the standard image of two or more disciplined national armies engaged in destroying each other within generally accepted rules of combat applies to only a small historical segment roughly 1650 to 1950 for Europe, a few much earlier periods for China, and even rarer intervals elsewhere in the world. Outside of those exceptional moments, autonomous raiding parties, temporary feudal levies, mercenary assemblages, bandits, pirates, nomads doubling as cavalry, mobilized villages, and similar conglomerate or part-time forces have fought most historical wars.

(b) Lethal contests shade over into *campaigns of annihilation* when one contestant wields overwhelming force or the object of attack is not an organization specialized in the deployment of coercive means. In recent decades, analysts have employed the term *genocide* for those campaigns in which attackers define their victims in terms of shared heritage and the term *politicide* for those in which victims belong to a common political category; so far, no commonly accepted term has emerged for similar campaigns aimed at members of religious or regional categories. The usual stakes in campaigns of annihilation are collective survival, on one side, and recognition as the sole party with the right to territorial control, on the other. Because of those stakes, such struggles tend to generate vast mobilizations of support extending far beyond the specialists in coercion who initiate them.

(c) In the other direction, lethal contests give way to *conspiratorial terror* when a small but well-organized set of actors begin attacking vastly more powerful targets by clandestine means—assassinations, kidnappings, bombings, and the like. When it has serious political effects, conspiratorial terror simultaneously demonstrates the vulnerability of apparently insuperable powers and the presence of a dangerous, elusive alternative to those powers. It thereby shakes up routine politics, shortens time horizons, and identifies possible allies for dissidents.

Distinctions among lethal contests, campaigns of annihilation, and conspiratorial terror rest on the degree of inequality among the damage-wielding parties. Another way to put it is this: lethal contests constitute the special case of coordinated destruction in which the parties approach parity. The special case looms large because obviously weaker parties usually avoid combat if they can get away, and they often seek allies to equalize forces on either side. Shows of strength, spying on enemies, and negotiations with potential coalition partners therefore figure significantly in the dynamics of lethal contests.

In coordinated destruction, struggles over exploitation and opportunity hoarding come doubly into play: (i) in control of the government; and (ii) in use of political power to establish, maintain, seize, alter, or destroy inequality-generating systems of social relations outside of government. Governments always engage in opportunity hoarding and usually engage in exploitation as well; they always involve members of categorically bounded networks' acquisition of access to resources that are valuable, renewable, subject to monopoly, supportive of network activities, and enhanced by the network's operating routines (opportunity hoarding). But they also commonly involve powerful, connected people's commandeering of resources from which they draw significantly increased returns by coordinating the efforts of outsiders whom they exclude from the full value added by that effort (exploitation).

The sharper the boundary and the greater inequality across that boundary, the weightier are the stakes of control over government for both incumbents and challengers. Coordinated destruction occurs when well-organized incumbents strike down resistance to their demands, when incumbents use force of arms to extend their jurisdictions, and when excluded parties organize on a sufficient scale to challenge incumbents' own armed force. These effects become stronger when the parties on either side of the boundary polarize—when cooperative arrangements and overlapping actors disappear—and/or when uncertainty about the other side's future actions increases on either or both sides. Following Sigmund Freud, Anton Blok (2001: 115–35) stresses the ironic, tragic "narcissism of minor differences" that comes into play as political entrepreneurs fortify the boundaries, empty the middle ground, and increase the uncertainty of fundamentally similar neighbors such as Bosnian Croats and Serbs or Rwandan Hutu and Tutsi.

In Algeria of the mid-1990s, Salafi Islamic purists broke with their more moderate allies in the struggle against the secularist regime. According to the leader of the *Groupe Islamique Armé* (GIA), Algerians divided opponents of the regime into three categories: (1) true freedom fighters who supported holy war; (2) those supposed Islamists who actually opposed holy war by "force, talk, or with the pen"; and (3) Islamists who supported democracy. Treating members of categories (2) and (3) as traitors, they drew their boundary at (1) versus everyone else, directing their most vicious violence not against the regime itself but against their neighbors in groups (2) and (3).

Thus they massacred whole villages of women and children that failed to enlist in their cause. On the whole, when control of governments is at stake the most savage violence pits close cousins, rather than truly alien peoples, against one another.

Outside the government, under some conditions the struggles over and within systems of exploitation and opportunity hoarding likewise take the form of coordinated destruction. Low-capacity regimes, especially undemocratic ones, live with greater vulnerability to coordinated destruction within their domestic politics because they allow greater scope for dissidents and rivals to organize their own violent specialists on a large scale. As Colombia's central state capacity has declined since the 1970s, for example, paramilitary forces have typically formed coalitions with rural landlords while guerrilla forces have typically formed coalitions with enemies of rural landlords. Both, however, have adopted kidnapping and taxes on the cocaine trade as means of support for their lethal activities. (As a result, Colombian kidnappings—which typically ran under 50 per year before 1985—... rose from 1,800 to 3,200 to 3,700 between 1998 and 2000; Ramirez 2001: 175.) Both sides have formed their own protection rackets and their own systems of exploitation; their private systems feed on existing nongovernmental systems of exploitation and opportunity hoarding (Echeverry *et al.* 2001; Walker 1999).

A ... remarkable change occurred within the broad category of coordinated destruction during the half-century following World War II. Where interstate wars among well-identified national armies had predominated for a century or more, shifts toward a much wider variety of coercive forces and toward campaigns of annihilation elevated civil war (broadly defined) to the chief setting of coordinated destruction. Decolonization, expansion of world trade in arms and drugs, reappearance of mercenary forces, and the weakening of central state capacity in many world regions all contributed to that change. As war shifted from interstate competition to internal struggle, paradoxically, external parties—both other states and international organizations—became more heavily involved as suppliers of military means, allies, aid givers, profiteers, and mediators.

These postwar shifts magnified the importance of two interlocked political phenomena that had receded in importance worldwide after the eighteenth century as Western states centralized at home and divided much of the non-Western world into colonies. The first practice was *subvention* by one state's rulers of rebellion and resistance to central rule in an adjacent state as a way of extending the intervening state's power. That practice did not entirely disappear during the nineteenth century, as recurrent intervention of the United States in Mexico (including the U.S. annexation of Texas) illustrates. But it became less common once internationally recognized boundaries, national and colonial, stood in place.

The second practice was outside *promotion* of political autonomy in resource-rich regions as a way of gaining privileged access to the resources in question. Again, massive Western interventions in China during the nineteenth century as well as twentieth-century U.S. interventions in Central America on behalf of American capital establish that the practice continued well past 1800. But it, too, became less prevalent where great powers agreed on the boundaries. Both practices revived in the decolonized world after World War II.

In the Congo we see convergence of two violence-generating practices: subsidy of rebellion by adjacent states and promotion of internal autonomy to facilitate seizure of resources. Resurgence of the two practices in parts of the world from which drugs, minerals, and cheap labor originate has [risen].

Rwandan genocide, furthermore, underlines the part that more general populations play in coordinated destruction when effectively linked or driven by political entrepreneurs and violent specialists. ... Distinct forms of social organization certainly set off coordinated destruction from other forms of collective violence (not to mention from nonviolent contention), but the case of interstate war should remind us how much advance planning, prior training, logistical preparation, and strategic coordination go into efforts at mutual destruction. That participants should then improvise furiously, feel rage, fear, shame, or satisfaction in the face of danger, or manufacture implausible stories about what they are doing does not distinguish them remarkably from those participating in any number of other high-risk activities: police patrols, unsafe sex, fire fighting, brain surgery, team sports, childbirth, drug running, corporate takeovers, and many more. In all these cases, established social ties, shared understandings, and interaction reper-toires channel the actors' behavior. Definable social processes—not impulse-ridden anarchy—determine who does damage to whom and how. Our job as analysts is to trace the more visible and robust of those social processes.

What social processes? ... Coordinated destruction, remember, refers to those varieties of collective violence in which persons or organizations special-ized in the deployment of coercive means undertake a program of actions that damage persons and/or objects. By definition, then, coordinated destruction results from the political engagement of at least one body of violent special-ists. That tautological statement sets the first part of an explanatory agenda: accounting for the creation or activation of forces specializing in coercion. In Rwanda, President Habyarimana's reluctant sponsorship of a Hutu Power militia left a deadly retaliatory force in readiness after his sudden death.

Programs of destruction, likewise present by definition, offer trickier problems of interpretation than does the presence or absence of violent spe-cialists; people tell different stories about their programs before, during, and after violent episodes, and they often modify these programs in the course of interaction. Nevertheless, the prior existence of a destructive program is usually detectable and an important facilitator of coordinated destruction. Such programs can take the form of concrete blueprints for annihilation, conspiratorial plans, or more general stigmatization of a social category—heretics, Jews, communists, Roma, gays, and so on—as falling outside of conventional legal protections.

Beyond tautology, coordinated destruction regularly results from the cre-ation of coalitions among previously segmented wielders of violent means. Political entrepreneurs therefore exercise great influence over the waxing and waning of coordinated destruction, for example by knitting scattered opponents of government exactions into common (if temporary) resistance fronts. In such circumstances, we find entrepreneurs carrying on their usual work of activating, connecting, coordinating, and representing—but now with violent interaction as the object of their efforts. Within governments, precisely parallel processes occur as advocates and opponents of destructive programs negotiate deployment of a government's own violent specialists. In general, coordinated destruction occurs when beneficiaries (governmental or nongovernmental) of exploitation and opportunity hoarding encounter connected resistance to those systems or to their control over those systems. If brokerage fails or multiple boundaries activate, it follows, coordinated de-struction mutates into opportunism and/or scattered attack.

Three complementary bundles of mechanisms select certain identities for collective action.

1 When networks of mutual aid segregate on either side of a boundary, a dispute that pits people on the two sides against each other (for whatever reason)—and then leads them to seek support from their fellows—redefines the dispute as categorical. ... Call this process *network-based escalation*.

2 Rather than being all-encompassing, political identities connect people with certain social settings and not with others; drawing them into those settings activates the identities. Holidays, weddings, funerals, enrollment in schools, election campaigns, calls to military service, and trips to fairs all place people in settings where identities that play little part in organizing daily life become salient, visible, and compelling. This second process promotes coordinated destruction to the extent that (a) the settings in question bring together members of paired categories that already have a history of conflict and (b) shows of group strength already belong to the repertoires attached to those settings. By itself, however, the process is likely to produce no more than intermittent and scattered violent incidents as a function of schedules attached to the relevant social settings. Call this process *setting-based activation*.

3 Political entrepreneurs (whatever their other talents and appeals) become skilled at evoking certain political identities and suppressing others. As they activate, connect, coordinate, and represent, they draw selectively on networks that will line up on their side of the appropriate boundary. The third process can operate quite independently of the first two, with leaders calling up members of a category who would rather evade service but cannot refuse (Tilly 2001). Alone or in conjunction with the first two processes, it can produce coordinated destruction on a large scale. If violent specialists are among those called, the chances of extensive damage increase. Call this process *brokerage*.

Coordination and salience—and thus the resemblance to war—rise as local struggles connect increasingly to divisions and changes at the national or international scale.

References

Blok, Anton. 1974. *The Mafia of a Sicilian Village, 1860–1960*. New York: Harper Row.
———. 2001. *Honor and Violence*. Cambridge: Cambridge University Press.

Chesnais, Jean-Claude. 1976. *Les Morts Violentes en France depuis 1826: Comparaisons Internationales*. Paris: Presses Universitaires de France.

Echeverry, Juan Carlos, Natalia Salazar and Veronica Navas. 2001. "El Conflicto colombiano en el contexto internacional." In *Economía, Crimen y Conflicto*. Bogata: Universidad Nacional de Colombia.

Fowerake, Joe and Todd Landman. 1997. *Citizenship Rights and Social Movements: A Comparative and Statistical Analysis*. Oxford: Oxford University Press.

Gambetta, Diego. 1993. *The Sicilian Mafia: The Business of Private Protection*. Cambridge, MA: Harvard University Press.

Shannon, Ulric. 2002. "Private Armies and the Decline of the State." In *Violence and Politics: Globalization's Paradox*. Edited by Kennon Worcester, Sally Avery Bermanzohn and Mark Unger. New York: Routledge.

Stanley, William. 1996. *The Protection Racket State: Elite Politics, Military Extortion and Civil War in El Salvador*. Philadelphia: Temple University Press.

Thomson, Janice E. 1994. *Mercenaries, Pirates and Sovereigns: State Building and Extraterritorial Violence in Early Modern Europe*. Princeton: Princeton University Press.

Tilly, Charles. 1993 "Speaking Your Mind without Elections, Surveys or Social Movements." *Public Opinion Quarterly* 47: 461–78.

———. 1998. "Where do Rights Come From?" In *Democracy, Revolution and History*. Edited by Theda Skocpol. Ithaca, NY: Cornell University Press.

———. 2001. "Do Unto Others," in Marco Guigni and Florence Passy (eds.) *Political Altruism? The Solidarity Movement in International Perspective*. Lanham, MD: Rowman and Littlefield.

———. 2002. *Stories, Identities and Political Change*. Lanham, MD: Rowman and Littlefield.

Varese, Federico. 2001. *The Russian Mafia: Private Protection in a New Market Economy*. Oxford: Oxford University Press.

Volkov, Vadim. 2002. *Violent Entrepreneurs: The Use of Force in the Making of Russian Capitalism*. Ithaca, NY: Cornell University Press.

Walker, William O. 1999. "The Limits of Coercive Diplomacy: U.S. Drug Policy and Colombian State Stability, 1978–1997." In *The Illicit Global Economy and State Power*. Lanham, MD: Rowman and Littlefield.

Terror, Terrorism, Terrorists

17

Charles Tilly

Some vivid terms serve political and normative ends admirably despite hindering description and explanation of the social phenomena at which they point. Those double-edged terms include *riot, injustice,* and *civil society,* all of them politically powerful but analytically elusive (Moore 1979; Vermunt and Steensma 1991; Cohen and Arato 1992; Brass 1996; Herzog 1998; Plotz 2000; Schweingruber 2000; Edwards, Foley, and Diani 2001; Ferree *et al.* 2002). They also include *terror, terrorism,* and *terrorists.* This brief survey shows how and why.

In his address to Congress nine days after the devastating attacks of September 11, 2001, U.S. President George W. Bush declared that "our war on terror begins with al-Qaida, but it does not end there. It will not end until every terrorist group of global reach has been found, stopped, and defeated" (State Department 2002a:i). Echoed Secretary of State Colin L. Powell in May 2002: "In this global campaign against terrorism, no country has the luxury of remaining on the sidelines. There *are* no sidelines. Terrorists respect no limits, geographic or moral. The frontlines are everywhere and the stakes are high. Terrorism not only kills people. It also threatens democratic institutions, undermines economies, and destabilizes regions" (State Department 2002a:iii). In the words of the president and the secretary of state, terror, terrorism, and terrorists become inseparable concepts, coherent entities, efficacious actors, and enemies to be eradicated.

Students of political processes and collective violence certainly should pay attention to such reification; it exerts a significant influence on world politics. But they should not incorporate the categories wholesale into their own descriptions and explanations of the political processes at hand.

In particular, social scientists who attempt to explain sudden attacks on civilian targets should doubt the existence of a distinct, coherent class of actors (terrorists) who specialize in a unitary form of political action (terror) and thus should establish a separate variety of politics (terrorism). This essay argues the following points instead:

- The word *terror* points to a widely recurrent but imprecisely bounded political strategy.
- We can reasonably define that strategy as *asymmetrical deployment of threats and violence against enemies using means that fall outside the forms of political struggle routinely operating within some current regime.*
- A great variety of individuals and groups engage in terror, thus defined, from time to time, most often alternating terror with other political strategies or with political inaction.
- Groups and networks specializing in terror and no other forms of political action do sometimes form, but they typically remain unstable and ephemeral.
- Most groups and networks that engage in terror overlap extensively with government-employed and government-backed specialists in coercion—armies, police, militias, paramilitaries, and the like.
- Even when they organize in opposition to existing governments, specialists in coercion typically adopt forms of organization, external connections, and sources of supply resembling those of government-employed specialists.
- Most uses of terror actually occur as complements or as byproducts of struggles in which participants—often including the so-called terrorists—are engaging simultaneously or successively in other more routine varieties of political claim making.
- Terror as a strategy therefore ranges from (1) intermittent actions by members of groups that are engaged in wider political struggles to (2) one segment in the modus operandi of durably organized specialists in coercion, including government-employed and government-backed specialists in coercion to (3) the dominant rationale for distinct, committed groups and networks of activists.
- Despite the publicity it has received recently, variety (3) accounts for a highly variable but usually very small share of all the terror that occurs in the contemporary world.

In fact, the State Department's own reporting on world affairs generally confirms this argument. The State Department tracks the world's vindictive violence from two distinct perspectives. Mandated by Congress, it issues separate annual reports on human rights and on global terrorism. Under the administration of John F. Kennedy, as Congress appropriated funds for foreign aid it also required the executive branch to report on human rights violations. In its current version, the annual human rights report draws information from American embassies across the world on local instances of government-backed torture, cruel punishment, irregular detention, drastic civil liberties restrictions, compulsory labor, child labor, and related abuses.

Issued in May 2002, the State Department's statement on human rights during 2001 made an obligatory reference to fighting terrorism, roughly equating governments that violate human rights with governments that promote international terror. It declared that its country reports capture "a world still reeling and reacting to the events of last September. Yet the reports' central mission remains the same—to give voice to those who have been denied the freedoms and rights provided for in the Universal Declaration on Human Rights. The reports confirm that the battle of ideas between those who suppress democracy and human rights and those who would see them flourish remains far from over. Only through the promotion and protection of human rights and fundamental freedoms can the international community be secure from the scourge of terrorism" (State Department 2002b:1). Nevertheless, the 2001 report on human rights, like its predecessors, focused on ways that governments mistreat (or tolerate the mistreatment of) their own citizens.

The State Department's annual human rights report complements the work of such organizations as Human Rights Watch and Freedom House by cataloguing specific abuses one country at a time (see Human Rights Watch 2000; Karatnycky 2000). Each one of these agencies issues an annual inventory of grim governmental actions and of governmental complicity with other people's assaults on citizens. By no means all of the abuses they report qualify as violence in the brute force sense of immediate infliction of physical damage. Only a minority of the violent events, furthermore, qualifies as terror defined as asymmetrical deployment of threats and violence against enemies using means that fall outside the forms of political struggle routinely operating within the current regime. But all of them constitute significant threats to the quality of life in the offending countries.

Since the 1980s, the State Department also sends Congress an annual document called *Patterns of Global Terrorism* (Johnson 2001). The State Department defines *terrorism* as "politically motivated violence perpetrated against noncombatant targets by subnational groups or clandestine agents, usually intended to influence an audience" (Ruby 2002:10). Any such definition has the disadvantage of requiring information on motivations and intentions; in fact, solid evidence on motivations and intentions rarely becomes available for collective violence. Still, the report's implicit selection principles single out attacks on noncombatant targets by other-than-regularly-constituted national military forces, especially when someone broadcasts political claims on behalf of the attackers. The annual reports actually describe two different kinds of events: (1) what they call *significant terrorist incidents,* attacks their specialists regard as crossing international lines—because the attackers came from the outside the country, because they received substantial backing from outside, or because they assaulted foreigners; and (2) other attacks by domestic groups on domestic targets.

On a fairly small scale, the State Department's locally knowledgeable observers probably report the bulk of qualifying actions in the first category for the world as a whole. Those are the events for which they supply synopses one by one and make annual counts. They surely miss the vast majority of the world's violent events in category 2 (cf. Bonneuil and Auriat 2000; Davenport 2000; Martinez 2001; Tilly 2003). Figure 17.1 displays the trend of events in the first category from 1980 through 2001 (State Department 2000, 2001, 2002a). Clearly, the overall trend ran downward. The State Department's count of international terrorist incidents reached a high point in 1988 and generally declined thereafter. The number of deaths in attacks rose from 233 to 405 to an estimated 3,547 (including 3,000 deaths assigned to September 11) from 1999 to 2001. Nevertheless, the 346 attacks of 2001 lay far below the frequencies of the 1980s, and the overall levels of casualties declined as well from the 1980s onward. (The similarly defined Enders-Sandler (2002:161) series for death-dealing events alone from 1970 to 1999 shows a second lethal peak during the early 1990s, and a steep decline thereafter.) From the later 1990s, around half of all tallied attacks consisted not of injuries to persons but of bombs directed at oil pipelines, especially pipelines carrying oil northward to the United States through Colombia. That fact in itself demonstrates that State Department specialists interpreted the "political motivation" required by their definition of terror rather broadly.

When they did voice demands, attackers described in the reports most often called for autonomy or independence for some subnational population or region, replacement of existing governments, or redress of wrongs done to some organization. On the whole, international terrorist incidents identified by State Department observers rose and fell with the activity of independence movements. Whether the minor rise that occurred during the later 1990s represents a new sort of political campaign remains to be seen. The overall trend still runs downward.

Unsurprisingly, the State Department's summaries of international terrorist incidents give special attention to attacks on American interests—American citizens, American service personnel attacked outside of their normal

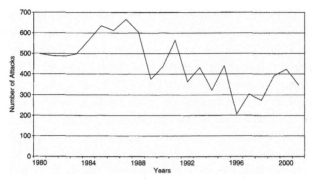

Figure 17.1 Total International Terrorist Attacks, 1980–2001

military activity, property owned by Americans or by the U.S. government, and U.S. territory itself. Thus, the airborne attacks of September 11 received exceptional attention in the year's report but still counted as just 4 of the year's 346 "significant terrorist incidents" (State Department 2002a). The previous year's report had singled out South Asia explicitly as a base for terrorism directed toward U.S. interests; had called special attention to the Afghan Taliban's provision of safe haven for Osama bin Ladin and his network; had linked the lethal bombing of the *U.S.S. Cole* in Yemen (October 2000) to bin Ladin; and had added, "The government of Pakistan increased its support to the Taliban and continued its support to militant groups active in Indian-held Kashmir, such as the Harakat ul-Mujahadin (HUM), some of which engaged in terrorism" (State Department 2001: Asia Overview 2). As mirrored in its annual reports on the subject, then, the State Department's working definition of terror singles out violence committed by relatively well-connected groups and directed against politically significant targets of other nationalities, especially of American nationality. Terrorists are the people who perform such acts, and terrorism is the fact of their performing it.

To Define Terror

Although definitions as such cannot be true or false, in social science useful definitions should point to detectable phenomena that exhibit some degree of causal coherence—in principle all instances should display common properties that embody or result from similar cause-effect relations. By that criterion, what violent events actually ought to qualify as terrorism? Beginning with citations from the 1790s, the *Oxford English Dictionary* gives two definitions for terrorism: (1) "government by intimidation as directed and carried

out by the party in power in France during the Revolution of 1789–94 ..."
and (2) "policy intended to strike with terror those against whom it is adopted." Both definitions point to the asymmetrical deployment of threats
and violence against enemies outside the forms of political struggle routinely operating within the current regime.

The word *terror* itself entered the West's political vocabulary as a name
for French revolutionaries' actions against their domestic enemies in 1793
and 1794. It referred to governmental repression, most directly in the form
of executions. About 17,000 legal executions occurred under the Reign of
Terror, and something like 23,000 more occurred illegally (Greer 1935). Some
scholars also argue that deaths in the fierce Vendée civil wars of 1793–1795
should count as consequences of the Reign of Terror; their inclusion would
bring the total up to the vicinity of 200,000 dead on all sides including regular
troops (Gerard 1999; Guenniffey 2000:234–35). At either extreme of the estimates, historians of the French Revolution continue to think of the original
Reign of Terror as state-organized or state-backed visitation of violence on
France's dissident citizenry during the two central years of radical revolutionary power.

Since the French Revolution, the word *terror* has expanded in scope.
Writers on terror continue to use it for governmental intimidation of
citizens, as in Joseph Stalin's use of executions to still dissent within the
Soviet Union (Mayer 2000). But they also use the term frequently to designate clandestine attacks on governmental targets by domestic opponents
such as Basque separatists, the Irish Republican Army, and Sri Lanka's
Liberation Tigers of Tamil Eelam (Schmid 2001). At times, furthermore,
such civil war practices as ethnic cleansing and genocide receive the designation terror (e.g. Taylor 1999). Thus, the term sprawls across a wide range
of human cruelties.

Amid the sprawl, is a coherent phenomenon at work? No useful generalization covers all the different sorts of political interaction for which observers, analysts, and participants sometimes use the term *terror*, much less for
terrorists and *terrorism*. But we can identify some order in the phenomenon
by means of four steps: (1) noticing that a recurrent strategy of intimidation occurs widely in contentious politics and corresponds approximately to
what many people mean by terror; (2) recognizing that a wide variety of individuals, groups, and networks sometimes employ that strategy; (3) relating
the strategy systematically to other forms of political struggle proceeding in
the same settings and populations; and (4) seeing that specialists in coercion
ranging from government employees to bandits sometimes deploy terror

under certain political circumstances, usually with far more devastating effects than the terror operations of nonspecialists.

Terror as a Strategy

Asymmetrical deployment of threats and violence against enemies outside the forms of political struggle routinely operating within the current regime does have a crude logic of its own. In addition to whatever harm it inflicts directly, it sends signals—signals that the target is vulnerable, that the perpetrators exist, and that the perpetrators have the capacity to strike again. The signals typically reach three different audiences: the targets themselves, potential allies of the perpetrators, and third parties that might cooperate with one or the other. Although some users of terror (for example, a minority of 19th-century anarchists) operate on the theory that destruction of evil objects is a good in itself, most terror supports demands for recognition, redress, autonomy, or transfers of power. Considered as a strategy, terror works best when it alters or inhibits the target's disapproved behavior, fortifies the perpetrators' standing with potential allies, and moves third parties toward greater cooperation with the perpetrators' organization and announced program.

Multiple Uses of Terror

From Mafiosi to ruthless governments, people who operate protection rackets intermittently deploy terror against enemies and uncertain clients (Gambetta 1993; Stanley 1996; Varese 2001; Volkov 2000, 2002). Whether or not they operate large-scale protection rackets, repressive governments frequently apply terror to threatening minorities. Weak, beleaguered governments commonly adopt the strategy of exemplary punishment: inflicting terrible public retaliation on those few enemies they manage to seize with the announced threat of visiting similar punishments on others who dare to challenge them. But dissidents seeking autonomy, striking at their rivals, or trying to bring down governments likewise sometimes engage in asymmetrical deployment of threats and violence against enemies by means that fall outside the forms of political struggle routinely operating within the current regime.

During the last few decades, religious and ethnic activists have been by far the most frequent nongovernmental strategists of terror (see, e.g. Kakar 1996; Gurr 2000; Beissinger 2001; Horowitz 2001).

Terror and Other Forms of Struggle

As these varied examples suggest, the strategy of terror appears across a wide variety of political circumstances, in the company of very different sorts of political struggle. Attacks of Irish Protestant and Catholic activists on each other and on governmental targets, for instance, frequently follow the strategy of terror, but they generally intersect with other forms of negotiation at international, national, and local levels (Jarman 1997; Keogh 2001). In many parts of the world, specialized military forces—governmental, nongovernmental, and antigovernmental—frequently engage in kidnapping, murder, and mutilation in addition to their occasional pitched battles with other armed forces.

Terror and Specialists in Coercion

The prominence of organized armed forces in certain types of terror lends itself to analytic confusion. It is all too easy to conflate terror-deploying governments, armies, militias, paramilitaries, and rebels with conspiratorial zealots. The State Department's general statements about human rights and terror in 2001 featured just such a conflation. We actually need a twofold distinction: first between violent specialists and others, and then between actors who deploy terror within their own operating territories and those who direct it elsewhere.

Figure 17.2 schematizes the two distinctions, assigning characteristic names to the four corners of a two-dimensional space. *Autonomists* stand for all those politically active groups whose members sometimes launch terror attacks on authorities, symbolic objects, rivals, or stigmatized populations on their own territories without becoming durably organized specialists in coercion. *Zealots* maintain similar connections with each other but commit their violent acts outside of their own base territories; they include long-term exiles who return home to attack their enemies. Governmental, nongovernmental, and antigovernmental *militias* maintain enduring organizations of coercive specialists and exercise terror within their base territories. Finally, *conspirators* organize specialized striking forces for operations away from base. (Terror-inflicting armies operating abroad also fit into this corner of the diagram, but they strike even more rarely than do mobile organizations of conspirators.) The diagram as a whole summarizes this paper's main point: A remarkable array of actors sometimes adopt terror as a strategy, and therefore no coherent set of cause-effect propositions can explain terrorism as a whole.

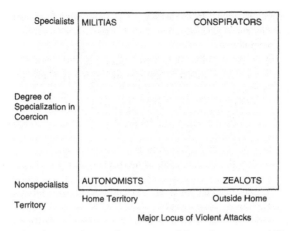

Figure 17.2 A Crude Typology of Terror-Wielding Groups and Networks

The crude typology distinguishes four rather different sorts of relations between the authors and victims of terror, hence four different varieties of politics. It also emphasizes a crucial fact about actually existing terror: Very little of it actually occurs in the diagram's upper-right-hand corner—where we find specialists in coercion who operate outside their home bases. Most terror occurs on the perpetrators' own home territory, and nonspecialists—zealots—inflict a significant share of the terror that does occur outside of home territory. The fact does not diminish the horror of September 11. But it does warn against analyzing all terror as if it consisted of closer or more distant approximations to that terrible series of attacks on the United States. Properly understood, terror is a strategy, not a creed. Terrorists range across a wide spectrum of organizations, circumstances, and beliefs. Terrorism is not a single causally coherent phenomenon. No social scientist can speak responsibly as though it were.

References

Beissinger, Mark R. 2001. *Nationalist Mobilization and the Collapse of the Soviet State.* Cambridge, UK: Cambridge University Press.

Bonneuil, Noel, and Nadia Auriat. 2000. "Fifty Years of Ethnic Conflict and Cohesion, 1945–94." *Journal of Peace Research* 37: 563–81.

Brass, Paul R., ed. 1996. *Riots and Pogroms.* New York: New York University Press.

Cohen, Jean L., and Andrew Arato. 1992. *Civil Society and Political Theory.* Cambridge, MA: MIT Press.

Davenport, Christian. 2000. "Introduction." In *Paths to State Repression: Human Rights Violations and Contentious Politics,* edited by Christian Davenport, 1–26. Lanham, MD: Rowman & Littlefield.

Edwards, Bob, Michael W. Foley, and Mario Diani, eds. 2001. *Beyond Tocqueville. Civil Society and the Social Capital Debate in Comparative Perspective.* Hanover, NH: University Press of New England.

Enders, Walter, and Todd Sandler. 2002, "Patterns of Transnational Terrorism, 1970–1999: Alternative Time-Series Estimates." *International Studies Quarterly* 46: 145–65.

Ferree, Myra Marx, William A. Gamson, Jürgen Gerhards, and Dieter Rucht. 2002. "Four Models of the Public Sphere in Modern Democracies." *Theory and Society* 31: 289–324.

Gambetta, Diego. 1993. *The Sicilian Mafia: The Business of Private Protection.* Cambridge, MA: Harvard University Press.

Gérard, Alain. 1999. *"Par principe d'humanité ..." La Terreur et la Vendée.* Paris, France: Fayard.

Greer, Donald. 1935. *The Incidence of the Terror during the French Revolution: A Statistical Interpretation.* Cambridge, MA: Harvard University Press.

Guenniffey, Patrice. 2000. *La Politique de la Terreur: Essai sur la Violence Révolutionnaire, 1789–1794.* Paris, France: Fayard.

Gurr, Ted Robert. 2000. *Peoples Versus States: Minorities at Risk in the New Century.* Washington, DC: United States Institute of Peace Press.

Herzog, Don. 1998. *Poisoning the Minds of the Lower Orders.* Princeton, NJ: Princeton University Press.

Horowitz, Donald L. 2001. *The Deadly Ethnic Riot.* Berkeley, CA: University of California Press.

Human Rights Watch. 2000. *World Report 2000.* New York: Human Rights Watch.

Jarman, Neil. 1997. *Material Conflicts: Parades and Visual Displays in Northern Ireland.* Oxford, UK: Berg.

Johnson, Larry C. 2001. "The Future of Terrorism." *American Behavioral Scientist* 44: 894–913.

Kakar, Sudhir. 1996. *The Colors of Violence: Cultural Identities, Religion, and Conflict.* Chicago, IL: University of Chicago Press.

Karatnycky, Adrian, ed. 2000. *Freedom in the World. The Annual Survey of Political Rights and Civil Liberties.* Piscataway, NJ: Transaction.

Keogh, Dermot. 2001. "Ireland at the Turn of the Century: 1994–2001." In *The Course of Irish History,* edited by Theodore W. Moody and Francis X. Martin, 321-344. 4th ed. Lanham, MD: Roberts Rinehart.

Martínez, Astrid, ed. 2001. *Economía, Crimen y Conflicto.* Bogotá: Universidad Nacional de Colombia.

Mayer, Arno J. 2000. *The Furies: Violence and Terror in the French and Russian Revolutions.* Princeton, NJ: Princeton University Press.

Moore, Barrington, Jr. 1979. *Injustice: The Social Bases of Obedience and Revolt.* White Plains, NY: M. E. Sharpe.

Plotz, John M. 2000. *The Crowd: British Literature and Public Politics.* Berkeley, CA: University of California Press.

Ruby, Charles L. 2002. "The Definition of Terrorism." *Analyses of Social Issues and Public Policy* 2.1: 9–14.

Schmid, Alex P., ed. 2001. *Countering Terrorism through International Cooperation.* Milan, Italy: International Scientific and Professional Advisory Council of the United Nations Crime Prevention and Criminal Justice Programme.

Schweingruber, David. 2000. "Mob Sociology and Escalated Force: Sociology's Contribution to Repressive Police Tactics." *Sociological Quarterly* 41: 371–89.

Stanley, William. 1996. *The Protection Racket State: Elite Politics, Military Extortion, and Civil War in El Salvador.* Philadelphia, PA: Temple University Press.

State Department. 2000. Office of the Coordinator for Counterterrorism, U.S. Department of State, "Patterns of Global Terrorism 1999," www.usis.usemb.se/terror/rpt1999/index.html (last accessed on November 10, 2016).

———. 2001. Office of the Coordinator for Counterterrorism, "Patterns of Global Terrorism 2000," www.bits.de/public/documents/US_Terrorist_Attacks/terrorpatterns 2000. pdf (last accessed on November 10, 2016).

———. 2002a. Office of the Coordinator for Counterterrorism, "Patterns of Global Terrorism 2001," www.state.gov/documents/organization/10319.pdf (last accessed on November 10, 2016).

———. 2002b. Bureau of Democracy, Human Rights, and Labor, "Country Reports on Human Rights Practices for 2001," www.state.gov/g/drl/rls/hrrpt/2001/8147pf.html (last accessed on Mar. 28, 2002).

Taylor, Christopher C. 1999. *Sacrifice as Terror: The Rwandan Genocide of 1994.* Oxford, UK: Berg.

Tilly, Charles. 2003. *The Politics of Collective Violence.* Cambridge, UK: Cambridge University Press.

Varese, Federico. 2001. *The Russian Mafia. Private Protection in a New Market Economy.* Oxford, UK: Oxford University Press.

Vermunt, Riël, and Herman Steensma, eds. 1991. *Social Justice in Human Relations.* 2 vols. New York: Plenum.

Volkov, Vadim. 2000. "The Political Economy of Protection Rackets in the Past and the Present." *Social Research* 67: 709–44.

——— 2002. *Violent Entrepreneurs: The Use of Force in the Making of Russian Capitalism.* Ithaca, NY: Cornell University Press.

Migration, Race, and Ethnicity

VI

Transplanted Networks

18

Charles Tilly

When Alexis de Tocqueville visited the United States in 1831, he saw a more homogeneous population and one less marked by immigration than we know today. That sense of homogeneity strongly influenced his analysis of American democracy. "All the new European colonies," he wrote of North America, "contained the seed, if not the whole grain, of full democracy" (de Tocqueville 1961: 1:28). In the early chapters of *Democracy in America*, Tocqueville insisted that the relative poverty of American immigrants made for equality of condition. He also remarked that the difficulty of putting American land into cultivation and the low yields once cultivation had begun formed barriers to the emergence of a landowning aristocracy. Thus, he thought, the United States had the means of establishing a uniquely egalitarian public life.

Toward the end of his first volume, however, Tocqueville recognized the presence of Indians and blacks in the midst of the white-run democracy. The first group he portrayed as fragmented but wild, the second as deracinated but temporarily docile. Tocqueville thought that the advance of Europeans across the continent would essentially wipe out the Indians. But he predicted great struggles issuing from the coexistence of blacks and whites:

> Whatever efforts southerners make to keep slavery, they will not succeed indefinitely. In a world of democratic liberty and enlightenment, slavery, squeezed into one corner of the globe, attacked by Christianity as unjust and by political economy as deleterious, cannot survive as an institution. Either the slave or the master will end it. In either case, we must expect a terrible outcome.
>
> (de Tocqueville 1961: 1:379)

To Tocqueville, writing in the 1830s, the Europeans of North America formed a fairly homogeneous mass, dominated by English-speakers who had created or assimilated to a local variant of English culture. In different ways, he thought, Indians and blacks lived in utter alienation from white Europeans. The United States, for him, faced serious problems that ultimately stemmed from previous migrations. But immigration itself did not seem to pose particular problems.

The next century made a big difference. Interpreting Americans to themselves and to his fellow Britons in 1944, D. W. Brogan conceded that the remarkable physical uniformity of American towns hid a great deal of ethnic (he said "racial") variety, a consequence of vast migrations. In the Swedish settlements of Minnesota, Detroit's Polish enclave of Hamtramck, and similar zones of intense immigration, large blocks of distinctive populations survived. "But more common," he remarked,

> is the town in which a dozen groups have to live together in close contact, in which a street of Germans borders on a street of Irish, in which the Italians and the Greeks are mingled in school and market, in which Jew and Gentile have to learn to get on together. It is in towns like these that the problem of Americanization is most acute, in which the well-meaning efforts of Rotary Clubs and women's organizations fail in face of the facts that seem to suggest that, whatever the legal fiction may be, there are first-class and second-class and even third-class Americans, that there is a scale descending from the "old stocks" down to [blacks].
>
> (Brogan 1994: 98)

By 1944 Tocqueville's dream of homogeneity and equality had little to do with American reality. For Brogan, as for most thoughtful Americans, immigration had created an acute problem, the problem of Americanization. Immigration, furthermore, intertwined with racial division to produce the further problem of stark inequality among racial and ethnic groups.

Some people thought the two problems were one: insufficient Americanization caused inequality, and assimilation would eradicate inequality. They merely disagreed over whether the Americanization in question meant obliterating distinctive ethnic and racial characteristics or extending basic rights and opportunities. By the first line of reasoning, the systems of rights and opportunities worked efficiently, once newcomers had acquired the appropriate skills, attitudes, and cultural traits. By the second, in contrast, the American system had room for a wide range of skills, attitudes, and cultural traits, once the groups in question had found their niches, made their presences known, and acquired their lawful rights.

Brogan had obliteration (or at least strong convergence) of old-country traits in mind, and thought it was happening. His contemporary Gunnar Myrdal, on the other hand, was less sure. He granted the existence of cultural assimilation but then stressed rights and opportunities: the rights of blacks presented white Americans with a dilemma (Myrdal 1944). Black-white relations were an American dilemma because Americans in general held strong commitments to equality of rights and opportunities, but whites had thus far chosen to define blacks out of the competition. The opening up of opportunity to successive immigrant groups, argued Myrdal, established that the United States had the capacity to extend opportunity to blacks as well.

Brogan or Myrdal? In the choice lie some critical historical questions with significant implications for public policy. What impact did the conditions of American immigration—including the forced immigration of blacks— have on inequality within the United States? To what extent did such consequences of immigration as the formation of distinctive ethnic communities sustain or alter American patterns of inequality?

Flows and Counterflows

Tocqueville was ordinarily a shrewd observer of social structure, yet he had little to say about immigration as an influence on American inequality. His lack of concern about immigration resulted in part from the fact that he visited the United States at the end of a lull in the flow of persons to there from Europe. The wars that engaged Europe and North America from the 1740s to 1815 had slowed transatlantic population movements. Meanwhile, slaveholders forced the large numbers of Africans who arrived during the same period to anglicize rapidly. The two trends favored the creation of a predominantly anglophone America.

Migration to North America formed only one stream of the great displacements within the populations of Eurasia and Africa that seem to have accelerated after 1500. (See McNeill 1984: 1–18; McNeill and Adams 1978.) Philip Curtin conveys a sense of that acceleration over the world as a whole. He shows that continental North America remained peripheral to the principal paths of tropical migration, including the slave trade. In the Western Hemisphere as a whole, "four times as many Africans as Europeans arrived in the Americas in the 1820s, and allowing for European repatriation, the two flows were of approximately the same strength in the 1830s. Not until

1840 did arrivals from Europe permanently surpass those from Africa" (Eltis 1983: 255; similarly, Sucheng Chan points out that North America figured only as a fringe area for the vast Chinese emigration. Healthy correctives to American megalomania in migration studies!) Nevertheless, the flows between Europe and the Americas constituted a major component of world migration from the sixteenth to the nineteenth centuries.

By the time of Tocqueville's visit, North America had been receiving immigrants—forced, voluntary, or in between—for two hundred years. The seventeenth-century arrival of European settlers introduced foreign diseases that devastated the native population; thus the migrants indirectly created the nearly open space into which they expanded (McNeill 1984: 16–17). During the seventeenth and eighteenth centuries, white migrants to North America came mainly from three colonizing powers: France, Spain, and Great Britain. The enslavement and importation of Africans by slavers from the three powers continued through much of the warlike era; indeed, at the prevailing rate of importation if the mortality of newly captured slaves had not been enormously higher than that of Europeans, by the 1820s the size of the black population of the United States (1.8 million in 1820 to 7.9 million whites) would have approached that of the white population (Eltis 1983: 278). American slaveholders, however, broke up homogeneous clusters of slaves and forced their captive Africans to adopt American manners and speech. The formation of the United States then left most of the French- and Spanish-speakers in separate North American colonies. Thus, a chiefly anglophone country came into being.

In the new United States, people of British stock predominated. In 1790 about 61 percent of the U.S. white population sprang from English origins, 10 percent from Irish, and 8 percent from Scots, for a total of almost 80 percent having origins in the British Isles. Yet Germans, Dutch, French, and Swedes also had appreciable percentages of the remainder (Thernstrom, Orlov, and Handlin 1980: 479). Even after the wartime lulls, the white population showed clear signs of its immigrant origins. And enslaved blacks were still arriving in large numbers. Only in retrospect do immigration and its consequences seem to belong peculiarly to the nineteenth and twentieth centuries.

After the wars ended, European immigration resumed at an unprecedented pace. British migrants increased unsteadily from 25,000 in 1821–1830 to 807,000 in 1881–1890, and Irish arrivals rose from 51,000 in 1821–1830 to 914,000 in 1851–1860; after a few slower decades, another peak of 655,000 Irish immigrants arrived between 1881 and 1890. As time passed, the balance shifted successively to Scandinavia, Germany, Austria-Hungary, Russia, and Italy, with Canada, Latin America, the Caribbean, and Asia becoming increasingly important during the twentieth century (Thernstrom, Orlov, and Handlin 1980: 480).

From the end of the slave trade until recently, then, American immigration consisted chiefly of flows back and forth between Europe and North America. Changes in the social organization of nineteenth-century Europe promoted a speeding up of long-established migratory currents. The extension of capitalist property relations greatly expanded the population that was available for long-distance migration. The separation of households from their means of production, the spread of wage labor, the rising labor productivity of agriculture, and the concentration of capital in cities combined to establish long-term, long-distance migration as an increasingly common response of Europeans to contraction at home and expansion elsewhere.

Capitalist growth probably also helps account for the great nineteenth-century acceleration of natural increase in much of Europe, which fundamentally altered the balance between available niches in farms or shops and the population eligible to fill those niches (Levine 1984). Constricted opportunity in Europe and relatively high wages in North America encouraged people who were already seeking work in the growing industrial and commercial towns of Europe to extend their searches beyond the Atlantic. Eventually, the decline of European fertility, mortality, and natural increase counteracted the effects of proletarianization and turned some European countries toward the importation of labor. But that shift occurred after the great waves of European migration to North America.

Not that the smoothly rational operation of an open, competitive, international labor market characterized by wage differentials accounts for the rhythm and timbre of American immigration. At the very least we need to recognize two facts about that immigration. First, it was and is extraordinarily selective by origin and type of migrant. Second, it usually did not draw on isolated individual decision makers but on clusters of people bound together by acquaintance and common fate. Nor were there clusters mere categories—skilled or unskilled, Jew or Gentile, Greek or Italian. To be sure, individuals did migrate to the United States, and sometimes alone. But they did so as participants in social processes that extended far beyond them. Of course, members of different categories of the European population migrated to the United States (and returned to Europe) at spectacularly different rates. But the categories we ordinarily apply to those differences poorly describe the actual groups that lived and organized transatlantic migration.

From the New Deal era to the immediate postwar period, American historians undertook a major revamping of ideas about immigration. Where earlier chroniclers had seen immigrants as foreign elements injected, and ultimately absorbed, into American life, the revisionists portrayed immigration as an indigenous American social process. The academic analysis had political overtones, for it argued against nativism and for the maintenance of equal opportunity. As Oscar Handlin, one of the major revisionists, put it, their approach started

> with the assumption that the entire population of the United States almost from the start was a composite, made up of elements from a multitude of sources. Among these heterogeneous multitudes those who had actually been born in other countries represented only the extreme of a condition that was general to the whole society. The differences between them and the native-born of various sorts, while real, were differences of degree rather than of kind.
>
> (Handlin, 1961: 11; Handlin 1963)

Not long after making the statement, Handlin published a general history of the United States, cunningly called *The Americans,* based on the premise that American history was more than anything else the tale of many peoples who became—or who are still becoming—one: *E pluribus unum.*

Historical work of the last quarter-century has not so much rejected that line of argument as expanded and refined it. (For a synthesis, see Bodnar 1985.) Where Handlin and his colleagues saw shock and subsequent assimilation, however, recent historians have commonly seen continuous processes of collective transformation involving the use of old social networks and categories to produce new ones. Rather than individual uprooting, disorganization, and adjustment, collective action and shared struggle. Rather than person-by-person striving, organized migration networks and labor markets. Rather than wholesale importation (and subsequent degradation) of cultural traits, collective fabrication of new cultures from old materials.

Networks and Categories in Migration

To put it simply: networks migrate; categories stay put; and networks create new categories. By and large, the effective units of migration were (and are) neither individuals nor households but sets of people linked by acquaintance, kinship, and work experience who somehow incorporated American destinations into the mobility alternatives they considered when they reached critical decision points in their individual or collective lives. Long-distance migration entails many risks: to personal security, to comfort, to income, to the possibility of satisfying social relations. Where kinsmen, friends, neighbors, and work associates already have good contacts with possible destinations, reliance on established interpersonal networks for information minimizes and spreads the risks. (See Taylor 1986: 147–71). Implicitly recognizing those advantages, the vast majority of potential long-distance migrants anywhere in the world draw their chief information for migration decisions (including the decision to stay put) from members of their interpersonal networks, and rely on those networks for assistance both in moving and in settling at the destination. Their activity then reproduces and extends the networks, especially to the extent that by migrating they acquire the possibility and the obligation to supply information and help to other potential migrants. Constrained by personal networks, potential migrants fail to consider many theoretically available destinations, and concentrate on those few localities with which their place of origin has strong links. The higher the risk and the greater the cost of returning, the more intense the reliance on previously established ties.

These general principles clearly apply to American immigration. Even when migration occurred one person at a time, migrants commonly drew on information from network members who had already gone to America. Virginia Yans-McLaughlin cites a typical report from among Italians in Buffalo:

> A local immigrant who joined his grandfather and cousins in 1906 recalled: "Immigrants almost always came to join others who had preceded them—a husband, or a father, or an uncle, or a friend. In western New York most of the first immigrants from Sicily went to Buffalo, so that from 1900 on, the thousands who followed them to this part of the state also landed in Buffalo. There they joined friends and relatives who in many cases had purchased the tickets for their steerage passage to America."
>
> (Yans-McLaughlin 1977: 58)

The frequency of remittances from emigrants to homefolks and of steamship tickets prepaid by people at the American destination reveals the extent of that mutual aid. As Ewa Morawska reminds us, a survey conducted by the U.S. Immigration Commission on 1908–1909 showed 60 percent of new immigrants from southern and eastern Europe arriving with prepaid passage.

Networks also provided other kinds of aid; as John Gjerde reports in his study of migrants from Norway's western coast:

> When immigrants arrived in a settlement, temporary housing was often provided for those who needed it. The communities settled by kinsmen also offered opportunities to work and accumulate capital at wages that were usually higher than those in Europe. Indeed, emigration was often funded by advance wages in the form of prepaid tickets. Unmarried men looking for work were often found in settlements peopled by former residents of their home community. A group of landless immigrants in 1883 used community ties to search for work, moving from one community settlement to another; eventually, they settled permanently in another Orsta community. Economic aid continued. One immigrant remembered that when he arrived in the Echo community in 1892, "we could get all we desired ... on credit only by showing that we were from Hjorundfjord."
>
> (Gjerde 1986: 22)

Such step-by-step moves eventually transplanted major segments of existing networks from the old country to the new, and modified the networks' structure in the process. Paradoxically, the high rate of return to many European areas had similar effects, for the returnees reinforced the ties between origin and destination, and thus facilitated further migration along the same lines. Like a honeysuckle vine, the network moved, changed shape, and sent down new roots without entirely severing the old ones. In that sense, networks migrated.

Categories, on the other hand, stay put. Although East Europeans retained some awareness of their divisions into Poles, Slovaks, Czechs, Rusyns, Ukrainians, Armenians, Lituanians, Latvians, Hungarians, Croatians, Serbs, Slovenes, and Jews (to quote Ewa Morawska's list), they did not simply carry these collective identities across the Atlantic like so many pieces of luggage. Where those labels did not simply represent outsiders' tags for collections of people who ordinarily identified themselves in quite other ways, they belonged to the situation at the origin and not necessarily at the destination. Which of these categories, and which of their subdivisions, actually survived the voyage depended on the population mix at the destination and on the previously established categories around which the people already at the destination organized their own lives.

Networks create new categories. In the experience of American immigration, sets of connected immigrants who did not have a common identity at the point of origin often acquired a new identification during interaction with others at the destination. In the United States, Piedmontese, Neapolitans, Sicilians, and Romans became Italians. But not always. That depended on the networks' size, density, and relationship to other groups.

Networks also transform existing categories. Kerby Miller shows how Irish identity, already formed in Ireland through opposition to the conquering English, altered in the United States under the influence of a bourgeoisie that promoted religiosity, nationalism, and political involvement. Although these three enthusiasms had actually been rare in the rural regions from which most Irish immigrants had departed, in the United States their lack came to seem un-Irish. Similarly, other groups of immigrants— Greeks, Zionist Jews, Armenians are examples—committed themselves more strongly to nationalist politics as Americans than had their ancestors in the old country. In none of these cases can we reasonably think of Americanization as straightforward assimilation to a dominant American culture. In each case members of networks whose identities and internal structures were themselves changing continuously negotiated new relations with other networks, including those in the country of origin.

Political identity was by no means the only sphere in which the simultaneous transformation of networks, identities, and relations with other groups occurred. In the world of employment, the prevalence of subcontracting in manufacturing and construction during the later nineteenth and earlier twentieth centuries epitomized the adaptation of networks initially formed by immigration. In subcontracting, the owner of a business delegates to a second party (most often a foreman or a smaller entrepreneur) the responsibility both for hiring workers and for supervising production, and the second partly delivers finished products to the owner. Migrant networks articulate neatly with subcontracting because they give the subcontractor access to flexible supplies of labor about which he or she can easily get information and over which she or he can easily exert control outside the workplace.

As a result of selective recruitment of workers, trades, shops, and divisions of large firms often display remarkable concentrations of particular racial and ethnic groups.

The "same" kinds of migrants establish very different relations to the populations at their destinations. Jewish immigrants, Ewa Morawska points out, were much more likely to become manual workers if they migrated to New York, Boston, Philadelphia, Baltimore, or Chicago than if they went to smaller towns; outside the major centers of Jewish settlement, Jews became self-employed much more often.

Similar contrasts appear on an international scale. With respect to wealth, education, previous work experience, and region of origin, the 2.3 million Italians who migrated to Argentina between 1860 and 1914 resembled the 4.1 million who migrated to the United States (Baily 1983: 303; for the general comparison, see also Klein 1983: 306–29). What is more, the great majority of both groups seem to have arrived via chain migration, with the idea of earning enough to return home. Immediately on arrival in the new land, both groups moved chiefly into unskilled labor. But Italians came to occupy much more prominent positions in Argentina (and especially Buenos Aires) than in the United States (and especially New York). Two factors made a large difference: first, investment opportunities for workers who saved money were greater in Argentina than in the United States; second, it was easier to move from unskilled to skilled jobs in Argentina. Both factors gave Italian immigrants who worked hard and saved in Argentina stronger reasons for remaining in their adopted country.

The network structure of migration makes implausible several standard ways of analyzing immigration: an assimilation of individuals to a dominant culture, as individual status-striving, or as the wholesale transplantation of preexisting groups. "Assimilation" becomes implausible because the paths of change vary enormously from stream to stream of migration, because the process is collective rather than individual, and because the network structure, multiplied, contradicts the idea of a single dominant pattern to which people might approximate themselves. Individual status-striving, although it surely occurs, accounts poorly for group changes after immigration because it misses the centrality of interpersonal connections to the fate of any particular group. Wholesale transplantation badly describes a process in which people greatly transform their social relations, and often create new group identities. Instead of a series of individual transformations in the direction of a dominant American culture, migration involves negotiation of new relationships both within and across networks. Instead of individual status-striving, collective efforts to cope. Instead of wholesale transplantation, selective re-creation of social ties.

Once we recognize the network structure of migration, some of the old, standard questions stop making sense. It is idle, for example, to ask whether in general migrants are smarter, braver, or more desperate than nonmigrants; some systems of social ties select in one direction, some in another. It is not very useful to classify migrants by intentions to stay or to return home, because intentions and possibilities are always more complex than that—and the migrants themselves often cannot see the possibilities that are shaped by their networks. Again, generalizations saying that skilled workers migrate longer distances than unskilled workers or that younger people migrate more frequently than older ones probably hold on the average but suffer enormous qualifications depending on the social organization of labor markets. In short, we ought to think of migration as we think of community structure: *not* reducible to individual characteristics and intentions. The decisive, recurrent regularities concern the structure of migration networks themselves.

Contrasting Types of Migration

The importance of social networks becomes clearer when we stop thinking about migration as a single homogeneous experience, and start recognizing its sharply contrasting forms. A rough but useful typology distinguishes colonizing, coerced, circular, chain, and career migration. The distinctions rest on the links between sending and receiving networks. We can usually distinguish two aspects of those links: (1) the extent to which migrants retain positions in the sending networks, and (2) the degree to which the move is definitive. An entirely temporary move in which the mover retains full membership in the sending network does not qualify as migration at all; we call it mobility. At the other extreme, a completely definitive move in which the mover loses all connection with the sending network is quite rare, despite its popularity as an image of the migrant uprooted; it almost never occurs except under extreme coercion.

The five types of migration overlap somewhat, but differ on the average with respect to both retention of positions in sending networks and permanence of the moves involved. *Colonizing* migration, in its pure form, simply expands the geographic range of a given population by moving intact segments of the population into territories they had not previously occupied; European farmers who moved to the American frontier, for example, often did so en bloc. *Coerced* migration entails obligatory departure, forced severing of most or all ties at the origin, and little or no personal connection between the migrants and people at the destination; Philip Curtin's description of the capture and shipping of slaves illustrates coerced migration very well, as does the shipping of convicts to the Caribbean. *Circular* migration consists of the creation of a regular circuit in which migrants retain their claims and contacts with a home base and routinely return to that base after a period of activity elsewhere in the circuit; many Mexican immigrants to the United States fit the pattern. *Chain* migration involves sets of related individuals or households who move from one place to another through a set of social arrangements in which people at the destination provide aid, information, and encouragement to the newcomers; Ewa Morawska's immigrants from southern and eastern Europe traveled largely in such chains. *Career* migration, finally, characterizes individuals and households that move in response to opportunities to change position within or among large structures, such as corporations, states, and professional labor markets.

Clearly the five types overlap. American immigration has taken all five forms, singly and in combination. Colonizing migration characterized the early decades of North America's settlement, and continued in some regions into the twentieth century. Coerced migration, which applies most evidently to the arrival of enslaved Africans, fits the experience of many Southeast Asian, Caribbean, and Central American refugees as well. The bulk of American immigration has fallen somewhere in the range from circular to chain migration. As John Bodnar says, return rates of 25 to 60 percent for major European groups reflect the intention of most immigrants to go back to their origins if and when they could accumulate the capital to reestablish themselves (Bodnar 1985: 53). Even impoverished Ireland had a return rate of 10 percent toward the end of the nineteenth century; young women who emigrated temporarily to earn money for dowry and liquidation of family debts were common enough in County Longford to merit a special name: "redeemers" (Hart 1985: 223–31). For many networks, North America simply represented one more extension of circuits that had long served the same purpose within Europe. To that extent, American immigration followed the model of circular migration.

Circular migration has some familiar correlates. Because it commonly rests on the maintenance of households in the area of origin, it rarely moves whole families and often draws disproportionately on one sex—for example, males for common labor, or females for domestic service. Males long predominated in Chinese migration to the United States, with the correlate that the few Chinese women who did migrate were frequently prostitutes; in the San Francisco of 1870, almost three-quarters of the 2,018 Chinese women enumerated in the census were recorded as prostitutes (Cheng 1984: 421). Circular migration often means some form of inexpensive collective living for the migrants, hard work, rigorous saving of wages, extensive remittances, and relatively little contact with the receiving population.

However, the networks of circular migration often transformed themselves into chains displaying a strong balance of movement in one direction.

Individual households were not the only ones to reorganize in the transition from circular to chain migration. The brokers and entrepreneurs of circular migration developed longer-term attachments and investments at the destination; helped create local networks of mutual aid in the search for jobs, housing, and sociability; formed patron-client networks that reinforced their own power; and lent money to their compatriots. These forms of mutual aid attached immigrants to American social structure. The immigrants did not necessarily "assimilate"; they did, however, construct social relations that helped ensure their survival on a strange terrain. In the process, they built migration machines: sending networks that articulated with particular receiving networks in which new migrants could find jobs, housing, and sociability. The machines worked efficiently, bringing in new labor from overseas when opportunities rose in the particular industries to which they were attached and sending people back when opportunity contracted or when they accumulated enough capital to reenter social life at the origin.

Obviously, similar mechanisms have operated in migration *within* the United States. Migration chains brought workers, both black and white, to Detroit's industry from Kentucky, Tennessee, and other southern states during both world wars, and Jews moved into the small-town retail trade of western Pennsylvania through elaborate chains of kinsmen and *Landsmänner*. Heavy reliance on migration chains in the search for jobs and housing produced the characteristically intense small-scale segregation of nineteenth-century American cities by place of origin. (See e.g. Nels Conzen 1976 and Zunz 1982)

Compared with the numbers involved in circular and chain migration, career migration has played a relatively small part in American immigration. In our own time, it is true, American medical services have drawn many doctors and nurses from overseas through professional networks, and multinational corporations have set up their own currents of intercontinental migration. But career migration looms much less large in American immigration than it does in migration within the United States. Across the seas, circles and, especially, chains predominate.

Networks and Solidarity

The social networks used and transformed by migration endure far beyond the time of displacement. They provide a setting for life at the destination, a basis for solidarity and mutual aid as well as for division and conflict. In recent years historians and sociologists of American communities have repeatedly shown how migrant groups cluster together as a result of housing searches mainly limited to the local network, job specialization depends largely on the initial contacts of a migrant population with the local labor market, formation of businesses and whole industries is dominated by people from a single origin, social and economic capital accumulates within boundaries set by immigration, and new, compelling identities take shape from the materials deposited by the migration process. Not that all groups huddled together with equal intensity, or maintained their networks with the same solidity; variation in those regards sets one of our major problems of explanation in American social experience.

Josef Barton's study of Italians, Rumanians, and Slovaks in Cleveland makes the variation clear. Migration patterns, he reports,

> had a significant impact on the development of ethnic settlements. The distinctive aspect of Italian migration was the predominance of major village chains. The settlement emerging as a result of this migration pattern formed around a stable core population from ten villages in the Abruzzi and Sicily. Immigrants from these two regions established a hegemony in the settlement, and the marriage choices of the arrivals reinforced the dominant regional groups. The pattern of parochial cultural loyalties that characterized Italian organizations reflected the community's peculiar demographic structure.
>
> The Rumanians and the Slovaks migrated in minor district streams, and village streams were much less important than in Italian migration. In both the Rumanian and Slovak settlements, efforts were made to maximize national rather than local ties, and mixed patterns of settlement and intermarriage across the boundaries of local groups facilitated these efforts. The resulting configuration of cultural loyalties was in sharp contrast to the Italian emphasis on village and regional organizations, for both Rumanian and Slovak societies oriented themselves strongly toward religious and national aims.
>
> (Barton 1975: 63)

Here we watch the initial conditions of migration setting the frame for the creation of a new social structure.

So long as they formed and reformed mainly within the limits set by the migration process, social networks also provided the basis for ethnic identity. Concentrating on the Irish in America, Kerby Miller shows how ethnicity—far from being a form of consciousness carried over from Ireland and gradually dissipated in the new environment—arose from the experience of living in the United States. Miller emphasizes the place of associational activities and institutional affiliations in transforming people's perceptions of themselves, of their collective histories, and of their relations to others.

Susan Olzak has generalized a parallel line of argument into a general model of ethnic conflict. "The central argument," she writes,

> It is the shifting dynamic of ethnic enclave solidarity coupled with rising levels of ethnic competition that raises the potential for ethnic conflict.
>
> (Olzak 1985: 3)

Evidence from American cities between 1877 and 1914 confirms Olzak's general line of argument (Olzak 1987a, 1987b). The perceptions that immigrant groups form of themselves and others vary considerably with their locations in the social structure.

Those perceptions, and the social practices that complement them, emerge from interaction with other groups, especially competitors and enemies. But they also develop through struggle within the group, as different sets of leaders and interpreters seek to impose their own definitions of the group's origins, character, interests, and destiny. External discrimination and conflict reinforce both processes. Thus, ethnicity acquires its Janus face, looking inward and outward at the same time.

Networks and Inequality

Networks brought into being by immigration serve to create and perpetuate inequality. Lest anyone think that solidarity and mutual aid have nothing but gratifying results, we should recognize two things: (1) members of immigrant groups often exploited one another as they would not have dared to exploit the native-born, and (2) every inclusion also constitutes an exclusion. American immigration produced a remarkable specialization of work by origin, although the precise specializations varied from one locality and migrant stream to another. John Bodnar provides a representative list:

> In Indiana oil refineries, Croatians held jobs in only three categories: stillman helper, firemen, and still cleaners. In the ready-made clothing industry, Jews predominated in small firms with minimal mechanization and segmentation of labor while Italians concentrated in large factories which tended to require less individual skills. Serbs and Croats in New York City were heavily involved in freighthandling. Italians dominated construction gangs and barber shops in Buffalo, Philadelphia, and Pittsburgh. By 1918, Italians represented 75 percent of the women in the men's and boy's clothing industry and 93 percent of the females

doing hand embroidery in New York City. Nearly all of the 3,000 employees in Peninsular Car Company in Detroit by 1900 were Polish.
Polish women dominated restaurant and kitchen jobs in Chicago by
1909, which they preferred to domestic employment. By 1920, one
study found an incredible 69 percent of Slovak males in coal mining
and about one-half of all Mexicans working as blastfurnace laborers.

(Bodnar 1985: 65. See also Portes and Manning 1986:
47–68; Waldinger 1986a, 1986b: 249–85.)

Any student of migration can supply further tales of occupational specialization by regional or national origin.

If we tune our categories finely enough, furthermore, we always find that
the specialization goes beyond occupation to include such matters as who
owns what kinds of firms, and which people work for others. Looking closely
at Jews, Italians, and blacks in New York since 1910, Suzanne Model demonstrates not only that Jews more often owned their own firms but also that
Jews more often worked for other people of the same origin (Model 1985).
Coethnic employment, as she calls it, was less common among Italians than
among Jews, and least common among blacks. Model also provides evidence
that coethnic employment, on the whole, contributed to higher incomes and
better jobs.

Longer-term effects, although more difficult to detect, probably mattered
as well. Coethnic employment most likely fostered capital accumulation
within an ethnic group, and thus facilitated investment in the occupational
and educational chances of the next generation. The self-exploiting Mama
and Papa, with their eyes on the kids' future, could carry out their self-
exploitation more easily where they ran their own businesses. They could
also use—and under-pay—the labor of women and children within their
households and kin groups. That happened especially when many people
from the same migrant origins moved into the same business.

Every one of these specializations, however, excluded someone else from
a particular occupation, trade, or business. In New York and elsewhere, part
of the tragedy of black life is that different groups of blacks lost control of the
few trades, such as barbering, in which they occupied strong positions during
the nineteenth century. For reasons no one seems to understand, they were
unable to establish new monopolies. Elsewhere in this volume, Model suggests that black families suffered most, in the long run, from the increasing
inability of breadwinners to place their children and kinsmen in sheltered,
relatively desirable occupational niches. That inability diminished parental
authority, speculates Model, and encouraged an individualistic self-reliance

that may have corresponded to American ideals but served blacks badly in the world of work.

Despite occasional exceptions such as Pullman-car portering, blacks differed from most other poor migrants in spreading across a wide range of jobs and industries, almost always in subordinate, insecure, and poorly paid positions. As a consequence, blacks have often found themselves competing unsuccessfully with the latest, poorest immigrants. This structural reality lies behind the ambivalent positions on immigration policy Lawrence Fuchs shows black leaders to have adopted.

The dialectic of inclusion and exclusion did not only set off blacks from whites; it also distinguished ethnic groups from one another, and established a rough hierarchy of advantage and opportunity. ...The hierarchy depended, to be sure, on the skills and resources different immigrant groups brought with them from their homelands, and on more general routines of discrimination by color, language, and religion in American life (Lieberson 1980).

But initial advantage and discrimination tell only part of the story. The most important teaching of recent work on immigration and ethnic experience concerns the ways in which the social organization of migration itself, the highly variable knitting together of sending and receiving networks, shaped the aspirations, opportunities, strategies, fortunes, and accomplishments of most Americans. That shaping continues today.

The history of American immigration therefore combines the general and the particular in a compelling way. On one side, it is everyone's history, a history in which chains of migrants formed over and over again to link distant places to the United States. On the other, its precise form differs from group to group, even from person to person; each of us has his own tale of migration to tell, ending networks and receiving networks could hardly be more specific, yet their junction and transformation follow well-defined general rules. Connections among persons established by nineteenth-century immigration still affect inequality today. In examining the history of immigration as individual experience or collective phenomenon, we are probing the roots, and the broken branches, of American democracy.

References

Baily, Samuel L. 1983. "The Adjustment of Italian Immigrants in Buenos Aires and New York, 1870–1914," *American Historical Review* 88.

Barton, Josef J. 1975. *Peasants and Strangers: Italians, Rumanians, and Slovaks in an American City, 1890–1950*. Cambridge: Harvard University Press.

Bodnar, John. 1985. *The Transplanted: A History of Immigrants in Urban America.* Bloomington: Indiana University Press.

Brogan, D. W. 1944. *The American Character.* New York: Knopf.

Cheng, Lucie. 1984. "Free, Indentured, Enslaved: Chinese Prostitutes in Nineteenth-Century America," in *Labor Immigration under Capitalism: Asian Workers in the United States before World War II,* ed. Lucie Cheng and Edna Bonacich. Berkeley: University of California Press.

Eltis, David. 1983. "Free and Coerced Migrations: Some Comparisons," *American Historical Review* 88.

Gjerde, Jon. 1986. "The Chain Migrations from the West Coast of Norway: A Comparative Study." Unpublished paper, Department of History, University of California, Berkeley.

Handlin, Oscar. 1961. "Immigration in American Life: A Reappraisal," in *Immigration and American History. Essays in Honor of Theodore C. Blegen,* ed. Henry Steele Commager Minneapolis: University of Minnesota Press.

———. 1963. *The Americans: A New History of the People of the United States.* Boston: Little, Brown.

Hart, Marjolein 't. 1985. "Irish Return Migration in the Nineteenth Century," *Tijdschrift voor Econ. en Soc. Geografie* 76: 223–31.

Klein, Herbert S. 1983. "The Integration of Italian Immigrants into the United States and Argentina: A Comparative Analysis," *American Historical Review* 88: 306–29.

Levine, David, ed. 1984. *Proletarianization and Family History.* Orlando, FL: Academic Press.

Lieberson, Stanley. 1980. *A Piece of the Pie: Blacks and White Immigrants since 1880.* Berkeley: University of California Press.

McNeill, William H. 1984. "Human Migration in Historical Perspective," *Population and Development Review* 10.

McNeill, William H. and Ruth S. Adams, eds. 1978. *Human Migration: Patterns and Policies.* Bloomington: Indiana University Press.

Model, Suzanne. 1985. "Ethnic Bonds in the Work Place: Blacks, Italians, and Jews in New York City." PhD dissertation, University of Michigan.

Myrdal, Gunnar. 1944. *An American Dilemma: The Negro Problem and American Democracy.* New York: Harper.

Nels Conzen, Kathleen. 1976. *Immigrant Milwaukee, 1836–1860.* Cambridge: Harvard University Press.

Olzak, Susan. 1985. "Ethnic Collective Action and the Dynamics of Ethnic Enclaves." Unpublished paper, Department of Sociology, Cornell University.

———. 1987a. "Have the Causes of Ethnic Collective Action Changed over a Hundred Years? Evidence from the 1870s and 1880s and the 1970s." Technical Report 87–6. Department of Sociology, Cornell University.

———. 1987b; "Labor Unrest, Immigration, and Ethnic Conflict in Urban America, 1880 through 1914." Technical Report 87–9. Department of Sociology, Cornell University.

Portes, Alejandro and Robert D. Manning. 1986. "The Immigrant Enclave: Theory and Empirical Examples," in *Competitive Ethnic Relations,* ed. Susan Olzak and Joane Nagel. Orlando: Academic Press.

Taylor, J. Edward. 1986. "Differential Migration, Networks, Information and Risk," *Research in Human Capital and Development* 4.

Thernstrom, Stephan, Ann Orlov, and Oscar Handlin, eds. 1980. *Harvard Encyclopedia of American Ethnic Groups.* Cambridge: Harvard University Press.

de Tocqueville, Alexis. 1961. *De la démocratie en Amérique,* 2 vols. Paris: Galimard.

Waldinger, Roger D. 1986a. *Through the Eye of the Needle: Immigrants and Enterprise in New York's Garment Trades.* New York: New York University Press.

———. 1986b. "Immigrant Enterprise: A Critique and Reformulation," *Theory and Society* 15.

Yans-McLaughlin, Virginia. 1977. *Family and Community: Italian Immigrants in Buffalo, 1880–1930.* Ithaca: Cornell University Press.

Zunz, Olivier. 1982. *The Changing Face of Inequality: Urbanization, Industrial Development, and Immigrants in Detroit, 1880–1920.* Chicago: University of Chicago Press.

19

Social Boundary Mechanisms

Charles Tilly

In Buenos Aires, each October, Bolivian immigrants of the Charrúa barrio stage the Fiesta of Our Lady of Copacabana, which attracts many native Argentines to its displays of Bolivian dance, crafts, costume, and cuisine. The gala festival gives usually downtrodden *bolivianos* a vital, visually attractive setting in which to assert their distinctiveness and even their superiority. An announcement of the 1996 fiesta in the local paper included these words:

> We Bolivians are landholders, while you Argentines—especially you porteños—are not landholders, but emigrants who came to occupy a territory. You are all descendants of foreigners; your ethnic group and your ancestors were European. Instead we own our own land, the land called Bolivia, as descendants of Aymaras and Quechuas. It is therefore important that we preserve our identity, since we own a specific territory, since our ancestors tilled that soil and the land is ours. People from Jujuy own their own land because the Incas formerly extended all the way to Tucumán. For these reasons it is important for us to maintain our identity because we are lords of that land, we are lords of all South America, we are the natives, we are not from Europe, we are not immigrants.
>
> (Grimson 1999:71–72)

Once you know that *porteños* means residents of Buenos Aires (a seaport region), that Argentina's Jujuy province abuts the Argentine-Bolivian border, and that the city of Tucumán dominates an Argentine province almost 400 miles south of the border, you begin to detect an audacious claim of authenticity, difference, and collective rights. Bolivian immigrants to Buenos Aires vary in the extent to which they stress indigenous origins, Catholic purity, or Bolivian nationality as their distinctive property. But at least on festive occasions, they draw a clear boundary between themselves and their Argentine neighbors.

Few people think the Inca Empire will revive and restore indigenous Bolivians to their ancestors' political glory. Yet the claims of Buenos Aires' Bolivian publicists draw on a discourse that elsewhere has figured recurrently in conquest, civil war, ethnic cleansing, international diplomacy, and demands for autonomy: we form a coherent, distinctive people, we were here first, and therefore we have prior rights to the territory. Most such claims fail, but they sometimes prevail, especially when backed by substantial armed force. More surprisingly, many populations that could in principle make such claims do so only intermittently, or never. Furthermore, through much of the year Bolivians who at their fiesta insist on a separate national identity deploy multiple other identities: worker, barrio dweller, woman, customer, even (vis-à-vis nonmigrant relatives in Bolivia) *porteño*. Neither prevailing identities nor distinctions between categories remain constant. On the contrary, they remain incessantly in play.

One aspect of these familiar circumstances deserves close attention: formation, transformation, activation, and suppression of social boundaries. Together, these alterations present the problem of explaining social boundary change.

We might think of everything about those within-boundary and cross-boundary transactions as peculiar to the recent history of Buenos Aires. Yet the boundary that separates *bolivianos* from *porteños argentinos* displays features readily recognizable across the world. People everywhere organize a significant part of their social interaction around the formation, transformation, activation, and suppression of social boundaries. It happens at the small scale of interpersonal dialogue, at the medium scale of rivalry within organizations, and at the large scale of genocide. Us-them boundaries matter.

Social boundary change sets a number of puzzling questions:

- Why and how do boundaries that at one point matter little or not at all for social life rapidly become salient bases of interaction, so much so that people who live peaceably with difference one month start killing across their boundary the next?
- Why and how does the opposite happen: that seemingly unbridgeable boundaries rapidly become irrelevant, or at least less salient?

- How do divisions between us and them change, such that yesterday's enemies become today's friends, at the same time as other previously less salient sets of people become enemies?
- Why does such a close relation exist between who "we" say we are and which others we identify as "not us"? How does that relation between their identity and ours work?
- How and why do such boundaries come to separate specific social sites from each other while usually remaining irrelevant to relations among a great many other social sites?

This chapter provides a preliminary inventory of robust mechanisms (1) causing boundary change, (2) consisting of boundary change, and (3) producing consequences of boundary change.

Social boundaries interrupt, divide, circumscribe, or segregate distributions of population or activity within social fields. Such fields certainly include spatial distributions of population or activity, but they also include temporal distributions and webs of interpersonal connections. We might therefore define a social boundary minimally as

> any contiguous zone of contrasting density, rapid transition, or separation between internally connected clusters of population and/or activity.

In this sense, as Lamont and Molnár (2002) argue, a symbolic boundary becomes a necessary component of a social boundary.

In the operation of a social boundary, we expect to find

1   distinctive relations between sites on one side;
2   distinctive relations between sites on the other side;
3   distinctive relations across the zone between those two; and
4   on each side, shared representations of the zone itself.

It makes no difference to my argument whether relations across the boundary are intense or intermittent, friendly or hostile, formal or informal. What matters is that the relevant social process exhibits all features simultaneously: distinctive relations on each side of a separating zone, distinctive relations across the zone, and shared representations of the zone.

Boundary change consists of formation, transformation, activation, and suppression of such four-part complexes. Boundary change figures importantly in a wide variety of phenomena, including the activation or deactivation of political identities, economic exploitation, categorical discrimination, democratization, and the alterations of uncertainty that promote or inhibit the outbreak of collective violence (McAdam, Tarrow, and Tilly 2001; Tilly 1998a, 2002, 2003). I argue that similar or identical causal mechanisms operate across a very wide range of boundary changes.

To avoid confusion concerning the proposed line of explanation, we must distinguish carefully between two clusters of mechanisms: (1) those that cause boundary change and (2) those that constitute boundary change and produce its direct effects. Figure 19.1 schematizes the distinctions and the argument's flow. Mechanisms *causing* boundary change singly or in combination include encounter, imposition, borrowing, conversation, and incentive shift. Mechanisms *constituting* boundary change include inscription, erasure, activation, deactivation, site transfer, and relocation. The two classes of mechanisms jointly produce some effects that on careless inspection appear to result from boundary changes alone, for instance, the initiation of ethnic cleansing as a consequence of imposition and activation; even if it occurs more or less simultaneously, the authoritative imposition of a boundary (a cause of boundary change) remains causally prior to activation of that boundary (a constituent of that change), which plays a direct causal role in the initiation of ethnic cleansing.

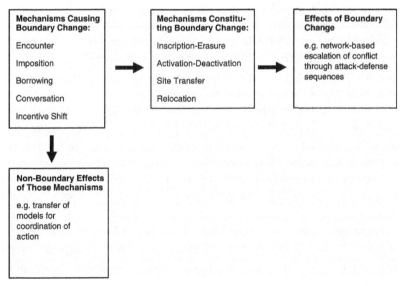

Figure 19.1 General Causal Relations in Social Boundary Mechanisms

Mechanisms That Cause Boundary Change

For all of its everyday employment in natural science, the term "mechanism" rarely appears in social-scientific explanations. Its rarity results, I think, partly from the term's unwanted suggestion that social processes operate like clockwork but mainly from its uneasy coexistence with predominant strategies of explanation in social science: proposal of covering laws for complex structures and processes, specification of necessary and sufficient conditions for concrete instances of the same complex structures and processes, identification of individual or group dispositions just before the point of action as causes of that action. As a practical matter, however, social scientists often refer to mechanisms as they construct partial explanations of complex structures or processes and as they identify parallels within classes of complex structures or processes. In the study of contentious politics, for example, analysts frequently invoke the mechanisms of brokerage and coalition-formation as well as some of the other mechanisms this chapter catalogs (McAdam, Tarrow, and Tilly 2001). If those mechanisms appear in essentially the same form with the same small-scale consequences across a wide range of circumstances, we can call them "robust."

Social mechanisms concatenate into processes displaying recognizable internal similarities but capable of producing variable overall outcomes depending on initial conditions, sequences, and combinations of mechanisms (Tilly 2001a). We are searching for robust mechanisms and processes that produce alterations in boundaries among social sites as well as other mechanisms and processes that produce the effects of boundary change. Let us begin with mechanisms that cause boundary change: encounter, imposition, borrowing, conversation, and incentive shift.

Encounter. When members of two previously separate or only indirectly linked networks enter the same social space and begin interacting, they commonly form a social boundary at their point of contact ... encounter plays a significant part in boundary change. As interaction intensifies between clusters of previously unlinked or indirectly linked social sites, boundaries between them become more salient (Olzak 1992, Olzak and Uhrig 2001).

Imposition. Authorities draw lines where they did not previously exist, for example distinguishing citizens from noncitizens, landowners from other users of the land, or genuine Christians from insufficiently pious persons.

Imposition, however, also operates on much smaller scales and for shorter durations. A foreman temporarily divides construction laborers into two squads, one for digging, the other for hauling. A schoolteacher lines up a class in competing teams—A, B, and C—for the day's spelling contest. A parent draws the line between those children who have cleaned their rooms properly (and will thus get their promised rewards) and those who have not (and will thus lose out this time). All these, and many more everyday routines, consist of imposing temporary boundaries. Those who impose such boundaries can, of course, rescind them, but I suspect that the mechanism is asymmetrical: once an imposed boundary falls into place, it leaves traces of its existence in the relevant social relations and representations even after it loses authoritative backing.

Borrowing. People creating a new organization emulate distinctions already visible in other organizations of the same general class, for example, by instituting a division between hourly wage workers and employees drawing monthly salaries. A great deal of inequality between members of different social categories results from borrowing, as those who create organizations such as schools, firms, and armies follow established models in recruiting categorically by gender, ethnicity, race, or religion to positions that differ significantly in the rewards they afford their occupants and the destinations to which they lead (Cohn 2000; Downs 1995; Levy 1997; McCall 2001; Reskin and Padavic 1994; Tilly 2001b). They are not *inventing* the boundary in question but installing a familiar sort of boundary in a new location. Borrowing repeatedly produces local boundary change as new forms of organization diffuse. In borrowing, organizers need not intend to produce categorical inequality for massive and durable inequality to result from their intervention.

Conversation. Conversation certainly includes ordinary talk, but it extends to a wider range of similar interactions among social sites, just as long as exchanges of signals modify relations among the parties (Tilly 1998b). In the course of routine interaction, participants incrementally alter relations between social sites by developing distinctive relations within at least two clusters, establishing distinctive relations across the zone between those clusters, and creating shared representations of that zone between them.

Incentive shift. Participants in boundary processes receive rewards or penalties that affect their pursuit of within-boundary relations, cross-boundary relations, and representations of the boundary zone.

Of course, these mechanisms sometimes occur jointly. Encounter and borrowing work together, for example, when members of two previously separate networks enter the same social space, begin interacting, and immediately adopt templates for their interaction that are available from elsewhere. Encounter and conversation together sometimes produce a cycle: first creation of a sharp boundary, then blurring or redefinition of that boundary as relations across it intensify. What is more, all these mechanisms have more or less equal and opposite counterparts, for example, the segregation that reverses effects of encounters. Blood feuds and violent ethnic conflict often feature surges of encounter, imposition, and borrowing that render boundaries powerfully salient, only to be followed by either complete separation or more routine conversation (Boehm 1987; Gould 1999; Horowitz 2001; Mamdani 2001; Petersen 2002; Varshney 2002).

Stepping up the level of magnification, we can always find more microscopic mechanisms within encounter, imposition, borrowing, conversation, and incentive shift. Looking closely at conversation, for instance, we will discover improvisation, turn-taking, meaningful hesitation, code switching, and much more (Burke 1993; Fitch 1998; Gal 1987; Gumperz 1982; Sawyer 2001).

For an observer of multiple social sites, then, my argument amounts to saying that each of the crucial mechanisms—encounter, imposition, borrowing, conversation, and incentive shift—produces indistinguishably similar effects on boundaries over a wide range of circumstances. The claim stands, obviously, as a hypothesis for investigation rather than as a postulate or a proven fact.

Mechanisms That Constitute Boundary Change

Encounter, imposition, borrowing, conversation, and incentive shift reliably cause social boundary change, but they do not *constitute* boundary change. Indeed, each of them produces similar effects across a wide range of nonboundary social processes. In other circumstances, for example, the combination of imposition with borrowing reproduces hierarchies or patterns of cooperation without significant activation of social boundaries; effective industrial leaders thus spread established forms of organization from one firm to the next (DiMaggio 2001). Figure 19.1 calls such consequences "non-boundary effects of those mechanisms." Other consequential mechanisms, however, actually occur as part of boundary change, and in combination produce the effects of boundary change. They include (1) inscription and its reversal, erasure; (2) activation and deactivation; (3) site transfer; and (4) relocation. We can review each in turn.

Inscription-erasure. Remember the elements of a social boundary: distinctive social relations on either side of an intermediate zone, distinctive relations *across* that zone, and, on each side, shared representations of that zone itself. Inscription heightens any and all of these elements; it differentiates social relations on either side more sharply from each other, differentiates relations across the zone more emphatically from those on either side, and/or increases the extensiveness of shared representations on either or both sides. Erasure reverses any or all of these changes.

Activation-deactivation. All persons and social sites live in the presence of multiple social boundaries at varying levels of activation or deactivation.

Inscription and activation sometimes operate simultaneously, as do erasure and deactivation. Inscription heightens the social relations and representations that comprise a particular boundary, while activation makes that same boundary more central to the organization of activity in its vicinity.

Site transfer. This mechanism maintains a boundary but shifts the exact locations of persons and social sites with respect to differentiated relations on either side of the boundary, cross-boundary relations, and/or representations of the boundary. Racial passing and religious conversion, for example, present two versions of site transfer in which individual persons or clusters of persons move from one side of a boundary to the other. Rites of passage similarly transfer people across boundaries without erasing those boundaries. Indeed, initiation ceremonies often reinforce the very boundaries across which they transfer individuals. Eric Wolf interpreted the Winter Ceremonials of American Northwest Coast peoples in just such a light:

> Among many North American Indian peoples, seekers after sacred power had visions in which they entered into contact with guardian spirits, who bestowed on them both supernaturally charged objects and instructions, and visionary encounters with spirits who endowed their clients with such powers were widespread on the Northwest Coast. The essential plot of the Winter Ceremonial conforms to this pattern in that a spirit kidnaps and consumes the initiand, and in so doing grants him supernatural powers; it then releases him back into normal life as a person transformed by that experience. Unlike the vision in much of North America, however, in the Kwakiutl ceremonial this visionary experience was neither open to all nor specific to the individual visionary. It was confined to sets of people who had acquired the prerogative to enter a sodality that impersonates the supernatural

in question, and that prerogative was acted out in a highly standardized and impersonal form, within an organized framework of impersonating performances.

(Wolf 1999:105)

The ceremony in question clearly transferred persons across the boundary of a privileged sodality while dramatizing the importance of that same boundary. It altered the relation of particular individuals to the boundary.

Not all site transfer, however, consists of individual movement across boundaries. Ethnic activists often strive for transfer of their entire category from one side to another of a racial or citizenship boundary, and sometimes succeed. In South Africa, leaders of mixed-race populations carried on a gingerly collaboration with Apartheid rulers that separated them from the increasingly unified black population and gave them distinctive political rights without rendering them white (Ashforth 1990; Jung 2000; Marks and Trapido 1987; Marx 1991). North American ethnic politics has long featured collective struggles and shifting governmental decisions concerning who qualifies as black, white, Latino, Anglo, Indian, Inuit, or otherwise (Cordero-Guzmán, Smith, and Grosfoguel 2001; Curtis 2001; Domínguez 1986; Omi and Winant 1994; Ong 1996; Pérez Firmat 1994; Peterson 1995).

Relocation. This mechanism combines two or more of the constitutive mechanisms: inscription, erasure, activation, deactivation, and/or site transfer. Within some set of social sites, it alters the major boundaries that are organizing action and interaction. In a simple and frequent scenario, one boundary deactivates while another activates: gender divisions fade while work divisions become more salient. In another, inscription and site transfer conjoin: Bosnian Serb leaders enforce a Serb-Muslim division in previously mixed populations, and families scramble to locate themselves on one side of the line or the other (Bax 2000; Malcolm 1996; Mazower 2000).

An unexpected but dramatic case in point comes from soccer violence. Unlike American football, soccer involves little outright violence on the field, most of it accidental and much of it punished as fouls. When soccer matches generate serious damage, spectators and supporters have usually started the trouble. More often than not, the violent performers consist of young male fans who have arrived in clusters; fortunately for the death rate, they rarely use weapons more lethal than clubs, broken bottles, and knives (Armstrong 1998; Bromberger 1998: chap. 3; Buford 1991). Deaths become frequent chiefly when police battle unruly fans (Giulianotti, Bonney, and Hepworth 1994).

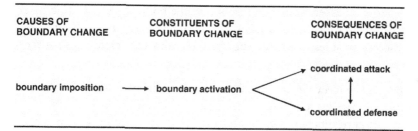

Figure 19.2 An Elementary Causal Sequence Involving Social Boundaries

Leaving aside the fights between rival groups of fans that recurrently take place outside of soccer stadiums, soccer violence on the field becomes serious when fans breach the boundary separating spectators from players and referees. That boundary gives way to another separating supporters of one team from supporters of another, easily distinguished by the colors and symbols they wear. Often, however, further relocation occurs as police struggle with all fans on the field regardless of their affiliation, and the previously hostile fans unite to fight back. On a small scale, soccer violence replays the sort of relocation that frequently occurs in the course of wars and revolutions.

Consequences of Boundary Change

As the evocation of wars and revolutions suggests, boundary change produces serious consequences across a wide range of social interaction. It facilitates or inhibits exploitation of one category by another. It likewise facilitates or inhibits mobilization in the forms of social movements or popular rebellions. It strongly affects the likelihood, intensity, scale, and form of collective violence (Tilly 2003). Instead of surveying the entire range of boundary change, however, let us trace some of the causal connections we have been examining through three quite different social processes: occupational sex-typing, ethnic cleansing, and immigrant adaptation. In each of them appears a causal sequence of the sort summarized in Figure 19.2.

In this elementary sequence,

- authorities draw lines among social sites where they did not previously exist;
- that boundary increases in salience as an organizer of social relations on either side, of social relations across it, and/or of shared representations;

- actors on at least one side respond to the boundary's activation by engaging in coordinated attacks on sites across the boundary; and
- actors on at least one side engage in coordinated defense against those attacks.

Occupational sex-typing. Job assignment by gender accounts for the bulk of male-female wage inequality in capitalist countries. A good deal of sex segregation results not from imposition but from borrowing, as managers set up new offices and firms on existing models, including the assignment of men to higher-paid job categories. But historically the gender composition of certain occupations has sometimes shifted rapidly.

Ethnic cleansing. Open physical attack identifies ethnic cleansing for what it is. ...Major European episodes during the twentieth century: Armenians and Greeks of Anatolia around World War I; Nazi extermination of Jews; the Soviet Union's forced deportation of Chechen, Ingush, and Crimean Tatars in 1944; expulsion of Germans from Poland and Czechoslovakia at the end of World War II; and Yugoslavia's successive episodes of the 1990s (Naimark 2001; see also Bax 2000, Petersen 2002, Rae 2002). Ethnic cleansing, for Naimark (2001:3), involves a deliberate program "to remove a people and often all traces of them from a concrete territory." At one extreme of ethnic cleansing lies expulsion, at the other extermination. All of the 20th-century episodes Naimark examines combined some of each.

Imposition played its part in all of Naimark's (2001) episodes, for example, in the Nazis' Nuremberg Laws (July 1935) identifying everyone with at least 25 percent Jewish ancestry as a Jew, depriving Jews thus defined of German citizenship, and strictly forbidding marriage of Jews with non-Jews. The Nazis activated the Jewish/non-Jewish boundary in a thousand demeaning and costly ways. Between their arrival in power (1933) and the start of World War II (1939), they exerted strong pressure on Jews to emigrate, leaving their goods behind. Systematic killing of Jews by German forces, however, did not begin until 1941; further activation of the Jewish–non-Jewish boundary then reorganized life—and death—on both sides.

The Nazis' overwhelming military and organizational strength meant that Jews' coordinated defense consisted chiefly not of counterattacks but of mutual aid, mutual concealment, and facilitation of escape for a fortunate few. In the process, Nazi leaders redefined the relevant boundary as separating good Germans not only from Jews but also from Bolsheviks.

Attacks on Jews and on Russians turned increasingly into campaigns of extermination.

Immigrant adaptation. With respect to levels of violence, immigrant adaptation generally lies between occupational sex-typing and ethnic cleansing—sometimes generating fierce attacks and counterattacks, but mostly working through competition and conflict on a lesser scale. Yet here, too, one recurrent causal path leads from imposition to activation to attack and defense. A striking case of the imposition-activation-attack-defense causal sequence appears in the experience of African-ancestry West Indian immigrants to the United States. They certainly come from unequal worlds, but ones in which the stark black-white distinction that prevails in the United States dissolves into a much more complex set of boundaries organized around class and ethnicity. "Racism," one New York immigrant told interviewer Vilna Bashi Bobb,

> is not really a priority there [in the West Indies], you know. You don't look at a black and white situation. You more look at an economic situation, you know. It doesn't matter really whether you're black or white or whatever it is. If you don't have the money you don't have the position in society that I'm talking about. If you have the money you have the position. But when I came here I realized that not only is there economics you have to deal with, you have to deal with the color of your skin, so that was kind of a shock to me.
>
> (Bashi 2001:215)

Caribbean immigrants to New York confront black-white boundaries long since imposed. But the activation of those boundaries varies significantly with their social situation. Migrants who move directly into New York's West Indian enclaves and work in West Indian establishments find themselves insulated from daily black-white distinctions and assimilation to the native-born African American population. Although those first-generation immigrants gradually become aware of American-style racism, Bashi argues, participation in the immigrant network shields them from its full activation:

> The network acts as a shield in three ways. One, it may limit interaction with whites who may behave in a racist manner. That is, although they are in the primary and secondary labor markets and not in ethnic enclaves, black West Indian immigrants work and live alongside other immigrants like them, because their social space is mainly limited to job and housing niches. Two, these niches bring to the West Indian immigrant population a degree of socioeconomic success relative to their native-born black counterparts, and thus socioeconomic separation

from them. Three, the labor market success that members receive along with access to these labor- and housing-market niches belies the racist stereotypes about the inability of black people to succeed in the United States.

(Bashi 2001:235)

The network also provides a basis for collective resistance to discrimination.

The children of West Indian immigrants, however, lose some of their parents' shielding from the activation of black-white boundaries. They grow up with New York accents, go to New York schools, enter the New York labor market, and often leave whatever remains of the immigrant enclave. They thus become subject to the same sort of attack—mostly day-to-day discrimination, but sometimes assault from nonblack gangs—that African Americans have long experienced. They become African American and mount their defense against attack in common with other African Americans. The long-standing black-white boundary activates for them. Although each migration stream has its distinctive properties, the sequence of imposition, activation, attack, and defense repeats itself in many immigrant experiences.

The theme should be familiar from the example of Bolivian immigrants to Buenos Aires. Long before any of the Bolivians observed by Alejandro Grimson arrived in the city, authorities had established a boundary between Argentine citizens and foreigners, not to mention the more specific boundaries separating *porteños* from others, Argentines from Bolivians, and Creoles from Indians. In Buenos Aires, the arrival of migrants from the Andes activates these boundaries, which in turn leads to the multiple forms of attack that Grimson (1999) documents, and generates defensive maneuvers on the part of bolivianos. At least in local festivals where Bolivians gather, those maneuvers include broadcast claims to cultural and historical superiority.

The claims do not prevail, but at least they assert a shared identity and propose an attractive story about the boundary that separates bolivianos from *porteños*. Grimson sums up,

> Faced with growing social asymmetries and with representations of inequality, immigrants try to broaden their identification as a way of activating networks of mutual aid and solidarity. This does not mean that narrower identities disappear, or stop being used as bases of high-risk relations if not of organizational connections. It means that as the process of moving and settling proceeds in a country they still experience as foreign, migrants seek to generalize their identities and to use their own cultural histories as they do so.

(Grimson 1999:181)

Instead of members of small clusters from particular villages, *porteños bolivianos* become just that: members of categories well defined by their separation from and connection to the social life of Buenos Aires. They become Bolivians. Their experience involves much more than the single-circuit imposition-activation-attack-defense. In one way or another, it includes our full range of causal mechanisms: encounter, imposition, borrowing, conversation, incentive shift, inscription-erasure, activation-deactivation, site transfer, and relocation, not to mention further consequences of those mechanisms. But that particular experience illustrates the great generality of boundary change as a social process.

References

Armstrong, Gary. 1998. *Football Hooligans: Knowing the Score*. Oxford, UK: Berg.

Ashforth, Adam. 1990. *The Politics of Official Discourse in Twentieth-Century South Africa*. Oxford, UK: Clarendon.

Bashi Bobb, Vilna. 2001. "Neither Ignorance nor Bliss: Race, Racism, and the West Indian Immigrant Experience." In *Migration, Transnationalization, and Race in a Changing New York*, edited by Héctor R. Cordero-Guzmán, Robert C. Smith, and Ramón Grosfoguel. Philadelphia: Temple University Press.

Bax, Mart. 2000. "Holy Mary and Medjugorje's Rocketeers. The Local Logic of an Ethnic Cleansing Process in Bosnia." *Ethnologia Europaea* 30:45–58.

Boehm, Christopher. 1987. *Blood Revenge: The Enactment and Management of Conflict in Montenegro and Other Tribal Societies*. Philadelphia: University of Pennsylvania Press. (Orig. pub. by University Press of Kansas, 1984.)

Bromberger, Christian. 1998. *Football, la bagatelle la plus sérieuse du monde*. Paris: Bayard.

Buford, Bill. 1991. *Among the Thugs*. New York: Vintage.

Burke, Peter. 1993. *The Art of Conversation*. Ithaca, NY: Cornell University Press.

Cohn, Samuel. 2000. *Race and Gender Discrimination at Work*. Boulder, CO: Westview.

Cordero-Guzmán, Héctor R., Robert C. Smith, and Ramón Grosfoguel, eds. 2001. *Migration, Transnationalization, and Race in a Changing New York*. Philadelphia: Temple University Press.

Curtis, Bruce. 2001. *The Politics of Population. State Formation, Statistics, and the Census of Canada, 1840–1875*. Toronto, Canada: University of Toronto Press.

DiMaggio, Paul, ed. 2001. *The Twenty-First-Century Firm. Changing Economic Organization in International Perspective*. Princeton, NJ: Princeton University Press.

Domínguez, Virginia R. 1986. *White by Definition: Social Classification in Creole Louisiana*. New Brunswick, NJ: Rutgers University Press.

Downs, Laura Lee. 1995. *Manufacturing Inequality: Gender Division in the French and British Metalworking Industries, 1914–1939*. Ithaca, NY: Cornell University Press.

Fitch, Kristine L.1998. *Speaking Relationally: Culture, Communication, and Interpersonal Connection*. New York: Guilford.

Gal, Susan. 1987. "Codeswitching and Consciousness in the European Periphery." *American Ethnologist* 14:637–53.

Giulianotti, Richard, Norman Bonney, and Mike Hepworth, eds. 1994. *Football, Violence, and Social Identity*. London: Routledge.

Gould, Roger V. 1999. "Collective Violence and Group Solidarity: Evidence from a Feuding Society." *American Sociological Review* 64:356–80.

Grimson, Alejandro. 1999. *Relatos de la diferencia y la igualdad. Los bolivianos en Buenos Aires*. Buenos Aires, Argentina: Editorial Universitaria de Buenos Aires.

Gumperz, John J. 1982. *Discourse Strategies*. Cambridge: Cambridge University Press.

Horowitz, Donald L. 2001. *The Deadly Ethnic Riot*. Berkeley: University of California Press.

Jung, Courtney. 2000. *Then I Was Black. South African Political Identities in Transition*. New Haven, CT: Yale University Press.

Lamont, Michèle, and Virág Molnár. 2002. "The Study of Boundaries in the Social Sciences." *Annual Review of Sociology* 28:167–95.

Levy, Yagil. 1997. *Trial and Error. Israel's Route from War to De-Escalation*. Albany: State University of New York Press.

Malcolm, Noel. 1996. *Bosnia. A Short History*. Rev. ed. New York: New York University Press. (Orig. pub. 1994.)

Mamdani, Mahmood. 2001. *When Victims Become Killers. Colonialism, Nativism, and the Genocide in Rwanda*. Princeton, NJ: Princeton University Press.

Marks, Shula, and Stanley Trapido, eds. 1987. *The Politics of Race, Class and Nationalism in Twentieth-Century South Africa*. London: Longman.

Marx, Anthony. 1991. *Lessons of Struggle. South African Internal Opposition 1960–1990*. New York: Oxford University Press.

Mazower, Mark. 2000. *The Balkans. A Short History*. New York: Modern Library.

McAdam, Doug, Sidney Tarrow, and Charles Tilly. 2001. *Dynamics of Contention*. Cambridge: Cambridge University Press.

McCall, Leslie. 2001. *Complex Inequality. Gender, Class, and Race in the New Economy*. New York: Routledge.

Naimark, Norman M. 2001. *Fires of Hatred. Ethnic Cleansing in Twentieth-Century Europe*. Cambridge, MA: Harvard University Press.

Olzak, Susan. 1992. *The Dynamics of Ethnic Competition and Conflict*. Stanford, CA: Stanford University Press.

Olzak, Susan, and S. C. Noah Uhrig. 2001. "The Ecology of Tactical Overlap." *American Sociological Review* 66:694–717.

Omi, Michael, and Howard A. Winant. 1994. *Racial Formation in the United States: From the 1960s to the 1990s*. 2nd ed. New York: Routledge.

Ong, Aihwa. 1996. "Cultural Citizenship as Subject-Making: Immigrants Negotiate Racial and Cultural Boundaries in the United States." *Current Anthropology* 37:737–62.

Pérez Firmat, Gustavo. 1994. *Life on the Hyphen: The Cuban-American Way*. Austin: University of Texas Press.

Petersen, Roger D. 2002. *Understanding Ethnic Violence. Fear, Hatred, and Resentment in Twentieth-Century Eastern Europe*. Cambridge: Cambridge University Press.

Peterson, Paul E., ed. 1995. *Classifying by Race*. Princeton, NJ: Princeton University Press.

Rae, Heather. 2002. *State Identities and the Homogenisation of Peoples*. Cambridge: Cambridge University Press.

Reskin, Barbara, and Irene Padavic. 1994. *Women and Men at Work*. Thousand Oaks, CA: Pine Forge.

Sawyer, R. Keith. 2001. *Creating Conversations: Improvisation in Everyday Discourse.* Cresskill, NJ: Hampton Press.

Tilly, Charles. 1998a. "Contentious Conversation." *Social Research* 65:491–510.

———. 1998b. *Durable Inequality.* Berkeley: University of California Press.

———. 2001a. "Mechanisms in Political Processes." *Annual Review of Political Science* 4:21–41.

———. 2001b. "Relational Origins of Inequality." *Anthropological Theory* 1:355–72.

———. 2002. *Stories, Identities, and Political Change.* Lanham, MD: Rowman & Littlefield.

———. 2003. *The Politics of Collective Violence.* Cambridge: Cambridge University Press.

Varshney, Ashutosh. 2002. *Ethnic Conflict and Civic Life: Hindus and Muslims in India.* New Haven, CT: Yale University Press.

Wolf, Eric R. 1999. *Envisioning Power. Ideologies of Dominance and Crisis.* Berkeley: University of California Press.

From Segregation to Integration

20

Charles Tilly

By 1720, French imperial forces had long since established a serious presence in North America. Although they had lost some ground to the aggressive English since 1700, the French still laid claim to the eastern part of what we now call Canada except for Hudson's Bay, Acadia, and Newfoundland, to northern sections of what we now call the American Midwest, and to a significant share of the Mississippi basin. Québec, Montréal, Detroit, St. Louis, Mobile, and New Orleans had all come into being as French cities and fortresses. French merchants, soldiers, and administrators controlled the major waterways linking the continental interior to Europe. Violence, intrigue, and venality intertwined in their imperial system of rule. The French held their ground until the 1760s under incessant pressure from Spanish and English competitors including frontier settlers. Defeat by the English in the Seven Years War (1756–1763) radically reduced France's North American territories. Up to then, nevertheless, the French still had some hope of becoming the dominant power in North America.

Despite their looming presence on the continent, the French never achieved more than contingent domination over the Indian populations they encountered from their earliest arrival in North America. They tried, but their very efforts to conquer Indian peoples or to push them aside for French settlements created new forms of connection among previously distinct villages, bands, tribes, and federations. Remember the three sorts of resources that rulers generally apply to subordinate populations:

coercion: all concerted means of action that commonly cause loss or damage to the persons, possessions, or sustaining social relations of social actors

capital: tangible, transferable resources that in combination with effort can
 produce increases in use value, plus enforceable claims on such resources
commitment: relations among social sites (persons, groups, structures, or positions) that promote their taking account of each other

French authorities deployed combinations of all three. They used coercion
aplenty as they conquered, but they also bought off Indians in generous ritual exchanges of gifts, and fostered commitment in their support of Catholic
missionaries among the Indians as well as their toleration of French-Indian
intermarriage.

Top-down French applications of coercion, commerce, and commitment
transformed Indian life, but did not insert Indians neatly into the French system of rule. Interacting with French conquerors, Indians developed skill in
concealment, clientage, dissimulation, and predation. In addition to general
Indian reluctance to accept European rule, the French discovered that British and Spanish paymasters were often willing to offer hard-pressed Indians
support for their resistance against the French. In compensation, French
paymasters similarly sought to buy away Indian supporters of the English
and French.

Up to the French defeat in the Seven Years War, repeated French efforts to
subordinate Indians, to integrate them durably into patron-client relations,
or even to bargain out brokered autonomy as if they were lesser sovereign
states sometimes worked in the short run. Over the long run, however,
those strategies usually generated not integration but concealment, predation, and (especially) dissimulation. As a consequence, French soldiers, administrators, and merchants expended a great deal of effort in negotiating
coexistence with the Indian populations in their territories. That negotiation produced what Richard White calls a "middle ground" of understandings and practices linking nominally sovereign French authorities to Indian
populations within their jurisdictions. In a more literal sense, the territory
between areas of dense French settlement and those of largely Indian population shifted as a mixed middle ground of encounter. As of the 1690s, the
middle ground extended around the Great Lakes.

French-Indian sexual relations, cohabitation, and marriages crisscrossed
the middle ground. In 1694, for example, prominent trader and notorious
libertine Michel Accault sought to marry Aremepinchieue, seventeen-
year-old daughter of a leading Kaskaskia chief in the Illinois territory.
Aremepinchieue, a fervent Catholic in defiance of her father's opposition to
the faith, refused to marry the nonpracticing Accault. She received backing from Jesuit Jacques Gravier, French missionary to the Illinois, who had

allied himself with Accault's enemies. Despite this configuration of conflicts, the principals worked out an astonishing dénouement: with the support of Father Gravier, Aremepinchieue agreed to marry Accault. Her conditions: he would return to the Catholic faith and her parents would accept Catholic baptism. The parties accepted. After this stunning example, and following concerted efforts on the part of French missionaries, by 1711 the Kaskaskias had almost all become Catholic (White 1991:74).

Aremepinchieue was not alone. By the 1720s, French men and Indian women had frequently been cohabiting, and sometimes marrying, for seventy years. Three generations or more of *métis* had therefore grown up in the middle ground. If White's identifications of the chief characters are right, the wedding of 1694 not only illustrated the creative character of French-Indian relations but also facilitated Indian intervention into French-on-French murders three decades later. In 1723, a French soldier insulted a French warehouse keeper named Perillaut, who replied by killing the soldier with his sword. French authorities condemned Perillaut to death. But Illinois Indians who had dealt extensively with Perillaut pleaded for his life. (As warehouse keeper, Perillaut took charge of distributing authorized gifts and military bounties to Indian groups.) First three Kaskaskia chiefs appeared with thirty warriors. Then followed a delegation of Cahokias including a much respected woman called Marie Rompiechoue, who—as her name suggests—was most likely the daughter or other close relative of the earlier Aremepinchieue.

The Kaskaskia chiefs had already allied their tribes closely with the French against their common enemies the Chickasaws and the Fox. The Indians offered the French a peace pipe. The French knew well that, by long-established Indian custom, to accept the pipe meant granting the giver's request. Led by a Catholic Indian spokesman, the Kaskaskias made a subtle, forceful argument: Chickasaws and Foxes would interpret the execution of Perillaut, friend of the Kaskaskias, as avenging their own dead in wars against the Kaskaskias and the French. In keeping with both Indian custom and Christian doctrine, they argued that the perpetrator's contrition, compensation to the victim's family, and a French pardon would resolve the situation more equitably. The chiefs reminded the French, furthermore, of the times that Kaskaskias had lost their lives avenging the French but, at French request, the Kaskaskias had not exacted blood revenge on their enemies.

French commander Boisbriant saw the point. He:

> insisted that the affair set no precedent, but he agreed to petition the king for Perillaut's pardon and release. Those Kaskaskias who 'have

died to avenge the Frenchman, cover the body of the one who has now been killed.' So ended the first recorded criminal case tried by the French in Illinois. Perillaut was free that May.

(White 1991:92)

This negotiation occurred in a world in which French military units freely massacred their Indian enemies and in which Indians at war commonly tortured, scalped, burned, and ate captured enemies. The Kaskaskias and French were not adopting a general strategy of nonviolence, but bargaining out conditions of rule.

We know too little of day-to-day Indian life between the 1690s and the 1720s to say confidently that the Kaskaskias as a whole formed a single connected trust network. French losses during the Seven Years War meant that France never integrated the Kaskaskias or other North American Indian nations durably into its regime. But confrontations of Indians with French around the American Great Lakes during that period surely included repeated encounters between regimes and trust networks. They illustrate a middle ground between total segregation and complete integration of trust networks.

From the top down, we see French officials experimenting with different combinations of coercion, capital, and commitment, sometimes achieving patronage or brokered autonomy, but never reaching full integration of Indians' trust networks into their system of rule. From the bottom up, we see Indians and *métis* mixing concealment, predation, and dissimulation with contingent forms of protection by French patrons. We watch the early stages of colonial domination.

Unequal Encounters

So far we have looked at trust networks mainly from the perspectives of their members. In the background we have noticed rulers applying various combinations of coercion, capital, and commitment in efforts to control visible trust networks and to draw essential resources from those networks. We have witnessed repeated encounters between trust networks and predators, including agents of government. We have examined how changes in external connections, boundaries, sustenance, and internal relations affect the day-to-day operation of trust networks. But we have not yet confronted the major processes by which trust networks actually become integrated into public politics: disintegration of existing networks, multiplication of populations outside of existing networks, and so on. How do these processes actually produce their political effects? Once again, it helps to distinguish bottom-up and top-down components of the processes, then break each of them into finer mechanisms.

"Bottom up" means simply as seen from the perspectives of trust networks. There are seven varieties of bottom-up strategies:

1   *concealment:* avoiding detection and manipulation by authorities
2   *dissimulation:* feigning conformity by adopting some available public identity, but minimizing both compliance and visibility of internal operations and resources
3   *clientage:* acquiring protection by intermediate authorities, thus reducing compliance and visibility, but usually at a price
4   *predation:* organizing enough externally effective force both to acquire resources and to defend against predation by others
5   *enlistment:* active integration into an existing regime's available niches
6   *bargaining:* establishing relations with major political actors on the basis of mutual contingent consent
7   *dissolution:* destruction of an existing network through either incremental departures or collective dismantling

Following encounters of a given trust network with political authorities over a substantial period, we often observe a sequence of these strategies, for example an integration process running *concealment—dissimulation—clientage—enlistment* for Val d'Aosta Waldensians as they went from clandestinity to membership in the Protestant establishment. In the opposite direction, *enlistment—clientage—dissimulation—dissolution* describes the changing position of many religious confraternities before and during the French Revolution.

Authorities deployed contrasting top-down strategies in seeking to control trust networks and resources within them. Figure 20.1 summarizes the main possibilities. Authorities first chose their *means of control:* a mixture of coercion, capital, and commitment ranging from exclusive reliance on coercion (nothing but application of means that damage and destroy) to exclusive reliance on commitment (nothing but appeals to shared means of communication and solidarity). But they also chose a *mode* of control: whether to *facilitate* a trust network's operation, to *tolerate* it, or to *repress* it. Some combinations of means and mode—for instance, facilitation by coercive means—seem unlikely at first glance, and did in fact occur no more than rarely. Rulers did, however, sometimes facilitate by coercive means, as when French authorities in North America annihilated enemies of their

Indian allies. To take the scheme's opposite corner, repression by means of commitment occurred every time the Catholic Church literally excommunicated a dissident, heretical trust network. Nevertheless, the diagonal arrow summarizes my main argument: stable integration of trust networks into systems of rule depends on a decline of coercive control combined with increasing reliance on capital and commitment. That shift entails movement from repression to toleration and facilitation.

Authorities' choices of means and modes obviously interacted with trust networks' strategies for dealing with authorities; however unequally, the two parties engaged in strategic interaction. Authorities faced with predatory trust networks such as pirates and bandits generally chose within a range running from repression by coercive means (attacking them directly) to facilitation by means of capital (enrolling them as privateers or mercenaries). Trade diasporas faced with regimes that stressed repression by coercive means generally chose within a range running from dissimulation by means of capital (bribery) to clientage by means of commitment (protection by kin or coreligionists). Hence, incessant negotiation took place among trust networks, rulers, and other political actors.

These negotiations located particular trust networks in our relation-means space. They differentiated evasive conformity, brokered autonomy, particularistic ties to rulers, patronage systems, totalitarianism, democracy, and theocracy. Thinking about the negotiations brings out similarities and dissimilarities in relations of trust networks to public politics. Totalitarianism and theocracy resemble each other greatly, in this view,

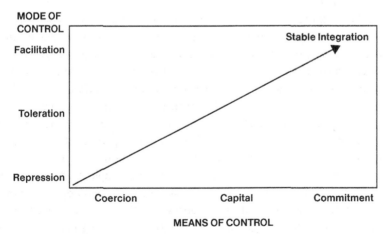

Figure 20.1 Top-Down Approaches of Rulers to Trust Networks

except that theocracy substitutes the commitment of common religious membership for totalitarian coercion. Brokered autonomy resembles other patronage systems, except that it involves the explicit recognition of a distinctive community and its representation. Evasive conformity and particularistic ties to rulers likewise operate in similar fashions, except that in evasive conformity the tie between ruler and trust network remains negotiated and contingent. Democracy differs from the rest, since all three of its ties—trust network to ruler, trust network to intermediary, and ruler to intermediary—work via negotiation and contingency. In that regard, we return to Margaret Levi's insight concerning contingent consent (Levi 1997: 21). Democracy entails contingent consent based mainly on combinations of material incentives with shared commitment.

Here is another way to interpret the range from high integration to high segregation. The top layer of high integration—totalitarianism, democracy, and theocracy—contains zones of direct rule, in which agents of the central government extend its writ effectively to local communities. The middle layer of negotiated connection—patronage and brokered autonomy—contains zones of indirect rule, in which powerful intermediaries enjoy substantial autonomy within their own domains. The bottom layer of segregation—evasive conformity and particularistic ties—contains zones of thin political control, backed neither by effective central agents nor by powerful autonomous intermediaries. The diagram therefore offers a restatement of this chapter's twin problems: What processes locate trust networks in different zones within the space, especially zones of direct rule, indirect rule, and thin control? What processes move trust networks from one zone to another?

At the bottom level, we find few people other than members of the ruling class relying on governmental agents for protection of their major valued long-term enterprises from risk. Instead, we find most people organizing such enterprises within autonomous trust networks and defending those networks as best they can from governmental intervention. In the middle level, we observe partial integration of trust networks into systems of rule, but always with protection by powerful intermediaries from the ruler's direct intervention. At the upper level, we discover people whose trust networks either extend into the government, depend on direct governmental intervention, or incorporate political actors (for example, trade unions, political parties, and commercial firms) that in turn depend on governmental connections for their continued operation. Only at the upper level do we therefore discover large numbers of citizens who regularly yield their children to military service, put their life savings into government-backed securities, and respond willingly to census takers. How and why do regimes at the top level ever come into existence?

This journey from bottom to top identifies some challenging difficulties in the analysis of segregation and integration. Rare is the trust network that migrates the whole distance from bottom to top or top to bottom without changing significantly in organization and membership. The forms, geographic locations, external relations, and very names of Indian villages and tribes altered continuously as they interacted with the conquering French. In the North American regions whose transformations during the seventeenth and eighteenth centuries Richard White studied, under today's U.S. and Canadian rule many tribes claim descent from entities that make appearances in White's account, but their organizations bear little relationship to those of their ancestors. We cannot hope for the neat experiment of observing the "same" trust network as it moves from level to level across the whole range.

If my arguments are correct, furthermore, at any given level we should see not only upward or downward movement of existing trust networks among segregation, negotiated connection, and integration but also creation of new trust networks and disintegration of old ones. We should observe effects of major transforming processes, processes in which segregated networks disintegrate or lose their members while politically connected trust networks form and expand. Despite these complexities, it will clarify our analysis if we break this chapter's task into segments. First, a look at actual trust networks inhabiting each of the three levels—segregation, negotiated connection, and integration—to see if they behave as the general argument says they should. Second, a broader survey of trust networks' disintegration and new creation. Finally, an examination of how the experiences of existing trust networks articulate with those larger processes of transformation.

Segregated Trust Networks

Let us start at the bottom and work our way to the top. Toward the bottom of our space, we should find rulers influencing trust networks by applying intermittent coercion or using particular ties of commitment. We should discover only thin political control, and should observe members of trust networks engaging in combinations of concealment, dissimulation, and predation. As we move toward the top, we should pass through a zone of indirect rule and negotiated connection on our way to another zone in which rulers are employing ample applications of capital and commitment as they establish direct rule. In that uppermost zone, we should notice trust networks adopting strategies of enlistment and bargaining, but also sometimes dissolving as rulers—including democratic regimes—encourage the formation of new, integrated trust networks.

One case per category will move us from significant segregation to extensive integration. ... The place of Islamist networks in most Middle Eastern countries provides a dramatic case in point. Through much of the Middle East, repressive regimes forbid political association and mobilization by means of formal organizations other than a few state-authorized political parties. They ban authoritative organizations that might dare to make public political claims. So doing, they increase the reliance of ordinary people on informal networks as vehicles for survival and influence (Singerman 1995).

The same impoverishment of formal public life drives activism underground. As Diane Singerman observes,

> The collusion among monarchical, dynastic regimes, the military, and intelligence forces has suffocated a wide range of mediating structures and formal organizations throughout the region, whether they are professional associations, regional clubs, neighborhood and community organizations, political parties, women's associations, human rights groups, youth groups, etc. The power and organizational vitality of society has been diminished by draconian laws of association and assembly, limitations on fund-raising, a censored press, and regulatory overkill. This has left the state, kinship, and religious institutions in place, offering few rights of citizenship, representation, voice, or political freedoms in return. Thus the ground for activism—no less Islamic activism—is littered with risks and formidable obstacles.
>
> (Singerman 2004:148–149)

Nominally Islamic regimes have little choice, however, but to tolerate (and keep a wary eye upon) ostensibly nonpolitical Islamic organizations such as medical clinics, schools, charities, and cultural societies. In relatively open Jordan:

> Informed by a concern with controlling religious discourse, the regime uses administration, repression, and legal mechanisms to create a web of disincentives for more critical Islamic groups, which as a result find formal organizations constraining in the struggle over sacred authority. Moderate Islamists with a strong relationship to the regime,

on the other hand, are allowed to act through formal organizations, so long as they limit their activities in accordance with the conditions of participation and do not challenge the state's Islamic discourse,

(Wiktorowicz 2001:83)

The same regimes, nevertheless, generally face covert opposition by networks of Islamists: activists who seek to impose strict religious rule over states they regard as having secularized and/or sold out to the secular West. Few Islamists plunge as deep into opposition as Osama Bin Laden and al-Qaeda, but many share Bin Laden's hope for a purified Islamic world.

As a consequence, Islamists themselves combine concealment and dissimulation; they keep their organized networks underground, but they infiltrate tolerated Islamic organizations, seeking both to influence those organizations and to recruit promising believers into their own networks. Shiites even have a word for outward but reluctant conformity to political authorities: *taqiyya* (Kepel 2002:38). Jordan's Salafi enthusiasts gain most of their new members from existing circles of pious but politically inactive Muslims (Wiktorowicz 2001:134–135).

One common path into ostensibly legitimate organization passes through religious discussion groups. In Yemen and elsewhere, religious women often participate in Qur'anic (Koranic) study groups, or *nadwas*. These nadwas, Janine Clark reports,

> form an important part of women's informal networks. These Qur'anic study groups provide religious solace and guidance, an education in reading and in Islam, an emotional outlet, a social life outside of the home, and a support group for the women who attend them. They also provide an arena where a woman can go for advice or find out where (or to whom) she can go to alleviate her problem. Nadwas furthermore form an important link in the transmission of knowledge and education and education from female religious scholars to the next generation. While girls generally learn about Islam at home, those with a desire for broader knowledge seek out a nadwa in someone's home.
>
> (Clark 2004:169)

These discussion groups typically have shifting memberships and lack formal structure. Yet they figure prominently in Islamist fundraising, charitable activity, and mutual aid. Nadwas establish "free spaces" where authorities that fear militant Islam have trouble entering and where women who live mainly sequestered lives can mingle (Evans and Boyte 1986; Polletta 1999;

Singerman 1995). For all their justified worries about religious extremism. Yemeni authorities can hardly forbid middle-class women from gathering for religiously respectable sociability.

Nadwas do not qualify in themselves as trust networks, but they provide an opportunity for members of Islamist trust networks to enter safe spaces where they can advance their ideas and recruit new members. This they do, not so much recruiting openly in the course of Qur'anic discussions as spotting likely members and inviting them to other nadwas in which Islamists play larger parts (Clark 2004:178). Thus a subversive network combines concealment and dissimulation under the cover of evasive conformity.

Islamist trust networks do not always remain underground and are often segregated from the regimes within which they live. Much to the dismay of revolutionaries and secular reformers who had risen against Iran's Shah, a dissident Islamist network centering on the Ayatollah Ruhollah Khomeini seized power in Iran as the Shah's secular opposition fragmented (Kepel 2002:36–42, 106–135; Parsa 2000:247–250). Although the Algerian government's ruthless military action eventually drove back the Islamist *Groupe Islamique Armé*, those zealots and their massacres of civilians shook the regime mightily during the 1990s (Kalyvas 1999). ... In these cases, precisely what conservative Muslim rulers throughout the Middle East feared actually materialized: previously segregated trust networks made military bids for national power. In Iran, Sudan, and Afghanistan, they even succeeded in building their own theocracies, at least for a while. The thin control, intermittent coercion, and particularistic ties that rulers exercise in our zone of segregation neither give rulers access to resources embedded in trust networks nor contain the political threats they sometimes pose.

Negotiated Connections

To exploit and contain trust networks, rulers across the world often reached into them by means falling far short of full integration. They struck deals with trust networks' patrons in two different ways: patronage systems and brokered autonomy. In patronage systems, trust networks remained under the protection and control of powerful intermediaries who took responsibility for containing them, but also drew resources from them to meet their own obligations vis à vis the regime. Such patrons often came from outside the trust network, thirteenth-century villagers in Spain's Galicia, for example, protecting themselves from the demands of León's king by seeking the patronage of powerful local monasteries. The villages became clients of patrons who in turn kept their distance from the king.

Brokered autonomy likewise involves patronage, but with a significant difference. In brokered autonomy, rulers grant formal recognition to a trust network, which retains distinctive rights and representation in return for negotiated payoffs going directly to the regime. In many parts of the world, trade diasporas established one relationship or the other to rulers of major commercial centers; either they lived under the patronage of some regional magnate, or they acquired formal licenses to trade as recognized foreign communities.

Seen from the top down, trust networks receiving protection from patrons escape from the ruler's repression, but gain relatively little toleration and even less facilitation from rulers. Recipients of brokered autonomy, in contrast, acquire toleration and at least a modicum of facilitation from rulers. From the trust network's bottom-up perspective, either arrangement centers on clientage rather than on concealment, dissimulation, or predation. Members of trust networks always pay something for the protection they receive, but who receives the payment makes a difference to the network's autonomy. Brokered autonomy provides greater guarantees that members can maintain their collective way of life.

Long before the nationalism of our time, Europeans frequently called beneficiaries of brokered autonomy "nations," with the implication of shared nativity rather than attachment to a particular nation-state. In Medieval Europe, the "nation" commonly meant a corporate group from the same geographic region, although it could also refer to members of a recognized religion. Among its several definitions of nation, the *Oxford English Dictionary* offers this one;

> In the mediaeval universities, a body of students belonging to a particular district, country, or group of countries, who formed a more or less independent community; still retained in the universities of Glasgow and Aberdeen, in connexion with the election of the Rector.
>
> ("nation," definition 1c.)

In universities, cities, and other centers of consumption, such nations often elected their own officials and public representatives, provided for their own security, judged their own members' derelictions, and, in time of want, took responsibility for their own food supply. At their interfaces with local authorities, these common-origin trust networks created authoritative organizations. The very arrangement gave authorities pretexts and means for expelling whole communities—including religious minorities organized as nations—in times of famine, epidemic, or war (Tilly 1975:437–440).

As we might expect, brokered autonomy often formed through an initial act of patronage by some authority. During the European Middle Ages, for example, regional potentates often recruited their own Jewish communities in order to organize their finances, promote trade, benefit from international connections, and produce taxable revenue, Polish rulers often welcomed Jews for their commercial skills and connections. Royal invitations to Poland's cities promoted a substantial movement of German-speaking Jews eastward. Yiddish (a dialect built largely on German) then became a common language in important parts of Northeastern Europe. Similarly, many Iberian Jews moved to North Africa and the Ottoman Empire, where their Muslim hosts opened special niches for them. (Iberian-origin Jews more often spoke the dialect called Ladino than Yiddish.)

A number of Jews also migrated to the more tolerant Italian city-states. Venice opened a new residential area for Jews, who had previously lived on the island of Giudecca—meaning "Jewish district"—in 1516. People called the new space Ghetto, "foundry" in Venetian, for the metal-working industry already established there. Afterward, the word *ghetto* applied to any city's Jewish quarter. From the two movements toward Poland and the Mediterranean springs the still common distinction between Ashkenazi and Sephardic Jews.

Lois Dubin has painstakingly reconstructed the acquisition of brokered autonomy by the Jewish community of Trieste. In 1382, the port city of Trieste, on the Adriatic's northeast coast, turned to the Habsburgs (by then hereditary Holy Roman Emperors) for protection from predatory Venice. During centuries of Venetian power and, to the south, Ottoman expansion, Trieste remained a small, minor connection between Vienna and the bustling Adriatic. During the early eighteenth century, however, Habsburg emperors began building their commercial presence in the Mediterranean region, including an expansion of trade with the still-formidable Ottoman Empire. Between 1719 and 1769, step by step the Habsburgs created, then expanded a tax-free port with open access to merchants of many nations. The effort succeeded: Trieste became a prosperous city, and the Habsburg empire's chief maritime center.

Jews lived in Trieste as early as the thirteenth century, and served as the city's authorized public bankers for centuries:

> In the sixteenth and seventeenth centuries, certain Jewish individuals and families, such as the Levis in 1556 and Ventura Parente in 1624, resided in Trieste on the basis of the privileges granted them by Holy

Roman emperors in return for their services of 'goods and blood' in time of war. These privileges promised sovereign protection and justice; unmolested practice of Judaism; the right of residence in any town where Jews already lived, including Vienna; unrestricted economic activities, including ownership of real property; the right of travel without distinguishing signs or special taxes; and immunity from any taxes not imposed on Christian merchants.

(Dubin 1999:18–19)

For their time, the Catholic Habsburgs were granting Trieste's Jews generous privileges. In Metz, for example, the French crown imposed stiff head taxes, additional fees, and obligations to supply and lodge royal troops on the Jewish community, yet did not give its Jewish merchants the secure right to travel within the kingdom (Miskimin 2002:48–50).

Both Habsburg rulers and Trieste's municipal authorities were engaging in deliberate toleration, with a dollop of facilitation thrown in. The authorities were offering Trieste's Jews a measure of protection against the exploitation, violence, and vindictive anti-Semitism to which Jews elsewhere in Europe often fell prey. From the perspective of the city's Jews, full enlistment in the empire's public life set too high a price even if it were possible, since it would have required assimilation and conversion to Catholicism. Nor were concealment, dissimulation, or predation viable strategies for the Jews of Trieste. Clientage was the price they paid for protection.

Protection had its limits. Like their French cousins, the Habsburgs tried to contain the empire's Jewish populations. In 1697, after much wrangling with leaders of the Jewish community, the city established a formal ghetto, surrounded by three streets and protected by three gates, in the *Portizza di Riborgo* quarter. But free port activity spurred Jewish migration to Trieste, increased the Jewish community's prosperity, and multiplied the number of Jewish households enjoying particular permission to reside outside the ghetto. By the time of the ghetto's formal abolition in 1785, the majority of Trieste's Jewish population had long since lived elsewhere.

Nevertheless, the Jewish community maintained its brokered autonomy into the nineteenth century. Jews could not become citizens of Trieste, or serve on its governing council; they counted among the city's multiple recognized *nazioni*. (The regime used the revealing term *Università* to designate the Jewish and other such nations.) They maintained authorized but separate communal institutions. Calling its members *li Hebrei di Trieste*, the Jewish community conducted religious services, maintained a Jewish cemetery, controlled Jewish immigration, and imposed discipline on its unruly members. As the community grew, however, it formalized its relation to the regime. In 1746, it proposed and received government approval of an elaborate statute centering on an assembly of all tax-paying heads of households run and represented by two elected Capi. The 1746 Statute also institutionalized the offices of scribe, chancellor, rabbi, cantor, and beadle (Dubin 1999:22–23). Within Trieste's Jewish trust network, they created an authoritative—and officially recognized—organization.

By 1782, the community was creating its own regime-authorized normal school: the *Scuola Pia Normale sive Talmud Torà*. The school took up space in the same ghetto building that also contained community offices, a kosher butcher, and a synagogue (Dubin 1999:103). In 1788, when the Habsburg state became the first European power to draft Jews into its army, Trieste's news received exemption despite their leaders' expressed willingness to collaborate with the measure (Dubin 1999:148–152). Meanwhile, Trieste's news successfully resisted the Habsburg state's efforts to impose German names and regulate marriage according to civil law. Not for another half century did the formal vestiges of brokered autonomy disappear.

Integrated Networks

Because we have until now concentrated on distant and contingent relations between trust networks and regimes, extensively integrated trust networks have rarely appeared in this book so far. We saw them in:

- the temporary integration of locally recruited military units into the Confederate Army
- accommodations between communities formed by chain migration and their local governments
- pirates who became privateers
- the (often reluctant) integration of parishes and confraternities into Europe's state churches

with the exception of migrant communities, none of these tells us much about integration between trust networks and the powerful states of our own time. Unexpected news on the subject comes from Russia's world of crime and violence. At considerable risk to his own safety, Vadim Volkov entered the world of violent entrepreneurs in the mid-1990s. He begins his book on the subject:

> This book was triggered by an observation. In 1995, on my way to work, I used to walk past a mansion in central Petersburg that housed

the headquarters of the Northwestern Regional Anti-Organized Crime Directorate (RUBOP). Each time I would observe the same scene: people of formidable physical proportions, with very short haircuts, wearing leather jackets or long dark overcoats, walked out of the RUBOP headquarters, got into black cars with tinted windows, and departed in various directions. Others parked nearby and entered the mansion. What struck me each time was that these people looked, moved, and gesticulated very much like those whom they were supposed to be fighting—members of organized criminal groups, the so-called bandits.

(Volkov 2002:ix)

That observation led Volkov to a remarkable journey through the underside of the Soviet Union's disintegration.

In Soviet times, the government maintained a huge domestic security force, of which the KGB—the Committee for State Security—was best known outside the country. But in the interstices of the authoritarian system lurked petty criminals and enforcers who often came from sporting clubs: wrestlers, boxers, weight lifters, and martial arts experts. Mikhail Gorbachev's reforms of the 1980s produced four major changes in Russia's domestic security situation. First, the government greatly reduced its own professional security forces, throwing a large number of specialists in the use of force onto the private labor market. Second, the government consequently relaxed its surveillance and policing, giving more scope to criminals on the small scale and the large. Third, the withdrawal of the large Soviet army from its stalemate in Afghanistan poured thousands of combat-hardened veterans into the civilian labor force, where legitimate employment was hard to find. Finally, private businesses multiplied at all scales from local markets to privatized national industries. In the absence of effective policing, opportunities for extortion and protection rackets increased throughout Russia's commercially active regions.

At the bottom and the top, the enforcers who offered protective services at a price commonly belonged to trust networks: sworn bands of criminals, groups of sportsmen, former colleagues in the shady work of government security services, and veterans who had fought together in Afghanistan. Russian rates of reported extortion soared between 1989 and 1992, leveled off, and only started to decline in 1996 (Volkov 2002:2–3). In a large Petersburg market, according to one of Volkov's informants:

In 1989 in Deviatkino all brigades stood side by side; initially, there were no clear divisions between *tambovskie, malyshevskie, Kazanskie* [gang names] and so forth, as happened later. Each brigade *poluchala* [received tribute] from *kommersanty* [businessmen, traders] who were not involved with other brigades. There was plenty of room for everyone. We also set up our own *kommersanty*, provided them with trading spots, and then protected them for a fee. The only rule was that we not assault or rob each other's *kommersanty*.

(Volkov 2002:15)

Later, in Petersburg and elsewhere, gangs began killing each other off as they competed for larger shares of the protection racket. In the process they developed increasingly elaborate hierarchies and divisions of labor.

Enforcers did not only engage in extortion and protection rackets. They also went into the businesses of debt collection, illegal commodities, sexual services, and physical protection for businessmen. A rough three-way division of labor emerged among 1) old fashioned bandits, thugs, and thieves, 2) local racketeers and, 3) increasingly organized operators of private protective services in major cities and at a national scale. Through the later 1990s, Volkov argues, category 3 moved increasingly into the public sphere as legitimate business, essentially substituting commercial services for the policing, protection, and contract enforcement the state itself had ceased to provide. They also began to operate their own legitimate businesses, whether legally or illegally acquired. Their leaders came disproportionately, in fact, from the ranks of retired state specialists in law enforcement. In the process, the more successful among them were using their trust networks to create formidable, and increasingly recognized, authoritative organizations.

Some sportsmen also made it to the top. Volkov tells the tale of Boris Ivaniuzhenkov, who became the Russian minister of sports in 1999:

it took him four days to accept the offer by then prime minister Sergei Stepashin (former head of the MVD and then of the FSB) that he become minister of sports. In police files, Ivaniuzhenkov is known as 'Rotan,' the right-hand man of Sergei Lalakin ('Lotchok'), the leader of the Podol'skaya criminal group. Born in the suburban town of Podol'sk near Moscow, Ivaniuzhenkov embarked on a dual career, achieving the title of master of sports in wrestling and a leading position in the local racketeering group. Podol'sk, he claims, 'is the only town where there were never any feuds. The situation was always stable.' In other respects, *podol'skie* went through the same evolution as many other similar organizations. They took control of the local market, trades, and businesses, consolidating power in the locale and expanding beyond it. The ability to maintain order and to give generously to charity ... brought the violent entrepreneurs popular support: Lalakin 'Lutchok' was made an honorary citizen of Podol'sk, and Ivaniuzhenkov ('Rotan') was elected to the Moscow *oblast'* legislature in 1997.

(Volkov 2002:187)

In the career of wrestler-gangster Lutchok we witness the integration of formerly criminal trust networks—those of the Podol'skaya gang—into public politics.

The violence-wielding trust networks studied by Vadim Volkov pursued spectacular paths toward integration into Russian public politics. As Margaret Levi's analysis of conscription should remind us most paths toward the same of integration have a more familiar air. They include governments' establishment of veterans' benefits, recognition or incorporation of mutual benefit organizations, protection of religious congregations, institutionalization of craft-based interest groups, formation of ties between governmental service providers and their clienteles, development of solidarities within political parties or publicly active voluntary associations, and political sponsorship of musical groups, sports teams, or ethnic clubs. All these paths to integration move away from the concealment, dissimulation, and predation that prevail at the bottom of our range from segregation to integration. Some pass through the clientage of the middle zone. Some respond to the dissolution of previously existing trust networks. But all of them involve enlistment and bargaining to a far larger extent than the bulk of the trust networks we have examined so far.

Origins of Integration

Let us step away from the trajectories of particular trust networks to survey processes by which such networks become integrated into public politics. When that integration occurs, we should expect to find people creating publicly recognized associations, mutual-aid societies, parties, unions, congregations, and communities, or seeking recognition for similar organizations that have existed underground, pursuing friendship, kinship, shared belief, security, and high-risk enterprises within such organizations, and a whole series of other things connecting locally consequential long-term activities and interpersonal ties to the vagaries of public politics. Historically, such reliance on public political actors and governmental agents for support of risky activities and relations has rarely occurred.

In our sweep across history, nevertheless, we have already encountered some historical circumstances in which that rare outcome actually emerged. Trust networks in the form of religious sects, kinship groups, or mercantile networks have occasionally established their own systems of rule (example: John Calvin's religious conquest of Geneva). Regimes have sometimes conquered other regimes that were already run by trust networks (example: Canadian or U.S. conquest and incorporation of intact Indian tribes). Political actors organized as trust networks have sometimes seized state power in established regimes (example: the Taliban in Afghanistan). Once in power, rulers have often created their own trust networks in the forms of dynastic marriage alliances and internal patronage systems (examples: almost all European monarchies before the nineteenth century).

High levels of integration have actually occurred. At least temporarily, totalitarian and theocratic regimes have managed extensive incorporation of existing trust networks into authoritarian systems of rule (example: Italian Fascist integration of those craft organizations they did not destroy). Democracies, finally, accomplish partial integration of trust networks into public politics (example: the repeated extension of benefits to U.S. military veterans from the Civil War onward, which not only created individual rights but tied veterans' organizations directly to the state; Skocpol 1998).

Reculer pour mieux sauter: Having stepped back, we make a heroic leap. Among these marvelously varied historical circumstances, do some common processes occur? The *outcomes* certainly have some common properties. In all of them, a government and/or a political actor exercising regular relations with that government (for example, a state church or trade unions with their own internal networks of mutual aid) connects trust networks to public politics. In all of them (as Figure 20.1 predicts), facilitation by rulers combines with rulers' reliance on commitment in addition to coercion and capital, with the result of a relatively stable integration of trust networks into political regimes.

How, in general, could that rare historical occurrence actually happen? Among all the possible transforming processes, here are the most promising candidates:

1   Existing segregated trust networks shrivel, disintegrate, or lose capacity to sustain their members' vital activities, thus making their constituencies more readily available for politically connected trust networks.
2   New risks and risky activities appear against which existing trust networks are incapable of defending their members.
3   Populations multiply outside of existing trust networks, thereby becoming available for politically connected trust networks.

4   Rulers or major political actors destroy existing trust networks, with similar effects.
5   Rulers or major political actors effectively integrate existing networks into public politics.
6   Rulers or major political actors create politically connected networks and recruit people to them.

We have seen how energetically members of trust networks across history have fought off these six processes, striving both to maintain their own networks and to shield them from political intervention. We have seen them defending their boundaries, securing external resources, monitoring members' external connections, and exerting control over internal social relations that might disrupt their networks' collective activities.

The major exceptions were members of ruling classes, who could bend the state to their own ends instead of fearing that its intervention in their trust networks would frustrate those ends. Even they typically moved into relations with governments and other major political actors tentatively, often relying on intermediaries with whom they had already established relations of trust as their initial connectors. Such intermediaries often included kin, churchmen, commercial collaborators, landlords, and local power holders who also occupied positions of power at a national scale. Those intermediaries served as brokers in the process of integration.

The new Dutch state, unlike its European rivals, already enjoyed excellent credit during the seventeenth century. The Netherlands' seventeenth-century revolt against Spain led to an ordering of public finances in that supremely commercial regime. In the process, Dutch burghers began investing furiously in government securities, thus tying their families' fates to that of the regime:

> In part, the Dutch success must be explained by the fact that the chief investors were magistrates and politicians themselves. They were close enough to their local receiver with whom they had contracted loans. At times, they were urged to invest by their political leaders so as to stimulate other buyers. The federal structure implied also a large degree of local political control. Other secure investments were found in land and houses, but already by 1700 the capital invested in government bonds exceeded all other.
>
> ('t Hart 1993:178)

The segmented structure of the Dutch Republic facilitated the work of brokers who simultaneously occupied municipal, provincial, and national positions of power. They helped make the Dutch Republic precocious in its integration of elite trust networks (Adams 1994a, 1994b; Davids and Lucassen 1995; Glete 2002). It took another two centuries before ordinary Europeans and North Americans began investing major parts of their savings in government securities.

Sooner or later, however, it happened widely. Ordinary people face risks and carry on risky long-term enterprises even when their available trust networks fail to give them adequate protection. In those circumstances, governments or political actors that can either shore up existing networks or create new alternatives to them become more attractive—or at least less unattractive—allies. As the Dutch example suggests, some additional circumstances increase the attractiveness of politically connected trust networks to a broad public: creation of external guarantees for governmental commitments, as when a peace treaty or an occupying power backs up a defeated government's finances; increase in governmental resources for risk reduction and/or compensation of loss, as when commercial expansion generates new tax revenues; and visible governmental meeting of commitments to the advantage of substantial new segments of the population, as when noncitizens not only become eligible for welfare benefits but actually receive them.

The Integration of Proletarians

In Western history of the last half millennium, one large process has swamped all others in its promotion of items 1 to 3 on our list of transforming processes: failure of existing trust networks, appearance of new risks, and multiplication of populations outside of existing trust networks. That process is proletarianization, an increase in the share of the total population depending on wages for survival and/or working at means of production over which they exercise little or no control. Europe experienced stupendous growth in its proletarian population after 1500. My own best guesses of total European population by category from 1500 to 1900 appear in Table 20.1. They suggest massive proletarianization, with a surprising proportion of it occurring in small towns and rural areas before the urban proletarianization of the nineteenth century.

Three major factors converged in producing this explosive growth: capitalist consolidation of control over the means of production, including agricultural land; multiplication of opportunities for wage labor in agriculture, cottage industry, and (later) in urban production of goods and services; and a natural increase in a proletariat that, on the average, married earlier and had

Table 20.1   Estimated Proletarianization of the European Population, 1500–1900

	Millions of people		
	1500	1800	1900
total population	56	150	285
nonproletarians	39	50	85
proletarians in cities	1	10	75
rural proletarians	16	90	125
% of total proletarian	30.0	66.7	70.2

Source: Tilly 1984:36.

more children than its counterparts in land-owning and tool-owning labor (Levine 1984; Tilly 1984).

Wage-earning proletarians became even more vulnerable to seasonal and longer-term economic swings than were most peasants and artisans. They survived more or less well when landlords and merchants hired them, but did badly in times of unemployment. Yet landlords and merchants could not do without them. Thus poverty became a problem for public policy at the municipal and national scales. Critics of the poor, including rulers, created a public mythology castigating vagabonds, wastrels, beggars, and idle lay-abouts for their lack of prudence and self-discipline. At the same time, however, authorities organized disciplined provision for the labor force in times of need. "In sum," comment Catharina Lis and Hugo Soly,

> during the late fifteenth and early sixteenth centuries the criticism of idleness and its counterpart, the exaltation of work, became major themes in the writings of both prominent men and middling people, laity and clergy, and Catholics and Protestants throughout western Europe. Their reaction was not limited to mere words. In the Netherlands (1531), France (1534), England (1531 and especially 1536), Scotland (1535), and Spain (1541), the central authorities proclaimed ordinances concerning begging and/or poor relief; detailed regulations were, however, relegated to the local governments. Between 1522 and 1545 some 62 towns created a coordinated system of public assistance: at least 30 in Germany, 15 or 16 in the Low Countries, 8 in France,

6 in Switzerland, and 2 in northern Italy. In nearly all towns two principles dominated: strict prohibition of begging for the able-bodied poor, regardless of age and sex, in order to compel them to accept work at any wage, and centralization of existing funds into a 'common box' to enable the selection and control of the 'true needy.'

(Lis and Soly 1984:168; see also Lis and Soly 1979)

The distinction between the worthy and unworthy poor hinged especially on the readiness of the worthy to perform disciplined low-wage work when the opportunity arrived. Moralists and authorities alike condemned idleness and improvidence. They both blamed poor people for profligacy. But at least local authorities recognized the necessity of tiding the worthy over recurrent bouts of unemployment, seasonal or longer term.

Few historians, alas, have documented interactions among proletarianization, poor relief, and trust networks. In a painstaking study of Amsterdam's poor relief between 1800 and 1850, Marco van Leeuwen has nevertheless established several crucial points. He uncovers an elaborate system of poor relief divided chiefly among Catholic, Calvinist, Jewish, and municipal authorities. Each one kept meticulous records of its clientele; hence the possibility of van Leeuwen's analysis. Each one imposed extensive conditions of membership, worthiness, and eligibility: were the applicants faithful and upright members of their religious congregations? Did they genuinely lack opportunities to earn wages honestly? Did they have secret accumulations of wealth? Could other people take responsibility for their welfare?

In 1809, such rules produced a clientele of 1,968 adults for the Ashkenazi Charity; two thirds consisted of the elderly, the infirm, widows with children, and/or families with three or more children (van Leeuwen 2000:107). Even in these cases, van Leeuwen shows, poor relief usually amounted to no more than a supplement, far short of enough money for survival. Amsterdam's poor households were surely relying on local trust networks, however fragile, for much of the rest.

Because Amsterdam's poor Jews concentrated in street vending, garment making, domestic service, and a few other low-paying trades, Jewish charities' clientele differed from those of other charitable organizations. Dockers led by far among the men aided by the municipal and Lutheran charities (van Leeuwen 2000:112). As an important port, Amsterdam swung from intense economic activity during the warm months to a frequent standstill during the winter. Van Leeuwen argues persuasively that Amsterdam's authorities adopted an implicit policy of fixing a mobile labor force in place by supplying just enough poor relief in the off season to allow dockers and similar workers to get through the year without emigrating. The same system permitted the authorities to exercise moral surveillance and control.

Not all of Amsterdam's workers, however, depended on public poor relief. Craftsmen generally belonged to guilds, which paid benefits far higher than poor relief to their sick, disabled, and aged members as well as to widows and children of deceased craftsmen. In 1811, Amsterdam had about 14,000 guild members in a total city population of about 200,000 (van Leeuwen 2000:167). As the nineteenth century wore on, voluntary mutual-aid societies, sickness benefit groups, and burial associations all became popular; by century's end, some 40 percent of the city's population belonged to a mutual-benefit association of some kind (van Leeuwen 2000:166). But all these varieties of trust networks operated with official sanction, under public scrutiny. Although van Leeuwen does not put it this way, he is describing the integration of popular trust networks into public politics. He is describing the early phases of a momentous transformation, a reversal of age-old segregation.

Citing van Leeuwen along the way, Peter Lindert has greatly generalized the story. Looking at a large number of countries, he has established how regularly economic expansion has led to formation of redistributive systems of social spending, especially as ordinary workers acquired political voice. "Since the eighteenth century," he remarks,

> the rise of tax-based social spending has been at the heart of government growth. It was social spending, not national defense, public transportation, or government enterprises, that accounted for most of the rise in governments' taxing and spending as a share of GDP over the last two centuries.
>
> (Lindert 2004:I, 20)

But wage-labor became more central to economies, first in the West and then across the world. As it did so, redistributive social spending skyrocketed. Most of that increase has occurred recently. Before the twentieth century, as the Amsterdam case illustrates, social spending never sufficed to maintain poor people in idleness, much less to entice them away from viable employment. Conservative critics to the contrary notwithstanding, Lindert challenges the view that welfare benefits sap initiative.

Lindert concludes that social spending stabilized the labor force and increased its productive capacity. Because it did so, even very high levels of expenditure occurred at little or no net cost to the whole economy. Amsterdam's city fathers were anticipating a strategy that eventually attracted capitalists and public authorities across the world. But capitalists and public authorities did not simply drift in an irresistible river. Which policies governments adopted, Lindert continues, depended closely on the organization of public politics. Great Britain led Europe in poor relief between the 1780s and 1834 because its great-landlords invested in retaining their agricultural labor force. But when the Reform Act of 1832 gave industrial capitalists new voice, a dramatic cutback in benefits occurred (Lindert 2004:I, 67–86).

References

Adams, Julia. 1994a. "The Familial State: Elite Family Practices and State-Making in the Early Modern Netherlands," *Theory and Society* 23: 505–540.
———. 1994b. "Trading States, Trading Places: The Role of Patrimonialism in Early Modern Dutch Development." *Comparative Studies in Society and History* 36(2):319–55.
Clark, Janine A. 2004. *Islam, Charity, and Activism: Middle-Class Social Networks and Social Welfare in Egypt, Jordan, and Yemen*. Bloomington: Indiana University Press.
Davids, Karel and Jan Lucassen, eds. 1995. *A Miracle Mirrored: The Dutch Republic in European Perspective*. Cambridge: Cambridge University Press.
Dubin, Lois C. 1999. *The Port Jews of Habsburg Trieste: Absolutist Politics and Enlightenment Culture*. Stanford, CA: Stanford University Press.
Evans, Sara M. and Harry C. Boyte. 1986. *Free Spaces: The Sources of Democratic Change in America*. New York: Harper & Row.
Glete, Jan. 2002. *War and the State in Early Modern Europe: Spain, the Dutch Republic, and Sweden as Fiscal-Military States, 1500–1660*. London: Routledge.
't Hart, Marojolein. 1993. *The Making of a Bourgeois State: War, Politics and Finance during the Dutch Revolt*. Manchester: Manchester University Press.
Kalyvas, Stathis N. 1999. "Wanton and Senseless? The Logic of Massacres in Algeria," *Rationality and Society* 11: 243–285.
Kepel, Gilles. 2002. *Jihad: The Trial of Political Islam*. Cambridge, MA: Harvard University Press.
van Leeuwen, Marco H. D. 2000. *The Logic of Charity: Amsterdam, 1800–1850*. London: Macmillan.
Levi, Margaret. 1997. *Consent, Dissent and Patriotism*. Cambridge: Cambridge University Press.
Levine, David. 1984. "Production, Reproduction, and the Proletarian Family in England, 1500–1851" in David Levine, ed., *Proletarianization and Family History*. Orlando, FL: Academic Press, pp. 87–28.
Lindert, Peter H. 2004. *Growing Public: Social Spending and Economic Growth Since the Eighteenth Century*. Cambridge: Cambridge University Press. 2 vols.
Lis, Catharina and Hugo Soly. 1979. *Poverty and Capitalism in Pre-Industrial Europe*. Atlantic Highlands, NJ: Humanities Press.
———. 1984. "Policing the Early Modern Proletariat, 1450–1850" in David Levine, ed., *Proletarianization and Family History*. Orlando, FL: Academic Press.
Miskimin, Patricia Behre. 2002. *One King, One Law, Three Faiths: Religion and the Rise of Absolutism in Seventeenth-Century Metz*. Westport, CT: Greenwood.

Parsa, Misagh. 2000. *States, Ideologies, and Social Revolutions: A Comparative Analysis of Iran, Nicaragua and the Philippines.* Cambridge: Cambridge University Press.

Polletta, Francesca. 1999. "'Free Spaces' in Collective Action," *Theory and Society* 28: 1–38.

Singerman, Diane. 1995. *Avenues of Participation: Family, Politics, and Networks in Urban Quarters of Cairo.* Princeton, NJ: Princeton University Press.

———. 2004. "The Networked World of Islamist Social Movements" in Quintan Wiktorowicz, ed., *Islamic Activism: A Social Movement Theory Approach.* Bloomington: Indiana University Press, pp. 143–163.

Skocpol, Theda. 1998. "Did the Civil War Further American Democracy? A Reflection on the Expansion of Benefits for Union Veterans" in Theda Skocpol, ed., *Democracy, Revolution, and History.* Ithaca, NY: Cornell University Press, pp. 73–101.

Tilly, Charles. 1975. "Food Supply and Public Order in Modern Europe" in Charles Tilly, ed., *The Formation of National States in Western Europe.* Princeton, NJ: Princeton University Press.

———. 1984. "Demographic Origins of the European Proletariat" in David Levine, ed., *Proletarianization and Family History.* Orlando, FL: Academic Press.

Volkov, Vadim. 2002. *The Monopoly of Force: Violent Entrepreneurs in Russia's Emerging Markets.* Ithaca, NY: Cornell University Press.

White, Richard. 1991. *The Middle Ground: Indians, Empires, and Republics in the Great Lakes Region, 1650–1815.* Cambridge: Cambridge University Press.

Wiktorowicz, Quintan. 2001. *The Management of Islamic Activism: Salafis, the Muslim Brotherhood, and the State Power in Jordan.* Albany: SUNY Press.

Narratives and Explanations

VII

Why Give Reasons?   **21**

Charles Tilly

The first observers simply tried to figure out what was happening. On the morning of September 11, 2001, at 8:19 AM, flight attendant Betty Ong called American Airlines' Southeastern Reservations Office in Cary, North Carolina. She phoned from American Flight 11, which had left Boston for Los Angeles at 8 AM. In North Carolina, Ong reached Nydia Gonzalez. Ong told Gonzalez that hijackers had taken over their flight, had stabbed two other flight attendants, had killed at least one passenger, and had sprayed her and others with a substance that made their eyes burn and gave them trouble breathing (9/11 2004:5).

At 8:27, Gonzalez relayed Ong's call to Craig Marquis, duty manager at American Airlines' operations center in Forth Worth, Texas. At about the same time, air traffic controllers reported that the flight had made a sharp turn south near Albany, New York. "'They're going to New York!' Mr. Marquis remembers shouting out. 'Call Newark and JFK and tell them to expect a hijacking,' he ordered, assuming the hijackers would land the plane. 'In my wildest dreams, I was not thinking the plane was going to run into a building,' Mr. Marquis says" (CBS News 2002:47). Veteran duty manager Marquis reasonably mapped the hijacking of Flight 11 into vivid previous episodes during which captors had demanded money, asylum, or release of political prisoners. They had grabbed the plane, he supposed, to hold the aircraft, its crew, and its passengers hostage for concessions. At nearly the same time, Boston air traffic controllers were telling the Federal Aviation Administration's Command Center that hijackers had probably taken over the plane (Duenes *et al.* 2004:A16). Continuing her whispered chronicle of events aboard the aircraft, at 8:38 Betty Ong reported that the plane was descending. Her call was cut off abruptly at 8:44 (9/11 2004:6).

The hijackers of Flight 11 soon proved Craig Marquis's reasons wrong. Two minutes after Gonzalez lost phone contact with Betty Ong, chief inspector Kevin McCabe of the U.S. Customs Service was looking east from his office window in Elizabeth, New Jersey. "He was sipping coffee and talking on the phone at 8:46," he later reported to Steven Brill, "when he saw the first plane hit the World Trade Center. Because he had seen how big the plane was, he thought it might be an attack. He flipped on the television, then called the Customs office in New York, which was at the Trade Center, to find out what was going on" (Brill 2003:1).

A few minutes after McCabe's call to headquarters, Bryant Gumbel was broadcasting for CBS News from Manhattan. He had just heard that an unidentified plane had crashed into the World Trade Center. At 8:52, his first eyewitness on the line was Stewart Nurick, who was waiting a table in a SoHo restaurant when "I literally saw a ... it seemed to be a small plane. ... I just heard a couple noises, it looked like it bounced off the building, and then I just saw a huge ball of fire on top of the building. And just lots of smoke and what looked to be debris or glass falling down" (CBS News 2002:16).

It was about two minutes past nine.

Gumbel switched to a third eyewitness, Theresa Renaud, who was watching the World Trade Center from her apartment at Eighth Avenue and Sixteenth Street, about two miles north of the Center. "Approximately ten minutes ago," reported Renaud,

> there was a major explosion from about the 80th floor—looks like it's affected probably four to eight floors. Major flames are coming out of the north side and also the east side of the building. It was a very loud explosion, followed by flames, and it looks like the building is still on fire on the inside.
>
> Oh, there's another one—another plane just hit. [gasps; yelling] Oh, my God! Another plane has just hit—it hit another building, flew right into the middle of it. My God, it's right in the middle of the building.
>
> GUMBEL: This one into [Tower 2]?
>
> RENAUD: Yes, yes, right in the middle of the building. ... That was definitely ... on purpose.
>
> GUMBEL: Why do you say that was definitely on purpose?
>
> RENAUD: Because it just flew straight into it.
>
> (CBS News 2002:18)

Filmmaker Jules Naudet, who had been producing a documentary on a downtown Manhattan fire company, had gone to the scene with the battalion chief after the first plane crashed into the World Trade Center. He was filming firefighters' actions in the lobby of the North Tower, the first tower hit, when the second aircraft struck the other tower: "Suddenly we heard an explosion coming from outside, and as I turned to look out the windows, I saw flaming debris falling in the courtyard and then heard a radio call announcing that Tower 2 had been hit by another plane. Any thought that this was simply a terrible accident vanished: New York was under attack" (CBS News 2002:23). Washington, D.C., was also under attack. A perplexing calamity had begun.

When commandeered commercial aircraft crashed into New York's World Trade Center, Washington's Pentagon, and a Pennsylvania field that September morning, people across the world began asking for reasons why. Why had someone perpetrated this vicious violence? Why had they targeted the United States? Why hadn't American authorities prevented the assault? Observers quickly shifted from simply making sense of what was happening to seeking reasons for the disaster. Direct participants faced the double challenge of finding reasons both for the terrible episode as a whole and for the specific incidents they had suffered, witnessed, or caused.

On the scene, emergency workers activated their routines without asking too many questions. Only as they worked did they start searching seriously for credible reasons for the disaster they were seeing. New York Fire Department Paramedic Gary Smiley, for example, was working overtime in downtown Brooklyn when the radio in his ambulance broadcast word that a plane had hit the 110-story North Tower (Tower 1) of the World Trade Center. The call had come at 8:48 AM. Within a few minutes, Smiley's crew rushed across the Brooklyn Bridge to Manhattan.

Smiley set up a triage area between the two towers. He was carrying an injured woman who had just left Tower 1 across the street when the woman started shouting "Plane." He looked up and saw the second aircraft hit the South Tower (Tower 2). It was 9:03 AM, just seventeen minutes after the first crash. Debris began falling on them, so partway across the street he pushed the woman to the ground and threw himself on top of her. A severed, burning human arm scorched his back. "It was chaos," he later reported. "Everyone was running around. Then it clicked in my head. I knew exactly what was going on. I was there in 1993 when they bombed the building. I ended up taking care of a hundred people across the street in the Millennium Hotel. So I knew this was an attack. That's what we started telling people, and that's what got them moving" (Fink and Mathias 2002:33). Smiley first figured out his own reasons for what was happening, then told other people those reasons. By his account, people not only accepted his reasons, but also acted on them at once. He moved his ambulance to a safer location, evaded the falling bodies of people who were jumping to their deaths from the highest floors of the North Tower, and started into the tower for rescue operations. At that point (9:50 AM) the South Tower fell into flaming ruins.

What Reasons for This Book?

As eyewitnesses at the World Trade Center and Pentagon searched for reasons, they followed an extremely general human routine. We might even define human beings as reason-giving animals. While, by some definitions, other primates employ language, tools, and even culture, only humans start offering and demanding reasons while young, then continue through life looking for reasons why.

Reasons provide organized answers to the question "Why does (did, should) X do Y?" X can be you as you tell me why you arrived late for our rendezvous, me as I explain my winning of the lottery, or the hijackers who piloted aircraft into the World Trade Center and the Pentagon. X need not be a person or people; X can be God, evil spirits, Islam, communism, or just plain Them. X sometimes means individuals, groups, organizations, categories, forces, or invisible entities. X produces Y.

The World Trade Center disaster provoked reason giving at multiple levels, including:

- Why did the hijackers seize the aircraft and crash them into the towers?
- Why did the buildings burst into flames and collapse?
- (In the case of a participant) Why did I behave as I did? Why did *we* (whatever the we) behave as we did?
- (In the cases of participants and observers) Why did other people (considered as individuals or as groups) behave as they did?
- What causes terrorism?
- What causes violence in general?

Moving among multiple levels, this book looks sympathetically but searchingly at reason giving. It asks how, why, and in what different ways people supply reasons for the things they do, that others do, that happen to them, or that happen to other people—not so much grand general reasons for life, evil, or human frailty as the concrete reasons that different sorts of people supply or accept as they go about their daily business, deal with hardship, pass judgment on each other, or face emergencies such as the 9/11 disaster.

This book focuses on the social side of reason giving: how people share, communicate, contest, and collectively modify accepted reasons rather than how individual nervous systems process new information as it comes in. It worries little about whether the reasons people give are right or wrong, good or bad, plausible or implausible. Instead, it concentrates on the social process of giving reasons. Nor does it spend much time on general intellectual discussions of why things occur as they do, much less on how to resolve broad disagreements about reasons for big events.

The attacks of 9/11 inspired plenty of debate. "There is no disputing," comment the editors of a volume concerning the implications of 9/11, "that the underlying significance of September 11 can only be comprehended when placed in its full context, yet the boundaries of that context are themselves hotly contested" (Hershberg and Moore 2002:1). Seriously proposed reasons for 9/11, the editors go on to say, include al-Qaeda fanaticism, misguided American foreign policy, peculiar characteristics of Middle Eastern regimes, collapse of a previously stable (if dangerous) world order, and more. All those themes sound quite familiar to me. Most of my own professional work involves sorting out reasons for political processes at a broad scale: why revolutions occur, what causes democratization and de-democratization, why terrorism takes its many forms, and so on. Instead of sorting out such broad political questions, however, this book concentrates on the social process of giving reasons at the person-to-person scale. Reason giving turns out to be momentous at this scale as well.

Giving of reasons, as we will soon see, connects people with each other even when observers might find the reasons flimsy, contrived, or fantastic. In uncertain situations such as the 9/11 attacks, most people first adapt reasons for what is happening from models they have already learned through interaction with other people. Available models vary dramatically from group to group, situation to situation, and relation to relation. Regardless of their content, however, reasons provide rationales for behaving one way or another and shared accounts of what is happening. They also make statements about relations between the people giving and receiving those reasons.

Varieties of Reasons

Whether public officials, emergency workers, or community college students, people do not give themselves and others reasons because of some universal craving for truth or coherence. They often settle for reasons that are superficial, contradictory, dishonest, or—at least from an observer's viewpoint—farfetched. Whatever else they are doing when they give reasons, people are clearly negotiating their social lives. They are saying something about relations between themselves and those who hear their reasons. Giver and receiver are confirming, negotiating, or repairing their proper connection.

Commonly given reasons fall into four overlapping categories.

1 *Conventions:* conventionally accepted reasons for dereliction, deviation, distinction, or good fortune: my train was late, your turn finally came, she has breeding, he's just a lucky guy, and so on
2 *Stories:* explanatory narratives incorporating cause-effect accounts of unfamiliar phenomena or of exceptional events such as the 9/11 catastrophe, but also such as betrayal by a friend, winning a big prize, or meeting a high school classmate at Egypt's pyramids twenty years after graduation
3 *Codes* governing actions such as legal judgments, religious penance, or awarding of medals
4 *Technical Accounts* of the outcomes in the first three: how a structural engineer, a dermatologist, or an orthopedic surgeon might explain what happened to Elaine Duch on the World Trade Center's 88th floor after a hijacked aircraft struck the building on 9/11

Each of the four ways of giving reasons has distinctive properties. Each of them varies in content depending on social relations between giver and receiver. Each of them, among other consequences, exerts effects on those social relations, confirming an existing relation, repairing that relation, claiming a new relation, or denying a relational claim. But the four sorts of reason giving differ significantly in form and content. Each can be valid in a way that the others cannot.

Conventions involve no pretense of providing adequate causal accounts. If I start explaining in detail why I spilled my coffee on your newspaper—how I had a bad night's sleep, have been worrying about my job, recently developed a tremor it is hard to control—you may well become impatient. "Oops, I'm such a klutz!" may suffice, especially if

I offer to get you a fresh newspaper. ("Sorry, I tripped on the rug" might also do.) Conventions vary enormously according to the social circumstances; given an identical dereliction, deviation, or good fortune, for example, a reason that satisfies a seatmate on the bus will usually not placate one's spouse. Conventions claim, confirm, repair, or deny social relations. They therefore differ greatly depending on the social relations currently in play.

Exceptional events and unfamiliar phenomena, however, call up different reasons why; they call up *stories*. People experiencing an egregious failure, a signal victory, a spectacular faux pas, a shared tragedy, or mysterious sounds in the night do not settle for "It was just the breaks." They, too, try to match reasons to the circumstances and social relations at hand, but now the reasons take on weight. Similarly, major life transitions such as marriage, divorce, or the death of a parent call for weightier accounts than conventions provide. In general, reasons for exceptional events complement explanations with at least hints of justification or condemnation: the company gave me a bigger bonus than you because I worked harder and sold more computers. Implied claims concerning the quality, intensity, durability, and propriety of relations between givers and receivers far exceed the claims tied to conventions.

Stories matter greatly for social life because of three distinctive characteristics. First, they rework and simplify social processes so that the processes become available for the telling; X did Y to Z conveys a memorable image of what happened. Second, they include strong imputations of responsibility, and thus lend themselves to moral evaluations: I get the credit, he gets the blame, they did us dirt. This second feature makes stories enormously valuable for evaluation after the fact, and helps account for people's changing stories of events in which they behaved less than heroically. Third, stories belong to the relationships at hand, and therefore vary from one relationship to another; a television interviewer gets a different story of a lost football game from the one that players tell each other.

Further, stories truncate cause-effect connections. They typically call up a limited number of actors whose dispositions and actions cause everything that happens within a delimited time and space. The actors sometimes include supernatural beings and mysterious forces—for example, in witchcraft as an explanation of misfortune—but the actors' dispositions and actions explain what happened. As a consequence, stories inevitably minimize or ignore the causal roles of errors, unanticipated consequences, indirect effects, incremental effects, simultaneous effects, feedback effects, and environmental effects (Tilly 1995, 1996). They conform to dominant modes of storytelling. In fact, most of the early reason giving for 9/11 took the form of stories.

In contrast to stories, *codes* need not bear much explanatory weight so long as they conform to the available rules. (When I served the U.S. Navy as a rule-wielding supply and disbursing officer, veteran Chief Petty Officer Edward McGroarty, who helped train me on the job, used to joke, "There's no reason for it: it's just policy!") Religious prescriptions, law codes, and prestigious systems of honors overflow with reasons, but those reasons describe how what happened conforms to the code at hand rather than what actually caused the outcome. Third parties such as judges, priests, and awards committees figure extensively in the giving of reasons according to codes.

When we wanted to copy some crucial and voluminous nineteenth century household records from Milan, Louise Tilly and I had an instructive encounter with codes proposed by Ragionier [Accountant] Ciampan, director of Milan's municipal archives. First the Ragionier dismissed us by insisting that only the city's mayor could authorize outsiders to use the records. When we pulled strings and actually returned with a letter from the mayor, I asked the Ragionier when I could start setting up my camera. The small man strode to a huge book of municipal regulations on their stand by the window, opened to a passage declaring that "no one external to the archives may photograph their contents," placed his hand on the great book, raised his other hand in the air, and declared, "I am bound by the law." We painfully copied the records by hand.

Finally, *technical accounts* vary enormously with regard to internal structure and content, but they have in common the claim to identify reliable connections of cause and effect. As he reflected on his futile attempt to kick open a fireproof door on the World Trade Center's 76th floor, Gerry Gaeta supplemented his initial story about the terrorists' foresight with a cause-effect account based on his expertise as an architect. Structural engineers center their cause-effect connections in mechanical principles, physicians in the dynamics of organisms, and economists in market-driven processes. Although engineers, physicians, and economists sometimes spend great energy in justifying their expertise when under attack, earnestly demonstrating that they reached their conclusions by widely accepted professional procedures, on the whole they center their giving of reasons on putative causes and effects. Whole professions and organized bodies of professional knowledge stand behind them.

Roughly speaking, then, reasons why distribute this way:

	Popular	Specialized
Formulas	Conventions	Codes
Cause-Effect Accounts	Stories	Technical Accounts

From left to right, the diagram represents the extent to which ordered, disciplined, internally coherent schemes dominate reason giving, with "popular" reasons being widely accessible, and "specialized" reasons relying on extensive training in the discourse. Top to bottom, the diagram runs from X-to-Y matching, in which criteria of appropriateness rather than causality prevail (formulas), to tracing of causal processes from X to Y (cause-effect accounts). Obviously, the scheme orders claims made by givers and/or accepted by receivers rather than any judgment of their adequacy by third parties, including you and me.

All four kinds of reasons commonly do relational work. The most invisible work simply *confirms* the relation between giver and receiver, visibly, reason giving often *establishes* relations, as in the case of an interviewer who explains the purpose of a survey when calling to ask about preferences in food, television, or politics. It sometimes *negotiates* relations, as when the author of a technical account displays professional credentials to make a claim on a listener's respect and compliance. Finally, much reason giving *repairs* relations, as someone who has inflicted damage on someone else tells a story to show that the damage was inadvertent or unavoidable and therefore, despite appearances, does not reflect badly on the relationship between giver and receiver. The phrase "I'm sorry, but ..." often starts a story that does relational repairs. Both formulas and cause-effect accounts do relational work.

Specialized reasons likewise vary strikingly from discipline to discipline; theologians elaborate both codes and technical accounts that differ deeply from those proposed by medical practitioners.

Sophisticated readers should guard against an easy and erroneous pair of assumptions: that popular reasons peddle inferior, ignorant, and excessively simplified versions of codes and technical accounts, and that truly sophisticated people therefore never resort to conventions or stories. We sophisticates easily make the mistake because we frequently have to translate our own codes or technical accounts into terms that people who work in other idioms will understand.

In everyday life, we all deploy practical knowledge. We draw practical knowledge not only from individual experience but also from the social settings in which we live. Practical knowledge ranges from logics of appropriateness (formulas) to credible explanations (cause-effect accounts). Appropriateness and credibility vary from one social setting to another.

Reason giving resembles what happens when people deal with unequal social relations in general (Bashi Bobb 2001; Burguière and Grew 2002; Fitch 1998; Gould 2003; Schwartz 1975; Scott 1990; Tilly 2001). Participants in unequal social relations may detect, confirm, reinforce, or challenge them, but as they do so they deploy modes of communication that signal which of these things they are doing. In fact, the ability to give reasons without challenge usually accompanies a position of power. In extreme cases such as high public offices and organized professions, authoritative reason giving comes with the territory (Abbott 1988). Whatever else happens in the giving of reasons, givers and receivers are negotiating definitions of their equality or inequality.

Here are some possibilities that the analogy between negotiation of inequality and reason giving suggests:

- Within their own jurisdictions, professional givers promote and enforce the priority of codes and technical accounts over conventions and stories.
- In particular, professional givers generally become skilled at translating conventions and stories into their preferred idioms, and at coaching other people to collaborate in that translation.
- Hence the greater the professionalization of knowledge in any social setting, the greater the predominance of codes and technical accounts.
- To the extent that relations between giver and receiver are distant and/ or giver occupies a superior rank, giver provides formulas rather than cause-effect accounts.
- Givers who offer formulas thereby claim superiority and/or distance.
- Receivers ordinarily challenge such claims, when they do, by demanding cause-effect accounts.
- Those demands typically take the forms of expressing skepticism about the proposed formula and asking for detail on how and why Y actually occurred.
- In the case of authoritatively delivered codes, however, a skilled receiver can also challenge the reasons given by deploying the code and demonstrating that giver has misused it.

- Even in the presence of distance and/or inequality, to the extent that receiver has visible power to affect giver's subsequent welfare, giver moves from formulas toward cause-effect accounts.

Most of us feel more comfortable challenging the reasons given by taxi drivers than those proposed by physicians. But in either case we are, among other things, negotiating definitions of the relations between us.

Working as a historian and social scientist, I inevitably give more attention to historical and social scientific analysis than to other ways of thought. But I hope that by the end of the book even readers who have their doubts about the explanatory power of history and social science will gain insight into what happens when people in their own worlds start giving, receiving, and negotiating reasons.

References

9/11. National Commission on Terrorist Attacks Upon the United States. 2004. *The 9/11 Commission Report.* New York: Norton.

Abbott, Andrew. 1988. *The System of Professions: An Essay on the Division of Expert Labor.* Chicago: University of Chicago Press.

Bashi Bobb, Vilna. 2001. "Neither Ignorance nor Bliss: Race, Racism, and the West Indian Immigrant Experience." In *Migration, Transnationalization, and Race in a Changing New York,* edited by Héctor R. Cordero-Guzmán, Robert C. Smith and Ramón Grosfoguel, 212–238. Philadelphia: Temple University Press.

Brill, Steven. 2003. *After: How America Confronted the September 12 Era.* New York: Simon and Schuster.

Burguière, André, and Raymond Grew, eds. 2002. *The Construction of Minorities: Cases for Comparison Across Time and Around the World.* Ann Arbor: University of Michigan Press.

CBS News. 2002. *What We Saw.* New York: Simon and Schuster.

Duenes, Steve, Matthew Ericson, William McNulty, Brett Taylor, Hugh K. Truslow, and Archie Tse. 2004. "Threats and Responses: On the Ground and in the Air." *New York Times,* June 18.

Fink, Mitchell, and Lois Mathias. 2002. *Never Forget: An Oral History of September 11, 2001.* New York: Harper Collins.

Fitch, Kristine L. 1998. *Speaking Relationally: Culture, Communication, and Interpersonal Connection.* New York: Guilford.

Gould, Roger V. 2003. *Collision of Wills: How Ambiguity about Social Rank Breeds Conflict.* Chicago: University of Chicago Press.

Hershberg, Eric, and Kevin W. Moore, eds. 2002. *Critical Views of September 11: Analyses from Around the World.* New York: The New Press.

Schwartz, Barry. 1975. *Queuing and Waiting: Studies in the Social Organization of Access and Delay.* Chicago: University of Chicago Press.

Scott, James C. 1990. *Domination and the Arts of Resistance: Hidden Transcripts.* New Haven: Yale University Press.

Tilly, Charles. 1995. "To Explain Political Processes." *American Journal of Sociology* 100: 1594–1610.

———. 1996. "Invisible Elbow." *Sociological Forum* 11: 589–601.

———. 2001. "Relational Origins of Inequality." *Anthropological Theory* 1: 355–72.

Credit, Blame, and Social Life

22

Charles Tilly

In Dostoevsky's chilling novel *Crime and Punishment,* poverty-stricken and ailing ex-student Rodion Romanovich Raskolnikov figures first as antihero, then finally as hero. At the book's very start, Raskolnikov descends the stairs from his shabby room to the St. Petersburg street. As he reflects on the crime he is contemplating, he mutters to himself:

> Hm ... yes ... a man holds the fate of the world in his two hands, and yet, simply because he is afraid, he just lets things drift—that is a truism ... I wonder what men are most afraid of ... Any new departure, and especially a *new word*—that is what they fear most of all ... But I am talking too much. That's why I don't act, because I am always talking. Or perhaps I talk so much just because I can't act.
>
> (Dostoevsky 1964[1866]:1–2)

Raskolnikov soon summons up the courage—or the frenzy—to commit a viciously violent act. With a stolen axe, he murders the aged pawnbroker Alyona Ivanovna, cuts a greasy purse from around the old woman's neck, fills his pockets with pawned objects from a chest underneath her bed, misses thousands of rubles in a nearby chest of drawers, and slaughters the old woman's long-suffering sister Lizaveta Ivanovna when Lizaveta arrives unexpectedly.

Raskolnikov then flees in panic down the stairs, almost gets caught on the way out, rushes to his miserable room, lies down feverish and exhausted, gets up to go out with his loot, hides it under a big stone in a faraway courtyard, and never retrieves his ill-gotten gains from their hiding place. Most of the novel revolves around changes in relations between Raskolnikov and other people as the imperial police close their net around him. Before the book's sentimental finale, Raskolnikov remains incapable of returning the love and admiration friends and family lavish on him despite his surly treatment of them.

With his brutal violence, Raskolnikov hopes confusedly to rise above credit and blame. Yet at his trial witnesses testify to a series of extraordinary charitable and even heroic acts Raskolnikov performed while at the university: supporting the old, ailing father of a dead classmate, rescuing children from a burning room, and more. Those deeds, his voluntary confession, and his debilitating illness win him a short prison sentence of eight years. But Raskolnikov takes no credit for charity and heroism. He identifies himself with heroes like Napoleon. They—he thinks—took their good deeds for granted. They did not hesitate to destroy for the larger good of humanity.

Later, in a Siberian prison for his crime, Raskolnikov reflects again:

> My conscience is easy. Of course, an illegal action has been committed; of course, the letter of the law has been broken and blood has been spilt; well, take my head to satisfy the letter of the law ... and let that be all! Of course, if that were the case, many benefactors of mankind who did not inherit power but seized it for themselves, should have been punished at their very first steps. But the first steps of those men were successfully carried out, and therefore *they were right*, while mine failed, which means I had no right to permit myself that step.
>
> (Dostoevsky 1964:521)

Although he is paying the penalty for his crime—hard labor in Siberia—Raskolnikov still refuses to accept the blame.

In his book's closing scenes, however, Dostoevsky breaks the somber spell. The love of Sonya, the former prostitute who has accompanied Raskolnikov to Siberia, redeems the antihero and starts him toward a new life. At the very end, Dostoevsky paints in the parallel with Christ's raising Lazarus from the dead. Life, for Raskolnikov, finally entails earning credit and taking blame. Perhaps the world's Napoleons can escape the binding of human relations, Dostoevsky tells us. The rest of us, Dostoevsky implies, have no choice but to take responsibility for our actions, good or bad.

The lesson cuts both ways: social life involves taking or giving credit and blame, but assignment of credit and blame also involves relations to other people. Nihilists, saints, and utilitarians may imagine worlds in which relations to specific other humans don't matter so long as accounts come out right with the cosmos, with the gods, or with humanity at large. They are rejecting their own humanity. Raskolnikov's very effort to escape credit and blame for his actions made the point. In so doing, he was denying his obligations to specific other people, including his mother, his sister, his companion Sonya, and his faithful friend Dmitri Prokofych Razumikhin. For the rest of us ordinary mortals, however, getting relations with specific other people right matters fundamentally.

Following that principle, this book examines how people assign credit and blame for things that go right or wrong. It shows that crediting and blaming are fundamentally social acts. They are doubly social. First, people living with others do not settle for Raskolnikov's indifference to responsibility. Instead, they insist that when things go right or wrong someone caused them, and should take responsibility for the consequences. They don't settle for attributing the consequences to luck or fate.

Second, people spend great effort in assigning that responsibility to themselves and others. They complain noisily when other people deny due credit or blame. How people give credit and blame to others (or, for that matter, demand credit for themselves) depends at first on any previously existing relations between the creditor and the credited, the blamer and the blamed. But the very acts of crediting and blaming then define or redefine relations between the parties. This book shows how.

Think of your own daily life. Simply listen to other people's conversations at lunch, during coffee breaks, or on the bus.

Stories about credit and blame don't simply spark the passing interest of stories about newly discovered dinosaurs, the latest movie star romance, or antique automobiles seen on the street. They call up empathy. They resonate because they raise issues in our own lives, whether or not we have any direct connection with the people involved. As we will see, in war, peace, politics, economics, and everyday social life, people care greatly about the proper assignment of credit and blame. This book asks how people actually assign credit and blame.

The Social Lives of Credit and Blame

The origins of the words "credit" and "blame" clearly communicate their social basis. Credit comes from the Latin *credere*, to trust or believe. The verb's past participle *creditum* meant a thing entrusted to someone else, including a loan. No credit could exist without a relation between the persons giving and receiving credit.

Blame comes from the Latin *blasphemare,* to revile or blaspheme. Blame only makes sense when some relation exists between the blamer and the blamed. (People do, of course, sometimes blame fate, their bad luck, evil spirits, the gods, or even themselves for their ill fortune. But even in these extreme cases they are talking about relationships between themselves and the originators of their misfortune.)

Persons who give or receive credit and blame care greatly about justice and its miscarriages. We observers, however, need not worry so much about whether they have acted correctly. This book does not seek general principles of right and wrong action. Here, we ask instead how people assign credit and blame, however appropriately they do so by our personal standards.

We could think of that as primarily a cognitive and emotional question: What mental and visceral stirrings lead an individual to conclude that she or someone else deserves credit or blame for something that has happened? That is how Charles Darwin set up the problem.

Darwin's third great book, *The Descent of Man,* focused on cognitive and emotional bases of morality. Darwin laid out four likely causes for the human moral sense: (1) instinctive sympathy of all higher animals for members of their own social groups, (2) memories of past actions and motives that reinforced the satisfaction from making enduring social instincts prevail over short-term desires, (3) reinforcement of the first two by language and communication with other group members, and (4) habit including "obedience to the wishes and judgment of the community" (Wilson 2006:818).

Although Darwin did not single out credit and blame directly, he did conclude that

> If any desire or instinct, leading to an action opposed to the good of others, still appears to a man, when recalled to mind, as strong as, or stronger than, his social instinct, he will feel no keen regret at having followed it; but he will be conscious that if his conduct were known to his fellows, it would meet with their disapprobation; and few are so destitute of sympathy as not to feel discomfort when this is realized.
>
> (Charles Darwin cited in Wilson 2006:829–830)

Psychologists and neuroscientists do not often use the word "instinct" these days. Now that they can simultaneously run experiments and watch the brain at work, however, they are confirming Darwin's general argument: Sociable moral principles evolved in the higher animals, and depend at least partly on relations to other group members, and on punishment proportionate to offenses (Cushman 2006; Hauser 2006). To some extent, furthermore, almost all human beings prefer to behave in ways that get approval from their fellows (Brennan and Pettit 2004). Most of us reject Raskolnikov as our model.

In thinking about credit and blame, we therefore face an interesting choice. We could concentrate on the deep individual psychological processes, inborn or learned, that go on as people assign credit and blame. Or we could focus on how people deal with each other as they assign credit or blame. This book takes the second tack. While giving due respect to built-in moral propensities, it emphasizes a fascinating trio of related questions: What social processes produce the singling out of this individual or that as worthy of credit or blame? Having singled out someone as worthy of credit or blame, what do people do about it? How does the assignment of credit and blame affect the lives of the people involved?

All of us have enough personal experience with credit and blame to check general explanations against our own observations. My only firing from a job, for example, took place in a Chicago suburb, Elmhurst, during World War II. As a young teenager, I earned precious pocket money in a neighborhood grocery store after school and on weekends by unloading incoming shipments, stocking shelves, sweeping floors, and helping with home deliveries.

One day a bigger, stronger stock boy and I were unpacking cartons of breakfast cereal and stacking them. We (self-serving memory says "he") invented the labor-saving method of pulling cereal boxes from the carton and throwing them to each other across about six feet of distance, shouting and laughing as we tossed boxes of Wheaties and corn flakes. The store's co-owner walked into the middle of our jamboree. He fired me, but not my partner, who got off with a warning. Although the boss probably had other reasons for getting rid of me, I felt an acute sense of injustice, not to mention the blame I faced when I reported the news to my parents, who were barely scraping by on my father's uncertain income. I haven't written this book to avenge that wrong, forgotten for more than sixty years. But it illustrates the personal impact of blame.

Credit and blame operate on a much larger and weightier scale than a teenager's work history.

Judging Credit and Blame

In firing an unsatisfactory worker, setting up a truth commission, and a thousand other assignments of credit or blame, people are making surprisingly similar judgments. They are making judgments of outcome, agency, competence, and responsibility. Truth commissions and other judges identify bad things that happened, look for their agents, decide whether the agents had the competence to produce the bad outcomes, and ask further whether the agents bear the responsibility for those outcomes because they acted with knowledge of the likely consequences.

Assigning credit or blame to someone, then, means identifying that someone as the agent who caused some outcome, whether meritorious or deplorable. It means making someone an effective agent.

Outcomes obviously vary in gravity. In the cosmic balance, a teenager's firing in the 1940s pales by comparison with the wrongs addressed by truth commissions.

Another important qualification: responsibility does not necessarily equal cause. Your judgment, my judgment, and a medical specialist's judgment as to what actually caused a given hospital patient to die often turn out to be irrelevant for the assignment of blame. Cause-effect connections usually play only a secondary and contingent part in determination of responsibility. That determination typically emphasizes judgments of intent and competence. Even legal proceedings for adjudication of responsibility normally center not on exactly what caused a given outcome, but on what the average competent person (whether doctor, lawyer, engineer, or ordinary citizen) is supposed to know and do.

Saving a life accidentally garners less credit than saving a life deliberately, especially if the lifesaver faces serious risks by doing so.

Advice books by famous successful corporate executives typically take credit in exactly that way. Through my own deliberate efforts, they say, I added to my corporation's value. Real estate mogul and TV star Donald Trump illustrates the genre. His brash, boastful book *How to Get Rich* tells you how to emulate him. If you do so, maybe you, too, will make five billion dollars:

> More and more, I see that running a business is like being a general. Calling the shots carries a great deal of responsibility, not only for yourself, but for your troops. Your employees' lives, to a large extent, are dependent on you and your decisions. Bad strategy can end up affecting a lot of people. This is where being a leader takes on a new

dimension. Every decision you make is an important one, whether there are twenty thousand people working for you or just one.

(Trump 2004:3)

To make big money, be decisive, daring, clear, and focused. Your competence will add value to the activity. Of course, it's a lot easier to take that sort of credit if you're a powerful boss, and everyone who knows otherwise remains under your thumb.

Blame operates in the opposite direction. The more an act decreases value, the greater the blame, but again only to the extent that the agent exercises competent responsibility for the act.

Far beyond the assignment of credit and blame, people across the world typically package their social experiences in stories: explanatory narratives incorporating limited numbers of actors, just a few actions, and simplified cause-effect accounts in which the actors' actions produce all the significant outcomes (Tilly 2002, 2006).

Stories matter greatly for social life in general because of three distinctive characteristics:

1   Stories belong to the relationships at hand, and therefore vary from one relationship to another; a mother gets a different story of a broken love affair than does a casual friend.
2   They rework and simplify social processes so that the processes become available for the telling; "X did Y to Z" conveys a memorable image of what happened.
3   They include strong imputations of responsibility, and thus lend themselves to moral evaluations. This third feature makes stories enormously valuable for evaluation after the fact. It also helps account for people's changing stories of events in which they behaved less than heroically.

As compared with scientific accounts of the same events or outcomes, everyday stories radically simplify cause-effect connections. They trot out a few actors whose dispositions and actions cause everything that happens within a limited time and place.

As a result, stories inevitably minimize or ignore the intricate webs of cause and effect that actually produce human social life.

The Politics of Credit and Blame

To be sure, all stories don't simplify equally. Dostoevsky's *Crime and Punishment,* after all, overflows with stories, many of which we only start to understand as other stories about Raskolnikov and his loved ones fall into place. But the great bulk of stories we hear and tell in everyday life convey their agents, causes, and effects in radically simplified ways: someone did something to someone else, and that caused some outcome.

Although deals and compromises fill the back streets of politics, its great plazas teem with stories of credit and blame. A great deal of public politics in the United States and elsewhere consists of taking or denying credit, assigning or resisting blame. The country's very founding document, the 1776 Declaration of Independence, adroitly combined credit and blame. Speaking for the "Representatives of the United States of America in General Congress Assembled," a final statement of complaints declared:

> Nor have we been wanting in attentions to our British brethren, we have warned them from time to time of attempts by their legislature to extend an unwarrantable jurisdiction over us, we have reminded them of the circumstances of our emigration and settlement here, we have appealed to their native justice & magnanimity, and we have conjured them by the tyes of our common kindred, to disavow these usurpations, which would inevitably interrupt our connections & correspondence, they too have been deaf to the voice of justice and of consanguinity; we must therefore acquiesce in the necessity which denounces our separation and hold them, as we hold the rest of mankind, enemies in war, in peace friends.
>
> (Maier 1997:240–241)

Here's the story: They—"our British brethren"—had the agency, responsibility, and competence to prevent the sad outcome, and therefore shared the blame with king and Parliament.

A Committee of Five drafted the Declaration: John Adams, Benjamin Franklin, Thomas Jefferson, Robert Livingston, and Roger Sherman. The five knew from the start that they had to levy strong enough charges against the British king and Parliament to justify the drastic step of repudiating British rule (Maier 1997:105–142). They took credit for American forbearance, and assigned blame primarily to the king. But they also blamed a parliament that failed to resist royal tyranny.

George Washington was away mustering the Continental Army in New York while his comrades were writing the Declaration. But as the successful rebels' first president (1789–1797), he worked both the back streets and the great plazas skillfully. As he approached the end of his second term on 18 September 1796, Washington delivered a farewell address we still read today as a model for public credit and blame. During his term, Washington had overseen the consolidation of the federal government and the securing of U.S. borders. But he had also faced the formation of political parties, the outbreak of a great European war, and a major Pennsylvania insurrection—the Whiskey Rebellion—against the government's fiscal authority. Echoes of all those events appear in the text of Washington's address to his countrymen.

Washington set a modest tone for his taking of credit:

> In the discharge of this trust, I will only say, that I have, with good intentions, contributed towards the organization and administration of the government the best exertions of which a very fallible judgment was capable. Not unconscious, in the outset, of the inferiority of my qualifications, experience in my own eyes, perhaps still more in the eyes of others, has strengthened the motives to diffidence of myself; and every day the increasing weight of years admonishes me more and more, that the shade of retirement is as necessary to me as it will be welcome. Satisfied that, if any circumstances have given peculiar value to my services, they were temporary, I have the consolation to believe, that, while choice and prudence invite me to quit the political scene, patriotism does not forbid it.
>
> (Washington 1796:2)

Thus he rebuffed any attempt to make him king or president for life. John Adams stood by, ready to take over from him.

Later in the address, Washington blamed without naming names. He warned against sectionalism, against advocates of involvement in foreign wars, against "faction":

> All obstructions to the execution of the Laws, all combinations and associations, under whatever plausible character, with the real design to direct, control, counteract, or awe the regular deliberation and action of the constituted authorities, are destructive of this fundamental principle [the duty of every individual to obey the established Government], and of fatal tendency. They serve to organize faction, to give it an artificial and extraordinary force; to put, in the place of the delegated will of the nation, the will of a party, often a small but artful and enterprising minority of the community; and, according to the alternative triumphs of different parties, to make the public administration the mirror of the ill-concerted and incongruous projects of faction, rather than the organ of consistent and wholesome plans digested by common counsels, and modified by mutual interests.
>
> (Washington 1796:4)

Despite advocating a small government with a modest military establishment, Washington called for obedience to that government's decisions, and blamed Americans who plotted against obedience.

More than two hundred years later, American politics still pivots on credit and blame. The al-Qaeda–coordinated attacks in New York and Washington, D.C., on September 11th, 2001, started an epidemic of credit and blame. As a New Yorker, I was not immune. At 6:50 AM the next day I sent out a message to my electronic mailing list on contentious politics. Nothing profound: my message called for students of the subject to avoid hysteria and to look systematically at causes and remedies of the sorts of terror we had just witnessed. The message closed:

> Those of us who study contentious politics should resist the temptation to concentrate on ideas of repression and retaliation, which demagogues will surely broadcast. We may be able to make a small contribution to explaining how such high levels of coordination emerge among damage-doers, and therefore how to reduce threats of violence to civilians in the United States and, especially, elsewhere.

A bit of blaming appeared in the reference to "demagogues." But the message only assigned credit to my fellow New Yorkers, who had generally shown sangfroid and solidarity.

Three days later, I followed up the message with another. This one offered predictions concerning what we would eventually learn about the New York and Washington attacks. It included unconditional predictions, for example that all plotters would eventually turn out to have ties, direct or indirect, to Osama bin Laden, but not all to be directly connected, or even known, to each other. It then went on to contingent if-then predictions, which ran as follows:

- Bombing the presumed headquarters of terrorist leaders will (a) shift the balance of power within networks of activists and (b) increase incentives of unbombed activists to prove their mettle.
- If the United States, NATO, or the great powers insist that all countries choose sides (thus reconstituting a new sort of Cold War), backing that insistence with military and financial threats will increase incentives of excluded powers to align themselves with dissidents inside countries that have joined the U.S. side, and incentives of dissidents to accept aid from the excluded powers.

- Most such alliances will form further alliances with merchants han-
  dling illegally traded drugs, arms, diamonds, lumber, oil, sexual services, and rubber.
- In Russia, Uzbekistan, Lebanon, Turkey, Sudan, Nigeria, Serbia, Algeria,
  and a number of other religiously divided countries, outside support
  for dissident Muslim forces will increase, with increasing connection
  among Islamic oppositions across countries.
- Bombing the presumed originator(s) of Tuesday's attacks and forcing
  other countries to choose sides will therefore aggravate the very conditions American leaders will declare they are preventing.
- If so, democracy (defined as relatively broad and equal citizenship, binding consultation of citizens, and protection from arbitrary actions by
  governmental agents) will decline across the world.

Although evidence on the connections with contraband trade and Muslim dissidents remains uncertain, none of these if-then predictions turned out flatly wrong. Of course, they missed some important points. In September 2001, for example, it never occurred to me that the 9/11 attacks would help justify an American invasion of Iraq. Considering that I made them in the shadow of 9/11, nevertheless, the predictions held up surprisingly well over the following years.

Most of the electronic responses to my posting that flooded in expressed support or offered friendly amendments to my predictions. A few, however, called me a paranoid subversive. About a year later, the White House issued a declaration that made my predictions look less paranoid than they might have seemed in the immediate aftermath of 9/11.

A document called the National Security Strategy (NSS), issued by President George W. Bush on 17 September 2002, claimed broad rights for the sole remaining superpower. It took credit for the victory of freedom and equality over "destructive totalitarian visions." It blamed the "embittered few" for current threats to "our Nation, allies, and friends" (White House 2002:3). It described Afghanistan as "liberated," Iraq and North Korea as "rogue states" in the process of acquiring weapons of mass destruction (White House 2002:5, 9). Although President Bush had bracketed Iran with Iraq and North Korea in the "axis of evil" identified by his speech of 29 January 2002, the NSS blamed Iraq and North Korea especially for the world's terrorist threats.

Six months before the U.S. attack on Iraq, the United States was declaring its right to prevent terrorism by outright military intervention. It blamed rogue states for their threat to peace, and claimed credit for the United States as the guarantor of world order. Like other American political centers, the White House was actively deploying credit and blame.

When a sharp us-them boundary separates blamer and blamed, the very actions for which A blames B are often actions for which B's supporters give B credit. That occurs most obviously in the case of war, where killing that looks barbarous to one side looks heroic to the other. In the world of nationalist struggles, critics often point out that one person's terrorist is another person's freedom fighter. In the world of city administration, what one side calls urban renewal opponents often call real estate profiteering.

Us-them boundaries cut across much of politics. As a result, disputes over whether a given action deserves credit or blame figure regularly in political debate. In the case of 9/11, almost all Americans (including me) deplore the suicide bombers' taking of innocent lives. But for Osama bin Laden's supporters, it still counts as a telling blow against American imperialism. For them, it deserves credit, not blame.

Credit and Blame Revisited

All these cases of political crediting and blaming identified relations between those who passed judgment and those who received judgment. Even my timid appeal to fellow students of contentious politics claimed a right to judge both Western politicians and the enemies they were condemning. In every case, furthermore, the judges were crediting or blaming some specific agent (sometimes themselves) for a particular good or bad outcome, which meant assigning them both competence and responsibility for that outcome. They were fulfilling the relational conditions for credit and blame.

We therefore have our work here cut out for us. The work: clarifying the social processes by which people arrive at assignments of credit and blame. Let me repeat that this book concentrates on *social* processes, in which people interact with each other.

References

Brennan, Geoffrey, and Philip Pettit. 2004. *The Economy of Esteem: An Essay on Civil and Political Society*. Oxford: Oxford University Press.

Cushman, Fiery. 2006. "The Declaration of Independence—A Lab Report." *Character 3*, no. 1: 50–61.

Dostoevsky, Feodor. 1964 [1866]. *Crime and Punishment*. New York: W.W. Norton.

Hauser, Marc D. 2006. *Moral Minds: How Nature Designed Our Universal Sense of Right and Wrong.* New York: HarperCollins.

Maier, Pauline. 1997. *American Scripture: Making the Declaration of Independence.* New York: Alfred A. Knopf.

Tilly, Charles. 2002. *Stories, Identities, and Political Change.* Lanham, MD: Rowman & Littlefield.

———. 2006. *Why?* Princeton: Princeton University Press.

Trump, Donald J. with Meredith McIver. 2004. *How to Get Rich.* New York: Random House.

Washington, George. 1796. "George Washington's Farewell Address." www.early america.com/earlyamerica/milestones/farewell/text.html.

White House. 2002. The National Security Strategy of the United States of America. www.whitehouse.gov/nsc/nssall.html.

Wilson, Edward O., ed. 2006. *From So Simple a Beginning: The Four Great Books of Charles Darwin.* New York: W.W. Norton.

Index

9/11 297, 300, 371–4, 394; credit and blame 392–3; reason giving 375–6

absolute poverty 250
abstract mobilization model 80
Accault, Michel 343–4
activation-deactivation 333
Adams, John 390–1
adaptation 232, 233
Advani, President Lal 267
Afghanistan, Taliban 297
agents of states, organized violence 134–6
aggregate inequality 253
Algeria: coordinated destruction 288; Islamist trust networks 352
American immigration see United States
American Northwest Coast peoples, Winter Ceremonials 333–4
Americanization 308
America's Reconstruction 200
Ames, Edward 129
Amsterdam, poor relief 364–5
Anjou (France) 32–3; military service 42; response to Revolution of 1789 36–41
anthropology 102
anti-Catholicism 98
antimobilization strategies 77
Aremepinchieue 343–4
Argentina: Bolivian immigrants 326–7; migrants 316
armies 134–5; French Revolution 176–8; indirect to direct rule 172–5; terror-inflicting armies 300; Third World states 149
artillery 131
Ashkenazi Charity 364

assets of poor people 250
assimilation 316
Association of Juchiteco Students (Mexico) 219
atomic bombs 146
authority, protection 125–6
authority-citizen interactions, collective violence 277
autonomists 300
autonomous goods 237–8
autonomous government 130
Ayodhya, India 267

Babri Masjid 267
Barère, Bertrand 29
bargaining 346; for military recruits 174; rights 181
barriers, inequality 245
Barton, Josef 320
Bax, Mart 209
Bean, Richard 131
Benita Galeana Women's Alliance 97
BJP (Bharatiya Janata Party) 267
Black Act of 1723 77
blacks, inequality 322–3
black-white boundaries 338
black-white differentials (United States) 254
black-white relations (United States) 307–9
blame 384–94
Blok, Anton 288
Bob, Clifford 95
Bobb, Vilna Bashi 337
Bodnar, John 318, 321
Boisbriant 344–5
Bolivia 149; immigrants 338; social boundaries 326–7

bolivianos 326–7
Bonaparte, Napoleon 190, 198
borrowing: category formation 278;
  boundary change 331
Bosnian Serb leaders 278; political
  entrepreneurs 281; Serb-Muslim division 334
bottom-up nationalism 280
bottom-up strategies, trust networks 346–7
boundaries: political identities 279; societies
  103–4
boundary change *see* social boundary change
bounded categories, durable inequalities 231–2
Bourdieu, Pierre 238
bourgeoisie 34; Sicily 56–7
bourgeois-organized workers coalition 179
bourgeois-worker-peasant coalitions 179
Bové, José 95
Brandenburg-Prussia, armies 136
Braudel, Fernand 127, 133
Brazil, military power 153
de Brienne, Loménie 35
Brill, Steven 372
Brinton, Crane 113
British Reform Act of 1832 179
Brogan, D. W. 308–9
brokerage 141, 291
brokered autonomy 348; trust networks
  353–4
Brougham, Henry 99
Buenos Aires 326–7
buffering 205
bureaucratic police forces 78
Bürgerschaft 172
Bush, President George W. 293, 393
Bustillo, Mario 219

cahiers de doléances 36
Cahokias 344
Calhoun, Craig 5
Calles, Plutarco Elias 213
Calvin, John 360
campaigns 92–9
campaigns of annihilation 286
Canada, suffrage rights 165
capabilities of poor people 250
capital 343
capital-intensive settings 145
capitalism, stages of 130
capitalized-coercion settings 145
Cárdenas, Lazaro 216
career migration 317–19
cargo system (Mexico) 219
Caribbean immigrants 337
categorical boundaries 245, 278
categorical boundary crossing 259
categorical inequality 205, 232–7
categorical pairs 233, 241

categories: durable inequalities *see* categorical
  inequality; of migration 312–17;
  population 107
category formation 277–8
Catholic Church, repression by means
  of commitment 347
Catholic Emancipation (1829) 98–9
Catholic Relief Act of 1778 98
Catholics 212–213
catnet, population 107
cause-effect connections, reason giving 378
chain migration 317–18
chains 241
challengers 62, 71
Chambliss, William 246
channels of mobility 260
characteristics of strikes 53
Charles I 143
Chartism 179
Chartist Movement 179
Chinese immigrants to United States 259
Chinese migration 318
Chouannerie 29
Chouans 29
Ciampan, Ragionier 378
circular migration 317–19
citizen/foreigner 234
citizenship 159–62; Europe 178–81; French
  Revolution 177; Great Britain 163–4; rights
  169–70
citizenship rights 169–70; European Union
  171–2
civil rights 170–1
civil rights movement (United States) 277
civil wars 146, 149
Clark, Janine 351
classification of forms of collective action 81–2
clergy, grievances 39–40
clientage 346
Coalición 220
Coalition of Workers, Peasants, and Students
  of Isthmus (COCEI) 219–20
coalitions 66, 71, 137, 179
Cobbett, William 72
COCEI (Coalition of Workers, Peasants,
  and Students of the Isthmus) 219–20
codes, reason giving 376, 378
coerced migration 317–19
coercion 342; terror 300–1
coercion-intensive settings 145; state making
  148
coercive resources 66
coethnic employment 322
collective action 74–5; contagion collective
  action 85; detecting 75–6; elections 87–8;
  forms of contention 80–1; identities
  for 291; measuring 75–6; Mexico 92–7;

repertoires of 82–5; spontaneous collective action 85; strikes 85–7; threats and opportunities 79–80
collective contention 278–9
collective reactions 81
collective violence 63, 275–7; coordinated destruction 286–91; internal collective violence 67; political entrepreneurs 280–5; political identities 279–80; violent specialists 282–5
Colombia, kidnappings 288
colonizing migration 317–19
Colors of Violence 268
commitment 343; expansion of commitment 65
communal hostility 270
Communes of Paris 190
compensation 240
competitive actions 81
Comte, Auguste 111
concealment 346
concentration of power in national states 67–8
conditions for: mobilization 74–6; revolutions 64–6
condottiere 151
confirming relations 379
Congo, coordinated destruction 289
consequences of social boundary change 335–9
conspiratorial terror 287
conspirators 300
constitutional approach, democracy 183
construction of democracy 158
consultation, democracy 186–7, 211
contagion collective action 85
contender for power 62
contenders 71
contention 269; collective action 80–1; collective contention 278–9; collective violence *see* collective violence; for power 79
contentious conversations 269–74
contentious politics 270, 278; collective violence 275
contentious repertoires 272
conventions, reason giving 376–7
conversations 269; social boundary change 331
coordinated destruction 286–91
coordination among violent actors 285
counterrevolutions, Vendée 27–30
credit 384–94
Crenshaw, Martha 117
Crime and Punishment (Dostoevsky) 383–4
criminal trust networks, public politics 358–9
Cromwell, Thomas 133
Curato, Frederico 56
Curtin, Philip 309, 317
Cyrenaica 152–3

Dahl, Robert 158, 159, 184–6
Darwin, Charles 386
Davenant, Charles 133
death, World War II 147
Declaration of Independence (United States) 390
Declaration of the Rights of Man and the Citizen 177
decolonization 138
de-democratization 187, 189; defined 208; distrust 220–1; Mexico 214–17; signs of 194–7; studying 202–6; Switzerland 197–202
deep improvisations 242
defensive mobilization 72
demilitarization of lords, England 128
demobilization 72
democracy 157–8, 164–6; conceptualizing 159–63; constitutional approach 183; construction of 158; consultation 186–7; elements of 186–7; Europe 162–3; Great Britain 163–4; India 193–5; polyarchal democracy 185; procedural definitions 184; process-oriented approaches 184–5; rights *see* rights; state capacity 187–9; studying 202–6; substantive approaches 183–4; threats to 221; top-down models 157; trust in 209–12
democratic dilemma of trust 210
democratization 187, 189; defined 208; France (1600–2006) 189–93; Mexico 212–17; signs of 194–7; studying 202–6; Switzerland 197–202, 205–6
demonstrations: Americans 83; England 88
The Descent of Man (Darwin) 386
destruction as conquest 286–91
detecting collective action 75–6
determinants of strikes (France) 53
development, inducing 112–13
differentiation 111–15
direct rule 172–5; nineteenth century 188–9
disorder 115–16
displacement effect 133
dispossessed react 81
dissimulation 346
dissolution 346
distrust, de-democratization 220–1
Dostoevsky, Feodor 383–4
Dubin, Lois 354–6
Duch, Elaine 376
Dufour, General Guillaume 200
durable inequalities 230–2, 242–7; categorical inequality 232–7
Durkheimian theories 74–5
Dutch Republic: citizenship 175–6; democracy 162–3; trust networks 361–2

Echeverría, President Luis 216
economic geographers 104
effigies, Stamp Act 88–9
El Salvador, violent specialists 283
elections 87–8
elements of inequality 237–9
Elton, G. R. 133
emigration, Vendée 44–5
emulation 232–3
encounters: category formation 278;
    mechanisms that cause boundary
    change 330
England: citizenship 161; demilitarization
    of lords 128; demonstrations 88; national
    debt 132–3; rights 170–1; stature,
    malnutrition 227–8
English Revolution of 1640 136, 143
enlistment 346
entitlements 240
entrepreneurial police forces 78
equalization 205
escapes from poverty 260
Estates General (1789, France) 36, 176–7
Ester, Comandanta 95
estimating relationships 110
ethnic activists 334
ethnic cleansing 298, 336
ethnic politics 334
ethnographers 102
Europe: citizenship 161–2; citizenship rights
    178–81; democracy 162–3; poor relief
    366; proletarianization 86, 363; state
    formation 150–1
European Fascists (1920s) 74
European immigration to United States 310
European Union, citizenship rights 171–2
evasive conformity 348
event catalogues 2
events, measuring collective actions 75–6
Executive Outcomes (South Africa) 283
expansion of commitment 65
exploitation 232–3, 242; governments 257
extermination, Jews 336
external state making 137–9, 151–2
extortion 129
extraction 134–6
EZLN (Zapista Army of National Liberation)
    95

facilitation 76–79
Fakir, Golam 269
family disputes 270–1
Federal Pact 198
feminist activists (Mexico) 97
Fiesta of Our Lady of Copacabana 326
Fillieule, Olivier 271
fit between political institutions and social
    situation, Sicilian revolution (1848) 57

Fogel, Robert W. 228
force 276
formation of: national states 136–7; states 143
Forment, Carlos 217–18
forms of contention, collective action 80–1
Fox, Jonathan 218
Fox, President Vicente 217
France: citizenship 162; democratization
    (1600–2006) 189–93; French Revolution
    see French Revolution (1789–1793); great
    disarmament (1620s) 128; indirect rule
    to direct rule 173; national debt 132;
    North American territories 342; policing
    (nineteenth century) 77–8; relations with
    Indians in North American territories
    342–5; Seven Years War 143; strike activity
    (1830–1968) 48–51; Vendée see Vendée
    (France)
Franklin, Benjamin 390
Freedom House 295
free-rider problem 73
French Revolution (1789–1793) 33–5, 190;
    first year of revolution 45–6; military
    recruits 42–3; Reign of Terror 298; rights
    176–8; Vendée see Vendée (France);
    Western France 35–6
French strike activity (1830–1968) 48–51
French-Indian relationships 342–5
Freud, Sigmund 288
Friendly Societies 78
Fuchs, Lawrence 323

Gaeta, Gerry 376
Galton's problem 102
Gamson, William 108
Garcia, Rafael 213
de Gaulle, Charles 190
gender, occupational sex-typing 336
gender boundaries 245
gender differentiation, nutrition 229–30
genocide 286, 298; Rwandans 289–90
German society 103
Germany, World War II 147
ghettos: Trieste 356; Venice, Italy 354
GIA (Groupe Islamique Armé) 288
gifts 240
Gillis, John 59
Gillray, James 227
giving reason see reason giving
Gjerde, John 314
Gonzalez, Nydia 371–2
goods 237–8
Goodwin, Jeffrey 260
Gorbachev, Mikhail 357
Gordon, Lord George 98
government 62, 71; boundaries separating
    challengers from polity members 277;
    exploitation 257; grievances 39; inequality

257–61; opportunity hoarding 258, 287; protection 125–6, 129–31; racket 118–19; repression 76; violence and 127–9
governmental repression 77
grant of legality, electoral association 88
Gravier, Jacques 343–4
Great Britain: anti-Catholicism 98; democracy and citizenship 163–4; organized labor 87; poor relief 366
Greer, Donald 44
grievances 37–40
Grimson, Alejandro 338
Groupe Islamique Armé (GIA) 288, 352
groups 107
Gumbel, Bryant 372
Gunnar, Myrdal 309

Habyarimana, President 290
Hadsburgs 354–6
Hamilton, Earl J. 132–3
Handlin, Oscar 312
Hart, Peter 208
hated poor 251
height, malnutrition 227–8
helpless poor 251
Henry IV 191
hierarchies 241, 253
high-capacity regimes 187
higher clergy, grievances 39–40
hijackings 83
Hindu militants (Ayodhya, India) 267
Hindu-Muslim conflicts 267–8, 273
Hispanic/white 234
Hobsbawm, E. J. 81
Holland 135; citizenship 175–6
Homans, George 2
homogenous populations 307–8
households 108; durable inequalities 235
HUM (Harakat ul-Mujahidin) 297
human capital 253
human rights 295
Human Rights Watch 295
human-capital theory 239
Huntington, Samuel, modernization and revolution 58–61
Hutu, political identities 279
Hutu Power militia, Rwanda 290
Hyderabad, India 268

Iberian Jews 354
identities: for collective action 291; political identities 273, 279–80
identity politics 279–80
Idris (Sanusi) 152–3
illegitimate versus legitimate force 116–19
immigrant adaptation 337
immigrants, durable inequalities 235
immigration (United States) 307–9

imposition, mechanisms that cause boundary change 330–1
incentive shift, social boundary change 331
income, measuring national income 112–13
India: Ayodhya 267; democracy 193–5; Hyderabad 268
Indians, relations with French in North American territories 342–5
indirect rule, to direct rule 172–5
individual passing 259
individual perspectives, inequality 252–6
individualistic analyses of inequality 239
individuals 106–7
inducing development 112–13
industrialism 52
inequality: building blocks of 241; categorical inequality 232–7; durable inequalities 230–2; elements of 237–9; individual perspectives 252–6; living standards 227–32; Marxists 254–5; migration networks 321–3; politics 257–61; revolutions 260
inequality-generating resources 255
inequality-producing queues 253–4
inscription-erasure 333
instability, pace of change 58–61
instinct 386
institutions, democracy 185
integrated networks 356–9
integration 348, 349, 359–62; versus differentiation 115; proletarians 362–6; of trust networks 211, 356–9
interactions, societies 105
interests 74
interim commissions 35
internal collective violence 67
internal state making 137–9, 151
international terrorist attacks 297
invention, category formation 278
I.R.A. (Irish Republican Army) 208–9
Iran, Islamist trust networks 352
Ireland: circular migration 318; trust in democracy 212
Irish migrants 320
Irish Republican Army (I.R.A.) 208–9
Islamic organizations, segregation 350–1
Islamist trust networks 352
Italian migration 320
Italy: immigrants 316; revolutions 67; sit-down strikes 84
Ivaniuzhenkov, Boris 358–9

Japan, World War II 147
Jefferson, Thomas 390
Jewish immigrants 315
Jews 354; Amsterdam 364; ethnic cleansing 336; migration 322; Trieste 354–6
Jordan, Islamic organizations 350–1

Juchitán, Mexico 219–20
judging credit and blame 388–9
jurés-priseurs 39

Kakar, Sudhir 268, 273
Kaskaskias 343–5
Kazakhstan 184
Kerensky, Alexander 2
Khan, Majid 268
Khomeini, Ayatollah Ruhollah 352
kidnappings, Colombia 288
kommersanty 358
Krauze, Enrique 216
Kriesi, Hanspeter 163
Kwakiutl ceremonial 333–4

labor 238–9; bin Ladin, Osama 297, 351, 394
Lalakin, Sergei 358–9
Lamont, Michele 328
Lane, Frederic 129, 130
large-scale social change 59
Latin America 165; external interventions 152
lead-lag model 59
legitimate force 276; versus illegitimate force
    116–19; governments 127–9
Lequinio 30
lethal contests 286–7
Levi, Margaret 359
li Hebrei di Trieste 355
Liberty Tree 89
Libya 152–3
Lindert, Peter 259, 365–6
Lis, Catharina 363–4
living standards, inequality 227–32
Livingston, Robert 390
local knowledge 241
long-distance migration 313
lords, first year of revolution (France) 46
Louis XIII 128, 191
Louis XIV 188, 191
low-capacity regimes 188

machine breaking 83
mafiosi 282
magnates, Europe 128
male/female 234
malfunctioning of the courts 39
malnutrition 227–32
manhood suffrage, Mexico 214
Maoist guerrillas 194
Marcos, Subcomandante 95
maritime states 131
Marquis, Craig 371–2
Marshall, T. H. 163, 170–1, 179
Marx, Karl 86, 111, 114, 238
Marxists, inequality 254–5
mass military mobilization, empowers classes
    supplying manpower 165

mass national armies, citizenship 178–9
McCabe, Kevin 372
McGroarty, Chief Petty Officer Edward 378
means of control, trust networks 346–7
measuring: collective action 75–6; national
    income 112–13
mechanisms that cause boundary change
    330–335
Medieval Europe, nations 353
members of polity 62, 71; threats and
    opportunity 80
mental events cause social behavior 105–9
mercenaries 173, 283
Mexico: collective action 92–7;
    democratization 212–17; tequio system
    219; trust networks 217–20
Middle Ages (Europe), brokered autonomy
    354
Middle East, segregation to integration
    350–1
middle ground 343
migrant networks 312–17
migrants, theory of the disruptive migrants
    116
migration: Italian migration 320; Jewish
    migration 322; long-distance migration
    313; networks 312–21; social boundaries
    326–9; types of 317–19; United States
    309–12
migration chains 319
migration patterns 320
military, historical perspectives 150–2
military conquest 149, 151–2
military conscription 39, 74
military demobilization 65–6
military power 138, 152–3
military recruits, bargaining for 174
military rule 152–3
military service, Vendée 41–3
militias 300
Mill, John Stuart 98
Miller, Kerby 315, 320
Mitterrand, Danielle 95
mobility 317; channels of mobility 260; poor
    251
mobilization 62, 72–9
mode of control, trust networks 346–7
Model, Suzanne 322
model of interaction see polity model
model of political conflict 62–3
modernization, revolutions and 57–61
Molnár, Virág 328
monetary transactions 240–1
Moore Jr., Barrington 2, 157, 168
morality 386
Morawska, Ewa 313, 315, 318
motivations for Vendée 29–30
Muslims, conflicts with Hindus 267–8, 273

NAACP (National Association for the Advancement of Colored People) 277
nadwas 351–2
NAFTA (North American Free Trade Agreement) 217
Naimark, ethnic cleansing 336
Napoleon 190, 198
national armies, French Revolution 176–8
national debt 132–3
national elections 87–8
national income 112–13
national interest 142
National Security Strategy (NSS) 393
national states: concentration of power 67–8; formation of 136–7
National Union of Autonomous Regional Peasant Organizations 219
nationalism 279–80
nationalization 142
nations, trust networks 353–4
Naudet, Jules 373
Naxalites 194
nazioni 355
Nazis: ethnic cleansing 336; internal collective violence 67
negotiated connections 348; trust networks 352–6
negotiated relations 379
negotiation, trust networks 347
negotiation of inequality, reason giving 380–1
Nelson, Joan 115
network-based escalation 291
networks: inequality in migration networks 321–3; migration 312–17; population 107; solidarity in migration 319–21; trust networks see trust networks
Newton, Sir Isaac 109
nineteenth century: direct rule 188–9; policing 77–8
North America, ethnic politics 334
North American Free Trade Agreement (NAFTA) 217
North American territories, France 342
Norway, immigrant 314
NSS (National Security Strategy) 393
Nurick, Stewart 372
nutrition, categorical inequality 236
nutritional deprivation 227–32

O'Brien, Conor Cruise 117
occupation of recruits, military service 42–3
occupational sex-typing 336
O'Connell's Catholic Association 72
offensive mobilization 72
offensive strikes 52–4
Olesen, Thomas 95, 96
Oliver, Andrew 88
Olson, Mancur 73

Olzak, Susan 321
Ong, Betty 371–2
opportunities, collective action 79–80
opportunity hoarding 232, 233, 287; governments 258
organization, mobilization 74
organizations 241
organized labor 87
organized violence, agents of states 134–6
organized workers-bourgeois coalition 179

pace of change, instability 58–61
Pakistan 297
PAN (Party of National Action), Mexico 217
Paris Commune of 1871 276–7
parish priests, grievances 39–40
Parsons, Talcott 113
particularistic ties 348
Partido Revolucionario Institucional (PRI) 216–17
Party of National Action (PAN), Mexico 217
Party of the Mexican Revolution 216
patrimonialism 140
patronage systems, trust networks 352
patron-client chains (Mexico) 217
Patterns of Global Terrorism 295
payments 240
Peacock, A. T. 133
peasant land invasions 81–2
peasants: French Revolution 176; Mexico 216–17; rights 175–6
Perillaut 344
Peru, peasant land invasions 81
Peterson, Paul 160–1
Place, Francis 72
Podol'sk (Russia) 358–9
Poland 354
policing, nineteenth century 77–8
policy interventions to facilitate exits from poverty 261–2
political actors 279–80; violent specialists 282–5
political conflict, model of 62–3
political entrepreneurs 291; collective violence 280–5
political identities 273, 279–80
political motivation, terrorism 296
political opportunity structure see POS (political opportunity structure)
political parties 87
political power, contention for 79
political rights 89–90, 170–1
political systems 89–90
politicide 286
politics: collective violence 275; contentious politics 270, 278; credit and blame 389–94; inequality 257–61; public politics 278
polity 62, 71, 159
polity model 71

polyarchal democracy 185
poor 250–1; public assistance 363–4
poor relief 364
population 107
porteños 326–7
POS (political opportunity structure) 93–4;
anti-Catholicism (Great Britain) 98
positional goods 237
postulates 100–1; differentiation is a
progressive master process 111–14;
equivalence of different forms of
disorder 115–16; illegitimate versus
legitimate force 116–19; mental events
cause social behavior 105–9; social change
is a coherent phenomenon 109–0; society
is a thing apart 101–5; stage theories
110–11
poverty 250; escapes from 260; policy
interventions to facilitate exits from
poverty 261–2; questionnaire for analyzing
escapes from poverty 256
Powell, Secretary of State Colin L. 293
power 79; concentration of power in national
states 67–8
practical knowledge 379–80
predation 346
predatory trust networks 347
predictions about September 11 attacks 392–3
preparatory mobilization 73
PRI (Partido Revolucionario Institucional)
216–17
principles for description of democracy,
democratization, and de-demoncratization
196–7
proactive collective actions 82
Proal, Herón 213
procedural definitions, democracy 184
process-oriented approaches, democracy
184–5
Production Consulation Committee (Mexico)
219
proletarian 86
proletarianization 86, 362–6
promobilization activities 76
promotion 289
protection 124, 134–6; government 129–31
protection rent 129
protectors 124–5
Protestant Association 98
Protestant-Catholic divide, Ireland 212
Prussia, peasants 175–6
Przeworski, Adam 158, 195
psychic impact of large-scale change, Sicilian
revolution (1848) 57
public assistance 363–4
public politics 278; trust networks 358–62
Putnam, Robert 209

al-Qadhdhafi, Mu'ammar 153
Québec Act of 1774 98
questionnaire for analyzing escapes from
poverty 256
Qur'anic study groups 351–2

Rab, Mahood 249–52
racial barriers 245
racial inequality 247
racism 337
racket 118–19
racketeers 124–5
Rapp, Richard 129
Raskolniko, Rodion Romanovich, (*Crime and
Punishment*) 383–5
ratchet effect 133
rational-action models 108
RDU (Rapid Deployment Unit), Washington
D.C. Metropolitan Police 246
reactive collective actions 81
reason giving 374–81
recruits for military service (Revolution of
1789) 42–3
redeemers 318
redistribution of wealth, state-directed 186–7
Reform Act of 1832 366
Reform Bill of 1832 72
reforms, Val-Saumurois 41
refugees 149–50
regimes 278; state capacity 187–9; violent
specialists 285
Regional Anti-Organized Crime Directorate
(RUBOP) 357
regions 104
Reign of Terror 298
Rejón, Manuel 218
relational 6, 15–16
relational repairs 379
relationships 107; estimating 110;
French-Indian relationships 342–5
relative goods 237–8
relocation 334
Remak, Joachim 200
Renaud, Theresa 372
repertoires of collective action 82–5
repression 76–9; repertoire of collective
action 84
repression by means of commitment,
Catholic Church 347
response to revolution, Anjou 36–41
responsibility, credit and blame 388
revolution 33
Revolution of 1789 (France) *see* French
Revolution (1789–1793)
Revolutionary Armies, France 176
revolutions 63–4, 260; conditions for 64–6;
English Revolution of 1640 136; French

Revolution (1789–1793) *see* French Revolution; modernization and 57–61; Sicilian revolution (1848) 55–7; war and 143 rich versus poor, mobilization 73–4
Richelieu 128, 173
rights 159, 168–70; bargaining 181; disappearance of 181; French Revolution 176–8; indirect rule to direct rule 172–5
riots, 1960s (United States) 117–18
rites of passage 333
Rivas, Attorney General Mario Zamora 283
robust social mechanisms 330
Romero, Archbishop Oscar 283
Rompiechoue, Marie 344
routinized, strikes 85–6
Roy, Beth 269
royalism 30
Rubin, Jeffrey 219
RUBOP (Regional Anti-Organized Crime Directorate) 357
Rueschemeyer, Dietrich 159, 165
Rumanians migration 320
rural landlords 288
Russia: integrated networks 356–7; peasants 175–6; public politics, criminal trust networks 358–9; *see also* Soviet Union
Rwanda: genocide 289–90; political identities 279

salience 285, 291
salt tax 37
scripts 241
Scuola Pia Normale sive Talmud Torà 356
segregation 348–9; Trieste 354–6; trust networks 349–52
selective re-creation of social ties 316
self-exploitation, migration 322
Sen, Amartya 169, 250
September 11 attacks 297, 300, 371–4, 394; credit and blame 392–3; reason giving 375–6
Serb-Muslim division 334
setting-based activation 291
Seven Years War 98, 143, 342–5
Sewell Jr., William H. 8
sex 229; French-Indian relations 343
shallow improvisations 242
shared stories about boundaries, political identities 279
Sherman, Roger 390
Sicilian revolution (1848) 55–7
significant terrorist incidents 296
signs of democratization and de-democratization 194–7
Simmel, Georg 107
Singerman, Diane 350
singling out individuals, credit and blame 387
sit-down strikes 84

site transfer 333
slave trade 311
slavery, United States 307, 310
Slovaks, migration 320
Smiley, Gary 373
Smith, Adam 238–9
soccer violence 334
social boundaries 326–9
social boundary change 327–9; consequences of 335–9; mechanisms that cause 330–2
social boundary mechanisms 326–9
social category 277
social change 109–10
social closure 231–2
Social Democrats, Sweden 87
social descriptions 107–8
social inequality 237
social inventions 241
social life: credit and blame 385–7; stories 389
social mechanisms 330
social movements 108
social networks *see* networks
Social Origins of Dictatorship and Democracy 168
social poor 251
social processes 109–10; differentiation 113–14
social relations: conventions 376–7; local knowledge 241–3; political identities 279; reason giving 379; scripts 241–3; stories 377–8
social relationships 106
social rights 170–1, 179–80
social spending 364
social units 107
socialism 86
sociological view of Vendée 31–2
sociétés de secours mutuels 78
societies 101–5; differentiation 111–14
society is a thing apart, pernicious postulates 101–5
sociology 101–3
Soly, Hugo 363–4
Sonderbund War 200
Sorkin, Pitirim A. 2, 60, 107
South Africa: Executive Outcomes 283; site transfer 334
South Asia, terrorism 297
South Korea 148, 153
Soviet Union 148; integrated networks 356–7; World War II 147; *see also* Russia
Soviety Union 142
Spain 135; Galicia 352–3
specialists in coercion, terror 300–1
specialization 142
specialized military forces, terror 299
specialized reasons 379
spillover from economic growth 260–1

spontaneous collective action 85
stage theories 110–11
Stalin, Joseph 298
Stamp Act 84, 88–9
standing armies 134–5
Stanley, William 283
state capacity 191; regimes 187–9
State Department (US); terrorism and human rights report 294–7
state formation 146–51
state making 129–39
state-certifying organizations 138
Statements of Grievances (*cahiers de doléances*) 36
states 159; formation of 136–7, 143; organized violence 134–6
stature, malnutrition 227–8
Steckel, Richard 228
Stepashin, Sergei 358–9
Stephens, Evelyn Huber 159, 165
Stephens, John 159, 165
stigmas, categorical inequality 245–6
Stinchcombe, Arthur L. 239
Stone, Oliver 95
stories: credit and blame 389; reason giving 376–8
strike activity (1830–1968) (France) 48–54
strikes 84–7; France 48–54
student massacre (Mexico) 216
substantive approaches, democracy 183–4
subvention 289
suffrage rights 165, 214
Sutton, F. X. 112
Sweden: birth weights 229; citizenship 161; citizenship for peasants 175–6; Social Democrats 87
Switzerland 163, 197–206

Taine, Hippolyte 35
Taiwan 148
Taliban (Afghanistan) 297
Tamayo, Sergio 92
Tanner, James 229
taqiyya 351
Tarkhania, Kumar 269
Tarrow, Sid 19, 20
tax rebellions 68
taxation: French Revolution 177; grievances 37–8; wars 133
taxes, salt tax 37
technical accounts, reason giving 376, 378
tequio system, Mexico 219
terror 294–301
terror-inflicting armies 300
terrorism 117, 293–9
terrorists 294, 297
Test and Corporation Acts (1828) 98–9
theory of the disruptive migrants 116

Third Republic (France) 190
Third World states 144–6; armies 149
Thompson, E. P. 77
threats: collective action 79–80; to democracy 221
Tilly, Louise 378
Tocqueville, Alexis de 33, 307–8, 310
top-down models: democracy 157; trust networks 346–7
top-down nationalism 280
trade unions 78; preparatory mobilization 73
transaction costs 241
triads 241
tributes 129
Trieste 354–6
Tripolitania 152–3
Trump, Donald 388–9
trust, democracy 209–12
trust networks 204, 208–9, 347; brokered autonomy 353–4; Dutch Republic 361–2; integration 356–9; integration into public politics 345–9; integration of 211; Islamist trust networks 352; Mexico 217–20; nations 353; negotiated connections 352–6; negotiation 347; patronage systems 352; segregation 349–52
twentieth century: social rights 179–80; state formation 151; war making 137
types of migration 317–19

umbrella effect, elections 88
United Nations 148; state formation 151
United States 142; atomic bombs 146; black-white differentials 254; black-white relations 307–9; Chinese immigrants 259; civil rights movement 277; Declaration of Independence 390; immigrant networks 313; immigration 307–9, 318; immigration and inequality 321–3; interventions in other countries 289; Italian immigrants 316; migration 309–12; military facilities throughout world 148; monopolization of legal tender 240; police forces 78; repertoire of collective action 83; riots (1960s) 117–18; slavery 307, 310; Stamp Act 88–9; State Department 294–7; suffrage rights 165; World War II 147
Universal Declaration on Human Rights 295
Università 355
urban 34
urban villagers 116
urbanization 31, 60
U.S.S. Cole 297
USSR (United of Soviet Socialist Republics), World War II 147
us-them boundaries, blame 394

Val d'Aosta Waldensians 346
Val-Saumurois 40–1
van Leeuwen, Marco 364–5
Vendée (France) 26–7; counterrevolution overview 27–9; emigration 44–5; first year of revolution 45–6; governement grievances 39; military service 41–3; motivations for 29–30; response to Revolution 36–41; Revolution of 1789 33–5; sociological view of 31–2; taxation grievances 37–8
Venice, Italy, Jews 354
violence 125–6, 276; government and 127–9; see also collective violence
violent specialists 282–5
Voices of the Poor 249–51
Volkov, Vadim 356–9
de Vries, Jan 132

wage-labor 365
Walpole, Sir Robert 77
war making 134–7
War of American Independence 143
War of the Vendée see Vendée (France)
Warren, Mark E. 210
wars 68–9, 125–6, 131–3; beginning of 140–43; civil wars 146, 149; revolutions and 143; taxation 133
Washington, George 390–1
waterways, state making 131–2

Weber, Max 172, 231
welfare systems 258
West Indian immigrants 337–8
Western France, Revolution of 1789 35–6
Western model, Third World states 144–6
White, Harrison 107
White, Richard 343
wholesale transplantation 316
Wilkes, John 98
Winter Ceremonials, American Northwest Coast peoples 333–4
Wiseman, J. 133
Wolf, Eric 72, 79, 333
women, Qur'anic study groups 351–2
working classes, democracy 165
World War I, Russia 143
World War II, impact on state formation 146–50
WUNC (worthy, united, numerous, and committed) 273

Yans-McLaughlin, Virginia 313
Yemen, Islamic organizations 351–2
Yiddish 354

Zapatista's rebellion, Mexican Revolution 81, 93–5
Zapotec identity (Mexico) 219–20
zealots 300
Zelizer, Viviana 240